THE
Recipes Only
COOKBOOK

THE
Recipes Only
COOKBOOK

by Carroll Allen
and the food writers of
Recipes Only Magazine

A McGRAW-HILL RYERSON/LORRAINE GREEY BOOK

McGraw-Hill Ryerson Limited
Toronto   Montreal

Recipes illustrated on the cover:
Creamy Fettuccine and Smoked Salmon
Lemon Lime Cheesecake
Gingered Carrot and Orange Soup
Buttered Green Beans with Almonds
Chicken with Apricots

A McGRAW-HILL RYERSON/LORRAINE GREEY BOOK

McGraw-Hill Ryerson Limited
330 Progress Avenue
Scarborough, Ontario
M1P 2Z5

Recipes Only Magazine Ltd.:
Lilia Lozinski – Publisher, *The Recipes Only Cookbook*
Carroll Allen – Editor, *Recipes Only Magazine*
Greg MacNeil – Senior Partner

Canadian Cataloguing in Publication Data
Allen, Carroll
  Recipes only cookbook

Includes recipes originally published in Recipes only magazine.
Includes index.
ISBN 0-07-549898-7

1. Cookery. I. Title.

TX715.A58 1989   641.5   C89-094289-7

Design consultants: Sarah Laffey and Georges Haroutiun
Jacket photograph by Robert Wigington
Jacket food styled by Kate Bush

Produced by
Lorraine Greey Publications Limited
Suite 303, 56 The Esplanade
Toronto, Ontario
Canada M5E 1A7

Printed and bound in Italy

ACKNOWLEDGEMENTS

This book was made possible by the
following people: the professional recipe creators
whose credentials appear on pages 252-3; Mary
Adachi, who did the copy editing; Julia Aitken, who
helped standardize the recipes; and Pauline Flick of
Brownridge Communication Strategies Inc., who did
hundreds of new nutritional analyses. Special thanks
are due Shiraz Bagli, who helped willingly and
cheerfully with anything that needed doing.

C.A.

CONTENTS

THE RECIPES

WHY ANOTHER COOKBOOK?

When we began to plan a *Recipes Only* cookbook, we had to think seriously about what kind of cookbook we wanted it to be. It would have lots of recipes, naturally, the very best from the hundreds published in *Recipes Only Magazine* over the past six years. We knew from our mail that readers valued and collected our recipes but frequently lent or lost the very ones they treasured most.

We decided our book would have lots of sample menus, too, menus for most of the occasions that arise in the life of the average cook, because we know that planning what to cook can sometimes be harder than the actual cooking. The zest for cooking bogs down as much in the everlasting daily question of "What will we have for dinner tonight?" as in any lack of culinary skill. The weariness a homemaker can feel at having to answer that question seven days a week, year in and year out, cannot be imagined by someone who simply brings a lively appetite to the table. As one *Recipes Only* reader wrote, it's amazing there aren't more homicides at 5:30 in the evening.

So to provide some answers to that dreaded question, we assembled more than 70 menus: for family dinners, family lunches and brunches, for company dinners when the guests are "almost family," for special occasions such as Christmas, Easter, Thanksgiving and birthdays or anniversaries, for breakfasts, picnics, barbecues and buffets. When you don't feel like cudgeling your brain to come up with a meal plan, you may find one that suits you between these covers.

We also know that in this era of not enough time and too much to do, you'd like to see at a glance how long a recipe is likely to take and how many it serves. So at the top of all our recipes we give the number of servings, the time required for preparation, cooking, marinating, chilling, as well as any other information you need before you begin. Since some cooks are whirlwinds in the kitchen, while others are leisurely and methodical, such times are only averages. You'll need to make allowances for your own style — tortoise or hare. Servings are geared to the average appetite, but if you're feeding ravenous eaters you may need to adjust our estimates. If, on the other hand, you're feeding people with bird-like appetites, you may have leftovers (and isn't that a blessing?).

Though more people now are acquainted with the millilitre than used to be, we still couldn't find anyone in our circle of friends and acquaintances who actually *cooked* with it: even teenagers who learn all about grams and millilitres in school tell us they use cups and teaspoons at home in the kitchen. So we've omitted metric measures from our recipes except when a package measurement may occur in metric only. In case you're looking for a pan in the store and don't know what size in centimetres to buy, you'll find a table at the back of the book.

It seems almost everyone is dieting in these self-conscious times — when not to be fit is considered one of the fairly major sins (and in some circles has replaced greed or adultery as a cause for raised eyebrows). So for all who are dieting, either to lose weight or put on muscle, to improve squash games or coddle arteries, we've provided an analysis of the major nutrients contained in each recipe. If, in the case of some desserts, a recipe provides nothing but plentiful calories, we think you're grown up enough to decide whether to pig out or not. Some readers tell us "light cuisine never caught on in this house," and even those who believe that healthy eating is the route to nirvana seem to binge every so often on a delectable dessert. Unrelieved virtue is pretty cold comfort and can lead to self-righteousness.

But still, what could justify publishing yet another cookbook? My office bookshelves are fairly buckling under the weight of cookbooks produced over just the past few years. North America almost seems to be in the grip of a feeding frenzy, just at a time when Third World famine is daily in the news. The word "foodie" has been coined to describe the person (of either sex) who can be heard at social gatherings extolling the delights of the shiitake mushroom and sun-dried tomato. In their presence we tend to remember nervously that in the last days of the Roman Empire the privileged lolled about peeling grapes and eating pheasants' tongues.

As might be expected in such a welcoming climate all manner of cookbooks abound: books wrapped in dust jackets glossy with glorious color; modest spiral-bound manuals; books for cooking Chinese, Mexican, Cajun, barbecue, microwave, vegetarian meals; books by chefs; "celebrity" books produced to aid good causes; books by nutritionists, doctors, gym instructors and cooking teachers; books devoted to honey, strawberries, herbs; books with recipes from famous restaurants and restaurants that would like to become famous.

Why add to this already ample supply? The answer seemed to come when we went back to what we had in mind when we started *Recipes Only Magazine*. We wanted a magazine for people who might or might not like to cook: for people who *had* to cook willy-nilly as well as those zealots blissfully devoted to their whisks and sauté pans. We were not a magazine for foodies; our readers seldom find time (nor think it important) to stuff mushrooms, let alone peel grapes. But there's no doubt that cooking can be one of life's richest pleasures. For many women, and these days men as well, cooking will always be a primary joy. I have a great-nephew who seems to have been born to cook. When he was only four, his older sister began a school essay (without any awareness of the absurdity) with the words: "My brother has always been a very good cook." He presumably added something special to his peanut butter sandwich or a little fruit to his cereal bowl. Some readers have told me that whenever they feel troubled or blue, they just need to start stirring, sifting or sautéeing to feel serene once again, and that God's in His Heaven and all's well with the world.

But truth to tell, many homemakers of both sexes are not such jubilant cooks. They do not approach the kitchen stove with a song in their hearts but with a resigned knowledge that it's getting on for mealtime and people have to eat. We thought it a shame that all such cooks don't have understanding aunts, mothers or neighbors to pass them reliable recipes across the back fence as they would have in bygone days when families tended to stay put. We'd like to inject some confidence and perspective into your culinary life — some sense that it's okay not to regard love of cooking as one of nature's basic instincts.

The basic instinct is for *eating*, not necessarily for cooking. Cooking is more like playing the violin; some people are virtuosos, some are good second-desk violinists, and some are tone deaf. A tone-deaf person would not be likely to take up violin playing, but many with no natural ability or affinity for cooking have to do it anyway. Perhaps this book will provide some challenging melodies for the virtuosos among you and encourage less-gifted cooks to rely on a sense of humor when things go wrong. We hope you'll find in the following pages some tunes you can master with your own pots, pans and spoons.

ON BECOMING A CONFIDENT COOK

What Kind of Cook Are You?

It's said that some people eat to live, while others live to eat. The former can be seen standing up at a street corner hot dog stand gulping lunch on the way to more interesting things. The latter will walk blocks for a ham sandwich at the one restaurant that thinly slices really good meat, and then slathers it with the zesty mustard it deserves. They are not on their way to something more interesting. Eating is their primary pleasure, and even when they're not hungry, they reminisce about marvellous meals they've had in the past or fantasize about ones they hope to have in the future — today's dinner with any luck. Likewise, some people cook in order to eat — survival cooks. Others cook for the sheer heavenly joy of it — artistic cooks.

Most of us fall somewhere between these extremes of gustatory enthusiasm and ennui. And when you scramble all the possible attitudes towards eating and cooking, you get a lot of different sorts of cooks. One who loves to eat *and* to cook will happily spend hours in the kitchen humming over a hot stove. One who loves to eat but hates to cook will contrive to eat someone else's cooking whenever possible. Someone who loves to eat and doesn't mind cooking will probably produce competent, unmemorable meals with a

minimum of fuss. (I belong, I confess, to this class.) People who hate to cook and only eat to stay alive will snatch meals on the run and will sometimes have to be reminded to do even that. Such people will never invite you to dinner, and you should be grateful.

People who love to cook even more than they love to eat are good friends to have — cozier than priceless gems. They will turn out marvellous, mouth-watering dishes and ask friends for dinner as casually as we'd invite them to a movie. The contributors to *Recipes Only Magazine* (and therefore to this cookbook) are such artistic cooks.

In coming to terms with the reality that much of our lives may be spent in the kitchen, it helps to acknowledge to ourselves which kind of cook we are — especially if we're thinking of entertaining. If you'd really rather converse with your friends than feed them, you'd best keep such parties as you feel obliged to have as simple and informal as possible. Otherwise, you may find yourself up to your armpits in pots and pans, grinding your teeth with resentment because they're all in the living room having fun. On the other hand, if you soar with the challenge of creating a splendid party your guests will talk about for weeks, why deny yourself and them the pleasure, just because few of them will be able to return in kind. They presumably have other endearing qualities.

Exploding the Gourmet Myth

In these days of advertisements for "gourmet" knives, "gourmet" spices, even "gourmet" kitchens, it's hard to keep our heads. It helps to remember that "gourmet" started life as a noun — not an adjective. Gourmet originally meant a *person* who is knowledgeable and discriminating about food and drink.

It's also helpful to remember in the midst of all this foodie hoopla that fine cuisine and fancy are not interchangeable. A bit of chicken or fish is not necessarily better because it's slathered in a sauce that took two hours to prepare. In a very costly restaurant, I was once served a rack of succulent Ontario lamb swimming in a fancy concoction of blueberry sauce. The lamb was so rare and slippery that in the course of trying to sever a sliver of it from the rubbery whole, my knife slid into the blueberry lake and a stream of blue sauce cascaded in a projectile arc, spraying the stark white wall just under the hanging fern. I would not have plotted such revenge for pretentiousness, but nevertheless I felt it was fitting. I did not concede that raw lamb in blueberry sauce, though billed as a "gourmet" delight, was fine cuisine.

Gourmets are connoisseurs, people who cultivate their taste buds, people who would rather eat a chunk of good cheese than a tarted-up, over-decorated, over-sauced and poorly cooked quail. The late Mme Jehane Benoit, who probably did more than any other Canadian to persuade us to enjoy our own excellent food, gave me my first lesson in the difference between "fancy" and "good" cooking. When she was asked to take a dish to a potluck dinner in her community, she chose to cook a beef tenderloin and serve it, lightly peppered, in its own pan juice. Beside it on the table was a magnificent ham, coated in a thick glutinous sauce and then wrapped in a heavy pastry. Madame knew that the cook had spent all day on her spectacular concoction, but felt that all she had accomplished was to virtually destroy a lovely ham. My father would have called it "gilding the lily." Mme Benoit's ten-derloin took moments to prepare and less than an hour to cook, and it was perfection.

Madame taught me another lesson that day 20 years ago when we talked. She and her husband, Bernard, raised sheep in the Eastern Townships of Quebec. Although she had been taught that mint was the herb to accompany lamb, she noticed that rosemary thrived in the same fields as the sheep did. So she tried rubbing lamb with rosemary before she cooked it and the result was (and is) delicious. Her advice was not to avoid experiment; half the fun in cooking is experimenting with new combinations. But not all experiments are successful, not all new combinations are a good idea. The menus of some of the new restaurants springing up like toadstools in our cities make it obvious that many cooks equate novelty with goodness, though it's not necessarily so. One restaurant dessert menu in my neighborhood featured smoked salmon cheesecake for a while. I just knew I could live out my life happily without trying that and I was half afraid it would arrive in a raspberry coulis (read "sauce"), so I never did. Evidently no one else did, either, because a few weeks later the menu featured smoked salmon pâté in the appetizer section of the menu and confided in brackets ("used to be called smoked salmon cheesecake").

No, novelty doesn't automatically make a dish good to eat. It took thousands of years of civilization to discover that some foods have a natural affinity for each other, enhance each other. If we're going to trifle with that, we should be reasonably sure before we serve the result to our friends that our experiment actually tastes good. When my kids occasionally got under my skin by nagging "What's for dinner? What's for dinner?" when I was already harried and couldn't decide, I used to threaten them with peanut butter and salami casserole. Though they loved peanut butter and loved salami, young as they were they knew that combination would not thrill them.

"Expensive" also isn't interchangeable with "good." Personally, I prefer home-grown mushrooms to many of the costly imported varieties. I even prefer them (and I might as well confess it and reveal myself as an utter clod among the foodies) to those costly truffles dug up by pigs in French forests. That doesn't make me a gourmet, but it doesn't automatically disqualify me, either. Perhaps the term "gourmand" (a polite word for glutton) most nearly describes me — I have yet to meet a food I actively dislike. But I don't like imported white asparagus as well as garden-grown green, and I think fresh green peas, parsnips and properly cooked turnip are hard to beat, and I can live quite comfortably without endive, which costs more. I prefer crisp leaf lettuce to radicchio. On the other hand, I could eat as many oysters as someone else is willing to pay for, and I can't even imagine what my limit of caviar would be; I only know that I've never even come close to finding it.

So costly food *can* be good, but so can cheap. It usually depends on how fresh it is and, when it needs cooking (I'd *never* cook an oyster), how lovingly it's cooked.

Another thing that's useful to understand about this "gourmet" business is that blue or pink food is not it. We don't often see blue, green or pink baby-shower sandwiches anymore and that's a mercy. Color co-ordination can go too far and is no substitute for tasty food. Pink cake, along with pink tablecloths, pink flowers and pink candles may be "cute" but will only get you a reputation for cuteness, not cooking. One of the truly inedible meals I've had lately (cold, over-cooked, dry chicken breast in a cold white sauce largely comprised of either library paste or cornstarch) was served in a dining room of breath-taking color co-ordination: deep blue tablecloths, red napkins, white candles (patriotic red, white and blue, get it?). A friend of mine once served blue spaghetti when her husband brought home unexpected guests once too often. They're now divorced and probably just in time to avert more serious retaliation.

So being a so-called gourmet cook doesn't mean putting sauce on everything, or creating a novel concoction no one's ever tried before, or mortgaging the house to buy caviar and truffles. It means doing the very best with what you have to work with: a perfectly cooked soft-boiled egg is more delectable by far than a tough leathery omelet. I achieved a certain reputation as a cook quite inadvertently (and certainly undeservedly) by baking a few loaves of bread. (More about the bread fluke in the Breads chapter.)

In a minute we'll get down to some specifics about entertaining. But before that, let's chart a course.

You Need to Have a Plan

Some joker (or sage?) once said, "Life is what happens to you while you're busy planning something else," and all too often that seems to be true. Nevertheless, we continue to plan: without a plan of some kind we feel we wouldn't stand a chance against life's vicissitudes but would be steered by every random current, blown by every sudden gust. Without a plan it's doubtful we'd be brave enough to get up in the morning.

Planning, of course, isn't everything. If we lock-step into a plan and march with blinders on, we'll never wander up the unexpected byway and stumble into the field of daisies. No, planning isn't everything, but in house-managing and cooking it's a lot, as anyone knows who has faced hungry, irritable children at the breakfast table with the news "We're out of milk."

Planning is at least half the secret of staying sane while feeding a family, and it may be even more than half the secret of hosting successful parties. And the underpinnings of planning are lists.

Those of you who've never had to run to the store for raisins or baking powder in the middle of preparing a recipe can probably skip this section altogether. You're already an organizer and have likely figured out long ago how to plan menus, make lists, shop for bargains, lay out ingredients. Nobody has to remind you to get the meat out of the freezer in the morning and to stop on the way home for bread. You almost seem to have been born knowing that you should put the potatoes in to bake a good while before you heat the broiler for the steak. Since you obviously weren't born with that knowledge, you must have watched your mother carefully.

But many mothers today are too busy at paying jobs to teach such things, and many children are too busy or too uninterested to learn. So many of us grope our way into cooking and meal-planning clumsily and slowly, forgetting crucial things, doing things backwards and upside down, blundering into disasters until we finally get the hang of it.

But even if you're the sort who has to run to the store for raisins when it's a raisin pie you're baking, don't despair of yourself. You may never be another Julia Child, but there's hope for you. You may not want to be Julia Child anyway but just aspire to orchestrate a meal so that the potatoes are cooked at the same time as the meat and the vegetables are neither mush nor rock-hard. And that's just the most basic kind of meal: add salad and dessert and the orchestration becomes more complex — a symphony orchestra rather than a string quartet.

Planning a whole week's menus is a feat I never quite accomplished. I usually got to Thursday's dinner before running out of ideas and patience. Maybe that was because the leftovers from the beginning

of the week would be pretty well used up by then and a fresh start was required. Friday tended to be an ad lib day with dinner determined by what was appealing *and* on special at the supermarket, and Saturday was immutably — because my family demanded it — hot dogs for lunch and hamburgers for dinner. There's no question that knowing on Sunday what the leftovers are likely to be can be a great comfort for the rest of the week: leftover Sunday roast means shepherd's pie or a stir-fry for Tuesday or Wednesday; leftover chicken, ham or turkey provides infinite possibilities for soups, pot-pies, pasta and rice dishes.

Even if this sort of planning is routine child's play for you, you may still be shaky about planning parties or large Christmas or Thanksgiving dinners, or dinners for your finicky aunts or your efficient, perfectionist friends. Perhaps the hardest meals to cook are for self-professed "gourmets" who have definite opinions about how garlicky the butter for an escargot should be, and who seem to know exactly when a soupçon of coriander would have elevated a dish to the "divine." You can sometimes profit from their expertise, provided your ears aren't stopped up with terror (or fury) in their presence. I'd positively quake to cook a meal for some of the superlative cooks of my acquaintance, in fact wouldn't cook for them unless the alternative was a firing squad. If I *had* to feed them, I'd take them to a restaurant — their choice.

And yet such nervous vapors are totally unreasonable. For I know that when I'm invited out to dinner I'm delighted to be with friends and grateful that someone else is cooking. If they chose to serve me only a peanut butter sandwich, I'd still be glad of their company. So why should we ever assume that people invited to our house are there to carp and criticize? The truth is they don't have to; we do a splendid job of that ourselves. "This sauce was much smoother last time. Today it seems a bit lumpy. And I don't think I put in enough nutmeg." Or "This cake didn't turn out as well as it should." Of course it didn't. Recipes *never* turn out as well when there's company. It's one of the laws of the universe — like the law of gravity.

Besides drawing attention to any actual imperfections there may be in the meal, such apologetic remarks leave guests feeling helpless and frustrated. Perhaps you're fishing for compliments — embarrassing for everyone. If they reassure you ("no, it's quite delicious"), they expose themselves as know-nothings who can't tell a good dish from a poor one, since you've already pronounced it under par. On the other hand, if they keep silent, they seem to be agreeing with your verdict. Either way they can't win and are uncomfortably aware of it. No-win games are not fun, so unless your meal is totally inedible for some freakish reason such as having caught fire or been mangled by the dog, just shut up and serve it. Save your post-mortems for the family where they might even engender some interest in the finer points of cooking.

But back to getting it planned, shopped for, cooked and on the table in the first place.

In Praise of Lists

Recipes are just lists of ingredients followed by lists of things to do with them. Everything in cooking depends on lists, either mental lists or pen-and-paper lists. Without realizing it, we started making lists inside our heads when we learned to put on our socks *before* we put on our shoes. We weren't born knowing that was the way it had to be done; we had to figure it out. I imagine God had a list before Creation.

1) Big Bang
2) Particles whirl in space
3) Particles gather together
4) Planets
5) Oceans — and so on.

Even if we subscribe to the seven-day version, if He had no plan we humans might have arrived on the scene at the same time as the dinosaurs and then where would we be? In a cold swamp with a lot of ferns and a brontosaurus breathing down our necks.

Yet many disparaging things have been said at the expense of list-makers. They are accused of being obsessive-compulsive by those irritating people who psychoanalyze everything. But in my experience, people who make lists, who write memos to themselves in the car at stoplights, are people who get things done. There have been times of intense pressure and confusion in my life when only a list that began "6:45 — get out of bed, 6:46 — clean teeth . . ." kept me moving forward at all.

So don't sneer at lists nor underestimate their value, even if your first cooking lists have to be as basic as 1) put kettle on to boil, 2) peel potatoes, 3) put potatoes on to cook, 4) get meat out of fridge. If the meat is still in the *freezer*, you didn't start your list soon enough. Next time start your list the night before with 1) get meat out of freezer.

So You Want to Have a Party

If lists are important to the ordinary daily running of a household, they're positively crucial to the success of entertaining. Without a pencil and pad of paper to impose some kind of system on the panicky recital of tasks that begins in my head at the thought of "guests" I'd never be brave enough to invite them. "Polish the silver, count the wine glasses, vacuum the baseboards, check to see if the tablecloth and napkins are clean and ironed." My inner nag starts carping at me even before I've decided on a guest list or a menu.

That's when I have to remind myself firmly of the principal rule of entertaining: *your job as a hostess is to make your guests feel comfortable — to ensure that they enjoy themselves*. It's not to outshine their parties; it's not to impress them with either your gleaming house or your cooking skill. It's to make them feel welcome, and they won't feel that at all if they arrive to find you frazzled, harried and frantic, no matter how impressive the surroundings or how delectable the meal. They'll feel they've put you to too much trouble and that both you and they wish they hadn't come.

This is where knowing what kind of cook you are — recognizing your limitations — is invaluable. You should choose a menu that's easily within your grasp to accomplish — preferably one you've cooked successfully before. Choose it with an eye to what can be made ahead, and unless you're a calm, confident virtuoso cook, keep it simple. If one dish is complicated, choose undemanding secondary dishes. Think of color when you make choices: cauliflower beside breast of chicken in a white sauce can look pretty boring. And think of what bright bit of garnish you can add to your serving dishes to give them a finished touch. But remember to garnish only with edibles because omnivores like me will eat everything put in front of them, including the garnish.

If you want to try a new menu, it's wise to experiment on the family first.

Diplomats and other such social personages keep logs of meals they have served, along with a list of the guests who were present. If you entertain frequently, that's a good idea. If you don't, it's unlikely anyone will remember, or care, what they had at your place two years ago. (Although that may not be true: evidently I served pork chops to my daughter's boyfriend the first three times she brought him home to dinner unexpectedly. Now that he's my son-in-law he feels free to remind me that for a time he thought that was all I could cook.)

It's considerate when making out a guest list to note any food allergies or dislikes your guests may have, and if they're relative strangers, ask them when you invite them. Two weeks ahead is not too long to plan a party, and even more time will make it go smoother.

Once you've decided on a list of people who either like each other or are likely to like each other, and have chosen a menu appropriate to your capabilities, you can start making more lists. List all the cleaning and tidying jobs you'd like to accomplish before your guests come. But resist the urge to do the spring cleaning you've neglected for years. Be satisfied to spruce up the areas your guests are going to see, and forget about tidying the linen closet or the garage or you'll be exhausted before you get to the important stuff.

From your menu, list all the groceries you have to buy and get non-perishable ones in plenty of time. Running to the store for drink mixes or wine or coffee at the last minute isn't necessary and doesn't make sense. Less durable foodstuffs and flowers to decorate the table should be bought as fresh as possible, a day or so ahead.

As you examine your menu, a logical order for doing things should begin to emerge and your lists can be divided up into categories: things to do a week ahead; things to do two days ahead; things to do one day ahead; things to do on "The Day" — right down to "turn on coffee while serving dessert."

I've never had the luxury of being able to stay out of the kitchen entirely when I'm giving a party. When I was growing up, my mother always had a hired girl (this was during the '30s Depression when people were willing to work for little more than room and board). So Mother cooked the food for her formal dinner parties, but then presided serenely over the table while someone else served up the many courses. For many years after I married, I attempted to duplicate my mother's impeccably run household single-handed. It took me a long time to realize that one person cannot do the work of two. I lowered my sights and began to plan simpler menus and, for the most part, buffet service. But I promise myself that one day I'll hire an agreeable teenager and brief her (or him) thoroughly to take over the kitchen when the first guest arrives.

What to Do When Disaster Strikes

Faced with a fallen cake or a failed recipe of any kind, the cook is beset with two compelling urges — to curse (or cry, depending on temperament) and then to throw the whole mess in the garbage. Indulge the first urge as fully as your conscience will permit, but do not yield to the second. Most failures are salvageable. What is a "failure" anyway? Something that didn't turn out the way you wanted it to. So doesn't that happen daily in some area of your life? And aren't you constantly switching to plan B? So look at the "failure" and let your mind range over the possibilities of what it might be good for, besides squirrel food.

I seem to have disasters clustered around baking powder. One of my earliest catastrophes occurred when two of my husband's disapproving (I thought) aunts were coming to lunch. Just as I was whipping up a batch of fresh biscuits to show them what a good little wife and housekeeper their nephew had lucked onto, I heard a terrifying squeal of car brakes at the front of the house. After I'd dashed to the door to assure myself a child was not under the car's wheels, I couldn't remember whether I'd already put the baking powder into the biscuits. I decided to put it in, and forgot about it while I agonized over the main dish.

I was so nervous at lunch that I didn't actually taste a biscuit until the aunts had already eaten one each. The biscuits were horrible. They tasted so strongly of baking powder that I almost choked on mine. When I apologized to the aunts and asked why on earth they hadn't complained, they smiled sweetly and said they hadn't wanted to spoil *my* day when I was trying so hard. That's when I learned a lot about the goodwill of guests (and aunts).

Probably nothing would have rescued those biscuits, but my next baking powder disaster turned into a success. I was baking a chocolate cake and chocolate chip cookies for a family birthday celebration, and the cake-batter and cookie dough were proceeding simultaneously in two separate bowls. I don't remember whether it was car brakes, the telephone or a knock at the door that distracted me this time (with four children there tended to be more distractions than tranquil moments), but there I was once again — had I put the baking powder into the cake batter? I was reasonably sure I had, so I poured the cake batter into layer pans and put it in the oven. It just sat there. After half an hour it was cooked, but hadn't risen a centimeter. Had I put the baking powder into the cookie dough by mistake? Following that hunch, I removed the cake from the layer pans and spread the cookie dough therein. Half an hour later I had two chocolate chip layers about an inch high. I combined them with the chocolate cake layers, which had the consistency of brownies. I spread icing between the layers, iced the tops and sides and presented it as my Special Birthday Invention. It was a great hit and the kids wanted to know when we could have it again. (Never, as it turned out, because I wasn't sure exactly what I'd done.) So it always saddens me when a reader writes to say she threw out something that had edible ingredients in it.

A custard that fails to thicken can become a sauce; a lemon pie filling that's runny can be a pudding; a cake that fails to rise can be cut into strips to make the base for a trifle. A crêpe that fails to hold its shape (and its filling) is still a crêpe — the taste is the same. Remember, if the ingredients are good, even your "failures" are edible in some form or another.

Shortly after I had stumbled into food-writing, I was asked by the editor of the *Star Weekly* Women's Section (yes, it was in those bad, old, women-are-only-interested-in-cooking days) to write a story about what I would serve Her Majesty the Queen if she were to come to my house. I was to cook the dinner just as if I was expecting her to sweep across my threshold, and a photographer would take pictures of the food.

After lengthy and nervous consultation with a sister-in-law who was the best cook I knew, I decided I'd serve the Queen a quintessentially Canadian dinner. The star of the show would be a whole salmon (I refuse to say from which coast, since I don't want half the country mad at me) poached in a subtle court bouillon and served cold with a homemade mayonnaise. I think fresh new green peas were to accompany it, but details are now lost in the mists of time. But it's the salmon I can now confess about. (I astounded myself by making a perfect mayonnaise just by following the recipe.)

When the salmon arrived, it was clearly about half as big again as any cooking vessel I had in the house. My next-door neighbor was a policeman who worked nights, and I woke him up at noon to ask if his wife had a large roasting pan. I was in luck — she had one of those oval, speckled roasting pans that I have since discovered are standard issue in most households. It was exactly the right size to contain my salmon, and I filled it with court bouillon (according to the recipe) and set it on to boil. I waited — and waited — and waited. The wretched thing wouldn't boil! I fiddled and cursed and sighed but couldn't produce a single bubble on the surface of that liquid. I decided to take emergency action: I phoned my sister-in-law. I was informed that she was out playing bridge. Where? I demanded. I got the phone number and interrupted the bridge game. She advised giving up on boiling and just plunging the salmon into the bouillon, which, I was able to report, was certainly *hot*. The salmon cooked just in time for the photographer, but it wasn't until I began to wash the dishes that the roasting pan suddenly came apart in my hands. It had a lid that had been nesting snugly inside the pan. I had been trying to boil water in the lid, with an insulating gap of air between it and the bottom of the roasting pan. And now you know what the readers of that old *Star Weekly* Women's Section were never told.

The opportunities for cooking mishaps are only equalled by the opportunities for misplaced commas in publishing. A day when we humans can avoid all pitfalls is a rare day. Since that early time of groping and catastrophes there've been years when hardly a day went by without a phone call either from a daughter or a niece (daughter of that helpful sister-in-law) with a strangled ''Help!'' as they came to grips with the reality of cooking. And my help isn't always enough.

I once nursed my niece through dinner-party preparations by telephone over a period of a couple of days, only to have her report later that her sole in a cream sauce exploded just as she was putting the finishing touches to it. I hadn't thought to warn her not to pour cold sauce over hot fish in a hot Pyrex dish. The dish cracked with a report like a gunshot, but ever resourceful, she dumped it quickly into another dish just in time to keep it from leaking all over the floor. As might be predicted, with that kind of savoir faire, she's become a superlative cook — almost a virtuoso — and has far outstripped her mentor. She loves cooking *and* she has a flair.

Anyone who wants to can learn to cook competently by following directions precisely, just as anyone can learn to draw a recognizable tree or house by adhering to the laws of proportion. But *great* cooking, like great painting, is only half science, rules and discipline. Few are the Michelangelos and Leonardo da Vincis. In the kitchen most of us occupy the territory somewhere between Julia Child and Peg Bracken (who wrote *The I Hate to Cook Book*). It's important to know it's okay to occupy that middle ground inhabited by good, dependable daily cooks.

MENUS FOR ALL OCCASIONS

Pan-Fried Turbot with Mushrooms and Shallots; Lemon Spring Rice; Green Beans with Bacon and Parmesan Cheese

Family Dinners

Serves 4

Pan-Fried Turbot with Mushrooms and Shallots 127
Lemon Spring Rice 161
Green Beans with Bacon and Parmesan Cheese 153
Ice cream or frozen yogurt

Serves 4

Individual Meat Loaves or Meat and Cheese Loaf 80, 84
Zucchini and Tomato Sauté 150
Baked potatoes
Blueberry and Raspberry Pie 209

Serves 4 to 6

Eggplant Spread 32
Ossobuco 82
Rice or mashed potatoes or boiled new potatoes
Stuffed Tomatoes with Shallots and Basil 156
Fresh fruit and Highland Cream 232

Serves 6

Apple and Winter Squash Soup 53
Cider- and Honey-Glazed Pork 97
Baked, boiled or mashed potatoes
Coleslaw 72
Baked Fudge Pudding 218

Hot or Cold Broccoli Soup; Fillet of Sole Montmorency; Salad with Blue Cheese Dressing; Pears in Red Wine

Dinners for Company

Serves 4

Quick Asparagus Soup 49
Roast Pork Tenderloin with Plum Sauce 90
Purée of Fall Root Vegetables 158
Roast or sautéed potatoes
Baked Fudge Pudding 218

Serves 4

Tapenade 40
Veal Chops with Tomato Tarragon Sauce 84
Broccoli with Creamy Dressing 158
Rice Pilaf 161
Apple Strudel 199

Serves 4 to 6

Hot or Cold Broccoli Soup 50
Fillet of Sole Montmorency 127
Salad with Blue Cheese Dressing 62
Boiled new potatoes
Pears in Red Wine 233

Serves 6

Artichoke Dip 34
Boeuf Bourguignon 80
Buttered noodles
Mixed Green Salad with Mustard Vinaigrette 63
Chocolate Pecan Pie 209

Serves 6

Eggplant Spread 32
Creamy Cannelloni with Chicken and Almonds 137
Julienne Vegetable Salad with Lemon Vinaigrette 75
Poached Pears in Raspberry Sauce 224

Serves 6 to 8

Hearty Country Meat Loaf with Sour Cream Gravy 86
Potato Croquette Casserole 150
Buttered Green Beans with Almonds 151
Coconut Cloud Cake 203

Quick Asparagus Soup; Broiled Lamb Chops with Lime, Mint and Chives; Zucchini and Tomato Sauté

Quick and Easy Menus

Dinner in an Hour

Serves 4

Chicken with Crabmeat Sauce 110
Danish Potato Salad 67
Tomato and Red Onion Salad with Savory 68
Melon with Ginger Sauce 228

Serves 4

Artichoke Dip with breadsticks 34
Pasta Shells with Salmon and Broccoli 140
Tomato and Basil Salad 67
Lemon Pudding 214

Serves 4 to 6

Skillet Orange Chicken with Green Beans 111
Buttered noodles
Mexican Corn Salad with Lime Dressing 76
Chocolate Fondue with fresh fruit and pound cake 214

Serves 4 to 6

Fresh Mussels Marinière 125
Autumn Fettuccine 142
Tomato and Red Onion Salad with Savory 68
Apple Crisp 217

Serves 8

Dill and Spinach Dip 36
Scallops and Snow Peas 120
Steamed rice
Tomato and Coriander Salad 62
Half-Hour Pudding 218

35-Minute Meals

Serves 4

Pasta with Quick Tomato Herb Sauce 136
Simple Caesar Salad 63
Rhubarb and Apple Compote 224

Serves 4

Pumpkin Soup 49
Chicken Risotto 113
Broccoli with Creamy Dressing 158
Bananas with Chocolate Fudge Sauce 228

Serves 4

Kidney Bean and Bacon Salad 73
Pasta with Spicy Sausage and Cream 142
Tomato and Basil Salad 67
Maple Oranges 230

Serves 4

Quick Asparagus Soup 49
Broiled Lamb Chops with Lime, Mint and Chives 106
Zucchini and Tomato Sauté 150
Rolls and butter
Melon with Ginger Sauce 228

Serves 4 to 6

Shrimp Curry 121
Steamed rice
Snow Pea and Mango Salad 70
Sautéed Bananas 231

Salad with Smoked Ham and Parmesan; Pasta with Spicy Tomato Sauce; Cherries with Sour Cream Dip

Dinners for Two

Salad with Smoked Ham and Parmesan 75
Pasta with Spicy Tomato Sauce 138
Cherries with Sour Cream Dip 226

Curried Apple and Avocado Soup 50
Grilled Chinese Chicken Salad 64
Fresh fruit and Highland Cream 232

Salmon with Ginger Lime Butter 124
Spiced Spinach 160
Strawberry Brûlée 232

Sirloin Steak with Pepper Sauce 88
Green salad with Garlic Vinaigrette 64
Tiny boiled potatoes and glazed carrots
Raspberry Sorbet 226

Fettuccine with Clam Sauce 136
Greens tossed with Garlic Vinaigrette 64
Strawberries Dipped in Chocolate 231

Chops with Herb Sauce 89
Zucchini Spaghetti with Basil 157
Instant Mocha Mousse 219

A Romantic Candlelight Dinner

Crab Legs with Herb Butter 129
Fluffy rice
Spiced Spinach 160
Orange Chocolate Mousse 219

Low-Calorie Menus

Serves 4

Pork Chops with Rosemary and Orange 96
Noodles
Peas Sautéed with Lettuce 151
Rhubarb and Apple Compote 224

Serves 4

Fish Fillets with Basil Butter 124
Grilled Zucchini with Tomatoes, Savory and Thyme 152
Steamed red potatoes
Navel Orange Slices in Spiced Red Wine 227

Serves 4

Chicken Breasts with Curried Cream Sauce 114
Buttered Green Beans with Almonds 151
Rice
Sherried Grapefruit Sorbet 226

Serves 4

Chilled Red Pepper and Mushroom Soup 59
Barbecued Lemon Chicken 109
Tomato and Basil Salad 67
Steamed rice
Rhubarb Sherbet 227

Microwave Menus

Serves 2

Curried Apple and Avocado Soup 50
Salmon with Ginger Lime Butter 124
Zucchini Spaghetti with Basil 157
Parsleyed noodles
Cheese and crackers

Serves 4

Meatballs Avgolemono 102
Zucchini and Tomato Sauté 150
Steamed rice
Sautéed Bananas 231

Serves 6

Eggplant Spread with crackers and Melba toast 32
Chicken with Bulgur Stuffing 109
Purée of Fall Root Vegetables 158
Baked or steamed potatoes
Mixed greens and tomato salad with
Garlic Vinaigrette 64
Poached Pears in Raspberry Sauce 224

Serves 8

Buffet

Herbed Crab Dip 40
Creamy Cannelloni with Chicken and Almonds 137
Sweet Potato Flan 154
Mixed Green Salad with Mustard Vinaigrette 63
Fruit Sherbet 227

Serves 8

Buffet

Baked Ham with Apricot Glaze 90
Tomato and Coriander Salad 62
Baked potatoes
Pumpkin Cheesecake 201

Barbecues

Barbecued Salmon Fillets 127
Grilled Zucchini with Tomatoes, Savory and Thyme 152
Lemon Spring Rice 161
Strawberry Rhubarb Tart 213

Serves 4

Barbecued Lemon Chicken 109
Tomato and Red Onion Salad with Savory 68
Baked potatoes
Chocolate Marble Cheesecake 196

Serves 8

Famous Maritime Hamburgers 83
Spinach and Mushroom Salad with Creamy
Buttermilk Dressing 68
Corn on the cob
Peaches Catherine 233

Serves 8 to 10

Herbed Crab Dip 40
Grilled Leg of Lamb with Aioli-Mustard Marinade 106
Watercress and Orange Salad 72
Baked potatoes
Rhubarb Mousse 233

Buffet Menus

Serves 4 or 5

Mulled Cider 44
Pork with Sage and Capers 100
Zucchini and Tomato Sauté 150
Rice Pilaf 161
Baked Apples with Ginger 228

Serves 8

Gratin of Scallops and Mushrooms 125
Rutabaga and Carrot Puff 155
Marinated Cauliflower Salad with Fresh Ginger 76
Refrigerator Rolls 173
Chocolate Clementine Mousse Cake 200

Serves 8

Onion Tartlets 39
Baked Ratatouille 133
Boiled rice
Celery Amandine 151
Pumpkin Biscuits 167

Serves 8 to 10

Lobster Butter on Melba toast rounds or crackers 39
Curried Chicken and Rice Casserole 108
Red Tomato and Apple Chutney 238
Onion and Pea Salad 71
Lemon Lime Cheesecake 204

Serves 12

Mulled Wine 41
Tourtière 93
Sweet Potato and Pecan Purée 158
Onion and Pepper Salad 68
Black Forest Cake 194

Serves 20

Eggplant Spread 32
Melba toast
Broccoli and Mushroom Dip 32
Crudités
Baked Ham with Apricot Glaze 90
Vegetable Lasagna 143
Large Mixed Green Salad with Mustard Vinaigrette 63
Refrigerator Rolls 173
Chocolate Torte 195
Pumpkin Cheesecake 201

Roast Turkey with Potato Dressing; Shredded Rutabaga Turnip; Cucumbers in Sour Cream; Pumpkin Biscuits

Special Occasion Menus

Christmas

Serves 12

Hot Rum Toddies 45
Lobster Butter 39
Salt Cod Pâté 39
Roast Turkey with Potato Dressing 111
Shredded Rutabaga Turnip 152
Cucumbers in Sour Cream 69
Broccoli and Carrot Vinaigrette 63
Pumpkin Biscuits 167
Steamed Cranberry Pudding with Sweet Butter Sauce 222

Serves 12

Creamed Crab with Mushrooms 33
Roast Turkey with Wild Rice and Sausage Stuffing 116
Creamed Potato Casserole 157
Apple Turnip Casserole 157
Onion and Pepper Salad 68
Cranberry Orange Cheesecake 192
Pralines 183
Swedish Nuts 191
Stuffed Dried Fruits 183

Easter or Spring Celebration

Serves 8

Smoked Fish Mousse with Melba toast and crackers 35
Stuffed Crown Roast of Pork 92
Parsnip Currant Puffs 154
Peas Sautéed with Lettuce 151
Oven-roasted potatoes
Mixed Green Salad with Mustard Vinaigrette 63
Maple Pecan Torte 193

Serves 8

Asparagus Bisque 58
Gratin of Scallops and Mushrooms 125
Mustardy Rack of Lamb 106
Minted Peas and Carrots Baskets 154
Boiled new potatoes
Marquises Glacées with Strawberries 224
Langues de Chat 189

Serves 8 to 10

Spinach Vichyssoise 54
Baked Ham with Apricot Glaze 90
Mustard Sauce 146
Watercress and Orange Salad 72
Sweet Potato Flan 154
Refrigerator Rolls 173
Rhubarb Mousse 233

Thanksgiving or Harvest Celebration

Serves 6

Gingered Carrot and Orange Soup 50
Capon with Corn Bread and Sausage Stuffing 118
Roast potatoes
Purée of Fall Root Vegetables 158
Classic Pumpkin Pie 210

Serves 8

Herbed Crab Dip 40
Glazed Ham with Pumpkin Maple Stuffing 93
Potato Croquette Casserole 150
Buttered Green Beans with Almonds 151
Harvest Fruit Pie 207

Serves 8

Harvest Pumpkin and Zucchini Soup 49
Stuffed Crown Roast of Pork with apple sauce 92
Roast potatoes
Rutabaga and Carrot Puff 155
Apricot Peach Pie 212

Birthday

Serves 4 to 6

Artichoke Dip and toast rounds 34
Boneless Pork Tenderloin with Apple Fennel Stuffing 91
Broccoli with Creamy Dressing 158
Birthday Chocolate Layer Cake and ice cream 198

Serves 6

Lili's Smoked Salmon Mousse 34
Mustardy Rack of Lamb 106
Gazpacho Salad 75
Boiled new potatoes
Maple Pecan Torte 193

Afternoon Tea

Serves 6

Scottish Scone 164
Strawberry jam
Apple Oatmeal Squares 184
Orange Date Loaf 167

Serves a Crowd

Pumpkin Biscuits 167
Apricot Citrus Bars 188
Maple Pecan Torte 193
Triple Decker Squares 187

Serves 8 to 10

Tea with milk or lemon
Brown Sugar Scones with honey 169
Cranberry Loaf 171
Lemon Loaf 166

Cocktail Parties

Elegant and Extravagant

Oysters on the Half Shell 35
Pickled Shrimp 37
Lobster Butter 39
Onion Tartlets 39

Cozy and Casual

Microwave Rumaki Canapés 40
Cucumber Cheese 37
Sausage Rolls or Onion Tartlets 34, 39
Salt Cod Pâté 39

Terrine with Orange and Pepper 38
Broccoli and Mushroom Dip 32
Eggplant Spread 32
Swedish Nuts 191

Lunches

Serves 4

Emerald Pasta Salad 71
Cracked Wheat and Citrus Salad 66
Chilled Chinese Pork 99
Apple Bran Streusel Muffins 168

Serves 6

Julienne Vegetable Salad with Lemon Vinaigrette 75
Mexican Corn Salad with Lime Dressing 76
Spicy Meat Loaf 89
Rolls
Melon with Blueberries 231

Serves 8

Gazpacho 57
Sausage Spinach Squares 101
Marinated Cauliflower Salad with Fresh Ginger 76
Pumpkin Chocolate Chip Cookies 184

Serves 8

A Winter Cross-Country Skiing Picnic

Harvest Pumpkin and Zucchini Soup 49
Sausage and Spinach Loaf sandwiches 98
Cranberry Oat Squares 188

Serves 12

A Co-operative Picnic

Broccoli and Carrot Vinaigrette 63
Cucumbers in Sour Cream 69
Stuffed Eggs 36
Tourtière 93
or Baked Ham with Apricot Glaze 90
Refrigerator Rolls 173
Almond Sponge Cake 203

Brunches

Serves 4

Orange juice
Spinach and Cheddar Strata 132
Broiled pork sausages
Lemon Oatmeal Muffins 169
Spiced Café au Lait 45

Serves 4 to 6

Baked Vegetable Omelet 135
Tomato Coulis 147
Melon with Ginger Sauce 228
Spiced Café au Lait 45

Serves 6 to 8

Tapenade 40
Endive and Hazelnut Salad with Tarragon Cream
Dressing 76
Brioche Ham and Cheese Tart 99
Cranberry Orange Cheesecake 192

Serves 6 to 8

Melon with Blueberries 231
Crêpe Quiche 178
Brown Sugar Scones 169
Pumpkin Apricot Marmalade or honey 237

Serves 8

Winter Fruit Salad with Citrus Yogurt Sauce 220
Ham and Cheese Strata 95
Bran Muffins 170
Coffee or tea

Breakfasts

Serves 2

Tomato and Mushroom Omelet with Thyme 132
Strawberry Rhubarb Muffins 166
Coffee or tea

Serves 4

Sliced Oranges
Crêpes Suzette 177
Spiced Café au Lait 45

Serves 3 or 4

Tomato Vegetable Mocktail 45
Savory Weekend Scrambled Eggs 131
Marmalade Muffins 173
Coffee or tea

THE RECIPES

APPETIZERS AND DRINKS

I doubt if my mother and grandmother would have understood appetizers. I'm almost certain they wouldn't have approved of them. "You'll spoil your dinner" is a warning that still rings in my ears whenever I see someone eating within an hour of dinnertime. Actually, during the years when I heard that admonition most frequently, it was impossible to spoil my dinner. My appetite as a teenager seemed to renew itself on the very act of eating thick chunks of warm homemade bread slathered in cold butter and topped off with about an inch of peanut butter. And that was *after* stopping at the Chinese restaurant on Main Street for a root beer float with the gang. Loaded with calories as they were, those were merely "appetizers," whetting my taste buds for the corn on the cob, baked potatoes and pie we were likely to have for what we called "supper": dinner was at noon and usually featured a large chunk of pan-fried steak or chop.

So the notion of an appetizer as an overture to the main event has a strong, if almost illicit, appeal. It's just close enough to eating between meals to be slightly sinful. My mother did serve soup as a first course at her sit-down dinner parties, but that was "the soup course" and not considered an appetizer. Come to think of it though, at these formal dinner parties cut-glass dishes of olives and celery were always passed while the soup was being served. Could these have been appetizers that didn't declare themselves?

Certainly times and styles have changed. Today, appetizers are often taken standing up, with drinks. Sometimes, as at cocktail parties, appetizers are all you get. They generally come in one-bite servings, but when they don't you're called upon to juggle a drink glass, a plate and a fork in a rather alarming fashion, while at the same time making bright conversation with your fellow jugglers. Some such appetizers are hot, others are drippy and some, alas, are both. The delicate scrap of tissue known as a cocktail napkin is often inadequate protection against the rivulets and crumbs so prone to ending up on the front of your dress. At such functions I always fill a plate and then selfishly commandeer a chair, if one's to be found, and devote myself to eating. Conversation can come later when the concentration is not distracted by food. If such gatherings titillate your appetite for dinner, you may have to make your own arrangements about that: either go home for it or head for the nearest restaurant.

Appetizers that start out on plates are usually served

Oysters on the Half Shell

as the prelude to a sit-down dinner or buffet table. A simple composed salad makes an appealing appetizer, as do pâté slices, or fish or seafood mousses, and they may even have been preceded by bite-size canapés with predinner drinks. My mother would definitely call this ''spoiling your dinner.''

It seems to me that drinking customs have altered somewhat in the last decade or so. You rarely see anyone holding a dark smoky glass of Scotch or a highball before dinner anymore, though it seemed 20 or 30 years ago that the rye-and-ginger highball or martini was the only drink North Americans understood — apart from beer. The only wines my parents were familiar with when I grew up on the Prairies were sherry and port, and these were taken with dessert and nuts at Christmas. Now the favored drinks at parties of all kinds seem to be white wines, spritzers, and even mineral water with a twist.

Is it possible that the wheel that brings us full circle in so many areas of life is bringing us back to the parties of my childhood where large cut-glass goblets of water and a handsome cut-glass pitcher of the same adorned our formal dinner tables? It seems not unlikely, given our evident taste for lighter drinks and our mis-

trust of what our taps provide, that alongside the wine, bottles of mineral water will become as familiar to the dinner table as they are to the bar.

In our Appetizers and Drinks section we've provided recipes for bite-size snacks for those occasions when you need canapés or hors d'oeuvres, as well as more formal plate-served preludes to a full meal. There are recipes for punches, hot drinks, refreshing drinks for hot days, mulled drinks for cold evenings and much, we hope, to add cheer to your parties.

Appetizers

BROCCOLI AND MUSHROOM DIP

Makes 2¼ cups
Preparation time: 15 minutes
Cooking time: 8 minutes

This delicious vegetable dip makes a nutritious snack served with crisp veggies or bread sticks.

2 cups	**chopped broccoli (include stalks)**
1 Tb	**vegetable oil**
1	**clove garlic, minced**
½	**onion, chopped**
1½ cups	**coarsely chopped mushrooms**
¾ cup	**low-fat cottage cheese**
¼ cup	**low-fat plain yogurt or light sour cream**
	salt and pepper to taste

▪ Cook broccoli in a pot of boiling water, just until tender-crisp, about 3 minutes. ▪ Drain and refresh under cold water. ▪ Drain again and set aside. ▪ Heat oil over medium heat in a non-stick skillet. ▪ Add garlic, onion and mushrooms and cook, shaking pan to prevent sticking, for 5 minutes or until onion is tender. Set aside. ▪ Combine cottage cheese and yogurt in a food processor, and process until smooth. ▪ Add mushroom mixture and broccoli. Season with salt and pepper to taste. ▪ Process with on/off motion just until mixed. ▪ Cover and refrigerate for up to 2 days.

calories/2 tablespoons: 23
vitamin C: good
low cal
low fat

SAVORY COEUR À LA CRÈME

Serves 8
Preparation time: 15 minutes
Setting time: 12 to 24 hours

Coeur à la crème is usually served as a dessert, but this savory version makes a simple yet rich appetizer.

1	**medium onion, chopped, *or* chopped chives to taste**
2 cups	**Ricotta cheese**
1 cup	**plain yogurt**
1 tsp	**salt or to taste**
	parsley sprigs for garnish
2 Tb	**caviar per person (optional)**

▪ Mince onion in a food processor or blender until fine but not reduced to mush. ▪ Add Ricotta, yogurt and salt and blend well. ▪ Line individual coeur à la crème pots with a double thickness of cheesecloth and pack mixture into pots. (Pottery ones are expensive, but you can buy heart-shaped tin molds and make your own holes in the bottom with a big nail and a block of wood. Just make sure you hammer from the inside out.) ▪ Place pots on a baking sheet with sides (to catch the drips) and chill overnight. ▪ To serve, unmold a pot onto a plate, one per serving, and top with a sprig of parsley. ▪ Spoon the caviar, if you wish, beside each coeur and pass warm French bread or interesting crackers. Best with a liqueur glass of freezer-chilled vodka.

calories/serving: 209
protein: excellent
calcium, iron, riboflavin, niacin: good
vitamin A: fair

EGGPLANT SPREAD

Makes 1½ cups
Preparation time: 10 minutes
Cooking time: 40 to 45 minutes
Chilling time: 4 hours or overnight

Most people will never guess that eggplant is the basis of this refreshingly cool appetizer. It is best made ahead of time for the flavors to blend.

1	**medium eggplant**
1	**medium onion, finely chopped**
1 to 2	**cloves garlic, minced**
1	**ripe tomato, peeled, seeded and finely chopped**
1 tsp	**sugar**
¼ cup	**olive oil**
2 Tb	**lemon juice**
	salt and pepper to taste
	few drops Tabasco sauce (optional)

▪ Prick eggplant in several places with a sharp knife. ▪ Place on baking sheet and bake in preheated 400°F oven until soft, 40 to 45 minutes, turning once during baking. ▪ Cool, cut in half lengthwise and scoop out flesh into a medium bowl. Discard skin. ▪ Stir in onion, garlic, tomato, sugar, oil and lemon juice. ▪ Purée in a food processor or blender as smooth as you wish. ▪ Season to taste with salt and pepper, and Tabasco. ▪ Cover and refrigerate at least 4 hours or overnight. Serve with sesame crackers, Melba toast or small pitas.
MICROWAVE DIRECTIONS: Pierce eggplant in several places with a fork. Place on paper towel and microwave on High 5 to 7 minutes or until tender when pierced. Let stand until cool. Continue as above.

calories/tablespoon: 15
vitamin C: good

Creamed Crab with Mushrooms

CREAMED CRAB WITH MUSHROOMS

Serves 12
Preparation time: 15 minutes
Cooking time: 12 to 15 minutes

This easy appetizer can be prepared ahead, then refrigerated before baking. Perfect for entertaining.

¼ cup	butter or margarine
3 cups	sliced fresh mushrooms
3 cups	coarsely crushed soda crackers
⅓ cup	melted butter or margarine
⅔ cup	mayonnaise
2	eggs, lightly beaten
¼ cup	finely chopped fresh parsley
	salt and pepper to taste
½ tsp	dry mustard
2 tsp	Worcestershire sauce
¼ cup	dry sherry
2 cans	(each 6 oz/170 g) crab, drained and broken up, *or* 2½ cups flaked cooked fresh crab
½ cup	grated Swiss cheese
	lemon wedges and fresh parsley sprigs for garnish

■ Butter 12 scallop shells or 6-ounce custard cups. ■ Heat ¼ cup butter or margarine in a skillet and add mushrooms. ■ Fry quickly until lightly browned, then remove from heat. ■ Combine cracker crumbs and ⅓ cup melted butter or margarine. ■ Set aside ⅔ cup crumb mixture. ■ Mix remaining crumbs, mayonnaise, eggs, parsley, seasonings, sherry, crab and mushrooms and divide among the shells or custard cups. ■ Mix the ⅔ cup reserved crumb mixture with the cheese and sprinkle over the crab mixture, using a generous tablespoon each. ■ Set shells or custard cups on a jelly roll pan or cookie sheet. ■ Bake in preheated 350°F oven until lightly browned and set, 12 to 15 minutes. ■ Garnish with lemon wedges and parsley sprigs and serve immediately.

calories/serving: 304
protein, niacin: good
iron, vitamin A, thiamin: fair

HOW TO COOK CRABS

To cook live crabs, bring a large kettle of lightly salted water to boil. Grasp crabs firmly by tail end and drop into boiling water. Cover and simmer 8 to 10 minutes per pound of crabs. Drain and rinse under cold running water.

Lili's Smoked Salmon Mousse

LILI'S SMOKED SALMON MOUSSE

Serves 6
Preparation time: 10 minutes
Chilling time: overnight

This mousse is a good way to stretch expensive smoked salmon and it always creates magic around the table.

6 oz	**smoked salmon**
3 cups	**whipping cream**
2 Tb	**lemon juice**
1 Tb	**chopped capers (optional)**
1 Tb	**chopped fresh dill**
	salt and white pepper to taste
4 to 6	**vine leaves**
	leaf lettuce for garnish

▪ Place smoked salmon in a blender or food processor. ▪ Purée. ▪ Gradually blend in whipping cream. ▪ Add lemon juice, capers, dill, salt and pepper all together. ▪ Blend. *Be careful not to overblend.* ▪ Oil a small soufflé mold and line with vine leaves. ▪ Pour in salmon mixture. ▪ Chill overnight. ▪ Unmold on curly leaf lettuce and serve with rice crackers.

calories/serving: 258
protein, vitamin A, niacin: good

ARTICHOKE DIP

Makes about 2½ cups
Preparation time: 10 minutes
Cooking time: 15 minutes

Serve this dip as an appetizer or as a nibble with drinks; it couldn't be easier to prepare.

1 can	**(19 oz/540 mL) artichoke hearts, drained**
1 cup	**mayonnaise**
1 cup	**grated Parmesan cheese**

▪ Chop artichoke hearts. ▪ Blend with mayonnaise and cheese. ▪ Spoon into a small, shallow, buttered casserole dish. ▪ Bake in preheated 350°F oven for 15 minutes. ▪ Serve warm with Melba toast or toast rounds.

calories/2 tablespoons: 99

SAUSAGE ROLLS

Pork sausages make tasty – and quick – sausage rolls. Simmer sausages in one inch of water for 7 minutes, drain and pat dry on paper towels. Wrap in puff pastry, brush with egg yolk and bake in preheated 400°F oven for 15 minutes.

SMOKED FISH MOUSSE

Serves 8
Preparation time: 10 minutes

Smooth, light and slightly smoky, this easy mousse is perfect for spreading on Melba toast, French bread or plain crackers. Or, if you wish, pipe mousse onto leaves of Belgian endive.

¾ lb	**smoked trout, salmon, whitefish or mackerel fillets, skin removed**
3 Tb	**each lemon juice, mayonnaise and heavy cream**
pinch	**each salt, black pepper and cayenne pepper**
	chopped fresh parsley and lemon slices for garnish

■ If using whole fish, buy approximately 1¼ lbs to yield ¾ lb fish fillets. ■ Cut fish into small pieces and purée in a food processor or blender. ■ Add lemon juice, mayonnaise, heavy cream, salt, pepper and cayenne. ■ Process 30 seconds or until smooth but not watery. ■ Transfer to a serving bowl, cover and refrigerate up to 1 day if making ahead of time. ■ Remove from refrigerator 30 minutes before serving. ■ Garnish with chopped fresh parsley and a lemon slice.

calories/serving: 129
protein: good

OYSTERS ON THE HALF SHELL

Preparation time: 30 minutes

The ultimate in appetizers; perfect for dinner à deux.

6	**fresh oysters per person**
	half a lemon per person
	freshly ground black pepper

■ Scrub oysters and open with an oyster knife. Discard top shells. ■ Arrange on oyster plates or individual serving plates and place a lemon half on each serving. ■ Pass the pepper grinder.

calories/6 oysters: 61
protein, iron, niacin: good

HOW TO OPEN AN OYSTER

To open an oyster first pad your hand with a folded tea towel or wear a thick oven mitt. Hold oyster, rounded shell down, in palm of your hand over a bowl to catch juices. Insert point of an oyster knife (or short sturdy kitchen knife) between shells near hinge. Twist knife to separate shells.

Stuffed Eggs and Pickled Shrimp

STUFFED EGGS

Makes 24
Preparation time: 15 minutes
Add a pinch of your favorite herb to vary this easy recipe.

12	hard-boiled eggs, shelled
¼ cup	mayonnaise (more if yolks seem dry)
	salt and pepper to taste
	chopped fresh parsley for garnish

▪ Slice eggs in half lengthwise. ▪ Remove yolks. ▪ Combine yolks and mayonnaise until smooth. ▪ Add salt and pepper to taste. ▪ Pile yolk mixture back into eggs. ▪ Sprinkle with parsley.

calories/serving: 112 (1 serving = 2 halves)
protein, niacin: good
iron, vitamin A: fair

DILL AND SPINACH DIP

Makes about 3 cups
Preparation time: 15 minutes
This all-purpose dip doubles as a base for salad dressing or a filling for cherry tomatoes.

1 pkg	(10 oz/284 g) frozen chopped spinach, thawed and squeezed dry
1 cup	mayonnaise
1 cup	sour cream
2 Tb	lemon juice
1 Tb	fresh dill *or* ½ Tb dried dill soaked in the lemon juice for 5 minutes
½ cup	chopped fresh parsley
½ cup	chopped fresh chives or green onion tops
	salt and pepper to taste

▪ Whirl all ingredients in a blender. ▪ Taste and adjust seasoning if necessary. Use in one of the following ways:
▪ As a dip with raw vegetables (carrots, celery, cucumber, radishes, etc.).
▪ Thin with yogurt or buttermilk to make a salad dressing.
▪ Cut off the tops of cherry tomatoes and hollow them out. ▪ Fill with dip. ▪ Serve speared on toothpicks.

calories/tablespoon: 42
vitamin A: fair

PICKLED SHRIMP

Serves 8
Preparation time: 30 minutes
Cooking time: 10 minutes
Marinating time: 24 hours

Marinating shelled shrimp in a spicy mixture overnight gives them an unusual and delicious flavor.

2¼ lbs	large shrimp (in shells)
¼ cup	chopped celery
3 Tb	salt
¼ cup	mixed pickling spices
1¼ cups	salad oil
¾ cup	white vinegar
1½ tsp	salt
1 Tb	celery seed
3 Tb	capers and their juice
¼ tsp	Tabasco sauce
4	large onions

▪ Bring 3 quarts of water to a boil with celery, salt and pickling spices. ▪ Add shrimp. ▪ Bring back to boil and let simmer 5 minutes. ▪ Combine salad oil, vinegar, salt, celery seed, capers and their juice and Tabasco to make marinade. ▪ Shell shrimp. ▪ Slice onions into rings. ▪ Layer shrimp and onions in a large bowl. ▪ Add marinade and let stand, refrigerated and covered, for 24 hours. ▪ Serve with toothpicks for spearing shrimp. ▪ Serve leftovers (if any) in shrimp salad, or stuff shrimp into hollowed-out cherry tomatoes and top with mayonnaise.

calories/serving: 275
protein, niacin: excellent
iron: good
calcium: fair

CUCUMBER CHEESE

Makes 1 cup
Preparation time: 5 minutes

Serve this refreshing cream cheese as a dip with vegetables, or spread on crackers.

1 pkg	(8 oz/250 g) cream cheese at room temperature
¼ cup	finely shredded and drained unpeeled cucumber
¼ tsp	Worcestershire sauce
dash	garlic salt

▪ Combine cheese, cucumber, Worcestershire sauce and garlic salt until smooth.

calories/tablespoon: 52

Winnipeg Goldeye Pâté

WINNIPEG GOLDEYE PÂTÉ

Serves 6 to 8
Preparation time: 20 minutes
Chilling time: ½ to 1 hour

A delicious pâté that uses one of Canada's best-known fish.

¾ lb	smoked Winnipeg goldeye
½ cup	mayonnaise
½ cup	plain yogurt
	lemon juice
	pepper
	Tabasco sauce (optional)

▪ Skin and bone goldeye. ▪ Put fish, mayonnaise and yogurt into a blender and blend until smooth. ▪ Turn out into a bowl and add lemon juice and pepper, and Tabasco to taste. ▪ Chill until firm, ½ to 1 hour. ▪ Serve with crackers as hors d'oeuvre; or split cherry tomatoes in four, not cutting quite through to bottom. Put mound of pâté in the middle of each and serve 3 or 4 on a lettuce leaf as an appetizer. Pass Melba toast squares.

calories/serving: 218 for 6 servings
164 for 8 servings
protein: good

Terrine with Orange and Pepper and Onion Tartlets

TERRINE WITH ORANGE AND PEPPER

Serves 8 to 10
Preparation time: 1 hour
Cooking time: 1 to 1½ hours

The zestiness of orange and black pepper gives this terrine a piquant flavor.

1	**small onion**
1 Tb	**butter, melted**
¾ lb	**ground pork liver**
¾ lb	**sausage meat**
¾ lb	**ground pork fat**
1	**clove garlic, crushed**
	salt and pepper
2 Tb	**Cognac or brandy**
1 Tb	**port wine**
1 tsp	**dried mixed herbs to taste (parsley, chervil, tarragon, chives)**
	julienne of orange peel
½ lb	**lean, boneless veal**
	bay leaf
	aspic (optional)

JULIENNE OF ORANGE:

	peel of 2 oranges, white pith removed
½ cup	**water**
½ cup	**sugar**
2 Tb	**crushed black peppercorns**

• To make julienne of orange, cut orange peel into narrow strips. • Combine orange peel, water and sugar in a saucepan and simmer gently, uncovered, for 15 minutes. • Cool to lukewarm, drain if necessary and coat strips with crushed pepper. • To make terrine, mince onion and simmer together with butter in a small covered saucepan, very gently on low heat. • Cool. • Combine pork liver, sausage meat and pork fat in a mixing bowl. • Add onion, garlic, and salt and pepper to taste. • Add Cognac, port and herbs. • Mix together thoroughly with your hands. • Spread julienne of orange in the bottom of a terrine or 6-cup loaf pan with a lid and cover with half the meat mixture. • Cut veal into strips and arrange lengthwise on top. • Add remaining meat mixture and top with a bay leaf. • Cover terrine and seal lid with a paste of flour and water. • Set terrine in a shallow pan of warm water and bake in preheated 350°F oven for about 1 hour and 15 minutes. • Remove lid and cover with waxed paper. • Put a weight (about 1½ lbs) on top. Cool. • Let stand overnight in the refrigerator before removing the weight. • Unmold when ready to serve. It will have a layer of fat: remove or not as you choose. If you wish, add a layer of aspic.

MICROWAVE DIRECTIONS: To make julienne of orange, cook orange peel, water and sugar in a glass container, uncovered, on High 5 to 6 minutes. Cool to lukewarm, drain if necessary and coat strips with crushed pepper. To make terrine, combine onion and butter in a large casserole. Cook on High 2 to 4 minutes. Add ground meats, pork fat, liquors and seasonings. Mix well, cover and cook on High 8 to 12 minutes, stirring once. If meat still looks pink, reduce power to Med/High and cook 4 to 5 minutes. Spread julienne of orange in bottom of terrine container. Cover with half the meat mixture. Lay strips of *cooked* veal on top. Add remaining meat mixture and refrigerate as regular recipe.

calories/serving: 730 for 8 servings
584 for 10 servings
iron, vitamin A, thiamin, riboflavin, niacin: excellent
protein, folate: good

HERB BUTTER

Herb-flavored butters are easy to make and delicious served on top of grilled fish or steaks. Blend softened butter with finely chopped fresh herbs to taste. Shape into ¾″ diameter sausage shape and wrap tightly in plastic wrap, twisting ends to seal. Chill until firm then cut in slices to serve.

ONION TARTLETS

Makes 2 dozen 1½" tarts
Preparation time: 30 minutes
Cooking time: 10 minutes

These delicious appetizers can be made ahead of time and slipped under the broiler at the last minute.

8	medium leeks, whites only
4	onions
2 Tb	butter
8	spinach leaves, finely chopped
6 Tb	finely chopped chives
⅔ cup	whipping cream
1 tsp	cayenne pepper or to taste
4 Tb	pine nuts
24	small tart shells

▪ Clean leeks and chop finely. ▪ Chop onions. ▪ Melt butter in a saucepan and add leeks and onions. ▪ Simmer very gently on low heat, covered, for 15 to 20 minutes. ▪ Add chopped spinach, chives, 8 tablespoons cream and cayenne. ▪ Simmer, uncovered, to reduce volume. ▪ Adjust seasoning if necessary. ▪ Add pine nuts and fill tart shells with this warm filling. ▪ Whip remaining cream and top each tart with a dollop of whipped cream. ▪ Slip tarts under the broiler for a minute, being careful not to scorch them.

MICROWAVE DIRECTIONS: Combine chopped leeks, onions and butter in a large container. Cover with plastic wrap and cook on High 10 to 15 minutes. Add spinach, chives, 4 tablespoons cream and cayenne. Cover and cook on Med/High 5 minutes. Proceed with regular recipe.

calories/tart: 125
vitamin A, vitamin C: fair

LOBSTER BUTTER

Serves 12
Preparation time: 10 minutes

Served on toast rounds or crackers this is seductive, almost addictive.

2 cups	cooked lobster meat, canned *or* from 4 tails
1½ cups	unsalted butter, melted
1 Tb	lemon juice
	salt to taste

▪ Pick over lobster meat and remove any cartilage. ▪ Process in a blender or food processor until smooth. ▪ Add melted butter to lobster and process until smooth. ▪ Add lemon juice and season to taste with salt. ▪ Process once again. ▪ Spoon into a small crock. ▪ Swirl a design on top. ▪ Serve with Melba toast or crackers.

calories/serving: 239 without crackers

Lobster Butter and Salt Cod Pâté

SALT COD PÂTÉ

Serves 12
Preparation time: 20 minutes
Soaking time: overnight
Cooking time: 20 minutes

No one will guess that the secret ingredient in this pâté is potato.

1 lb	salt cod
2	medium potatoes
½ cup	light cream
½ tsp	summer savory
1	clove garlic, finely chopped
½ cup	olive oil

▪ Place salt cod in a large non-metallic bowl. ▪ Cover with cold water. ▪ Soak for 24 hours, changing the water 3 or 4 times. ▪ Drain cod and cut into small pieces. ▪ Peel and dice potatoes. ▪ Place cod and potatoes in a large saucepan, cover with cold water and bring to boil. ▪ Reduce heat and simmer for 15 minutes, or until potatoes are tender. ▪ Drain and remove bones and skin from cod. ▪ In a food processor or blender process cod, potatoes, cream, summer savory, garlic and olive oil with on/off motion until smooth, being careful not to overprocess. ▪ Serve warm or chilled on crackers or bread.

calories/serving: 169
protein, niacin: excellent
calcium, iron: fair

TAPENADE

Makes 2 cups
Preparation time: 20 minutes

This delicious French spread or dip comes from southern France.

1 can	(7 oz/198 g) flaked white tuna
6	anchovy fillets, drained and minced
3	cloves garlic, minced
½ cup	black olives, pitted, finely chopped
2 Tb	capers, well-drained, finely chopped
2 Tb	red wine vinegar or lemon juice
½ tsp	freshly ground black pepper
½ cup	extra-virgin olive oil
3 Tb	chopped fresh parsley for garnish

▪ Combine tuna, anchovies, garlic, olives, capers, vinegar or lemon juice, and pepper in a food processor, blender or with a mortar and pestle. ▪ Beat in olive oil slowly and steadily (mixture should be consistency of thick mayonnaise). ▪ Taste and adjust seasoning if necessary. ▪ Place in an attractive bowl and sprinkle with parsley. ▪ Serve with crackers, toast, French stick or as a dip with vegetables.

calories/tablespoon: 41
protein, niacin: fair

MICROWAVE RUMAKI CANAPÉS

Makes about 24
Preparation time: 30 minutes
Cooking time: 10 to 13 minutes

Try the popular Oriental appetizer prepared this way for a change.

½ lb	chicken livers
½ cup	water
1 tsp	chicken bouillon
6	slices bacon
1 Tb	soy sauce
½ tsp	onion powder
½ tsp	dry mustard
¼ tsp	grated nutmeg
¼ cup	dry sherry
dash	hot pepper sauce (optional)
1 can	(7¾ oz/220 g) water chestnuts, drained and chopped finely
	olive or pimento slices for garnish

▪ In a 1-quart casserole, combine chicken livers, water and bouillon. ▪ Cook in microwave on High 4 to 5 minutes, stirring once, or until no longer pink. ▪ Drain. ▪ Cook bacon on paper towel on High 5 to 6 minutes or until crisply cooked. ▪ Crumble and set aside. ▪ Put livers, soy sauce, onion powder, mustard, nutmeg and sherry in a blender or food processor. ▪ Blend until smooth. ▪ Transfer to a bowl. ▪ Add hot pepper sauce sparingly. ▪ Stir in water chestnuts and bacon. ▪ Spread thickly on toast triangles or crackers. ▪ Arrange on a paper-lined plate and reheat in microwave on Med/High 1 to 2 minutes or until heated through. ▪ Garnish with a slice of olive or pimento. The canapés can be prepared in advance then reheated and garnished just before serving.

calories/canapé: 27
vitamin A: good

HERBED CRAB DIP

Serves 8
Preparation time: 10 minutes

Pita bread is great to serve with dips because it's firm and easy to form into little cups. If you can find the tiny pita breads, cut them into halves; the pockets are perfect.

4 oz	herbed cream cheese (e.g. Boursin or Rondelé)
⅓ cup	mayonnaise
⅓ cup	sour cream
3½ oz	frozen snow crab, picked over and shredded
¼ tsp	black pepper
1 Tb	lemon juice
	pita bread cut into quarters

▪ Beat cheese until creamy and stir in mayonnaise and sour cream. ▪ If crab is very wet, squeeze out excess moisture. ▪ Stir in crab. ▪ Add pepper and lemon juice. ▪ Taste and adjust seasoning if necessary. (Cheese and crab are usually quite salty.) ▪ Serve with pita bread.

calories/serving: 133

Drinks

CRANBERRY ORANGE SANGRIA

Serves 12
Preparation time: 5 minutes

Although some of this can be prepared ahead of time, it's easier just to chill all the ingredients individually and then combine at the last minute.

1 bottle	(40 oz/1.14 L) cranberry cocktail
1 bottle	(750 mL) dry red wine
1 can	(6¼ oz/178 mL) frozen orange juice concentrate, thawed
1	orange
1 bottle	(750 mL) soda water, chilled
1 cup	fresh cranberries

- Combine cranberry cocktail, wine and orange juice in a large pitcher and stir until well mixed. - Slice orange thinly and cut each slice in half. - Add soda water to cranberry mixture just before serving. - Pour into goblets and garnish with fresh cranberries and orange slices.

calories/serving: 142
vitamin C: excellent

MULLED WINE

Serves 24
Preparation time: 10 minutes
Cooking time: 25 minutes

A perfect wintertime warmer. Because of the spices, rather ordinary wine can be used to make this special drink.

2	lemons
4 bottles	(each 750 mL) red wine
8 cups	water
½ cup	sugar
12	whole cloves
1 tsp	whole allspice
1	cinnamon stick
½ tsp	Angostura bitters
	cinnamon sticks for garnish

- Grate and juice lemons, then combine with remaining ingredients, except cinnamon sticks, in a large kettle. - Heat to just below boiling point, reduce heat and let stand over low heat for 20 minutes. - Strain into a heat-proof punch bowl. - Ladle into mugs and serve with cinnamon sticks to stir.

calories/serving: 109

Fresh Rhubarb Punch

FRESH RHUBARB PUNCH

Serves 8 to 10
Preparation time: 10 minutes
Cooking time: 10 minutes

Celebrate the arrival of spring with a glass of this tangy punch. Truly delicious.

3 cups	diced rhubarb
1 cup	sugar or to taste
3 cups	water
1 cup	pineapple juice
2 cups	ginger ale or sparkling white wine
3 Tb	freshly squeezed lemon juice

- Combine diced rhubarb, sugar and water in a medium saucepan. - Stir to blend and cook over medium heat until fruit is very soft. - Remove from heat and chill thoroughly. - Liquefy in a food processor or blender. - Combine rhubarb mixture with pineapple juice, ginger ale and lemon juice. - Serve in tall glasses over ice.

calories/serving: 150 for 8 servings
120 for 10 servings
vitamin C: excellent

SHANDY

Shandy is a welcome thirst-quencher on a hot day. Fill a large jug with ice cubes and add cold beer and old-fashioned ginger beer or fizzy lemonade in the ratio of two to one.

MOCK GROG

Serves 8
Preparation time: 15 minutes
Steeping time: 15 minutes
This exciting hot drink has a coffee base accented with chocolate, citrus peel and spices.

1	orange
1	lemon
4	cinnamon sticks, broken into pieces
1½ tsp	whole cloves
½ tsp	anise seeds
⅓ cup	sugar
¼ cup	chocolate syrup
8 cups	hot, strong coffee
	softly whipped cream

■ Pare the peel from the orange and lemon and cut into wide strips. ■ Lay them on a board, colored side down. ■ Cut away and discard all the white inside the peel, then cut the colored part into short, thin strips. ■ Combine orange and lemon peel, spices, sugar, chocolate syrup and hot coffee in a large carafe or kettle. ■ Set over low heat and let steep 15 minutes. Do not boil. ■ Strain into mugs and top with dollops of whipped cream.
calories/serving: 90

JUNE WINE

Serves 25
Preparation time: 10 minutes
Chilling time: 2 hours 30 minutes
A fine punch for a June wedding. Less expensive wines are quite suitable for this.

4 cups	small strawberries
1½ cups	icing sugar
½ cup	lemon juice
½ cup	brandy
2 bottles	(each 750 mL) chilled dry white wine
2 bottles	(each 750 mL) chilled champagne-type wine

■ Wash and hull strawberries (reserve some for garnish) and put them in a bowl. ■ Sprinkle with icing sugar, lemon juice and brandy. ■ Stir gently, cover and let stand in the refrigerator until well chilled (about 2 hours). ■ Stir occasionally. ■ Add white wine and let stand 30 minutes or until serving time. ■ At serving time, set a punch bowl inside a larger bowl filled with crushed ice. ■ Pour well-chilled punch into the punch bowl (do not add ice). ■ Add champagne. ■ Serve in punch cups with one or two strawberries in each serving.
calories/serving: 144
vitamin C: excellent

GIN JULEP

Serves 1
Preparation time: 2 minutes
A refreshing version of the traditional Southern mint julep.

5	sprigs fresh mint
1 tsp	sugar
1 oz	gin
	ice cubes or crushed ice
	good squeeze lemon or lime juice
¾ cup	tonic water
1	slice lemon or lime

■ Chop 4 sprigs of mint and mash with sugar in the bottom of a tall glass. ■ Add gin and stir well. ■ Fill with ice. ■ Add a good squeeze of lemon or lime juice. ■ Fill to top with tonic water. ■ Give drink a good stir and garnish with remaining fresh mint and lemon slice.
calories/serving: 145

BERRY BANANA SHAKE

Makes 3 cups
Preparation time: 5 minutes
Yogurt and fruit team up with vanilla ice cream in this nutritious shake.

1 cup	sliced fresh strawberries
1 cup	plain yogurt
1 cup	vanilla ice cream
1	large ripe banana, peeled and chopped
	thinly sliced strawberries and chocolate chips for garnish (optional)

■ Place strawberries, yogurt, ice cream and banana in container of blender. ■ Blend until smooth. Mixture may appear too thick at first; stop machine and stir with spatula; continue to purée. ■ Serve in tall glasses. ■ Garnish with sliced berries and chocolate chips, if you wish.

Variations: *Substitute raspberries for strawberries. For a refreshing dessert, freeze mixture in small bowls in freezer compartment. Let stand 10 minutes to soften slightly before serving.*
calories/serving: 199
vitamin C: excellent
protein, calcium: good
riboflavin, niacin: fair

Gin Julep and Berry Banana Shake

Orange Spritzers

CHEERY RED PUNCH

Serves 50
Preparation time: 15 minutes
Chilling time: several hours

This fruit punch is delightfully exotic in taste. If you wish to add alcohol for those who aren't driving, try leaving one half "as is" and adding about 16 ounces white rum or vodka to the other half.

1 cup	sugar
9 cups	water
1 can	(48 oz/1.36 L) pineapple juice
3 cups	cranberry juice cocktail
2 cups	orange juice
1 cup	lemon juice
½ cup	maraschino cherry juice
½ cup	halved maraschino cherries
	red food coloring (optional)
6 cups	ginger ale
	orange slices

▪ Combine sugar and 1 cup water in a saucepan and set over high heat. ▪ Stir until sugar dissolves, then reduce heat and simmer 10 minutes. ▪ Cool. ▪ Combine sugar syrup with fruit juices, cherries, 8 cups water and enough food coloring to tint mixture a pleasant red. ▪ Chill. ▪ At serving time, pour mixture into a large bowl set inside a larger bowl filled with crushed ice and add ginger ale. ▪ Garnish with orange slices.

calories/serving: 60
vitamin C: excellent

ORANGE SPRITZERS

Serves 8
Preparation time: 5 minutes

Here's a fine refresher. If you wish, replace half the carbonated water with dry white wine.

2 cups	chilled carbonated water (either mineral or soda)
2 cups	chilled orange juice
2 cups	chilled apple juice
	ice cubes
8	lemon slices

▪ Combine carbonated water, orange juice and apple juice. ▪ Fill 8 tall glasses with ice cubes and pour juice mixture over. ▪ Slip a lemon slice onto the rim of each glass and serve immediately.

calories/serving: 60
vitamin C: excellent
low cal

MULLED CIDER

Serves 6
Preparation time: 5 minutes
Cooking time: 35 minutes

For a special touch, float clove-studded crab apples on this fragrant mulled cider and add rum to taste just before serving.

8 cups	apple cider
5	cinnamon sticks
8	whole cloves
2 Tb	sugar

▪ Place ingredients in a large saucepan and stir over low heat until sugar dissolves. ▪ Simmer, uncovered, for 30 minutes. ▪ Discard cinnamon sticks and cloves. ▪ Pour into a heat-proof bowl.

calories/serving: 191

PINEAPPLE DAIQUIRI

Serves 4
Preparation time: 5 minutes

An adult slush puppy!

½ cup	canned pineapple chunks, drained
6 oz	light rum
¼ cup	lime juice
1 tsp	sugar
8	ice cubes

▪ Place all ingredients in a blender and whirl until smooth. ▪ Pour into chilled wine glasses.

Variations: *Replace pineapple with a ripe banana, sliced peaches or tropical fruit nectar.*
calories/serving: 123
vitamin C: fair

SPICED CAFÉ AU LAIT

Makes 8 cups
Preparation time: 7 minutes

For a festive touch, top each mug with a dollop of whipped cream and a few tiny chocolate chips or chocolate shavings.

8 Tb	ground coffee, preferably dark roast
½ tsp	each ground cinnamon, ground cloves
7 cups	cold water
	sugar
2 cups	warm milk or light cream

▪ Combine coffee, cinnamon and cloves. ▪ Place coffee mixture in filter or basket if using percolator. ▪ Pour water through or let brew in regular way. ▪ Pass sugar bowl and pitcher of warm milk or cream. ▪ Serve immediately.

calories/serving: 16 with 2% milk
37 with half-and-half cream

TOMATO VEGETABLE MOCKTAIL

Serves 3
Preparation time: 10 minutes

This vitamin-rich drink is delicious before a patio dinner. Add a splash of vodka for an alcoholic beverage.

2 cups	tomato juice
1	thin slice lemon, with peel
1	large stalk celery, chopped
1	slice green pepper, ½" thick
1	peeled slice cucumber, ½" thick
1 Tb	chopped fresh Italian parsley
	salt to taste
	Worcestershire and Tabasco sauce to taste
1 cup	crushed ice
	whole celery stalks, with leaves, for garnish (optional)

▪ Place all ingredients except crushed ice and whole celery stalk in container of blender. ▪ Cover and process until mixture is smooth. ▪ Add ice and continue to process until ice is liquefied. ▪ Serve at once in cocktail glasses, garnished with a celery stalk, if you wish.

calories/serving: 32
vitamin C: excellent
iron, vitamin A, niacin: fair
low cal

Hot Rum Toddies

HOT RUM TODDIES

Serves 12
Preparation time: 10 minutes
Cooking time: 25 minutes

A bracing drink for a blustery day.

10 cups	water
3	2" cinnamon sticks
6	whole cloves
12	whole allspice
10	cardamom pods
½ tsp	grated nutmeg
18 oz	rum
¾ cup	honey
6	lemons

▪ Combine water, cinnamon, cloves, allspice, cardamom and nutmeg in a large saucepan. ▪ Bring to boil. Reduce heat, cover and simmer for 15 minutes. ▪ Remove from heat and strain liquid. ▪ Discard spices. ▪ Refrigerate spice water until you are ready to assemble and serve the toddies. ▪ To prepare the toddies reheat spice water to boiling point. ▪ In each mug combine 1½ ounces rum, 1 tablespoon honey, juice of ½ lemon and ¾ cup spice water. ▪ Stir well and serve immediately.

calories/serving: 175

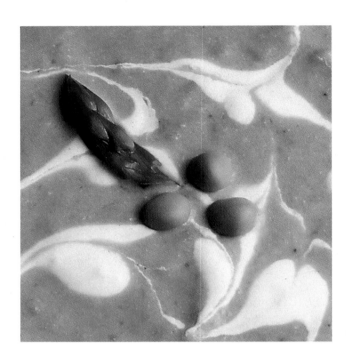

SOUPS

I t's no wonder we take tureens of soup to people who are ill or in trouble. Soup is still the primary comfort food in our scheme of things. And without soup, life would be a good deal drearier. Whenever I was home from school with the flu, someone could be counted on to bring a tray with a bowl of tomato soup and a plate of salty crackers to my bedside. Then the decision was whether to crumble the crackers into the soup to make a thick, mushy stew or to opt for the delight of a spoon of scalding soup alternated with a bite of crispy cracker.

If the illness was thought to be more serious, and cream of tomato soup too rich, it was chicken noodle soup on the tray. Families could be roughly divided into Campbell's or Heinz camps on these occasions. Homemade soups were not a spur-of-the-moment dish, so were not available unless you were sick for more than one day.

But hearty, homemade soups were very much a part of life: thick barley and vegetable soups, soups with rice or noodles and shreds of lamb or beef left over from the Sunday roast. Golden chicken and turkey soups, dense with slithery noodles, appeared inevitably a couple of days after roast chicken or turkey. Great bloody beef knucklebones were free at the butcher shop, and I brought them home wrapped in slick butcher's paper so Mother could set them on to simmer for stock.

Such soups were not served *before* a meal; they *were* the meal, usually accompanied by thick slices of home-made bread. I made such serious soups for my children in the '50s when it was considered an eccentricity to do so. We had entered the ''streamlined'' age — the precursor to the age of technology — and canned and packaged foods were thought to be superior just be-cause they were faster. One lunchtime I overheard my son's playmate whisper pityingly as I sat them down to bowls of split-pea soup made from the Sunday ham bone, ''Are you too poor to buy Campbell's?'' Well, no we weren't, and we ate our share of canned soups over the years. In fact, with four children home for lunch every day, canned soups were part of our basic survival kit. Soup-and-a-sandwich was probably served for most schoolday lunches on our suburban street. But because we were all economizing (two-income families were rare in the '50s) about once a week we'd gather the leftover bones and vegetables and brew a great kettle of homemade soup. Such soups needed to sim-mer for hours and then be cooled on the back porch

or in the fridge so the meat fat would rise to the top and congeal like a solid lid that could be lifted out and discarded with the bones. Then you added noodles or rice or lentils, and perhaps some fresh vegetables, tasted it all for seasoning and hoped this batch of soup would turn out to be one of the memorable ones — and if it did, that you could remember how you made it.

Like much else, soup has changed since then. Most people don't have time, or don't know how, to convert chewed-over bones into a life-sustaining jolt of taste, energy and comfort.

Nowadays soup is more often a prelude to a meal, the curtain-raiser. And marvellous they are, too — the silky, creamy soups made from puréed vegetables and pinches of fresh herbs, the delicate, ambrosial broths with bits of fire or crunch suspended in the depths. We even have cold soups and fruit soups (is fruit soup really melted sherbet, or is sherbet frozen fruit soup . . . best not to inquire). With a blender or a food processor, a little imagination and an instinct for seasoning, you can make soup from whatever you please. My husband mastered two things in the kitchen — chocolate fudge and soup. It was never the same soup twice, and it tended to grow into larger and larger

kettles as he thought of more and more things he'd like to add, but it was *filling* soup and nobody ever turned down a bowl of it.

We hope you'll regard our soup recipes as a jumping-off place and go on to great soup inventions of your own.

Corn and Crab Chowder

CORN AND CRAB CHOWDER

Serves 8
Preparation time: 15 minutes
Cooking time: 30 minutes

This warming chowder would make a perfect finish to an outdoor evening of skiing, skating or tobogganing. Serve with some crusty bread and a hearty cheese.

¼ cup	unsalted butter
1	small onion, diced
1	potato, peeled and diced
3 cups	corn kernels, off the cob or frozen
3 cups	chicken stock
	salt and pepper to taste
1 cup	heavy cream
7 oz	frozen, cooked crabmeat, picked over and shredded
2 Tb	chopped fresh parsley or green onions for garnish

▪ Melt butter in a Dutch oven or large pot. ▪ Add onion and cook gently until very tender and fragrant. ▪ Add potato, corn and stock. ▪ Bring to boil. ▪ Reduce heat, cover and cook gently 15 minutes. ▪ Purée half of soup until smooth. ▪ Stir back into remaining soup in Dutch oven. ▪ Add salt, pepper and cream. ▪ Bring to boil. ▪ Add crab, reduce heat and cook 5 minutes. Soup can be made ahead to this point and reheated just before serving. ▪ Serve sprinkled with parsley.

calories/serving: 217
protein, vitamin A: good
fiber: moderate
vitamin C, thiamin, niacin: fair

CRUNCHY TOPPING

For a quick crunchy topping to sprinkle on soups, salads or vegetables, combine 2 cups rolled oats and ½ cup melted butter with grated Parmesan cheese, garlic and herbs to taste. Bake in a shallow pan in a preheated 350°F oven until golden. Or, sprinkle unbaked mixture over a casserole before cooking.

HARVEST PUMPKIN AND ZUCCHINI SOUP

Serves 8
Preparation time: 30 minutes
Cooking time: 45 minutes

This is a delightful fall soup. If you don't peel the zucchini, the soup will be green in color; if peeled it will be pumpkin-colored.

3 cups	peeled, cubed pumpkin or squash
3 cups	cubed zucchini
2	medium potatoes, peeled and cubed
1	large onion, sliced
2 cups	chicken stock
2 Tb	vegetable oil
2 Tb	chopped fresh parsley
2	cloves garlic, chopped
¾ cup	2% milk
1 tsp	dried basil *or* 2 Tb chopped fresh
	fresh mint leaves or chopped fresh parsley for garnish

▪ Combine pumpkin, zucchini, potatoes, onion, chicken stock, oil, parsley and garlic in a large saucepan. ▪ Cover and simmer, stirring occasionally, for 45 minutes, or until vegetables are tender. ▪ If stock simmers down, add water to reach original level. ▪ Purée mixture in batches in a food processor or blender. ▪ Return to saucepan. ▪ Add milk and basil and reheat. ▪ Garnish each serving with mint leaves or chopped parsley.

calories/serving: 99
vitamin A, vitamin C, niacin: good
fiber: moderate

QUICK ASPARAGUS SOUP

Serves 4
Preparation time: 10 minutes
Cooking time: 15 to 20 minutes

Broccoli is also tasty for this, but in the spring fresh asparagus makes a special pale green soup.

3 cups	chopped asparagus
2 Tb	butter or margarine
½ cup	chopped onion
1	small carrot, chopped
1	small clove garlic, chopped
2 Tb	flour
2 cups	chicken stock
2 cups	milk
	salt, white pepper and grated nutmeg to taste

▪ When preparing asparagus, wash well and discard coarse stalk ends. ▪ Heat butter in a medium saucepan. ▪ Add onion, carrot and garlic and cook, stirring, over medium heat 5 to 7 minutes. ▪ Add flour and cook, stirring, about 2 minutes. Do not brown. ▪ Remove saucepan from heat and whisk in stock and milk. ▪ Return to heat and cook, stirring, until mixture barely comes to boil. ▪ Add chopped asparagus and cook over medium heat until tender, 15 to 20 minutes. ▪ Purée mixture in a blender or food processor until smooth. ▪ Return to heat. ▪ Season with salt, white pepper and nutmeg.

calories/serving: 195
vitamin A, vitamin C, niacin: excellent
calcium, thiamin, riboflavin: good

PUMPKIN SOUP

Serves 4 to 6
Preparation time: 5 minutes
Cooking time: 20 minutes

With a food processor or blender and some good rich stock, hearty soups can be whizzed together in minutes.

2 Tb	butter
1	large onion, finely chopped
1	clove garlic, crushed
1	medium potato, finely chopped (unpeeled)
3 cups	chicken stock
¼ tsp	grated nutmeg
¼ tsp	curry powder
½ tsp	dried marjoram
1 tsp	sugar
	salt and pepper to taste
1 Tb	lemon juice
1½ cups	pumpkin purée (about 1 lb fresh or a 14 oz/398 mL can)
½ cup	heavy cream

▪ Melt butter in a large saucepan and fry onion, garlic and potato over medium heat until onion is transparent. ▪ Stir in remaining ingredients, except lemon juice, pumpkin and cream. ▪ Increase heat and bring to boil. ▪ Reduce heat, cover and simmer for about 10 minutes, or until vegetables are tender. ▪ Leave to cool slightly. ▪ Purée in a food processor or blender and return to saucepan. ▪ Stir in lemon juice and pumpkin and heat through. ▪ Adjust seasoning and pour into soup bowls. ▪ Swirl a little cream into each before serving.

calories/serving: 259 for 4 servings
173 for 6 servings
vitamin A: excellent
iron, vitamin C: fair

GINGERED CARROT AND ORANGE SOUP

Serves 6
Preparation time: 15 minutes
Cooking time: 30 to 40 minutes

A colorful soup with just a hint of orange and ginger. Make ahead of time, if desired, and reheat with cream just before serving.

2 Tb	butter
3	leeks, well cleaned and sliced
5	large carrots, sliced
1 Tb	finely chopped ginger root or to taste
4 cups	chicken stock
	grated peel and juice of 1 orange
1 cup	light cream
	salt and pepper to taste
	snipped chives or chopped green onions for garnish

■ Melt butter in a large saucepan over medium heat. ■ Add leeks and cook, stirring often, until softened but not browned, about 5 minutes. ■ Add carrots and ginger and sauté for 1 minute. ■ Add chicken stock, cover and bring to boil. ■ Reduce heat and simmer, covered, until carrots are tender, 20 to 30 minutes. ■ Remove from heat, stir in orange juice and peel. Purée mixture, in batches, in a food processor or blender if you wish. ■ Return to saucepan and add cream. ■ Heat, but do not boil. ■ Season with salt and pepper. ■ Garnish each bowl with chives.

calories/serving: 176
vitamin A, vitamin C: excellent
niacin: good
fiber: moderate

HOT OR COLD BROCCOLI SOUP

Serves 4 to 6
Preparation time: 10 minutes
Cooking time: 15 minutes

This recipe is equally delicious made with spinach, cauliflower or zucchini.

1	bunch broccoli
3 Tb	butter
1	onion, chopped
3 Tb	flour
3 tsp	curry powder or to taste
4 to 6 cups	stock (beef, chicken or vegetable)
	salt and pepper to taste
	cream (optional)

■ Cut off coarse stems and peel remaining stems of broccoli. ■ Steam broccoli until tender, about 10 minutes. ■ Melt butter and sauté onion gently in a heavy saucepan. ■ Stir in flour and cook 1 minute. ■ Add curry powder. ■ Stir and cook 1 minute. ■ Add hot stock and stir until boiling. ■ Purée cooked broccoli in a food processor and add to hot stock. ■ Taste for seasoning. Serve hot or cold with cream added to taste.

calories/serving: 163 for 4 servings
109 for 6 servings
vitamin C, niacin: excellent
vitamin A: good
iron, riboflavin: fair
fiber: moderate

CURRIED APPLE AND AVOCADO SOUP

Serves 2 to 3
Preparation time: 5 minutes
Cooking time: 15 minutes
Chilling time: at least 30 minutes

A lovely, pale green, summery soup. Serve chilled in glass mugs topped with a sprig of mint. To chill quickly, place in freezer for 15 minutes.

2 Tb	butter
1	small onion, chopped
¼″ slice	ginger root, peeled and crushed
1 tsp	curry powder or to taste
½	green apple, peeled and chopped
1 tsp	sugar
2 cups	chicken stock
½	avocado, peeled, pitted and chopped
¼ cup	heavy cream
½ tsp	grated nutmeg
	salt and pepper to taste
	mint sprigs for garnish

■ Melt butter in a medium saucepan. ■ Sauté onion in butter until soft but not brown. ■ Add ginger, curry powder and apple. ■ Cook for 1 minute. ■ Add sugar and chicken stock. ■ Bring to boil. ■ Reduce heat and simmer for 10 minutes. ■ Purée soup until smooth in a food processor or blender. ■ Add avocado and purée again. ■ Pour mixture into a bowl and stir in cream, nutmeg, salt and pepper. ■ Refrigerate until serving time or place in freezer for 15 minutes if needed immediately. ■ Garnish with mint sprigs.

MICROWAVE DIRECTIONS: Place onion and butter in a small casserole dish. Cook on High 2 minutes. Add ginger, curry powder and apple. Cook for further 2 minutes. Add sugar and chicken stock. Cook on High 3 minutes, or until liquid boils. Reduce to Medium for 5 to 6 minutes. Continue with above instructions.

calories/serving: 353
vitamin A, vitamin C, niacin: good

Turkey Barley Soup

TURKEY BARLEY SOUP

Number of servings depends on amount of water.
Preparation time: 10 minutes
Cooking time: stock, 2 hours
soup, 1 hour

This recipe is similar to hearty Scoth broth and can be a meal in one dish. Barley will thicken the soup as it stands. If made the day before, it may need to be thinned with stock or water when reheated.

1	turkey carcass
	cold water
1	onion, quartered
2	carrots, cut into 2″ chunks
2	stalks celery, cut into 2″ chunks
½ cup	pearl barley
1 cup	diced carrots
1	onion, coarsely chopped
2 cups	diced turnip
	diced cooked turkey
	salt and pepper to taste
2 Tb	chopped fresh parsley for garnish

■ Break up turkey carcass to fit a large saucepan; cover with water. ■ Add onion, carrots and celery. ■ Cover and bring to boil. ■ Skim any scum that rises to top; discard. ■ Reduce heat and simmer, uncovered, for 2 hours. ■ Strain soup into another large saucepan, reserving carcass but discarding vegetables. ■ Pick any meat off carcass and reserve. ■ Return stock to simmer, stir in barley and simmer, covered, for 30 minutes. ■ Add diced carrots, onion and turnip and simmer for a further 30 minutes, or until vegetables are tender. ■ Add turkey. ■ Season well with salt and pepper and garnish with parsley.

calories/1-cup serving: 95
vitamin A: excellent
vitamin C: good
niacin: fair
fiber: moderate
low fat
low cal

Curried Pea and Asparagus Soup

CURRIED PEA AND ASPARAGUS SOUP

Serves 6
Preparation time: 40 minutes
Chilling time: 4 hours or overnight

Catch the last of the fresh asparagus with the first of the pea crop for this flavorful chilled soup.

1 lb	peas in pods
1 lb	asparagus
¼ cup	butter
½ cup	chopped shallots *or* 1 small onion and 1 clove garlic, chopped
2 tsp	curry powder
1 tsp	grated lemon peel
1	medium potato, peeled and chopped
4 cups	chicken stock
1 cup	light cream
1 Tb	fresh lemon juice
	salt and white pepper to taste
	sour cream or yogurt for garnish

■ Wash and shell peas and reserve 2 or 3 empty pods. Reserve 2 tablespoons of the shelled peas for garnish, if you wish. ■ Wash asparagus well, discard coarse stalk ends and cut into 1″ pieces. ■ Melt butter over medium-low heat in a large saucepan. ■ Add shallots and cook, stirring often for about 3 minutes until soft but not brown. ■ Blend in curry powder, lemon peel, potato and stock. ■ Bring to boil. ■ Add peas, reserved pods and asparagus. ■ Bring to boil. ■ Reduce heat to low, cover and simmer about 7 minutes, or until vegetables are tender. ■ Remove pods. ■ Purée soup in batches in a blender or food processor. (A blender makes a smoother soup.) ■ Stir in cream, lemon juice, salt and white pepper. ■ Cover and refrigerate at least 4 hours or overnight. ■ After chilling, taste and add more lemon juice or seasoning if necessary. ■ If too thick, thin with additional chilled cream or milk. ■ Stir well. ■ Serve in chilled bowls. ■ Garnish each serving with a dollop of sour cream or yogurt and raw peas.

calories/serving: 216
protein, iron, vitamin A, vitamin C: good
fiber: moderate
thiamin, niacin: fair

CURRIED CELERY SOUP WITH SHRIMP

Serves 6
Preparation time: 30 minutes
Cooking time: 1 hour 15 minutes

Fresh shrimp are perfection, but most of us make do with frozen ones.

½ to ¾ lb	medium shrimp, fresh or frozen
3 Tb	butter
¾ cup	chopped onion
1½ cups	cubed peeled potato
3 cups	sliced green celery
3 cups	chicken stock
¾ tsp	curry paste *or* 1 tsp curry powder, to taste
	water
	dry white wine or lemon juice
pinch	each dried thyme and oregano
1	small bay leaf
¼ tsp	salt
	fresh celery leaves
1½ to 2 cups	milk or light cream

▪ Melt butter over moderate heat in a large heavy pot – enamelled cast iron is excellent – and gently cook onion, potato and celery for a few minutes until onion is translucent. ▪ Add chicken stock, bring to boil, then reduce heat and simmer, uncovered, for 40 minutes or so, until vegetables are completely tender. ▪ Stir in ¾ teaspoon curry paste for last 10 minutes of cooking. (The exact amount will depend on the strength of your paste; it shouldn't overwhelm the flavor of the soup. If you're using curry powder, stir it into the vegetables, blending well, before adding stock.) ▪ While vegetables are simmering, shell and devein shrimp. ▪ Refrigerate shellfish while you make a fumet by putting the shells into a medium saucepan, covering with cold water and a splash of white wine – or a good squeeze of lemon juice – adding salt and herbs, and cooking at a gentle boil for 20 minutes. ▪ Line a sieve with a damp paper towel and strain the fumet. ▪ Rinse the saucepan and return the strained liquid to it. ▪ Let vegetable mixture cool a little, then purée in a food processor or food mill and sieve to remove any celery strings. ▪ Rinse soup pot and return purée to it. ▪ Make a chiffonade for garnish by dropping whole celery leaves into boiling water, lifting them out immediately with a skimmer, patting dry with a paper towel, then cutting crosswise into very fine shreds. (Do this before completing the soup.) ▪ Gradually add milk or light cream to vegetable purée until it reaches the consistency you like. ▪ Correct seasoning and heat just to the simmering point. ▪ Meanwhile, bring fumet to boil, drop in shrimp, reduce heat and poach for 1 to 2 minutes, depending on size, until shrimp turn pink. Drain immediately, discarding fumet, and cut shrimp into halves lengthwise. ▪ Either ladle the soup into warmed individual bowls, adding a few shrimp pieces and some celery leaf chiffonade to each, or pour into a warmed tureen and distribute shrimp and chiffonade over the surface. Serve at once.

calories/serving: 217 using homogenized milk
protein, niacin: excellent
calcium, iron, vitamin C: good
riboflavin, vitamin A: fair

APPLE AND WINTER SQUASH SOUP

Serves 6 to 8
Preparation time: 20 minutes
Cooking time: 30 minutes

The addition of apples lends a subtle sweetness to this creamy squash soup. For best results use buttercup, butternut or hubbard squash.

¼ cup	butter
1	large onion, chopped
2 cups	peeled, diced apples
4 cups	peeled, diced winter squash *or* 3 cups cooked squash, fresh or frozen
4 cups	chicken stock, homemade or canned
1 cup	light cream
1½ tsp	salt
	pepper to taste
	ground cinnamon or chili powder to taste

▪ Melt butter in a large saucepan or soup pot. ▪ Add onion and apples and cook, uncovered, stirring for about 5 minutes or until soft and tender. Do not allow them to brown. ▪ Stir in squash and chicken stock. ▪ Bring to boil. ▪ Reduce heat and simmer gently for 20 to 30 minutes, or until squash is tender. ▪ Purée soup in a blender, food processor or food mill. ▪ Return to saucepan, add cream, salt and pepper. ▪ Heat thoroughly, stirring over low heat, but do not boil. Serve sprinkled with ground cinnamon or chili powder.

calories/serving: 248 for 6 servings
186 for 8 servings
vitamin A, vitamin C: excellent
niacin: fair
fiber: moderate

SPINACH VICHYSSOISE

Serves 8 to 10
Preparation time: 20 minutes
Cooking time: 40 minutes
Chilling time: 6 hours or overnight

A classic soup is made even better with fresh-tasting spinach.

¼ cup	butter
2 cups	sliced leeks (white part of 3 large)
¼ cup	finely chopped celery and leaves
2	cloves garlic, minced
4 cups	sliced, peeled potatoes (4 medium)
5 cups	chicken broth
2 Tb	fresh lemon juice
1 tsp	salt
¼ tsp	white pepper
1 lb	fresh spinach
2 cups	light cream
	thin lemon slices for garnish

▪ Melt butter in a large saucepan over medium heat. ▪ Add leeks, celery and garlic and cook over low heat for about 20 minutes, stirring often. ▪ Do not brown. ▪ Stir in potatoes, broth, lemon juice, salt and pepper. ▪ Bring to boil, reduce heat and simmer mixture, covered, for about 10 minutes, or until potatoes can easily be pierced with a fork. ▪ Stir in spinach, bring back to boil and simmer 5 more minutes. ▪ Purée in a blender or food mill or push through a sieve into a large bowl. (A food processor will spoil the soup's texture.) ▪ Cool. ▪ Add cream and taste for seasoning. Stir in more salt, white pepper and lemon juice if necessary. ▪ Cover and chill for several hours or overnight. ▪ After chilling, adjust seasoning if necessary, and if too thick, stir in more cream. ▪ Serve in chilled bowls or glasses and float thin slices of lemon on each serving.

calories/serving: 293 for 8 servings
237 for 10 servings
vitamin A, vitamin C: excellent
iron, protein: good
calcium, thiamin, riboflavin, niacin: fair

FREEZING SOUP

When freezing a casserole or soup that you're planning to defrost in the microwave, spoon into a freezer bag standing in a microwave-safe dish large enough to take the recipe. Press out air, seal and freeze in bowl. When frozen solid, remove from bowl and store in freezer. To defrost, peel off bag and place frozen casserole or soup in the original bowl — it will fit perfectly. Defrost in microwave according to manufacturer's instructions.

MINESTRONE

Serves 6 to 8
Preparation time: 20 minutes
Cooking time: 3 hours

Omit the pasta and you can make this traditional Italian soup ahead of time and freeze it.

STOCK:	
2 Tb	oil
1 lb	oxtails or beef bones
8 cups	water
1	bouquet garni (celery top, parsley and bay leaf tied together)
1	small onion

SOUP:	
2 Tb	oil
1	onion, chopped
4	slices bacon, chopped
1	clove garlic, chopped
2	carrots, chopped
1	stalk celery, chopped
1 can	(19 oz/540 mL) tomatoes, drained and chopped
½	head cauliflower, chopped
½ lb	green beans, quartered
2	bouillon cubes
½ lb	spinach, cleaned and chopped
1 cup	uncooked small pasta, any shape
	grated Parmesan cheese
1 Tb	finely chopped fresh parsley for garnish

▪ To make stock, heat oil in a large heavy pot. ▪ Add bones and brown well. ▪ Add water, bouquet garni and onion. ▪ Simmer for 2 to 3 hours. ▪ Strain. (If you wish, the stock may be made with just bouillon cubes, but the flavor will not be nearly as nice.) ▪ To make soup, heat oil in a large heavy pot. ▪ Add onion, bacon and garlic and cook until softened. ▪ Add carrots and celery. ▪ Cook, stirring frequently, for 5 minutes. ▪ Stir in tomatoes, cauliflower and green beans. ▪ Add prepared reheated stock and bouillon cubes. (The bouillon cubes strengthen the flavor of the stock.) ▪ Heat through and simmer until vegetables are tender. ▪ Add spinach and cook until softened. (Freeze at this point, if you wish.) ▪ When ready to serve, cook pasta until just tender but firm. ▪ Heat soup and stir in pasta. ▪ Adjust seasoning. ▪ Serve with grated Parmesan cheese, a sprinkling of parsley, and crusty rolls on the side.

calories/serving: 276 for 6 servings
208 for 8 servings
vitamin A, vitamin C: excellent
fiber: high
protein, iron, thiamin, niacin: good
calcium: fair

Minestrone

Quick Fish Chowder

QUICK FISH CHOWDER

Serves 4
Preparation time: 10 minutes
Cooking time: 20 to 25 minutes

One of the handiest foods to have in your freezer is a package of fish fillets. Here's a quick soup to make from your favorite fresh or frozen fish.

5	slices bacon, chopped
1	onion, chopped
3	potatoes, diced
2 cups	water
2 cups	milk
1 lb	fish fillets
1 cup	kernel corn, frozen or canned
	salt and pepper to taste
	chopped fresh parsley for garnish

▪ Cook bacon in a heavy saucepan over medium heat until crisp, about 3 minutes. ▪ Pour off fat. ▪ Stir in onion and cook 3 to 5 minutes until soft. ▪ Add potatoes and water. ▪ Simmer, covered, until potatoes are tender, about 10 minutes. ▪ Stir in milk, fish and corn. ▪ Cook until fish flakes, about 5 minutes. ▪ Season with salt and pepper and sprinkle with parsley.

calories/serving: 359
protein, vitamin C, niacin: excellent
calcium, thiamin, riboflavin: good
iron, vitamin A: fair

COLD MELON SOUP

Serves 10
Preparation time: 20 minutes
Chilling time: 4 hours or overnight

No cooking is necessary for this quick and delicious soup.

1	large ripe cantaloupe
1	large honeydew melon
½ cup	light rum
⅓ cup	fresh lime juice
3 Tb	sugar
1 tsp	grated lime peel
½ tsp	salt
pinch	ground ginger
	sprigs of fresh mint or lemon balm for garnish

▪ Cut each melon in two and scoop out seeds. ▪ With a melon-ball scooper, scoop out one-quarter of the flesh of both melons and set aside. ▪ Peel and cut rest of the flesh into chunks. ▪ Place in a blender with remaining ingredients and blend in batches until really smooth. ▪ Transfer to a large container and fold in reserved melon balls. ▪ Cover and refrigerate until very cold, at least 4 hours or overnight. ▪ Serve in chilled bowls or wine goblets. ▪ Garnish each with a sprig of mint or lemon balm.

calories/serving: 109
vitamin C: excellent
vitamin A: good
low fat
low cal

CREAMY CUCUMBER SOUP

Serves 4
Preparation time: 15 minutes
Chilling time: at least 1 hour

Cucumber and mint give sparkling flavor to this refreshing soup that can be made in minutes in a food processor or blender. Serve the soup in chilled bowls.

1	English cucumber
2 cups	plain yogurt
1 cup	heavy cream
1 Tb	chopped fresh mint *or* ½ Tb dried mint
1	clove garlic, crushed
½ cup	milk
	salt and white pepper to taste
	sprigs of fresh mint or chopped green onion tops for garnish

▪ If using dried mint, put in a cup with enough hot water to cover. ▪ Leave for 5 minutes, then strain and discard water. ▪ Peel cucumber and cut in half lengthwise. ▪ Scoop out and discard seeds. ▪ Cut cucumber into chunks and put in a food processor or blender with yogurt, cream, mint and garlic. ▪ Process until smooth. ▪ Pour soup into a large bowl and stir in milk. ▪ Taste and adjust seasoning. ▪ Chill at least 1 hour in refrigerator before serving. ▪ Pour into individual bowls and garnish each with a sprig of fresh mint or chopped green onion tops.

calories/serving: 312
calcium: excellent
vitamin A, riboflavin, protein: good
vitamin C, niacin: fair

GAZPACHO

Serves 6 to 8
Preparation time: 10 minutes
Chilling time: several hours

Gazpacho, a cool Spanish soup filled with vegetables, is ideal for the hot summer months.

4	medium tomatoes, chopped *or* 1 can (19 oz/540 mL) stewed tomatoes
1	medium onion, chopped
1	medium cucumber, chopped
1	small sweet pepper, chopped
1	small hot pepper, finely chopped
1	clove garlic, crushed
4 Tb	finely chopped fresh parsley
3 cups	water
2 Tb	olive oil
2 Tb	lemon juice
2 tsp	salt
½ tsp	pepper
	lemon slices, chopped fresh cilantro or parsley for garnish
2 cups	croutons
½ cup	chopped green olives

▪ Process all ingredients except lemon slices, croutons and olives in a food processor until vegetables turn to liquid, or if you prefer a crunchy gazpacho, chop in the blender to desired texture. ▪ Place in a large bowl. ▪ Chill thoroughly before serving. ▪ Garnish with a lemon slice or with chopped cilantro or parsley. ▪ Serve croutons and olives in separate dishes.

calories/serving: 174 for 6 servings
130 for 8 servings
vitamin C: excellent
vitamin A: good
iron, niacin: fair

Noodles with Mushrooms

NOODLES WITH MUSHROOMS

Serves 4
Preparation time: 10 minutes
Cooking time: 15 minutes

Noodles served in a bowl with broth and seasonings is a staple dish in China and makes a quick and easy lunch. Use regular mushrooms, oyster mushrooms or eight dried Chinese mushrooms soaked in water.

8 oz	thin noodles
2 cups	chicken or beef stock
1 Tb	vegetable oil
1 cup	sliced mushrooms
1½ tsp	minced garlic
¼ cup	water
½ cup	chopped green onions
2 Tb	soy sauce
2 Tb	sherry
1 Tb	vinegar
1 tsp	sesame oil
dash	hot chili oil or hot pepper sauce

▪ Cook noodles in a large pot of boiling water for about 5 minutes, until tender yet firm. ▪ Drain. ▪ Meanwhile heat stock. ▪ Heat oil in a wok or heavy frying pan or skillet over medium-high heat, add mushrooms and garlic and stir-fry for 2 minutes. ▪ Add water, onions, soy sauce, sherry, vinegar, sesame oil and hot chili oil to taste. ▪ Bring to boil. ▪ Divide noodles into 4 soup bowls. ▪ Spoon broth, then mushroom mixture, into each bowl. ▪ Serve with a salad and crusty bread.

calories/serving: 280
thiamin, niacin: excellent (using enriched noodles)
vitamin C, riboflavin: good

ASPARAGUS BISQUE

Serves 6 to 8
Preparation time: 20 minutes
Cooking time: 35 minutes

This tasty soup can be made with fresh asparagus when it's at its best. Or try it with two 10-ounce packages of frozen.

2 lbs	fresh asparagus
2 Tb	butter or margarine
4	green onions with tops, chopped
1	medium potato, peeled and diced
6 cups	chicken stock
1 tsp	salt or to taste
¼ tsp	white pepper or to taste
½ tsp	paprika
½ tsp	Worcestershire sauce
¼ cup	chopped fresh parsley
1 Tb	snipped fresh dill *or* 1 tsp dried dill
2	egg yolks
½ cup	light cream

▪ Snap off and discard tough lower stems of asparagus and wash stalks. ▪ With a vegetable peeler, scrape skin and scales from lower part of stalks. ▪ Cut off tips and set aside. ▪ Cut stalks into ½" pieces. ▪ Heat butter or margarine in a large saucepan over medium heat. ▪ Add onions and stir 2 minutes. ▪ Add potato, chicken stock, seasonings, asparagus pieces (not tips), parsley and dill. ▪ Cover and simmer 30 minutes, or until vegetables are very tender. ▪ Meanwhile, steam asparagus tips until just tender, about 3 minutes. ▪ Purée soup a little at a time in a blender and return to saucepan. ▪ Beat egg yolks and cream together, then stir in some of the hot soup. ▪ Stir mixture slowly into soup and stir until very hot but not boiling. ▪ Ladle into soup bowls and add some asparagus tips to each serving.

calories/serving: 180 for 6 servings
135 for 8 servings
vitamin C: excellent
vitamin A, protein: good
iron, thiamin, riboflavin, niacin: fair

ICED TOMATO AND BASIL SOUP

Serves 12
Preparation time: 20 minutes
Cooking time: 55 minutes
Chilling time: 6 hours or overnight

Here is a wonderful example of the happy marriage between tomatoes and basil. Use only fresh basil for best results. Serve with homemade Melba toast or tiny pitas sprinkled with Parmesan cheese and toasted.

2 Tb	butter
2 Tb	olive oil
3	onions, sliced
3 or 4	sprigs parsley
2	stalks celery with leaves, sliced
2	cloves garlic, minced
2	bay leaves
½ cup plus 1 Tb	finely chopped fresh basil
1 tsp	salt
1 tsp	brown sugar
¼ tsp	black pepper
pinch	cayenne pepper
¼ cup	flour
5 cups	hot chicken stock
12	ripe tomatoes, unpeeled and sliced
	fresh basil leaves for garnish

■ Heat butter and oil in a large pot over medium heat until butter is melted. ■ Add onions and stir for 2 or 3 minutes. ■ Stir in parsley, celery, garlic, bay leaves, 1 tablespoon basil, salt, brown sugar, black pepper and cayenne. ■ Reduce heat to low, cover and cook 20 minutes. ■ Stir occasionally. ■ Stir in flour and cook, stirring often, for 3 minutes. ■ Remove from heat and, stirring constantly, add hot stock and cook until thickened. ■ Stir in tomatoes and bring to boil. ■ Reduce heat, cover and simmer 20 minutes. ■ Stir in ½ cup basil and simmer, uncovered, 2 or 3 minutes. ■ Pass soup through a food mill fitted with a fine disc or through a sieve into a large clean bowl. ■ Chill, covered, several hours or overnight. ■ Stir well, taste and add more salt and pepper if necessary. ■ Serve in chilled bowls or wine goblets. ■ Garnish each serving with small basil leaves.

calories/serving: 97
vitamin C: excellent
vitamin A, niacin: fair

Iced Tomato and Basil Soup

CHILLED RED PEPPER AND MUSHROOM SOUP

Serves 4 to 6
Preparation time: 20 minutes
Cooking time: 35 minutes
Chilling time: 4 hours or overnight

Although your guests may not guess what is in this flavorful soup, they will certainly find it appealing.

¼ cup	butter
1	onion, chopped
2	cloves garlic, minced
4	sweet red peppers, seeded and chopped
1 lb	mushrooms, finely chopped
3 cups	chicken stock
2 tsp	paprika
1 tsp	sugar
2 Tb	fresh lemon juice
¼ tsp	cayenne pepper
	salt and pepper to taste
	slices of fresh mushroom or thin slices of lemon for garnish

■ Melt butter in a large saucepan over medium-low heat. ■ Add vegetables and cook, stirring often, until softened, about 10 minutes. ■ Stir in stock, paprika and sugar. ■ Bring to boil. ■ Reduce heat and simmer, uncovered, for 20 minutes. ■ Purée in batches in a blender. ■ Strain through a sieve or pass through a food mill into a large bowl. ■ Stir in lemon juice, cayenne, salt and pepper. ■ Chill, covered, at least 4 hours or overnight. ■ Taste and add more seasoning if needed. ■ Serve in chilled bowls. ■ Garnish each serving with a slice of mushroom or lemon.

calories/serving: 183 for 4 servings
123 for 6 servings
vitamin C, niacin: excellent
riboflavin: good
iron, vitamin A: fair

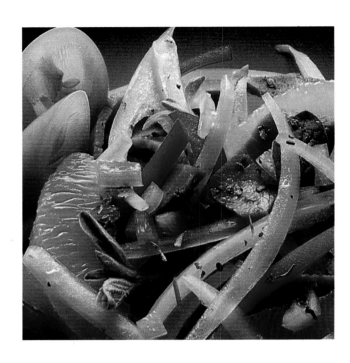

SALADS

S alads present the cook with two questions: What *is* a salad really? and Should you serve it before, during or after the main course?

Salad in Canada *used* to be a chunk of iceberg lettuce accompanied by a wedge of hard pink tomato and drenched in a commercial bottled dressing (French, Thousand Island, or Italian? the waitress would ask before plunking down the chosen bottle). Sometimes this salad had a radish or a sliver of carrot, and sometimes instead of bottled dressing it came with a waxed thimbleful of sticky yellow stuff that pretended to be mayonnaise. We were not big salad eaters. No wonder.

Now, it seems, a salad is whatever you say it is. It can be as simple as a plate of sliced tomatoes drizzled with olive oil and sprinkled with fresh basil. Or it can contain so many slivers of ham, chicken, bacon, beef, fish, egg, greens, peas, carrots, beets, cheese, beans, broccoli, asparagus, spinach, pasta, onions, croutons, nuts that a person could get a total day's requirement of nutrients at one salad bar and in one gigantic bowl. Salads have become like soups: we can put into them anything we fancy and they can be a meal unto themselves. For any assembly of ingredients to be called a salad, all that seems to be required is the drizzling of

oil over it; even vinegar and lemon juice are optional. Herbs, fresh or dried, are frequently added to the oil/ vinegar drizzle, as are garlic, mustard, pepper and pinches of various spices. Some cooks with a flair for the dramatic and questionable culinary sincerity (usually men it must be said) can't resist the temptation to ''create'' and turn the simple task into a theatrical event, whisking together the dressing in front of their seated guests with the air of a magician about to produce a rabbit from the depths of a hat.

I confess to being an ad libber. I shake together the oil and vinegar with whatever combination of herbs and spices takes my fancy that day. Since I seldom measure when making a dressing, I've never made exactly the same dressing twice, and it must be admitted that some are more successful than others. In my own defense, though, I point out that I don't perform this experiment in public.

Since not all oils and vinegars are created equal, whole books have been written about olive oils, oils steeped in walnut, wine vinegars of various hues and herbal infusions. I have been too busy reading British mystery novels to take part in this lively debate and can't pretend to be au courant of the salad dressing

trends. The only firm conclusions I've drawn are these: balsamic vinegar *does* taste rather nice, red wine vinegar makes red salad dressing so it's best not to use it unless you're aiming at red, and olive oil today is much nicer than the thick green stuff my mother used to advise me to put on my prairie-sun-dried hair. But the contributors to this book know *all* about the esoterica of combining oil and vinegar, and their dressings on the following pages are delicious.

The ''composed'' salad, whether revival or invention, deserves our support. The basic theory of the composed salad seems to be that you put on a plate two or three (or even more) edibles that look attractive together (a couple of snow peas seems a popular place to start) and you create a kind of still-life picture. Then you drizzle it with the requisite oil and/or vinegar/lemon juice combination and call it a salad. The results are almost always fair to look upon and, if you make a sensible selection, tasty to eat.

But *when* in the course of a meal should salad appear? There are advocates of the *before* school of thought and those who think it lacking in refinement to serve a salad at any juncture other than as a refreshing palate awakener between the main course and dessert. Some

think it positively *crude* to serve a salad alongside a main course and have only contempt for those of us who like to alternate bites of mashed potatoes and gravy with nibbles of lettuce. I refuse to be squelched. In my time I've served salad before, I've served it alongside and I've served it after . . . without apology. In the matter of feeding ourselves I believe *we*, not fashion, should be pleased. The salads in the next few pages are pleasing. Serve them as you choose.

Tomato and Coriander Salad

TOMATO AND CORIANDER SALAD

Serves 6 to 8
Preparation time: 20 minutes

Perhaps more than any other herb, fresh coriander leaves give salads, soups and stews a delightful taste.

5	**firm ripe tomatoes, sliced into wedges**
1	**small bunch fresh coriander leaves, washed and finely chopped**
1	**small onion, finely chopped**
1	**very small hot pepper, finely chopped**
1	**clove garlic, crushed**
1 tsp	**salt**
½ tsp	**black pepper**
3 Tb	**lemon juice**
2 Tb	**olive oil**

▪ Place all ingredients in a salad bowl and gently toss just before serving.

calories/serving: 83 for 6 servings
62 for 8 servings
vitamin C: excellent
vitamin A: fair

SALAD WITH BLUE CHEESE DRESSING

Serves 4 to 6
Preparation time: 5 minutes

Green salad can be a bore, but this one isn't.

	romaine, spinach, chicory and/or endive
	fresh or dried basil to taste
½ cup	**olive and corn oil, mixed**
3 Tb	**red wine vinegar**
1 Tb	**Dijon mustard**
3 Tb	**blue cheese**
	salt and pepper to taste
2	**hard-boiled eggs**

▪ Wash and spin-dry salad greens. ▪ Combine basil, oils, vinegar, mustard and cheese in a food processor and blend. ▪ Add salt and pepper, if you wish. ▪ Just before serving, toss greens with dressing. Press hard-boiled eggs through a sieve and sprinkle over salad. ▪ Toss again at the table.

calories/serving: 358 for 4 servings
240 for 6 servings
vitamin A, vitamin C, folate: good
iron, niacin: fair
fiber: moderate

MIXED GREEN SALAD WITH MUSTARD VINAIGRETTE

Serves 8
Preparation time: 15 minutes
A delicious, refreshing salad to accompany many meals.

1	**head Boston lettuce**
1	**bunch watercress**
2	**heads Belgian endive**
MUSTARD VINAIGRETTE:	
1 Tb	**Dijon mustard**
	salt and pepper to taste
2 Tb	**white wine vinegar**
⅓ cup	**olive oil**

▪ Stir together mustard, salt and pepper until smooth in a small bowl or measuring cup. ▪ Beat in vinegar; then slowly beat in oil. Dressing can be prepared ahead and refrigerated, covered, up to 2 days. Bring to room temperature before using. ▪ Wash and dry lettuce and watercress. ▪ Remove any tough stems from watercress. Greens may be prepared to this point a day ahead. Wrap in paper towels, place in plastic bag and refrigerate. ▪ Just before serving, rinse endive, cut out core and break into individual leaves. ▪ Tear lettuce into bite-size pieces. ▪ Toss with endive leaves and watercress in large salad bowl. ▪ Stir dressing to recombine, pour over top, toss again and serve.

calories/serving: 91
vitamin C: good

BROCCOLI AND CARROT VINAIGRETTE

Serves 12
Preparation time: 30 minutes
This salad can be prepared several hours in advance.

3	**large bunches broccoli**
6	**carrots**
1 cup	**salad oil**
⅔ cup	**fresh lemon juice**
1 tsp	**sugar**
1½ tsp	**salt**
2	**cloves garlic, crushed**

▪ Wash broccoli and carrots. ▪ Separate broccoli florets. ▪ Peel carrots and stems of broccoli. ▪ Slice broccoli stems and carrots diagonally. ▪ Place vegetables in a large bowl. ▪ Combine remaining ingredients in a small bowl. ▪ Stir briskly and pour over vegetables. ▪ Toss vegetables in dressing. ▪ Cover and refrigerate until ready to serve.

calories/serving: 130
vitamin A, vitamin C: excellent
fiber: moderate

Simple Caesar Salad

SIMPLE CAESAR SALAD

Serves 4 to 6
Preparation time: 10 to 15 minutes
If you're using a mustard that has an egg in its ingredients, such as homemade, you can eliminate the egg yolk in this lemony dressing. Be sure the greens are very dry before tossing.

1	**head romaine lettuce**
4	**croutons**
1	**large clove garlic, minced**
3 or 4 drops	**Worcestershire sauce**
1 tsp	**mustard (homemade, German or Dijon)**
1	**egg yolk (optional)**
3 Tb	**lemon juice**
½ cup	**vegetable oil or light olive oil or a combination**
	croutons for garnish
	salt and pepper to taste
¼ cup	**grated Parmesan cheese**

▪ In a bowl mash croutons into crumbs with a wooden spoon. ▪ Add garlic, Worcestershire sauce, mustard and egg yolk (if using) and blend into a thick paste. ▪ Whisk in lemon juice. ▪ Very slowly add oil, by drops, whisking until smooth and thick. If mixture is too thick, add more lemon juice. ▪ Wash and dry lettuce leaves very well. ▪ Tear into bite-size pieces. ▪ Toss well with dressing to coat and garnish with croutons. ▪ Sprinkle with Parmesan cheese.

calories/serving: 344
vitamin A, vitamin C: excellent
iron: good

GRILLED CHINESE CHICKEN SALAD

Serves 2
Preparation time: 10 minutes
Cooking time: 8 minutes
Marinating time: 15 minutes

Grilled chicken stars in this Chinese-type salad. The chicken can be served warm or cold. You can make double the quantity and eat one recipe hot the first day and the other cold later. For the warm salad, slice the chicken and place on top of salad just before serving. Vary the vegetables depending on what is available.

2	boneless chicken breasts, skin removed
1	large carrot, shredded
2 cups	grated English cucumber, drained
2 cups	shredded iceberg lettuce
2	green onions, chopped, for garnish

MARINADE:

1 Tb	white wine or lemon juice
1 tsp	olive oil
1 Tb	soy sauce
1 tsp	finely chopped ginger root

VINAIGRETTE:

2 Tb	red wine vinegar
1 Tb	sugar
2 Tb	sesame oil
2 Tb	vegetable oil
2 Tb	soy sauce
1 tsp	finely chopped ginger root
1 tsp	Dijon mustard
	salt to taste

■ Mix marinade ingredients together and pour over chicken breasts. ■ Marinate for 15 minutes. ■ Preheat broiler. ■ Broil chicken 4 minutes each side, or until juices are clear. ■ Cool, then cut into ¼″ slices. ■ Whisk together vinegar, sugar, sesame oil, vegetable oil, soy sauce, ginger, mustard and salt in a bowl. ■ Arrange vegetables on serving plate. ■ Place sliced chicken on top. ■ Pour vinaigrette over. ■ Just before serving toss together. ■ Garnish with green onions.

calories/serving: 503
protein, vitamin A, vitamin C, niacin: excellent
iron: good
fiber: moderate
thiamin, riboflavin: fair

SALADE NIÇOISE

Serves 6
Preparation time: 30 minutes
Cooking time: 10 to 20 minutes
Standing time: overnight

This classic salad is a favorite at our house during warm weather.

2 cups	sliced green beans, 1½″ diagonal slices
½ lb	asparagus, cut diagonally into 1″ lengths
6	small (*or* 3 medium) new potatoes, boiled, peeled and sliced into ½″ slices
1	large red onion, sliced very thinly
1	large green pepper, seeded and cut into thin rings
2 cups	sliced celery, ½″ diagonal slices
1 cup	black olives
	Garlic Vinaigrette
1	head romaine lettuce
2 cans	(each 6 oz/170 g) tuna
6	hard-boiled eggs, peeled and quartered
4	medium tomatoes, quartered

■ Cook green beans just until tender, about 5 minutes. ■ Refresh under cold running water. ■ Drain well. ■ Cook asparagus just until tender, about 5 minutes, and proceed as with beans. ■ Combine beans, asparagus, potatoes, onion, green pepper, celery and olives in a large bowl. ■ Pour on Garlic Vinaigrette and stir gently to combine. ■ Refrigerate overnight in a covered container, stirring once or twice. ■ To serve, line a shallow salad bowl with lettuce broken into large bite-size pieces. ■ Drain marinated vegetables and reserve dressing. ■ Spoon vegetables onto lettuce. ■ Break up tuna slightly and arrange it with the eggs and tomatoes on top. ■ Sprinkle with reserved dressing.

calories/serving: 558 (including Garlic Vinaigrette)
protein, iron, niacin, vitamin C: excellent
vitamin A, thiamin: good
riboflavin: fair

GARLIC VINAIGRETTE

2 tsp	Dijon mustard
	salt and pepper to taste
2	cloves garlic, crushed
¼ cup	tarragon vinegar
2 Tb	fresh lemon juice
¾ cup	olive oil

■ Combine mustard, salt, pepper, garlic, vinegar and lemon juice. ■ Whisking constantly, add oil.

calories/tablespoon: 83

Salade Niçoise

Cracked Wheat and Citrus Salad

CRACKED WHEAT AND CITRUS SALAD

Serves 4 to 6
Preparation time: 15 minutes
Standing time: 1 hour

Filled with an interesting variety of textures and flavors, this colorful salad goes nicely with pork, veal or poultry.

1 cup	bulgur (cracked wheat)
2 cups	cold water
2	oranges, preferably seedless
1	large red onion, thinly sliced
½ cup	finely chopped fresh parsley
½ cup	black olives, pitted and cut into halves
¼ cup	olive oil
2 Tb	fresh orange juice
2 Tb	fresh lemon juice
1 tsp	finely grated orange peel
1 tsp	sugar
	salt to taste
pinch	cayenne pepper
	spinach leaves

■ Rinse bulgur in cold water. ■ Combine with 2 cups cold water and let stand at room temperature 1 hour. ■ Line a sieve with rinsed cheesecloth and drain bulgur. ■ Pull up the corners of the cloth around wheat and squeeze firmly to make sure all excess moisture is removed. ■ Peel oranges, remove pith and slice crosswise. ■ Reserve 3 slices for garnish and cut remainder into quarters. ■ Stir together prepared bulgur, orange pieces, onion, parsley and olives in a large bowl. ■ In a small bowl or cup, stir together oil, orange and lemon juices, grated peel, sugar, salt and cayenne. ■ Stir gently into salad. ■ Cover and chill until serving time. ■ Salad can be made one day ahead. ■ To serve, line a platter with spinach leaves and mound salad on top. ■ Garnish with reserved orange slices.

calories/serving: 339 for 4 servings
226 for 6 servings
vitamin C: excellent
iron, thiamin, niacin: fair
fiber: moderate

CRACKED WHEAT

Cracked wheat is a favorite staple in the Middle East. The nutritious grain can be used in place of rice in many dishes, and also makes a tasty breakfast cereal.

HAM, RICE AND AVOCADO SALAD

Serves 4
Preparation time: 25 minutes

This delicious main-course salad is sure to become a favorite. Ingredients can be varied according to what you happen to have in the refrigerator. Cook the rice ahead of time or use Minute Rice for an even speedier dish.

3 Tb	olive oil
1½ Tb	wine vinegar
1 tsp	dried tarragon
1	clove garlic, crushed
	salt and pepper to taste
1 tsp	sugar
2 Tb	lemon juice
2	ripe avocados
1½ cups	long-grain rice, cooked
12 oz	cooked ham, unsliced
2 cups	sliced button mushrooms
2	large stalks celery, chopped
2 Tb	horseradish sauce
2 Tb	chopped fresh parsley
1¼ cups	mayonnaise
2	tomatoes, cut into wedges
1 Tb	capers
6	black olives, pitted and sliced

▪ Mix together oil, vinegar, tarragon, garlic, salt, pepper, sugar and half the lemon juice. ▪ Let stand to blend flavors. ▪ Halve avocados and remove peel and stones. ▪ Chop flesh into ½″ cubes and toss in remaining lemon juice. ▪ Mix together cooked rice, avocado and dressing and spoon into a shallow serving dish. ▪ Chill. ▪ Cut ham into ½″ cubes and mix in a bowl with mushrooms and celery. ▪ Stir horseradish sauce and parsley into mayonnaise. ▪ Add to ham mixture and stir to coat well. ▪ Pile ham salad on top of rice and avocado salad and garnish with tomato wedges, capers and black olives. ▪ Serve chilled with warmed cheese croissants.

calories/serving: 839 (using extra lean ham and diet mayonnaise)
999 (using regular ham and mayonnaise)
protein, vitamin C, thiamin, niacin: excellent
iron, vitamin A, riboflavin: good

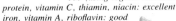

DANISH POTATO SALAD

Serves 4
Preparation time: 5 minutes
Cooking time: 15 to 20 minutes

Choose small, even-size potatoes.

1½ lbs	new potatoes
4	slices bacon, chopped
1	small onion, finely chopped
1 Tb	flour
1 cup	water
3 Tb	lemon juice
1 Tb	Dijon mustard
1 Tb	Worcestershire sauce
1 Tb	liquid honey
¼ tsp	celery salt

▪ Wash potatoes but do not peel. ▪ Put into a pot with cold salted water and bring to boil. ▪ Reduce heat and simmer for 10 to 15 minutes until just tender. ▪ Drain well, transfer to a heated serving dish and keep warm. ▪ Meanwhile fry bacon in its own fat over high heat until crisp. ▪ Remove from pan with slotted spoon and drain on paper towel. ▪ Add onion to fat remaining in pan and fry gently for 2 minutes. ▪ Blend in flour and cook for 1 minute. ▪ Whisk in water until mixture is smooth, then stir in remaining ingredients. ▪ Bring to boil, reduce heat and simmer, stirring all the time, until thickened. ▪ Add bacon to potatoes, pour on hot dressing and serve at once.

calories/serving: 220
vitamin C: excellent
thiamin, niacin: good
fiber: moderate

TOMATO AND BASIL SALAD

Serves 4
Preparation time: 5 minutes

To add a little color and counteract the richness of a creamy pasta sauce, this fresh-tasting tomato salad fits the bill.

4	ripe tomatoes, cut into wedges
12	pitted black olives
2 Tb	fresh basil, chopped
1 tsp	sugar
	black pepper to taste

▪ Mix together tomatoes and olives in a salad bowl. ▪ Sprinkle with remaining ingredients, being very generous with the pepper, and toss well. ▪ Serve at room temperature.

calories/serving: 66
vitamin C: excellent
vitamin A: fair

TOMATO AND RED ONION SALAD WITH SAVORY

Serves 4
Preparation time: 15 minutes
Standing time: 1 hour

Attractive yet simple, this marinated salad makes a delightful change from tossed salad. If you grow your own savory, garnish with fresh sprigs, including the delicate edible mauve flowers.

2	large ripe tomatoes
1	medium red onion
	fresh savory sprigs for garnish

DRESSING:

1 tsp	homemade or Dijon mustard
1 tsp	red wine vinegar
	juice of ½ lemon
⅓ cup	vegetable oil
1 Tb	chopped fresh savory or basil
	salt to taste

▪ Cut tomatoes into ½″ thick slices. ▪ Cut onion into thin slices. ▪ Overlap each tomato slice with 2 onion rings on a white plate. ▪ Set aside. ▪ Whisk mustard with vinegar and lemon juice. ▪ Slowly add oil by drops, whisking until smooth and slightly thick. ▪ Blend in chopped savory and salt. ▪ Drizzle dressing over tomato and onion slices. ▪ Let stand at room temperature 1 hour or several hours in refrigerator. ▪ Bring to room temperature before serving. ▪ Garnish with fresh savory sprigs with flowers if available.

calories/serving: 174
vitamin C: good

SPINACH AND MUSHROOM SALAD WITH CREAMY BUTTERMILK DRESSING

Serves 6 to 8
Preparation time: 15 minutes

Low on calories but high on flavor, this crunchy salad is delicious with grilled beef, lamb or chicken.

1 cup	buttermilk
½ cup	mayonnaise
2	cloves garlic, crushed
2 tsp	Dijon mustard
	salt and pepper to taste
1 pkg	(10 oz/284 g) fresh spinach
½ lb	mushrooms, sliced
2 cups	bean sprouts
5	slices crisply cooked bacon, crumbled

▪ Whisk together buttermilk, mayonnaise, garlic, mustard, salt and pepper until quite frothy. Dressing can be made ahead, covered and refrigerated up to 8 hours. ▪ Wash and dry spinach well, remove any thick stems and tear into bite-size pieces. ▪ Toss in a large salad bowl with mushrooms and bean sprouts. Salad can be prepared ahead, covered and refrigerated without dressing 2 to 3 hours. ▪ Just before serving, pour dressing over spinach mixture and toss gently to coat. ▪ Sprinkle with bacon.

calories/serving: 222 for 6 servings
166 for 8 servings
vitamin C: excellent
iron, thiamin, riboflavin, niacin: good
fiber: moderate

ONION AND PEPPER SALAD

Serves 12
Preparation time: 30 minutes (15 minutes with food processor)
Standing time: several hours

Onions, peppers and celery aren't unusual in a salad – but ginger is. Here preserved ginger, Dijon mustard and lemon juice make this a salad that really sings.

8	green peppers
2	Spanish onions
1	whole bunch celery
⅓ cup	finely chopped preserved ginger
1½ tsp	salt
½ tsp	black pepper
1 Tb	Dijon mustard
½ cup	olive oil
¼ cup	lemon juice
	lettuce

▪ Chop peppers, onions and celery quite small: use a food processor for onions and celery, if you wish. ▪ Put them in a bowl with ginger and salt, cover and refrigerate for several hours, then drain well. ▪ Combine remaining ingredients except lettuce, pour over vegetables and toss lightly. ▪ Chill. ▪ Line a large salad bowl with lettuce at serving time and pile in the salad.

calories/serving: 132
vitamin C: excellent

HOW TO STORE LETTUCE
Washed lettuce leaves will stay fresh and crisp if you place the leaves between layers of paper towels, seal them in a plastic bag and store in the refrigerator.

Tuna Salad with Fresh Dill

TUNA SALAD WITH FRESH DILL

Serves 5
Preparation time: 15 minutes

Use this easy-to-make tuna salad as part of a summer salad plate, served perhaps in a hollowed-out tomato or papaya half. Or use for sandwich fillings, or as an hors d'oeuvre stuffed into cherry tomatoes, mushrooms or hollowed-out cucumber rounds.

1 can	(6.5 oz/184 g) tuna, packed in water
¼ cup	diced celery
¼ cup	chopped fresh dill
2 Tb	chopped fresh parsley
2 Tb	chopped chives or green onions
2 Tb	light mayonnaise
2 Tb	low-fat plain yogurt
½ tsp	Dijon mustard
	black pepper to taste

▪ Mash tuna with juices. If you only have tuna packed in oil, drain thoroughly and add more yogurt to taste. ▪ Add celery, dill, parsley, chives, mayonnaise, yogurt and mustard. Season with pepper. ▪ Mix well.

calories/serving: 86
niacin: excellent
protein: good

CUCUMBERS IN SOUR CREAM

Serves 12
Preparation time: 15 minutes
Chilling time: 2 to 3 hours

In this old Lunenburg County dish, the cucumbers are salted and the liquid drained.

2	English cucumbers
2 tsp	salt
2 cups	sour cream or whole milk yogurt
1 to 2 Tb	lemon juice
3	green onions, chopped
	freshly ground pepper
2 tsp	chopped fresh mint (optional)

▪ Thinly slice unpeeled cucumbers into rounds. ▪ Place slices in layers in a bowl, sprinkling each layer with salt. ▪ Place a small plate on cucumbers and press with a weight. ▪ Refrigerate for a few hours. ▪ Pour off liquid and dry slices with paper towels. ▪ Combine sour cream or yogurt, lemon juice, green onions, pepper and mint in a small bowl. ▪ Mix in the cucumber slices. ▪ Taste for seasoning and add salt if necessary. ▪ Chill for 30 minutes before serving.

calories/serving: 71 using sour cream
34 using yogurt

Sauerkraut Apple Salad

SAUERKRAUT APPLE SALAD

Serves 8
Preparation time: 15 minutes
Chilling time: 2 hours
Good with baked beans.

4 cups	**sauerkraut, washed and drained**
½ cup	**chopped celery**
1 cup	**grated carrot**
3	**large red apples, unpeeled, cored and diced**
¾ cup	**sugar**
½ cup	**vegetable oil**
½ cup	**vinegar**

▪ Combine sauerkraut, celery, carrot and apples.
▪ Stir sugar, oil and vinegar together. ▪ Pour over salad. ▪ Mix thoroughly and chill for two hours.
▪ Before serving, drain excess dressing.

calories/serving: 259
vitamin A, vitamin C: excellent
iron: good
fiber: moderate

SNOW PEA AND MANGO SALAD

Serves 6
Preparation time: 15 minutes
Cooking time: 1 minute

This easy, colorful salad is great with barbecued pork or chicken. If you wish, three large nectarines or a small cantaloupe can be substituted for the mangoes, and sugar snap peas can replace the snow peas, if you're lucky enough to find them.

1 lb	**snow peas, trimmed**
2	**peeled mangoes, thinly sliced**
½ cup	**finely diced red pepper**
3 Tb	**fresh lemon or lime juice**
	salt and pepper to taste
½ cup	**vegetable oil**

▪ Blanch peas 1 minute or until color is set (sugar snap peas take longer). ▪ Immediately drain and refresh under cold running water. ▪ Drain well.
▪ When cool, combine in a bowl with mangoes and red pepper. ▪ Whisk together lemon juice, salt and pepper. ▪ Whisking constantly, add oil. ▪ Pour over snow pea mixture. ▪ Toss gently so that everything is evenly coated with dressing. Salad can sit, covered, up to 2 hours in refrigerator. If it sits longer, the peas lose their color.

calories/serving: 243
vitamin C: excellent
vitamin A: good
iron: fair
fiber: moderate

EMERALD PASTA SALAD

Serves 4 to 6
Preparation time: 15 minutes
Cooking time: 5 to 10 minutes
Chilling time: 1 hour

Serve this pretty pasta dish as an unusual appetizer or side salad. Its bright green color would look beautiful next to a salad of tomatoes or beets.

3 cups	uncooked pasta shells
	oil
1 to 2 Tb	vinaigrette dressing
1	large ripe avocado
	grated peel and juice of 1 lime
1	clove garlic, crushed
1 tsp	honey
	salt and pepper to taste
3 to 4 Tb	milk
4	green onions, chopped
2 Tb	chopped fresh parsley

▪ Cook pasta in boiling, salted water, with a little oil added, until just tender. ▪ Drain well and toss in vinaigrette to coat while still warm. ▪ Transfer to a salad bowl and leave to cool. ▪ Halve avocado and remove stone. ▪ Scoop out flesh into a food processor or blender and add grated lime peel, juice, garlic, honey, salt, pepper and most of milk. ▪ Purée until smooth, then turn out into a bowl. ▪ Thin avocado dressing with a little milk if necessary and stir in onions and parsley. ▪ Add to pasta, toss well and serve chilled.

calories/serving: 358 for 4 servings
239 for 6 servings
thiamin, niacin: good
vitamin C: fair

ALMOND CELERY SALAD

Serves 6
Preparation time: 10 minutes

A recipe you'll find invaluable for its ease and good flavor, this salad can be made two or three days before serving.

1	large bunch celery
⅓ cup	ground, toasted, blanched almonds
2 Tb	fresh lemon juice
1 tsp	dry mustard
½ tsp	dried tarragon
	salt and pepper to taste
⅓ cup	olive oil
	lettuce leaves
1 or 2	medium red onions, thinly sliced

▪ Keeping stalks together, wash bunch of celery by running cold water into the top of the stalks. ▪ Cut through the whole bunch in thin crosswise slices. Include leaves. ▪ Place in a large glass bowl. ▪ Combine almonds, lemon juice, mustard, tarragon, salt and pepper in a small bowl. ▪ Whisking continuously, add olive oil. ▪ Pour over celery and stir gently to coat. ▪ Cover and refrigerate, stirring occasionally. ▪ To serve, line a round serving plate with lettuce leaves. ▪ Arrange the onion slices to overlap around the edge, leaving an outside border of lettuce. ▪ Mound the celery mixture in the center, just covering the inside edges of the onion slices.

calories/serving: 170
vitamin C: good
fiber: moderate

ONION AND PEA SALAD

Serves 8 to 10
Preparation time: 20 minutes
Chilling time: up to 3 hours

Turn ordinary ingredients into a pretty and interesting spring salad. Look for tiny white, red or gold onions in the import section of your supermarket or greengrocer.

1 pkg	(10 oz/238 g) pearl onions
1 lb	frozen tiny peas, thawed
	leaf or Boston lettuce
	chopped chives or green onion tops for garnish
DRESSING:	
1 cup	sour cream
½ cup	mayonnaise
2 Tb	chopped fresh chives or green onions
2 tsp	finely chopped fresh chervil *or* ½ tsp dried chervil
	salt and white pepper to taste

▪ Drop whole, unpeeled onions into boiling water and boil for 3 minutes. ▪ Rinse in cold water. ▪ Cut off root end with a sharp knife, peel off thin outer skin and place onions in a large bowl. ▪ Combine thawed peas with onions. ▪ Stir together sour cream, mayonnaise, chives, chervil, salt and white pepper in a small bowl. ▪ Stir dressing into onion-pea mixture, cover and refrigerate up to three hours. Before serving, line a large salad bowl with lettuce leaves. ▪ Mound onion-pea mixture on lettuce. ▪ Garnish top with a light sprinkling of chopped chives.

calories/serving: 193 for 8 servings
155 for 10 servings
vitamin C: good
fiber: high

COLESLAW

Serves 4 to 6
Preparation time: 30 minutes

In the Kitchener-Waterloo area of Ontario, coleslaw is usually offered as an alternate for sauerkraut or salad.

4 cups	chopped cabbage
1	small onion, finely chopped
2 tsp	sugar
1 tsp	vinegar
½ cup	thick sour cream
	salt and pepper to taste
	paprika, cayenne pepper, mustard or horseradish to taste (optional)

■ Put chopped cabbage and onion through a food chopper or processor, using a medium blade that won't extract the juice. ■ Mix sugar, vinegar, sour cream, salt and pepper together. ■ Pour mixture over cabbage and onion and combine them. ■ Sprinkle with paprika or cayenne, if you wish. ■ If you want more nip, add a pinch of mustard or a teaspoon of horseradish. ■ Serve it on your plate with meat and potatoes or in a little side dish.

calories/serving: 81 for 4 servings
53 for 6 servings
vitamin C: excellent
fiber: moderate

CHILLY YOGURT MINT CUCUMBERS

Serves 4
Preparation time: 10 minutes
Standing time: 30 minutes
Chilling time: 1 hour

Serve this low-cal salad as a cooling accompaniment to spicy barbecued lamb or seafood.

2	small cucumbers *or* 1 large
	salt
4	green onions, sliced
6	red radishes, thinly sliced
1 cup	plain yogurt
2 Tb	finely chopped fresh mint
1 Tb	chopped fresh parsley
1	clove garlic, crushed
1 tsp	vinegar or fresh lemon juice
¼ tsp	each sugar and pepper
2 Tb	vegetable oil
	leaf lettuce
¼ cup	chopped peanuts
	sprigs of mint for garnish

■ If skins are tough, peel cucumbers. ■ Cut in half lengthwise. ■ Scrape out seeds if necessary and slice thinly crosswise. ■ Place in colander and sprinkle lightly with salt. ■ Let drain 30 minutes to get rid of excess water and any bitterness. ■ Dry and transfer to a large bowl. ■ Toss with green onions and radishes. ■ Stir together yogurt, mint, parsley, garlic, vinegar, sugar and pepper in a small bowl. ■ Slowly whisk in oil. ■ Mix with vegetables. ■ Taste for seasoning and add more salt if needed. ■ Cover and refrigerate 1 hour to chill, but no longer. ■ To serve, line a shallow bowl with lettuce, mound cucumber mixture on top and sprinkle with chopped peanuts. Garnish with sprigs of mint.

calories/serving: 160
vitamin C: good
niacin, calcium: fair

WATERCRESS AND ORANGE SALAD

Serves 8 to 10
Preparation time: 15 minutes

Watercress is a true herald of spring. If it's not available, substitute tender young spinach leaves or fresh coriander (also called cilantro or Chinese parsley).

3	bunches watercress
4	seedless oranges
1 Tb	sugar
½ cup	toasted, slivered almonds
¼ cup	fresh lemon juice
¼ cup	minced shallots or onion
½ tsp	curry powder or to taste
	salt and pepper to taste
½ cup	olive oil

■ Remove stems from watercress; wash and dry well. ■ Wrap in paper towels and place in a plastic bag in the refrigerator if doing ahead of time. Or, if using immediately, arrange on a large salad platter. ■ Peel oranges and remove all white pith. ■ Cut in thin crosswise slices and arrange in overlapping pattern on top of watercress. ■ Sprinkle with sugar and almonds. ■ Stir together lemon juice, shallots, curry powder, salt and pepper in a small bowl. ■ Slowly whisk in oil and pour all over salad. ■ Serve immediately. (The dressing itself can be made ahead of time, covered and left at room temperature. Whisk just before pouring onto salad to blend in oil again.)

calories/serving: 207 for 8 servings
166 for 10 servings
vitamin C: excellent
vitamin A: fair
fiber: moderate

CURRIED CHICKEN AND PASTA SALAD

Serves 8
Preparation time: 20 minutes
Cooking time: 20 minutes

There's lots of crunch and plenty of flavor in this brightly colored salad.

6	chicken breast halves
¼ cup	cider vinegar
	water
½ lb	snow peas or sugar snap peas
4 cups	uncooked pasta shells
1	large red pepper, cut into julienne strips
½ cup	coarsely chopped walnuts
½ cup	raisins
1½ cups	mayonnaise
½ cup	sour cream
4 tsp	curry powder or to taste
2 tsp	ground cumin
	salt and pepper to taste

▪ Poach chicken breasts by simmering in vinegar combined with enough water to cover, 15 to 20 minutes or until tender. ▪ Set aside to cool in poaching liquid. ▪ When cool, cut or pull chicken apart into bite-size pieces. ▪ Remove stems and strings from peas. ▪ Blanch 1 minute in a large saucepan of boiling water. ▪ Refresh under cold running water and drain well. ▪ Cool. ▪ Cook pasta in boiling, salted water until just tender. Drain well. Cool. ▪ Stir together chicken, peas, pasta, red pepper, walnuts and raisins in a large bowl. ▪ Stir together mayonnaise, sour cream, curry powder, cumin, salt and pepper in a small bowl. ▪ Stir gently into chicken mixture. If making ahead, cover and refrigerate. Serve in a lettuce-lined bowl.

calories/serving: 567
protein, niacin, vitamin C: excellent
iron, thiamin: good
riboflavin: fair

TOASTED ALMONDS

Toasted almonds are not only a crunchy addition to a salad, but make an attractive garnish too. To toast, spread nuts in a single layer in a shallow roasting pan. Bake in 300°F oven 15 minutes until just beginning to color.

Kidney Bean and Bacon Salad

KIDNEY BEAN AND BACON SALAD

Serves 4
Preparation time: 10 minutes
Cooking time: 5 minutes

Canned beans of all kinds make excellent salads. If you need to increase the quantities in this recipe, use a variety of beans.

1 can	(19 oz/540 mL) red kidney beans
4	slices bacon, chopped
4 Tb	salad oil
2 Tb	lemon juice or wine vinegar
2 tsp	Dijon mustard
1	large clove garlic, crushed
	salt and pepper to taste
1	small onion, sliced into rings

▪ Drain and rinse kidney beans and place in a large bowl. ▪ Fry bacon in its own fat until crisp. ▪ Remove and drain on paper towels, then add to beans and mix well. ▪ Whisk together oil, lemon juice, mustard, garlic, salt and pepper until smooth. ▪ Add to beans and toss well. ▪ Spoon salad into 4 individual dishes and serve topped with onion rings.

calories/serving: 283
protein, iron, niacin: good
vitamin C: fair
fiber: very high

Oriental Pork and Noodle Salad

ORIENTAL PORK AND NOODLE SALAD

Serves 4
Preparation time: 20 minutes
Cooking time: 15 minutes
Chilling time: 20 minutes
A flavorful taste of the Far East.

¾ lb	boneless lean pork loin
⅓ cup	rice vinegar
¼ cup	soy sauce
1 Tb	minced ginger root
1	clove garlic, minced
pinch	sugar
½ lb	broccoli, cut into small florets
2 Tb	peanut or vegetable oil
3	dried hot chilies
½ lb	dried rice noodles or fettuccine
½	sweet red pepper, diced
2 tsp	sesame oil
	black pepper to taste

▪ Cut pork against grain into thin ¼″ julienne strips. ▪ Place in a small bowl and stir in vinegar, soy sauce, ginger, garlic and sugar. ▪ Set aside at room temperature for 15 minutes. ▪ Blanch broccoli in a large saucepan of boiling water, about 3 minutes or until just tender. ▪ Drain in colander and refresh under cold running water. ▪ Drain well again and transfer to a large bowl. ▪ Heat oil in a large skillet and sauté chilies 1 minute. ▪ Reserving marinade, drain pork. ▪ Add pork to skillet and sauté over medium-high heat 3 to 4 minutes or until no longer pink. ▪ With slotted spoon, remove to bowl containing broccoli. ▪ Pour marinade into skillet and bring to boil. ▪ Cook 1 minute. Set aside. ▪ Hold noodles down inside a large paper bag and cut into 4″ lengths with sturdy kitchen shears before cooking. ▪ Cook noodles in a large saucepan of boiling salted water, about 4 minutes or until tender but firm. ▪ Drain and rinse under cold running water. ▪ Drain well again and stir into pork-broccoli mixture. ▪ Stir in red pepper. ▪ Pour marinade over top. ▪ Stir in sesame oil and pepper. ▪ Toss well, cover and refrigerate at least 20 minutes. ▪ Toss again just before serving. ▪ Pick out and discard chilies.

calories/serving: 450
protein, thiamin, niacin, vitamin C: excellent
iron: good
vitamin A, riboflavin: fair

GAZPACHO SALAD

Serves 4 to 6
Preparation time: 15 minutes
Standing time: 2 hours

With all the refreshing flavor and color of the Spanish soup of the same name, this layered salad is perfect with beef or lamb hot off the barbecue. If you have fresh herbs available, use them finely chopped, substituting three times the amount of dried.

¼ cup	red wine vinegar
1	clove garlic, crushed
½ tsp	sugar
¼ tsp	each crushed dried basil and oregano
pinch	crushed dried rosemary
	salt and pepper to taste
½ cup	olive oil
2	large tomatoes, sliced
1	small Spanish onion, thinly sliced
1	green pepper, in thin rings
1	cucumber, thinly sliced
2	stalks celery, sliced diagonally

- Stir together vinegar, garlic, sugar, basil, oregano, rosemary, salt and pepper in a small bowl.
- Slowly whisk in oil. ▪ In a large glass bowl, preferably with straight sides, alternate layers of tomatoes, onion, green pepper, cucumber and celery slices until all vegetables are used. ▪ As you proceed, drizzle each layer with some of the dressing, being sure to stir dressing often to keep blended. ▪ Cover and refrigerate 2 hours. ▪ Drain to serve if you wish.

calories/serving: 312 for 4 servings
208 for 6 servings
vitamin C: excellent
fiber: moderate

JULIENNE VEGETABLE SALAD WITH LEMON VINAIGRETTE

Serves 6
Preparation time: 20 minutes

A colorful and crisp salad, this is best made ahead of time for flavors to blend.

1 cup	sliced green beans, 1½″ lengths
1 cup	julienne strips of carrot
1 cup	julienne strips of zucchini
1 cup	julienne strips of celery
	salt and pepper to taste
	lettuce leaves

LEMON VINAIGRETTE:

2 Tb	olive or walnut oil
¼ cup	lemon juice
2 Tb	chopped fresh parsley
2 Tb	chopped green onion tops or chives
1	clove garlic, minced

- Blanch green beans in boiling water for 1 minute.
- Immediately drain and plunge into cold water.
- Drain when cool and dry well. ▪ Combine green beans, carrot, zucchini and celery. ▪ Combine vinaigrette ingredients in a small bowl. ▪ Pour over vegetables and toss well. ▪ Season with salt and pepper. ▪ Cover and refrigerate until serving time.
- To serve, arrange lettuce leaves on plates. Divide salad between plates.

calories/serving: 69
vitamin A: excellent
vitamin C: good
fiber: moderate

SALAD WITH SMOKED HAM AND PARMESAN

Serves 2
Preparation time: 10 minutes
Standing time: 30 minutes

It's always better to buy good Italian Parmesan cheese in one piece and grate it yourself – it's fresher and better tasting.

1 cup	thinly sliced red onion
1 Tb	cider vinegar
6	leaves romaine lettuce
6	leaves red leaf lettuce
6	leaves Boston lettuce
3	slices smoked ham, chopped
2 oz	Parmesan cheese, coarsely grated or shredded

VINAIGRETTE:

2 Tb	white wine vinegar
1 tsp	Dijon mustard
1 Tb	finely chopped fresh basil *or* 1 tsp dried basil
⅓ cup	olive oil

- Marinate onion slices in vinegar for 30 minutes.
- Set aside. ▪ Wash, dry and tear romaine, red leaf and Boston lettuce into bite-size pieces. ▪ Combine all lettuces in salad bowl. ▪ Sprinkle with smoked ham. ▪ Whisk together wine vinegar, Dijon mustard and basil. ▪ Slowly add olive oil, whisking constantly. ▪ Set aside. ▪ Just before serving toss salad with onion slices, Parmesan and vinaigrette.

calories/serving: 500
protein, calcium, vitamin C, thiamin, niacin: excellent
iron, vitamin A, riboflavin: good
fiber: moderate

MARINATED CAULIFLOWER SALAD WITH FRESH GINGER

Serves 8
Preparation time: 10 minutes
Cooking time: 6 minutes for vinaigrette
Standing time: at least overnight

Pouring a hot vinaigrette over raw cauliflower leaves it with lots of crunch.

1	large head cauliflower, in small florets
½ cup	dry white wine
½ cup	white wine vinegar
½ cup	water
½ cup	olive oil
1	clove garlic, minced
2 Tb	sugar
1 Tb	minced ginger root
	salt and pepper to taste
1	large green pepper, cut into chunks
1 cup	small cherry tomatoes
¼ cup	coarsely chopped fresh parsley

▪ Put cauliflower in a heat-proof bowl. Set aside. ▪ Stir together wine, vinegar, water, oil, garlic, sugar, ginger root, salt and pepper in a small saucepan. ▪ Bring to boil, stirring, and boil 3 minutes. ▪ Pour over cauliflower and toss to coat well. ▪ Stir often until cooled to room temperature. ▪ Add green pepper, tomatoes and parsley. ▪ Cover and refrigerate at least overnight and up to 2 days, tossing often. ▪ Remove to serving bowl with slotted spoon.

calories/serving: 167
vitamin C: excellent

MEXICAN CORN SALAD WITH LIME DRESSING

Serves 4 to 6
Preparation time: 10 minutes

Hearts of palm, available in specialty sections of supermarkets, add an exotic touch that turns a simple everyday salad into company fare. Serve with roast beef or poultry.

4 cups	cooked corn kernels
1 cup	canned hearts of palm slices
¼ cup	diced sweet red pepper
¼ cup	chopped onion
	spinach or lettuce leaves (optional)

LIME DRESSING:

2 Tb	fresh lime juice
1 tsp	chili powder or to taste
½ tsp	finely grated lime peel
	salt and pepper to taste
⅓ cup	olive oil

▪ Stir together corn, hearts of palm slices, red pepper and onion in a large bowl. ▪ Stir together lime juice, chili powder, lime peel, salt and pepper in a small bowl. ▪ Slowly whisk in olive oil. ▪ Gently stir dressing into corn mixture. ▪ Use immediately or cover and refrigerate for up to three days. ▪ To serve, transfer to a pretty glass serving bowl or mound on a platter lined with spinach or lettuce leaves if you wish.

calories/serving: 316 for 4 servings
212 for 6 servings
vitamin C: excellent
fiber: high
niacin: good
thiamin: fair

ENDIVE AND HAZELNUT SALAD WITH TARRAGON CREAM DRESSING

Serves 6 to 8
Preparation time: 20 minutes

This salad will easily become a favorite, and the dressing is delicious on lettuce as well.

½ cup	hazelnuts
6	Belgian endives

DRESSING:

3 Tb	raspberry or red wine vinegar
	salt and pepper to taste
½ tsp	Dijon mustard
1 tsp	dried tarragon *or* 1 Tb fresh tarragon
⅓ cup	heavy cream
⅓ cup	extra-virgin olive oil

▪ Preheat oven to 350°F. ▪ Spread hazelnuts on a cookie sheet and toast lightly for about 10 minutes. ▪ After removing from oven, cool slightly and then rub in a tea towel to remove as much of the brown skins as possible. (Don't worry if some remains.) ▪ Chop hazelnuts coarsely and reserve for garnish. ▪ Separate leaves of endives and cut into halves either horizontally or vertically, depending on the way you wish the salad to look. ▪ Wash in cold water and dry thoroughly. ▪ Whisk vinegar, salt, pepper, mustard and tarragon together. ▪ Whisk in cream. ▪ Gradually beat in oil. ▪ Taste and season as desired. ▪ Toss dressing with endives and sprinkle with toasted hazelnuts.

calories/serving: 226 for 6 servings
169 for 8 servings
vitamin C: fair

Mexican Beef and Orange Salad

MEXICAN BEEF AND ORANGE SALAD

Serves 6
Preparation time: 20 minutes
Chilling time: 2 hours

If you make this easy salad from leftover roast beef, no one will complain about having to eat leftovers.

1½ lbs	**lean cooked roast beef**
½	**Spanish onion**
2	**oranges**
2	**hot yellow peppers**
½	**sweet red pepper**
	leaf or Boston lettuce
	sprigs of fresh coriander (optional)
DRESSING:	
⅓ cup	**white wine vinegar**
½ tsp	**each dried oregano and cayenne pepper**
	salt and black pepper to taste
1 cup	**olive oil**

▪ Cut roast beef into thin julienne strips and place in a large bowl. ▪ Cut onion into very thin slices and toss with beef. ▪ Peel oranges and, holding over bowl, cut into segments between membranes. ▪ Discard membranes and toss segments with beef mixture. ▪ Seed peppers, cut into slivers and toss with beef. ▪ Stir together vinegar, oregano, cayenne, salt and pepper in a small bowl. ▪ Gradually whisk in oil and pour over beef mixture. ▪ Toss gently but well. ▪ Cover and refrigerate at least 2 hours before serving. ▪ To serve, line platter with lettuce leaves. ▪ Drain and arrange beef mixture on top. ▪ Garnish with sprigs of fresh coriander.

calories/serving: 529
protein, vitamin C, niacin: excellent
iron: good
thiamin, riboflavin: fair

BEWARE OF HOT PEPPERS

Take care when handling hot peppers, the irritating juices can be very painful if they get into your eyes. Wear rubber gloves when preparing them, or wash your hands well immediately afterwards.

MAIN DISHES

A main dish is the soul and heart of a meal. Around it we may build frills and embellishments — appetizers, salads, desserts, garnishes, as we choose — but every meal needs a solid identifiable core even if, as in the case of a simple pub lunch, the center is simply a chunk of cheese.

I'm no food historian, but reasonable conjecture tells us that at the beginning of human history there would usually be only one dish at a meal. Our ancestors of the plains, caves and forests presumably ate what they could gather, catch or stun on any given day. Anthropologists believe they grazed their way through life, digging up a root here, picking a handful of berries there and, if they'd developed a taste for flesh, keeping a keen eye out in case the meat course hove into view. It's certain they gnawed on the haunch of whatever beast or bird they'd been fleet enough or clever enough to capture, without the dimmest notion that it might be more delectable still with a little sauce à l'orange. Nor, presumably, were they concerned with serving a green and a yellow vegetable to balance the meal nutritionally. If someone stumbled upon a patch of blueberries, it was blueberries for dinner.

Though no sane person would choose to return to foraging for dinner, chasing it or constructing ambushes for it, still it must have made for fewer and simpler decisions. Before the discovery of fire, no one even had to cook.

The experts who study our current habits tell us we're becoming grazers again, wolfing down doughnuts mid-morning, nibbling in front of the TV set, fixing a little something for a bedtime snack. Perhaps they're right, but the people I know still expect to eat one serious meal a day (and call it "dinner" whether they eat it at noon or in the evening) and they still plan that meal around a main dish.

The nature of "main dish" seems to have changed somewhat in many households in the past decades. An infinite variety of pastas with vegetable, meat or seafood sauces have grown popular, as have rice dishes, quiches and vegetarian inventions.

When I was growing up and asked "What's for dinner?" I took it for granted the answer would be some combination of meat and potatoes: steak and baked, ham and scalloped, roast beef/veal/pork with roast potatoes, chicken with mashed. "Supper" was another matter altogether — a meal for using up leftovers or gorging on corn on the cob. But dinner simply wasn't

Lamb Shanks in Red Wine

dinner without some variation of meat and potatoes on the menu. Indeed, meat-and-potatoes has become a metaphor for basic, important bedrock matters: when we wish to clear away irrelevant or confusing complications, we call it "getting down to the meat-and-potato issues."

In my early homemaking days, eating customs began to change. Dinner in the middle of the day was largely replaced by lunch in families where the father didn't come home at noon. And we discovered that dishes like spaghetti and meatballs and chili con carne for dinner were not only slightly exotic and sophisticated, they were beloved by children and made the meat go further. But they were still main dishes and the meal was built around them. Casseroles were all the vogue for a while (every cook had her version of canned tuna casserole), and some wizard thought up the idea of marketing chicken "parts," which made chicken-for-dinner a whole lot quicker. We were persuaded that broiled steak was tastier than pan-fried, and we tried valiantly to provide one green and one yellow vegetable at every dinner.

With the recent influx of immigrants and imported food from all over the world, we're now faced with a bewildering array of choices when asked the question "What's for dinner?" Our answer will be governed obviously by personal taste, the state of our food budget, what's available in our local stores and how fond we are of cooking. We hope you'll find in our Main Dishes section lots of recipes to inspire you and stimulate your imagination. Embellish them with as many extra courses and frills as you like, follow them with elaborate desserts or no desserts at all; they're the foundation stones for building your own personal meals. And it's always comforting to know we can fall back on good old meat and potatoes, so you'll find plenty of those.

Beef

BOEUF BOURGUIGNON

Serves 6
Preparation time: 20 minutes
Cooking time: 2 hours

A wonderful dish for a crowd. Increase the amount of meat just a little and you'll have plenty for eight, especially if you pass lots of French bread for sopping up the good gravy. For best flavor, make two or three days ahead (up to garnish point) and refrigerate. Can be frozen.

3 lbs	rump of beef, cut into 1½" cubes
5 Tb	butter
2 Tb	vegetable oil
2	onions, sliced
¼ cup	flour
2 cups	dry red wine
2 cups	beef stock
2	shallots, finely chopped
3	cloves garlic, finely chopped
2 tsp	tomato paste
1	large stalk celery, cut into pieces
6	large sprigs parsley
¼ tsp	dried thyme
	salt and pepper to taste
½ lb	tiny silver onions
½ lb	boneless pork (fat and lean), cut into ¼" cubes
½ lb	small mushrooms, cut into halves
	chopped fresh parsley

▪ Trim all excess fat from beef. ▪ Heat 2 tablespoons butter and oil to very hot in a Dutch oven. ▪ Add beef cubes and brown quickly on all sides over high heat. ▪ Add sliced onions and continue cooking over high heat, stirring constantly, until onions are lightly browned. ▪ Sprinkle in flour and stir until flour is lightly browned. ▪ Add wine, stock, shallots, garlic, tomato paste, celery, parsley, thyme, salt and pepper. ▪ Bring to boil, turn down heat, cover and simmer until meat is tender, about 2 hours. ▪ While meat is cooking, peel and boil silver onions until barely tender. ▪ Drain and dry on paper towelling. ▪ Fry cubes of pork in a large skillet until crisp. ▪ Lift out of pan with a slotted spoon and set aside. ▪ Discard fat in pan. ▪ Add 1 tablespoon butter to pan, add cooked silver onions and shake over high heat until the onions are golden. Add more butter if necessary. ▪ Lift onions out and add 2 tablespoons butter and the mushrooms to the pan. ▪ Fry, stirring constantly, 2 minutes. ▪ Lift out of pan and set aside. ▪ Heat a large deep platter in the oven shortly before meat is tender. ▪ Remove from oven and set oven at 350°F. ▪ Lift meat out of gravy onto hot platter with slotted spoon. ▪ Strain gravy over meat and garnish the edge of the platter with bits of pork, silver onions and mushrooms. ▪ Slip into oven for 5 minutes to be sure everything is hot. ▪ Sprinkle with parsley and serve.

calories/serving: 607
protein, iron, niacin: excellent
vitamin A, vitamin C, thiamin, riboflavin: good

INDIVIDUAL MEAT LOAVES

Serves 4
Preparation time: 10 minutes
Cooking time: 35 to 40 minutes

When family members get after-school jobs or join the track team, you soon find everyone wants supper at a different time. These little loaves can be reheated quickly for latecomers and make good lunch-bag fare the next day.

1 lb	ground beef
1	small onion, minced
½ cup	fine dry breadcrumbs
¼ cup	each lemon juice and milk
1	egg, lightly beaten
2 Tb	chopped fresh parsley
1 Tb	Worcestershire sauce
½ tsp	dry mustard
	salt and pepper to taste
8	slices side bacon

▪ Mix together all ingredients except bacon. ▪ Form into 8 small rolls 3" × 1½". ▪ Wrap 1 slice of bacon spiral-style around each roll. Place on greased rack in broiler pan and bake in preheated 350°F oven for 35 to 40 minutes, or until rolls are brown and meat is cooked through.

calories/serving: 408 (204 per loaf)
protein, niacin: excellent
iron: good

BOEUF BOURGUIGNON

Shallots and silver onions add a unique and subtle flavor to traditional Boeuf Bourguignon, but they can be hard to find. The white parts of green onions make a good substitute for shallots; in place of silver onions use the smallest yellow onions you can find and peel them down to about one inch in diameter.

Shredded Beef and Green Pepper Sauté

SHREDDED BEEF AND GREEN PEPPER SAUTÉ

Serves 2 to 3
Preparation time: 15 minutes
Standing time: 10 minutes
Cooking time: 5 minutes

A touch of hot chili pepper adds extra flavor to this quick stir-fry. Mixing the beef with cornstarch makes it beautifully tender.

8 oz	flank steak
1½ tsp	cornstarch
2 Tb	soy sauce
5 Tb	vegetable oil
1½	green peppers
1	dried chili pepper
SAUCE: 3 Tb	water
½ tsp	cornstarch
1 tsp	soy sauce
½ tsp	sesame oil
	pepper

■ Cut beef into thin strips about 2½″ long. ■ Combine cornstarch, soy sauce and 1 tablespoon vegetable oil in a bowl. ■ Mix well, then stir in beef. ■ Let stand 10 minutes or up to 1 hour. ■ Seed green peppers. ■ Cut into strips. ■ Seed chili pepper and chop finely. ■ Combine sauce ingredients. ■ Heat remaining oil in a wok or heavy frying pan over high heat. ■ Add beef and stir-fry for 2 minutes or until cooked. ■ With slotted spoon remove to side plate. ■ Add green and chili peppers. ■ Stir-fry for 2 minutes or until tender-crisp. ■ Return beef to pan. ■ Add sauce and stir-fry for 1 minute or until sauce thickens. ■ Serve with rice or buttered noodles.

calories/serving: 500 for 2 servings
333 for 3 servings
protein, vitamin C, niacin: excellent
iron: good

Ossobuco

OSSOBUCO

Serves 4 to 6
Preparation time: 15 minutes
Cooking time: about 1 hour and 20 minutes

This dish, whose name means marrow bone, is cooked in many parts of Italy, but it is classically Milanese.

3 lbs	**veal knuckles or shank of beef, cut 1½″ thick**
⅓ cup	**flour**
	salt and white pepper to taste
¼ lb	**butter**
1	**clove garlic, crushed**
1	**carrot, thinly sliced**
	grated peel of ½ lemon
2 Tb	**tomato paste**
1 tsp	**dried basil**
1 cup	**dry white wine**
	rich meat stock to cover knuckles halfway
3 Tb	**chopped fresh parsley**

■ Wipe meat with a damp towel. ■ Combine flour, salt and pepper; rub into meat, coating it well on all sides. ■ Sauté meat in butter in a large heavy frying pan or Dutch oven until brown on all sides. ■ Add crushed garlic, carrot, half of grated lemon peel, tomato paste, basil and wine. ■ Add meat stock to cover knuckles halfway. Simmer gently, covered, about 1 hour. ■ Turn pieces once while cooking. ■ Reduce liquid with lid off for 10 minutes. ■ Sprinkle with parsley and remaining grated lemon peel and serve with tiny spoons for guests to extract marrow.

calories/serving: 419 for 4 servings
279 for 6 servings
vitamin A, niacin: excellent
protein, iron, vitamin C: good

FAMOUS MARITIME HAMBURGERS

Serves 8
Preparation time: 10 minutes
Cooking time: 10 to 15 minutes

These are a great Maritime secret said to be fit for the gods.

1½ lbs	medium ground beef
⅔ cup	undiluted evaporated milk
1	egg
½ cup	fine cracker crumbs
	salt and pepper to taste
1 tsp	dry mustard
¼ cup	minced onion
½ cup	minced green pepper

▪ Combine all ingredients in a mixing bowl using your hands. ▪ Mix well. ▪ Form into patties. (May be frozen: remove from freezer a few hours before grilling.) ▪ Barbecue over medium coals about 5 to 7 minutes on each side.

calories/patty: 275
protein, niacin: excellent
iron: good
riboflavin: fair

HUNGARIAN VEAL STEW

Serves 4 to 6
Preparation time: 20 minutes
Cooking time: 1½ to 2 hours

This gently seasoned dish is wonderful the first time around, and leftovers can be frozen and served without apology — especially if you zing up the flavor with a pinch or two of thyme, added while the stew reheats.

3 lbs	lean stewing veal, cubed
3 Tb	vegetable oil
2	large onions, minced
2 Tb	sweet paprika
2 or 3	cloves garlic, minced (optional)
1 tsp	salt
2	medium sweet red peppers, cored and diced

▪ Heat oil in a heavy casserole or Dutch oven and cook onions until lightly browned. ▪ Remove from heat and stir in veal, paprika, garlic and salt. ▪ Cover and return to very low heat. The meat should cook in its own and the onions' juices. ▪ Check occasionally, and if it seems to be drying out, add a few tablespoons of water. ▪ After half an hour, stir in diced sweet peppers, cover again and continue to cook slowly, adding a little more water only if moisture evaporates. ▪ When meat is tender, sauce should be a rich dark red and gold, neither too thin nor too thick. If it is on the thin side, remove meat

Famous Maritime Hamburgers

to a warm dish, quickly reduce juices over moderately high heat, then return veal to warm for a few minutes. ▪ Correct seasoning and serve with rice or boiled potatoes.

calories/serving: 576 for 4 servings
384 for 6 servings
protein, iron, vitamin C, niacin: excellent
riboflavin: good
thiamin: fair

FILET OF BEEF CHAROLAIS WITH VEGETABLES

Serves 4 to 6
Preparation time: 15 minutes
Cooking time: 40 minutes

Even cold leftovers of this dish are delicious.

3 to 4 lbs	filet of beef
	butter
	salt and pepper to taste
⅓ cup	consommé
2 Tb	tomato paste
¼ cup	dry sherry, Cognac or red wine
	cooked green beans, peas, cauliflower and broccoli florets, potato balls rolled in butter and parsley, and broiled tomato halves

▪ Have meat at room temperature. ▪ Trim filet, rub with butter, salt and freshly ground pepper. ▪ Roast beef in preheated 500°F oven. Rare beef will take approximately 5 to 6 minutes a pound, 10 minutes a pound for medium-rare. ▪ During roasting, add 2 tablespoons butter two or three times. ▪ Remove filet to a large hot platter. ▪ Add consommé, tomato paste and sherry to the roasting pan and heat. ▪ Keep hot in gravy boat. ▪ Garnish platter with cooked vegetables.

calories/serving: 718 for 4 servings (without vegetables)
480 for 6 servings
protein, iron, niacin: excellent
riboflavin: good
thiamin: fair

MEAT AND CHEESE LOAF

Serves 4
Preparation time: 10 minutes
Cooking time: 1 hour and 15 minutes

A quick and easy meat loaf with a good flavor.

1 lb	**lean ground beef**
1 cup	**milk**
½ cup	**fine cracker crumbs**
½	**onion, chopped**
½	**green pepper, chopped**
1	**egg, lightly beaten**
	salt and pepper to taste
pinch	**ground mace**
¾ cup	**diced mild Cheddar cheese**

■ Combine all ingredients except cheese in a large bowl. ■ Gently mix in cheese and pack into a 9″ × 5″ loaf pan and bake in 350°F oven for 1 hour and 15 minutes, or until browned and meat is cooked through.

calories/serving: 406
protein, niacin: excellent
iron, calcium, riboflavin, vitamin C: good

CABBAGE ROLLS

Serves 6 to 8
Preparation time: 30 minutes
Cooking time: 2 hours
Standing time: 20 to 30 minutes

Cabbage rolls require work ahead of time, but you can put your feet up while they're reheating.

24 to 30	**cabbage leaves (2 heads)**
1 lb	**ground beef**
1	**small onion, finely chopped**
½ cup	**raw long-grain rice**
	salt and pepper to taste
2	**medium onions, sliced**
½ cup	**brown sugar**
1 can	**(14 oz/396 mL) tomato sauce**
1 can	**(19 oz/540 mL) tomatoes, drained**
	juice of 2 lemons

■ Steam or simmer cabbage until leaves can be separated. ■ Remove leaves and cool in cold water. ■ Keep a few extra cabbage leaves to line bottom of baking dish. ■ Shave thick part of leaf stem with a sharp knife. This will make rolling the leaves easier. ■ Combine beef, onion, rice, salt and pepper. ■ Place 1 to 2 tablespoons of filling on the bottom, stem end, edge of leaf. ■ Roll leaf envelope fashion and set aside. ■ Repeat with remaining leaves. ■ Line a large baking dish or roasting pan with extra cabbage leaves. ■ Place cabbage rolls on leaves. ■ Mix remaining ingredients together and pour over.

■ Cover with foil and bake in preheated 350°F oven for 1 hour. ■ Uncover, baste with juices and bake a further ¾ to 1 hour. ■ Baste occasionally. ■ Remove from oven and let stand for 20 to 30 minutes before serving. ■ Serve with sour cream and bread.

calories/serving: 391 for 6 servings
290 for 8 servings
protein, vitamin C, niacin: excellent
iron, vitamin A, thiamin: good
calcium, riboflavin: fair
fiber: moderate
low fat using lean ground beef

VEAL CHOPS WITH TOMATO TARRAGON SAUCE

Serves 4
Preparation time: 20 minutes
Marinating time: 1 hour
Cooking time: 15 minutes

Grilled or sautéed veal chops (tender Provimi if possible) are delicious served with this quick sauce. Serve with rice or noodles and a green vegetable such as broccoli or beans.

4	**veal chops**
	juice of 1 lemon
2 Tb	**vegetable oil**
1 Tb	**chopped fresh tarragon *or* 1 tsp dried**
	freshly ground pepper to taste
SAUCE:	
1 Tb	**vegetable oil**
1	**clove garlic, minced**
2	**green onions, chopped**
1	**stalk celery, chopped**
1	**medium carrot, chopped**
3 cups	**peeled, seeded and chopped tomatoes**
2 Tb	**chopped fresh tarragon**
	salt and pepper to taste

■ Combine lemon juice, oil, tarragon and pepper and drizzle over veal chops in flat dish. ■ Marinate, covered, 1 hour at room temperature or several hours in refrigerator. ■ Heat 1 tablespoon oil in saucepan. ■ Add garlic, onions, celery and carrot and cook 2 minutes, stirring, to soften. ■ Add tomatoes and cook, stirring, over medium heat 10 to 15 minutes or until reduced to about 1½ cups and slightly thickened. ■ Blend in tarragon. ■ Add salt and pepper. ■ Keep warm. ■ Remove chops from marinade and grill over hot barbecue coals, or sauté over high heat in greased, heavy skillet 3 to 4 minutes on each side, to desired doneness. ■ Serve hot chops with sauce.

calories/serving: 342
protein, iron, vitamin A, niacin, vitamin C: excellent

Meat and Cheese Loaf

Beef Tenderloin with Béarnaise Sauce

HEARTY COUNTRY MEAT LOAF WITH SOUR CREAM GRAVY

Serves 6 to 8
Preparation time: 20 minutes
Cooking time: 1 hour and 20 minutes

This rich, satisfying meat loaf will remind you of hearty country feasts.

3	slices white bread
1 cup	milk
2 Tb	butter
¾ cup	chopped mushrooms
1	small onion, finely chopped
2	cloves garlic, minced
1 lb	ground beef
1 lb	ground pork
2	eggs, lightly beaten
2 Tb	catsup
1 Tb	Worcestershire sauce
½ tsp	each dried marjoram and thyme
	salt and pepper to taste
3	slices side bacon
	chopped fresh parsley for garnish

SOUR CREAM GRAVY:

¼ cup	pan drippings
2 Tb	flour
1 cup	beef stock or water
1 cup	sour cream
	salt and pepper to taste

▪ Tear bread into small pieces and soak in a large mixing bowl with milk while you prepare rest of loaf. ▪ Melt butter in a small skillet and sauté mushrooms, onion and garlic until soft, about 3 minutes. ▪ Let cool. ▪ Mix vegetables and meat into bread mixture with your hands. ▪ Add eggs, catsup, Worcestershire sauce, marjoram, thyme, salt and pepper; mix by hand in a circular motion. ▪ Form into a free-form 9″ × 5″ loaf. ▪ Drape with bacon and place on greased rack in broiler pan. ▪ Bake in preheated 375°F oven for about 1 hour and 15 to 30 minutes, or until browned and meat is cooked through. The internal temperature should be 160°F. ▪ Lift off rack and keep warm while making gravy. ▪ Pour ¼ cup of the pan drippings into a small saucepan. ▪ Stir flour into drippings until smooth. ▪ Cook, stirring, over medium heat 3 minutes. ▪ Gradually stir in stock and bring to boil. ▪ Reduce heat and cook until thickened. ▪ Stir in sour cream; heat through but do not boil. ▪ Season with salt and pepper. ▪ Transfer to heated sauce boat and sprinkle with parsley.

calories/serving: 479 (meat loaf only)
protein, thiamin, niacin: excellent
iron, riboflavin: good
Sour Cream Gravy: calories/tablespoon: 26

BEEF TENDERLOIN WITH BÉARNAISE SAUCE

Serves 6
Preparation time: 15 minutes
Cooking time: 15 to 20 minutes
Standing time: 10 minutes

Since Béarnaise sauce disappears faster than you can say chateaubriand, this recipe makes a generous amount. Serve the sauce with a whole tenderloin for six or more, or with individual broiled steaks. Filet mignon (small filet), tournedos or thick chateaubriand cut for two or three are all excellent choices.

2 lbs	tenderloin of beef
2 Tb	melted butter
	fresh parsley or watercress for garnish

BÉARNAISE SAUCE:

⅓ cup	dry white wine
⅓ cup	white wine vinegar or tarragon vinegar
1 Tb	chopped shallots
1 Tb	crumbled dried tarragon *or* 2 Tb chopped fresh tarragon
1 tsp	crumbled dried chervil *or* 2 Tb fresh chervil
4	whole peppercorns, crushed
pinch	salt
4	egg yolks, beaten, at room temperature
½ lb	unsalted butter, slightly softened
1 Tb	chopped fresh tarragon
	salt and cayenne pepper to taste

▪ Preheat oven to 500°F. ▪ Place meat on rack in shallow roasting pan and brush with butter. ▪ Insert meat thermometer and place in oven. ▪ Turn heat down to 425°F. Roast to desired doneness; for rare, thermometer registers 130° to 140°F. ▪ While beef cooks, make sauce. ▪ Combine wine, vinegar, shallots, tarragon, chervil, peppercorns and salt in a small heavy saucepan. ▪ Simmer 10 minutes or until mixture is reduced to 2 tablespoons. ▪ Strain into a small saucepan, pressing with back of spoon to extract all juices. ▪ Let cool slightly. This herbal reduction can be made in advance and refrigerated, but bring to warm room temperature before continuing. ▪ Place saucepan with reduction over warm water in bottom of double boiler on low heat. Do not allow water to boil. ▪ Add egg yolks to reduction and whisk constantly until sauce thickens. ▪ Still whisking, add softened butter in small pieces, about 1 tablespoon at a time. If mixture thickens too quickly, remove from heat. ▪ When all the butter is incorporated and sauce is thick and creamy, re-move from heat and blend in chopped tarragon. ▪ Add salt and cayenne pepper. ▪ When beef is cooked, let it stand on a warm platter for 10 minutes before carving. ▪ Sauce can be kept up to an hour in top of double boiler, as long as it does not overheat. ▪ Should it separate because of overheating, remove from heat and rapidly whisk in a few drops of lukewarm water. ▪ Serve the sauce warm, not hot, spooned over beef slices. ▪ Can be served with sautéed mushroom caps and crisp, seasonal vegetables. ▪ Garnish with fresh parsley or watercress.

calories/serving: 600
protein, iron, niacin: excellent
vitamin A, thiamin, riboflavin: fair

MARINATED FLANK STEAK

Serves 4 to 5
Preparation time: 5 minutes
Marinating time: 3 hours to 3 days
Cooking time: 8 to 10 minutes

It only takes a few minutes to make the marinade and the steak can be refrigerated in the marinade for one to three days.

1 lb	flank steak

MARINADE:

¾ cup	vegetable oil
¼ cup	soy sauce
¼ cup	brown sugar
2 Tb	vinegar
2	cloves garlic, minced
2 Tb	chopped onion
1 Tb	grated ginger root *or* 1 tsp ground ginger

▪ Score one side of the steak by making shallow cuts in a crisscross design. ▪ Combine marinade ingredients and pour over the meat. ▪ Cover and refrigerate for 1 to 3 days, or leave at room temperature for 3 to 4 hours. ▪ Broil or barbecue 4 to 5 minutes on each side. ▪ Slice in thin strips across the grain. Good hot or cold. ▪ For a different flavor, use Herbed Marinade instead:

HERBED MARINADE:

⅓ cup	red wine vinegar
¼ cup	vegetable oil
1 tsp	dried marjoram
1 tsp	dried thyme
1	bay leaf, crumbled
1	small onion, chopped
2	cloves garlic, minced
	freshly ground pepper

calories/serving: 314 for 4 servings
251 for 5 servings
protein, niacin: excellent
iron: good
riboflavin: fair

Chili Deluxe

CHILI DELUXE

Serves 6 to 8
Preparation time: 20 minutes
Cooking time: 1 to 1½ hours

This is rich, thick chili made with chunks of meat instead of ground beef, then served with a colorful array of condiments.

2 lbs	lean stewing beef
4 Tb	oil
1	medium onion, chopped
1	clove garlic, chopped
1 to 2 Tb	chili powder or to taste
½ tsp	dried oregano
1	small carrot, grated
1 can	(5½ oz/156 mL) tomato paste
1 can	(19 oz/540 mL) tomatoes
1 cup	water
	salt to taste
1 can	(19 oz/540 mL) kidney beans, drained

CONDIMENTS:

grated Cheddar cheese, sour cream, chopped onion, tomato, green pepper and hot pepper

■ Trim beef well and cut into ½″ cubes. ■ Heat 2 tablespoons oil in a large heavy pot. ■ Add beef a little at a time and brown well. ■ Remove and set aside. ■ Add remaining oil. ■ Stir in onion and garlic and cook until just softened. ■ Add browned beef, chili powder, oregano and carrot and mix well. ■ Stir in tomato paste, tomatoes (breaking up tomatoes), water and salt. ■ Heat through. ■ Simmer until beef is very tender, approximately 1 to 1½ hours. ■ Just before serving stir in kidney beans and heat through. ■ Taste for seasoning. ■ Serve in deep warm bowls and let everyone help themselves to condiments. ■ If freezing chili, don't add beans. ■ Stir beans in when reheating chili.

calories/serving: 438 for 6 servings
327 for 8 servings
protein, iron, vitamin C, niacin: excellent
vitamin A, thiamin, riboflavin: fair
fiber: moderate

SIRLOIN STEAK WITH PEPPER SAUCE

Serves 2
Preparation time: 10 minutes
Cooking time: 10 minutes

This particular pepper steak will draw rave reviews. For those of you watching your waistline, omit the cream and add one tablespoon of unsweetened applesauce and two tablespoons thinly sliced sautéed mushrooms to the sauce. Follow all other directions as given. The applesauce creates an intriguing flavor.

2	strip sirloin or T-bone steaks, about 1″ thick
1 Tb	crushed black peppercorns
pinch	salt
2 Tb	flour
1 Tb	brown sugar
1 Tb	butter
2 tsp	green peppercorns packed in brine, drained
½ tsp	crushed white peppercorns
1 Tb	brandy
½ cup	heavy cream

■ Rub both sides of steaks with crushed black peppercorns and a pinch of salt. ■ Dredge steak with 1 tablespoon flour and 1 tablespoon brown sugar. ■ Heat heavy frying pan and add butter. ■ When butter is almost brown, add steaks and cook for 2 minutes to a side for rare, longer for well-done. ■ Remove steaks to warm platter. ■ To pan juices, add 1 tablespoon flour and brown. ■ Add green peppercorns, crushed white peppercorns and brandy. ■ Simmer for a minute. ■ Turn heat down and slowly stir in cream. ■ Pour over steaks and serve immediately with tiny glazed carrots and small boiled potatoes.

calories/serving: 540 using 18% table cream
protein, iron, niacin: excellent
vitamin A, thiamin, riboflavin: good

SPICY MEAT LOAF

Serves 6 to 8
Preparation time: 40 minutes
Cooking time: 40 minutes

Kubba – meat loaf – is one of the best-known dishes in the eastern Arab world, where it is considered to be the king of all foods.

1 cup	**fine bulgur**
1 lb	**freshly ground lean beef**
1	**medium onion, chopped**
1 tsp	**salt**
½ tsp	**crushed dried mint leaves**
¼ tsp	**black pepper**
¼ tsp	**ground cumin**
¼ tsp	**ground cinnamon**
pinch	**cayenne pepper**
3 Tb	**butter**
STUFFING:	
1½ Tb	**butter**
2 Tb	**pine nuts or slivered almonds**
½ cup	**ground beef**
1	**medium onion, finely chopped**
½ tsp	**salt**
¼ tsp	**ground coriander**
pinch	**black pepper**
pinch	**allspice**

▪ Soak bulgur in cold water for 10 minutes. ▪ Force out all the water through a cheesecloth or by pressing by hand. ▪ Process bulgur and remaining ingredients, except butter, in a food processor until thoroughly mixed. ▪ Set aside. ▪ To make stuffing, melt 1½ tablespoons butter in a frying pan. ▪ Add nuts and sauté over medium heat until they turn golden brown. ▪ Add meat and stir-fry for about 10 minutes. ▪ Add remaining stuffing ingredients and stir-fry until onions turn limp. ▪ Set aside. ▪ Divide the kubba into two portions. ▪ Spread one portion on the bottom of a buttered 8″ × 11″ baking pan. ▪ Cover evenly with stuffing. ▪ Top evenly with the remaining kubba. ▪ Cut into 2″ squares and dot with 3 tablespoons butter. ▪ Bake in preheated 350°F oven for 40 minutes. ▪ Serve hot or cold.

MICROWAVE DIRECTIONS: Prepare meat loaf as instructed. To make stuffing, melt butter in a casserole dish for 30 seconds, add nuts, cook on High 2 minutes. Add meat, cook further 1 to 2 minutes. Add onions, cook 1 minute or until soft. Assemble meat loaf in a casserole dish. Cook on High 10 minutes.

calories/serving: 324 for 6 servings
243 for 8 servings
protein: excellent
iron: good
niacin, riboflavin, thiamin: fair

CHOPS WITH HERB SAUCE

Serves 2
Preparation time: 5 minutes
Cooking time: 20 minutes

Stuffing the chops with Brie gives them an unusual flavor. The sauce is simple to make as long as you remember to whisk the butter off the heat. Too much heat and the sauce will separate.

2	**veal or pork chops, 1″ thick**
2 oz	**Brie**
1 Tb	**olive oil**
1 Tb	**butter**
	salt and pepper to taste
SAUCE:	
¼ cup	**white wine**
2 Tb	**raspberry or red wine vinegar**
1 tsp	**lemon juice**
1 tsp	**dried tarragon *or* 1 Tb chopped fresh**
1 tsp	**dried thyme *or* 1 Tb chopped fresh**
½ tsp	**dried rosemary *or* 2 tsp chopped fresh**
¼ cup	**unsalted butter, softened**

▪ Make a pocket approximately 2″ long in the side of each veal chop. ▪ Remove rind from Brie, cut into pieces and stuff inside pockets. ▪ Heat oil and butter until sizzling in a heavy oven-proof skillet. ▪ Brown chops about 2 minutes per side. ▪ Season with salt and pepper. ▪ Remove chops to baking pan and bake in preheated 425°F oven for 12 minutes. ▪ When chops are ready, place on serving dish and keep warm. ▪ Skim any fat from skillet, reserving juices. ▪ Pour in wine, vinegar, lemon juice and herbs. ▪ Boil on high heat until reduced by half or until liquid thickens slightly. ▪ Remove from heat and whisk in butter, 1 tablespoon at a time. Sauce will emulsify. ▪ Serve chops with herb sauce on top.

calories/serving: 710
protein, iron, niacin: excellent
vitamin A, riboflavin: good

EXTENDING MEAT LOAF
Rolled oats added to meat loaf mixture is a good extender: it also makes the meat loaf tender and adds fiber.

Pork

BAKED HAM WITH APRICOT GLAZE

Serves about 10
Preparation time: 15 minutes
Cooking time: 2½ hours

"Fully cooked" smoked hams are greatly improved by a short cooking time to finish them off. A spicy apricot-honey mixture goes on for the last few minutes to give a seductive and delicious glaze.

1	fully cooked smoked ham (about 7½ lbs, bone in)
	whole cloves
	watercress or parsley and fruit for garnish
GLAZE:	
½ cup	apricot jam
¼ cup	liquid honey
2 Tb	fresh lemon juice
1 Tb	cornstarch
¼ tsp	ground cloves
pinch	ground cinnamon

■ Remove any rind and excess fat from ham. ■ Place ham, fat side up, on a rack in a shallow pan. Score outside layer of fat diagonally in both directions to make 2″ diamonds. Do not cut too deeply or the cuts will open out. ■ Insert whole cloves at corners or centers of diamonds. ■ Insert meat thermometer (if using), being careful it doesn't touch the bone, and bake in preheated 325°F oven for about 2½ hours, or until internal temperature is 135°F to 140°F. ■ Meanwhile stir together apricot jam, honey, lemon juice, cornstarch, ground cloves and cinnamon in a small saucepan. ■ Over medium heat, bring to boil, stirring constantly. ■ During last 30 minutes of baking, spoon glaze on ham and baste occasionally. ■ Serve ham on a heated platter garnished with watercress or parsley and whole apricots, if available. Other fruit like kumquats, figs, grapes or plums are also attractive.

MICROWAVE DIRECTIONS: Cook on Medium 10 to 12 minutes per pound, fat side up, in a roasting dish covered with plastic wrap, or in a roasting bag. Shield outer rim with foil to prevent overcooking. Cook glaze in a heat-proof bowl on High 2 to 3 minutes.

calories/serving: 419
protein, thiamin, niacin: excellent
iron, riboflavin: good

ROAST PORK TENDERLOIN WITH PLUM SAUCE

Serves 4
Preparation time: 30 minutes
Cooking time: 50 minutes

Pork tenderloin roasts quickly without any waste. Here it is moist and tender under a spicy plum sauce.

1 lb	pork tenderloin
1 lb	blue or purple plums (prune, damson or valor)
⅓ cup	cider vinegar
½ cup	brown sugar or to taste
½ tsp	ground cinnamon
¼ tsp	salt
pinch	each ground cloves, cardamom and allspice
small pinch	cayenne pepper
	black pepper to taste

■ Wipe pork and set in a small shallow pan on rack. ■ Set aside at room temperature while preparing sauce. ■ Combine plums and vinegar in a small saucepan. ■ Bring to boil, reduce heat to low, cover and simmer 10 to 15 minutes, or until plums are very soft. ■ Put plums and juice through a sieve or food mill, or remove pits and purée in a food processor. ■ Return purée to pan with sugar (½ cup for damson and perhaps ⅓ cup for others), cinnamon, salt, cloves, cardamom, allspice and cayenne. ■ Bring to boil, lower heat to medium and cook, uncovered, 15 minutes or until thickened, stirring occasionally. ■ Meanwhile roast pork, uncovered, in preheated 350°F oven for 15 minutes. ■ Sprinkle with black pepper and spoon some of the thickened plum sauce over top, keeping remaining sauce warm. ■ Continue roasting about 35 minutes longer, or until no longer pink inside, basting with plum sauce twice more. ■ Cut into thin slices to serve, and pass any remaining sauce in a heated sauce boat.

calories/serving: 361
protein, thiamin, niacin: excellent
vitamin C: good

STORING SPICES

Buy spices in small amounts and store them in a cool, dark place in airtight containers. Use them up within a year as they lose their pungency if kept too long.

Boneless Pork Tenderloin with Apple Fennel Stuffing

BONELESS PORK TENDERLOIN WITH APPLE FENNEL STUFFING

Serves 4 to 6
Preparation time: 25 minutes
Cooking time: 50 minutes

Moist and delicious, this stuffing is so good you may want to double the recipe and simply bake the extra stuffing topped with bacon in a small casserole for 50 minutes.

1½ lbs	pork tenderloins
4	slices bacon, cut into halves
STUFFING:	
2 Tb	butter
1	medium onion, finely chopped
¾ cup	finely chopped fennel or celery
2	apples, unpeeled and shredded
1 Tb	red currant jelly
½ tsp	fennel seeds
	salt and pepper to taste
¼ cup	fine dry breadcrumbs

▪ To make stuffing, melt butter in a large saucepan and sauté onion and fennel for 3 minutes until slightly tender. ▪ Stir in shredded apples, jelly, fennel seeds, salt and pepper. ▪ Cook for about 5 minutes, stirring often, until apples are tender and most of liquid has evaporated. ▪ Remove from heat and stir in breadcrumbs. ▪ Cut the tenderloins lengthwise but do not cut right through. Meat should open like a book. ▪ Between sheets of waxed paper lightly pound meat with a cleaver or rolling pin to flatten slightly. ▪ Spread stuffing down cut side of meat. ▪ Fold narrow ends of tenderloins into stuffing and fold sides together, gently shaping into round shape. ▪ Wrap bacon slices around outside and secure with metal skewers or string. ▪ Place on rack in roasting pan. ▪ Bake in preheated 325°F oven for about 50 minutes, or until juices run clear when meat is pierced with a knife. ▪ If crisp bacon is desired, broil briefly.

calories/serving: 482 for 4 servings
321 for 6 servings
protein, thiamin, niacin: excellent

Stuffed Crown Roast of Pork

STUFFED CROWN ROAST OF PORK

Serves 8
Preparation time: 25 minutes
Cooking time: about 2½ hours

This majestic roast is really quite easy to prepare and serve.

6 to 7 lb	**crown roast of pork**
1 Tb	**vegetable oil**
1½ tsp	**dried sage**
¾ tsp	**pepper**
8 oz	**bulk pork sausage**
1	**onion, finely chopped**
1	**stalk celery, chopped**
1	**clove garlic, minced**
1	**red apple, unpeeled and chopped**
1½ cups	**fresh breadcrumbs**
¼ cup	**chopped fresh parsley**
⅓ cup	**orange juice**
1	**egg, beaten**
1 tsp	**grated orange peel**
½ tsp	**salt**
¼ tsp	**crushed dried thyme**
¼ cup	**maple syrup**
2 cups	**chicken stock or water**
1 Tb	**cornstarch**
	watercress or parsley and orange slices for garnish

▪ Stir together oil, 1 teaspoon of the sage and ½ teaspoon of the pepper in a small bowl. ▪ Set aside. ▪ Cook sausage meat with onion, celery and garlic in a large skillet over medium heat until vegetables are soft and meat is no longer pink, about 10 minutes, stirring often. ▪ Pour off any excess fat from pan and stir in apple, breadcrumbs, parsley, 2 tablespoons of the orange juice, egg, orange peel, salt, thyme and remaining sage and pepper. Recipe can be prepared to this point up to 4 hours ahead. Let stuffing cool, then cover and refrigerate stuffing and pork roast separately. Let return to room temperature before proceeding. ▪ Place crown roast bone side up, on small piece of foil in a shallow roasting pan. ▪ Brush inside and out with oil-sage mixture. ▪ Fill center with stuffing, mounding on top. ▪ Cover stuffing with foil and individually wrap bone tips with foil to prevent burning. ▪ Roast in preheated 400°F oven for 15 minutes. ▪ Reduce heat to 325°F and roast 1 hour and 15 minutes. ▪ Combine remaining orange juice and maple syrup. ▪ Remove foil from stuffing and brush pork all over with half maple syrup mixture. ▪ Continue roasting about 45 minutes longer, or until internal temperature reaches 160°F, brushing all over once more with remaining maple syrup mixture. ▪ Remove from roasting pan and set on platter. Let rest 15 minutes loosely covered with foil. ▪ Remove foil from bone tips and decorate with paper frills, if desired, before serving. ▪ Garnish platter with watercress and orange slices, cut halfway through and twisted. ▪ Slice between ribs to serve. ▪ While roast is resting, place roasting pan over medium-high heat and add chicken stock or water to pan. ▪ Bring to boil, scraping up any brown bits in bottom of pan. ▪ Stir cornstarch together with 2 tablespoons cold water in a small bowl and add to pan, stirring constantly until thickened and smooth. ▪ Season to taste with salt and pepper. ▪ Pass in heated sauce boat with roast.

calories/serving: 546
protein, iron, thiamin, niacin: excellent

GLAZED HAM WITH PUMPKIN MAPLE STUFFING

Serves 8 to 10
Preparation time: 30 minutes
Cooking time: 2 hours

This is a wonderful main course for a party as it is presliced and easy to reheat and serve. If you don't want to prepare your own Pumpkin Bread, use a commercial fruit and nut quick bread or muffins.

1	**boned, rolled, cooked ham (about 4 lbs)**
⅔ cup	**apricot jam or preserves**
¼ cup	**Dijon mustard**
2 Tb	**maple syrup or honey**
2 Tb	**soy sauce**
¼ tsp	**pepper**
STUFFING:	
2	**onions, chopped**
¼ cup	**butter or oil**
2	**stalks celery, chopped**
2	**eggs**
1 tsp	**salt**
4 cups	**cubed Pumpkin Bread (see Breads and Quick Breads), dried out or baked until dry in low oven**
½ cup	**chopped dried apricots**
½ cup	**raisins**
¼ cup	**butter (optional)**

▪ Trim ham of excess fat and pat dry. ▪ Combine jam, mustard, maple syrup, soy sauce and pepper. ▪ Coat ham with half of glaze mixture. ▪ Place in a roasting pan and bake in preheated 375°F oven for 1 hour until nicely glazed. ▪ Cool. ▪ Meanwhile prepare stuffing. ▪ Cook onions in butter until tender and lightly browned. ▪ Add celery and cook 5 minutes longer. ▪ Place in a large bowl and beat in eggs and salt. ▪ Toss with bread cubes. ▪ Stir in apricots and raisins. ▪ Moisten with ¼ cup melted butter if mixture appears dry. ▪ Adjust seasoning to taste. ▪ When ham is cool, slice into ½″ slices. ▪ Spread each slice with some stuffing. ▪ Reassemble ham, with slices on a slight angle, on a large baking dish or oven-proof platter. ▪ Spread remaining glaze on top. ▪ Refrigerate until ready to serve. ▪ Bake, covered, in preheated 350°F oven for 30 minutes. ▪ Uncover and bake 20 to 30 minutes longer until nicely glazed on top.

calories/serving: 873 for 8 servings
699 for 10 servings
(using ¹/₂ of pumpkin recipe)
protein, iron, thiamin, niacin: excellent
vitamin A: good

Tourtière

TOURTIÈRE

Serves 12
Preparation time: 30 minutes (includes making and rolling pastry)
Cooking time: 1½ hours

A French Canadian Christmas Eve tradition for generations. Serve with a homemade chili sauce or hot pepper jelly.

2 lbs	**ground pork**
1 cup	**water**
2	**onions, chopped**
2	**cloves garlic, minced**
2 tsp	**dried sage leaves, crumbled**
1 tsp	**each salt, mace and dried thyme**
½ tsp	**each dry mustard, allspice, grated nutmeg and freshly ground black pepper or to taste**
2 cups	**fresh breadcrumbs**
	pastry for two 9″ double-crust pies
1 Tb	**milk**

▪ Combine pork, water, onions, garlic and seasonings in a large saucepan. ▪ Bring to boil, reduce heat and simmer, uncovered, stirring often, until pork is no longer pink and most of liquid has evaporated, about 45 minutes. ▪ Remove from heat, stir in breadcrumbs and let cool to room temperature. ▪ Line pie plates with pastry. ▪ Divide pork mixture between two pie shells and cover with top crusts. ▪ Trim, seal and flute edges. ▪ Slash steam vents. ▪ Brush with milk and bake in preheated 425°F oven for 10 minutes. ▪ Reduce temperature to 350°F and bake for 25 to 35 minutes, or until golden brown and filling is bubbly. If tourtière is made ahead and frozen, bake an additional 15 to 20 minutes, or until heated through.

calories/serving: 568
protein, thiamin, niacin: excellent
iron: good
riboflavin: fair

Pork Tacos

PORK TACOS OR TOSTADAS

Serves 4
Preparation time: 15 to 20 minutes
Cooking time: 10 minutes

A tostada is a flat tortilla, with toppings; a taco is a folded tortilla filled with a variety of foods such as grated cheese, shredded lettuce and meat sauce. Use this meat sauce as a basis for either, and let each person top or fill his or her own taco or tostada.

1 lb	ground pork
1	medium onion, chopped
1	clove garlic, minced
1 can	(7½ oz/213 mL) tomato sauce
2 tsp	chili powder
1 tsp	dried oregano
½ tsp	salt
½ tsp	ground cumin
¼ tsp	crushed red pepper flakes
8	6″ corn tortillas, tacos or tostadas
	bottled taco sauce or chili salsa

TOPPINGS: grated Cheddar cheese
shredded lettuce
sliced avocado
chopped tomato
chopped green olives or
green pepper
sour cream

▪ Cook pork in a large skillet over medium heat until brown. ▪ Pour off fat. ▪ Add onion and garlic and cook until tender. ▪ Stir in tomato sauce, chili powder, oregano, salt, cumin and crushed red pepper flakes. ▪ Simmer for 5 to 10 minutes. If mixture becomes dry, add a little water. ▪ Spoon into serving dish. ▪ Place bowls of various toppings on table. ▪ Let each person spoon some meat mixture and taco sauce into a tortilla, then add cheese, lettuce and other toppings.

calories/serving: 314 without toppings
protein, niacin: excellent
iron, potassium: good
thiamin: fair

TORTILLAS
Packaged crisp tortillas can be served cold or warmed through in a preheated 300°F oven for 5 minutes. Soft tortillas should be fried, one at a time, in hot oil for 30 seconds until golden. Drain them on paper towels and keep warm in low oven.

HAM AND CHEESE STRATA

Serves 8
Preparation time: 15 minutes
Cooking time: 40 minutes

Easy to make, this colorful one-dish breakfast main course must be prepared the night before.

6	slices firm, homemade-style white bread
2 tsp	Dijon mustard
¼ cup	melted butter
8	slices Black Forest ham, slivered
1 cup	shredded mild Cheddar cheese
¼ cup	chopped fresh parsley
3	eggs
½ tsp	salt
1½ cups	milk
½ cup	sour cream
dash	Tabasco sauce
2 Tb	butter

■ Remove crusts from bread and cut each slice in half on diagonal. ■ Spread each with mustard, then dip one side of each in butter. ■ Arrange half the slices, butter side down, in an ungreased 13″ × 9″ baking dish. ■ Sprinkle evenly with half of ham slivers, cheese and parsley. ■ Arrange remaining bread slices, butter side up, on top and repeat with remaining ham, cheese and parsley. ■ Beat together eggs, salt, milk, sour cream and Tabasco sauce. ■ Pour evenly over top. ■ Dot with butter, cover with foil and refrigerate overnight. ■ Next morning, bake, covered, in preheated 350°F oven 30 minutes; uncover and bake about 10 more minutes or until puffed and golden. ■ Remove from oven and let sit 5 minutes before cutting into squares.

calories/serving: 307
protein, thiamin, niacin: excellent
calcium, vitamin A: good
riboflavin: fair

PORK CHOPS WITH ROSEMARY AND ORANGE

Serves 4
Preparation time: 5 minutes
Cooking time: 5 minutes
This fast and easy recipe also works well using veal or turkey scaloppine.

1 lb	fast-fry or thinly sliced pork chops
2	oranges
2 tsp	butter or margarine
2 tsp	dried rosemary
	salt and pepper to taste

■ Trim fat from pork chops. ■ Peel and slice one orange. ■ Squeeze juice from other. ■ Heat a heavy-bottomed skillet over high heat. ■ Add butter and when sizzling add pork chops and cook about 2 minutes or until brown. ■ Turn. ■ Sprinkle with rosemary, salt and pepper, and brown on other side. ■ Add orange juice and slices and stir to scrape up brown bits on bottom of pan. ■ Cook 1 to 2 minutes. ■ To serve, arrange chops on plate and pour juice and orange over top.

calories/serving: 215
protein, thiamin, niacin: excellent
iron: good
riboflavin: fair

PORK SATAY

Serves 6
Preparation time: 15 minutes
Marinating time: 1 hour
Cooking time: 12 to 15 minutes
For authentic barbecue flavor, satays should be broiled over a charcoal fire. Indonesian sweet soy sauce and hot pepper sauce (Sambal Oelek) will give a more authentic taste to the dish and are available at Oriental grocery stores.

2 lbs	pork tenderloins
1	onion, coarsely chopped
1 Tb	grated ginger root
2	cloves garlic, crushed
1 tsp	ground coriander
2 Tb	strained lime juice
2 Tb	sweet soy sauce
2 Tb	water
1 Tb	hot pepper sauce
2 Tb	cooking oil
2	limes, cut into wedges

■ Cut pork into ½″ cubes. ■ Blend remaining ingredients, except oil and lime wedges, in a blender until smooth. ■ Pour contents into a deep bowl.

■ Add pork cubes and marinate at least 1 hour at room temperature. ■ Remove pork from marinade and thread it tightly on bamboo skewers. (To avoid scorching, soak skewers in water and cover their tips with foil.) ■ Brush with oil and broil over a hot, open charcoal fire until cooked, 12 to 15 minutes, turning often and basting with marinade. ■ Serve garnished with lime wedges (speared onto ends of skewers, if desired) and Peanut Sauce on the side.

calories/serving: 294
protein, thiamin, niacin: excellent
iron, riboflavin: fair

PEANUT SAUCE

Makes about 2 cups
Preparation time: 10 minutes
Cooking time: 15 minutes
Half a cup of crunchy or smooth peanut butter can be substituted for the peanuts, but the latter lend a fresher flavor.

1 cup	dry roasted peanuts
1 Tb	cooking oil
1	medium onion, chopped
2	cloves garlic, crushed
1 Tb	hot pepper sauce or hot chili peppers, chopped
1	bay leaf
2 Tb	lime juice
2 Tb	soy sauce
½ tsp	grated ginger root
2 Tb	coconut cream
2 cups approx.	chicken stock or water

■ Grind peanuts in a blender. ■ Heat oil in a heavy saucepan. ■ Sauté onion, garlic and pepper sauce or chili peppers until soft. ■ Add ground peanuts, remaining ingredients and half the stock. ■ Simmer until sauce thickens. ■ Add more stock until sauce is of pouring consistency. ■ Serve with satays.

calories/tablespoon: 37

COCONUT CREAM

Coconut cream is a popular ingredient of eastern cuisines. It's sold in cans or in solid form in packages. The latter can be diluted with warm water to make a cream or added directly to sauces or curries. You can prepare your own coconut cream by steeping grated fresh coconut meat or packaged, unsweetened shredded coconut in hot milk for several minutes. Strain through a sieve, pressing out all liquid.

CIDER- AND HONEY-GLAZED PORK

Serves 6
Preparation time: 10 minutes
Marinating time: overnight
Cooking time: 2 hours

Marinated, glazed and baked in the oven, pork chops, ribs or hocks are shiny, brown and succulent. The marinade is also delicious with chicken pieces.

6	large pork chops *or* 6 lbs pork ribs *or* 6 pork hocks
1 to 2 Tb	flour or cornstarch

MARINADE:

3 cups	apple cider
½ to 1 cup	honey
2 Tb	lemon juice
1 tsp	salt or to taste
½ tsp	dried thyme
1½ tsp	dry mustard
2 tsp	dried sage

■ Arrange meat in a large pan. ■ Blend marinade ingredients and pour over meat. Marinate in a cool place for several hours or overnight, turning occasionally. ■ Remove meat from marinade, saving liquid. ■ Arrange meat in one layer in a large baking pan. ■ Bake in preheated 350°F oven for 20 minutes, then baste meat generously with marinade. ■ Bake a further 1½ hours, basting every 20 minutes with marinade, until meat is tender and marinade has turned into a golden-brown sticky glaze. ■ Remove pieces of meat to a hot serving platter. ■ Brown pan drippings to make gravy or sauce, using the marinade and some water if you think the flavor is too strong. ■ Thicken with flour or cornstarch blended with a little water. ■ Simmer 2 minutes, stirring. ■ Serve over meat and baked, boiled or mashed potatoes. ■ If there is any marinade left over, it can be frozen.

calories/serving: 431 for pork chops
587 for pork ribs
protein, thiamin, niacin: excellent
iron, riboflavin: good
calories/serving: 304 for pork hocks (lower calorie count due to lower yield
of meat per serving)
protein: excellent
iron, niacin: fair

Ginger Pork with Carrots and Celery

GINGER PORK WITH CARROTS AND CELERY

Serves 4 to 5
Preparation time: 15 minutes
Cooking time: 7 to 10 minutes

Fresh ginger adds a delicious flavor to this quick and easy pork stir-fry. The carrots and celery look nicest cut into thin strips; if you're in a hurry, slice in a food processor.

1 lb	boneless pork, cut into thin strips
2 Tb	minced ginger root
2 Tb	soy sauce
2 tsp	cornstarch
1 Tb	sherry
¼ cup	vegetable oil
1½ cups	sliced carrots
1½ cups	sliced celery
1	onion, sliced
2 Tb	water

■ Combine half the ginger with soy sauce, cornstarch and sherry. ■ Mix well. ■ Add pork and mix. ■ Let stand 5 minutes or up to 1 hour. ■ Heat half the oil in a wok or heavy frying pan over high heat until nearly smoking. ■ Add pork mixture and stir-fry 2 to 3 minutes until pork is cooked. ■ Remove and set aside. ■ Add remaining oil to pan. ■ Add carrots, celery, onion and remaining ginger. ■ Stir-fry for 1 minute. ■ Add water if necessary to prevent scorching and stir-fry until vegetables are tender-crisp. ■ Return pork to pan and stir to mix. ■ Serve with rice.

calories/serving: 367 for 4 servings
294 for 5 servings
protein, vitamin A, thiamin, niacin: excellent
vitamin C: good
riboflavin: fair

Sausage and Spinach Loaf

SAUSAGE AND SPINACH LOAF

Serves 6
Preparation time: 10 minutes
Cooking time: about 1 hour and 15 minutes

This is an unusual variation on everyone's favorite – meat loaf.

½ pkg	(10 oz/284 g) spinach
1 lb	bulk pork sausage meat
½ lb	ground veal
1	egg, lightly beaten
¼ cup	finely chopped onion
1 Tb	lemon juice
¼ tsp	each dried thyme, dry mustard and dried basil
	salt and pepper to taste

▪ Wash spinach and cook, covered, in water that clings to leaves, for about 2 minutes or just until wilted. ▪ Drain well in a sieve; squeeze dry with your hands. ▪ Chop finely. ▪ Set aside. ▪ Combine sausage meat, veal, egg, onion, lemon juice, thyme, mustard, basil, salt and pepper. ▪ Blend in spinach. Pack into 8″×4″ loaf pan and bake in preheated 350°F oven for 1 hour and 15 to 30 minutes, or until well browned and meat is cooked through. ▪ The internal temperature should be 160°F. ▪ Turn out and cut into slices to serve.

calories/serving: 296
protein, vitamin A, thiamin, niacin: excellent
iron: good
riboflavin: fair

LEMONY PORK

Serves 4
Preparation time: 20 minutes
Cooking time: 1 hour 40 minutes

The richness of pork needs a sharp flavor to complement it.

2 Tb	vegetable oil
2 lbs	stewing pork, in 1″ cubes
2	large onions, sliced
1	clove garlic, crushed
2	lemons, peeled and chopped
1	small green pepper, seeded and sliced
1 can	(19 oz/540 mL) tomatoes
2 tsp	Worcestershire sauce
2 tsp	paprika
1 tsp	dried rosemary
	salt and pepper to taste

▪ Heat oil in a flame-proof casserole dish and cook pork over high heat until well browned. ▪ Remove with a slotted spoon and set aside. ▪ Add extra oil to dish, if necessary, and fry onions and garlic over moderate heat until onion is transparent. ▪ Return pork to dish and top with lemons and pepper. ▪ Mix together remaining ingredients and pour into dish. ▪ Cover tightly and cook in preheated 350°F oven for 1½ hours, until pork is tender. ▪ Serve with baked potatoes and a green vegetable.

calories/serving: 608
protein, iron, vitamin C, thiamin, riboflavin, niacin: excellent
vitamin A: fair

CHILLED CHINESE PORK

Serves 2 to 4
Preparation time: 10 minutes
Marinating time: 6 hours
Cooking time: 1 hour
Chilling time: overnight

Leftovers with an Oriental twist.

2 lbs	boneless roast pork
½ cup	hoisin sauce

- Trim all fat from roast. - Cut meat into 3″ cubes.
- Toss with hoisin sauce and allow to marinate 6 hours at room temperature. - Separate chunks. - Cook in preheated 300°F oven for 1 hour. When cooled, slice thinly and refrigerate overnight.

calories/serving: 632 for 2 servings
316 for 4 servings
protein, thiamin, niacin: excellent
riboflavin: good
iron: fair

BRIOCHE HAM AND CHEESE TART

Serves 8
Preparation time: 30 minutes
Rising time: 1 to 1½ hours
Cooking time: 1 hour

This is an unusual tart, not unlike a quiche, but it has a wonderful buttery yeast crust.

CRUST:

1 tsp	sugar
¼ cup	warm water
1	envelope dry yeast *or* 1 cake yeast
2	eggs
¼ cup	milk
2 cups	flour
1 tsp	salt
⅓ cup	unsalted butter, softened

FILLING:

2 Tb	unsalted butter
1	onion, chopped
1	clove garlic, minced
2	eggs
2	egg yolks
1 cup	heavy cream
	salt and pepper to taste
¼ tsp	grated nutmeg
8 oz	cooked ham, diced
8 oz	Swiss cheese, grated
2 Tb	grated Parmesan cheese

Brioche Ham and Cheese Tart

- Dissolve sugar in warm (not hot) water and mix in yeast. - Allow to rest 10 minutes or until mixture bubbles up. - Stir mixture down and beat in eggs and milk. - Combine flour and salt and beat in. - Beat in soft butter and knead about 5 minutes. This can be done in a mixer or by lightly greased or floured hands. The dough will be sticky, but do not worry. - Place dough in a buttered bowl. - Cover with plastic wrap and allow to rise in a warm place until doubled, about 1½ hours. - While dough is rising, prepare filling. - Melt butter in a skillet and cook onion and garlic until tender and fragrant. - Cool. - Combine eggs, yolks, cream and seasonings. - Reserve. - Butter a 9″ springform pan and refrigerate. This will make it easier to pat dough into pan. - When dough is ready, punch down and knead lightly. - Place dough in pan and pat into bottom and up the sides. - Spread onion mixture over dough and sprinkle with ham and cheese. - Pour custard mixture over all and sprinkle with Parmesan. - Bake in preheated 400°F oven for 55 to 60 minutes. - Allow to rest 10 minutes in pan before removing sides and serving. - If preparing ahead, reheat at 325°F for 45 to 50 minutes.

calories/serving: 553
protein, calcium, thiamin, niacin: excellent
iron, vitamin A, riboflavin: good

Pork Loin with Cranberry Stuffing

PORK LOIN WITH CRANBERRY STUFFING

Serves 6 to 8
Preparation time: 30 minutes
Cooking time: 1½ hours

Vary the stuffing, if you wish, by using corn bread instead of white or whole wheat crumbs.

3 lbs	pork tenderloins
2 Tb	butter
STUFFING: 2 Tb	butter
1	small onion, chopped
½ cup	chopped raw cranberries
½ tsp	celery seed
½ tsp	dried sage
½ tsp	dried thyme
¼ tsp	allspice
3 cups	day-old breadcrumbs
	salt and pepper to taste

■ To make stuffing, melt 2 tablespoons butter in a large saucepan and sauté onion until tender but do not brown. ■ Stir in cranberries, celery seed, sage,

thyme and allspice. ■ Add breadcrumbs and stir until evenly mixed. ■ Season with salt and pepper. ■ Cut the tenderloins lengthwise but do not cut right through. Meat should open like a book. ■ Pound lightly with a cleaver or rolling pin to flatten slightly. ■ Spread stuffing on one side of meat, fold other side to cover stuffing and tie with cotton string. ■ Place meat on rack in roasting pan. ■ Rub with butter. ■ Bake in preheated 325°F oven for 20 to 30 minutes to the pound for approximately 1 hour. ■ Baste several times with pan juices. ■ Let stand for 10 minutes before serving.

calories/serving: 681 for 6 servings
507 for 8 servings
protein, thiamin, niacin: excellent
iron, riboflavin: good

PORK WITH SAGE AND CAPERS

Serves 4 to 5
Preparation time: 15 minutes
Cooking time: 1½ to 2 hours

This dish from the Languedoc area in the south of France is delicious served with braised fennel or celery. Fluffy mashed potatoes or egg noodles go well too.

2 lbs	lean pork shoulder, cubed
2 Tb	vegetable oil
2	medium onions, chopped
1 scant cup	dry white wine
1 Tb	chopped fresh sage leaves *or* 1 tsp dried sage, crumbled
2 sprigs	fresh thyme *or* ½ tsp dried thyme
1	bay leaf
	salt and pepper to taste
1 to 2 Tb	capers, rinsed and drained
	chopped fresh parsley

■ Dry pork cubes with paper towels. ■ Sauté pork in oil in a flame-proof casserole or Dutch oven until nicely browned. Do this in two or three batches, if necessary, removing meat as it browns. ■ When pork is browned, add onions, lower heat and cook until softened. ■ Pour in wine and let it simmer for a few minutes, scraping up any brown bits from sides and bottom of pan. ■ Return meat to casserole and stir in sage, thyme, bay leaf, salt and pepper. ■ Cover and cook over low heat for 1 to 1½ hours until tender, stirring occasionally. ■ When meat is done, remove from pan with slotted spoon. ■ Quickly bring juices to boil and boil to reduce by half. ■ Return meat to pan, add capers and allow to heat through. ■ Remove thyme sprigs and bay leaf, sprinkle with parsley and serve from the casserole.

calories/serving: 584 for 4 servings
470 for 5 servings
protein, thiamin, niacin: excellent
iron, riboflavin: good

GINGER LIME PORK CHOPS

Serves 4
Preparation time: 5 minutes
Marinating time: at least 1 hour
Cooking time: 20 minutes

For the juiciest and most flavorful results, choose chops that are about one inch thick.

4	thick pork loin chops
2	limes
¼ cup	vegetable oil
1 Tb	grated ginger root
1 tsp	ground coriander
½ tsp	ground cumin

■ Trim fat from pork chops. ■ Place in single layer in dish. ■ Grate peel and squeeze juice from limes. ■ Combine juice and peel with oil, ginger, coriander and cumin and mix well. ■ Pour over chops, cover and refrigerate for at least 1 hour, or preferably overnight, turning occasionally. ■ Barbecue over medium hot coals about 8 to 10 minutes on each side or until faintly pink on inside, basting often with marinade.

calories/serving: 237
protein, thiamin, niacin: excellent
iron: fair

SAUSAGE SPINACH SQUARES

Serves 8
Preparation time: 20 minutes
Cooking time: 40 minutes

These savory squares can be prepared ahead of time and served warm or cold with a tossed salad or rice.

3 Tb	vegetable oil
1	onion, chopped
1 lb	sweet Italian sausages, or breakfast sausages, removed from casings and crumbled
2 pkgs	(each 10 oz/284 g) frozen spinach, defrosted, squeezed dry and chopped
1 cup	saltine cracker crumbs
4	eggs
½ cup	milk or cream
	salt and pepper to taste
1 cup	grated Cheddar cheese

■ Heat oil in a large skillet. ■ Add onion and cook until lightly browned. ■ Add sausage and break up well with a spoon. ■ Cook 10 minutes until sausage colors. ■ Drain off any excess fat and discard. ■ Stir in spinach and cook a few minutes, combining ingredients well. ■ Cool slightly. ■ Stir in cracker crumbs. ■ Beat eggs with milk or cream, salt, pepper and cheese. ■ Stir in sausage-spinach mixture.

■ Spoon into a buttered 9″ square baking dish. ■ Bake in preheated 350°F oven 35 to 40 minutes or until set in the center. This can be made ahead and served cold or at room temperature, cut into squares. Or it can be reheated at 350°F for 20 minutes. Allow to rest 10 minutes before cutting.

MICROWAVE DIRECTIONS: Mix sausage and onion together in a large casserole. Cook on High 5 minutes. Break up well, add spinach, cook further 3 minutes. Stir in remaining ingredients. Spoon into ungreased dish, cook on Medium 10 minutes. Shield around edges of dish with foil, shiny side towards dish, to prevent corners from overcooking. Cook 10 minutes on Medium, or until center is almost set. Let stand, covered, about 10 minutes.

calories/serving: 315
protein, vitamin A, niacin: excellent
calcium, iron, thiamin: good
riboflavin: fair

SCALLOPED SWEET POTATO AND APPLES WITH PORK CHOPS

Serves 4
Preparation time: 15 minutes
Cooking time: 1 hour and 40 minutes

Pork chops are ideal in an all-in-one pot dinner; the preparation is quick and easy.

4	pork chops, 1¼″ thick
2	large sweet potatoes, peeled and sliced
2	large apples, peeled, cored and sliced
2	large onions, sliced
¼ cup	melted butter
1 Tb	brown sugar
¼ cup	flour
¼ tsp	grated nutmeg
	salt and pepper to taste
1 can	(12 oz/341 mL) beer

■ Brown pork chops evenly on both sides in their own fat in a large skillet over medium-high heat. ■ Layer sweet potatoes, apples and onions alternately in a greased 12-cup shallow casserole. ■ Sprinkle with half the butter and brown sugar. ■ Lay pork chops on top in a single layer. ■ Mix flour, nutmeg, salt and pepper into remaining butter. ■ Stir in beer. ■ Pour over pork chops. ■ Cover and cook in preheated 350°F oven 1½ hours.

calories/serving: 525
protein, vitamin A, vitamin C, thiamin, niacin: excellent
iron, riboflavin: good

Lamb

LAMB SHANKS IN RED WINE

Serves 6
Preparation time: 20 minutes
Cooking time: 3½ hours

A perfect example of how a cheaper cut of meat can be rendered mouth-wateringly tender by long, slow cooking.

6	lamb shanks (about 1 lb each)
	oil and butter
1 Tb	flour
1 Tb	tomato paste
2	carrots, finely chopped
2	medium onions, finely chopped
18	cloves garlic
	salt and pepper to taste
1 tsp	dried thyme
1 bottle	(750 mL) red wine
1 can	(1¾ oz/50 g) anchovies in oil, drained

■ Use a round flame-proof dish large enough to take the 6 shanks, arranged like the spokes of a wheel, the meaty part towards the outside of the dish. ■ Heat a little oil and butter in the dish. ■ Add shanks and sprinkle with a little flour. ■ When golden underneath, turn them. The flour will then be underneath and will cook. ■ Coat golden side of shanks with a little tomato paste. ■ When golden on second side, turn them again; tomato paste will be underneath. ■ Add carrots and onions and 6 cloves of garlic and continue cooking until vegetables are golden. ■ Pour off excess fat. ■ Add salt, pepper and thyme. ■ Add just enough red wine to almost cover shanks. ■ Bake in preheated 275°F oven, uncovered, for 3 hours. Turn shanks 3 or 4 times during cooking. ■ Meanwhile soak remaining 12 cloves of garlic in boiling water. The lamb is ready when you can prick it easily with a fork. ■ Put shanks very delicately (they are now rather fragile) on a round serving dish like the spokes of a wheel again. ■ Purée cooking juices and vegetables in a food processor or blender. ■ Transfer to a saucepan and simmer until reduced and thickened slightly. ■ Pour over shanks. ■ Put 2 anchovy fillets on each shank, crosswise, and sprinkle dish with the 12 cloves of garlic. ■ Cover and heat in oven at 275°F for about 15 minutes. ■ Serve with noodles.

calories/serving: 548
protein, iron, vitamin A, niacin: excellent
vitamin C, thiamin, riboflavin: good

MICROWAVE MEATBALLS AVGOLEMONO

Serves 4
Preparation time: 15 minutes
Cooking time: 11 to 14 minutes

Avgolemono is a Greek sauce with a creamy texture and the tang of lemon. Here it transforms meatballs into something special.

MEATBALLS:

1 lb	ground lamb
1	small onion, finely chopped
2	cloves garlic, minced
½ tsp	dried mint flakes
½ tsp	dried parsley flakes
½ tsp	salt (optional)
½ tsp	ground cumin
¾ tsp	dried oregano
¼ tsp	pepper
1	egg, lightly beaten

AVGOLEMONO SAUCE:

1 Tb	butter
1½ Tb	flour
2 cups	chicken broth
	juice and grated peel of 1 lemon
3	egg yolks, lightly beaten

■ Mix together all meatball ingredients. ■ Form into 12 to 14 balls. ■ Place on microwave meat rack. ■ Cook on High 8 to 10 minutes or until no longer pink. ■ Rearrange if necessary for even cooking. ■ Remove from rack to serving dish. Keep warm. ■ Melt butter on High 30 seconds in a 4-cup glass measure. ■ Add flour and mix well. ■ Stir in chicken broth, lemon juice and grated peel. ■ Cook on High 2½ to 3½ minutes or until thickened, stirring 2 or 3 times. ■ When cooked, add 1 tablespoon of sauce to egg yolks and beat thoroughly. ■ Stir egg yolks into sauce and beat thoroughly. ■ Pour sauce over meatballs and serve with rice or noodles.

calories/serving: 401
protein, niacin: excellent
iron: good
vitamin A, vitamin C, thiamin, riboflavin: fair

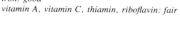

Sweet and Sour Grilled Lamb Sausage with Red Onions

SWEET AND SOUR GRILLED LAMB SAUSAGE WITH RED ONIONS

Serves 4
Preparation time: 5 minutes
Cooking time: 10 minutes

Lamb sausages are delicious grilled on the barbecue; they become crispy and brown on the outside and juicy inside, while absorbing the delicious smoky flavor.

1 lb	lamb sausages
2	red onions
	vegetable oil
½ cup	apricot jam
1 Tb	vinegar
1 Tb	Dijon mustard
1 tsp	Worcestershire sauce

▪ Slice onions into ¾" slices and place in hinged wire basket or push a small metal skewer through each to keep slices together. ▪ Place on greased barbecue grill about 4" from medium-hot coals or on medium-high for barbecue with controls, and grill about 10 minutes, turning often and brushing with oil. ▪ Grill sausages about 8 minutes, turning often. ▪ Combine jam, vinegar, mustard and Worcestershire sauce in a small saucepan. ▪ Place on hottest part of cooking rack and heat, stirring, until jam melts. ▪ Brush on onions and sausage for last 4 minutes of cooking. ▪ Pour remaining sauce over sausages to serve.

calories/serving: 490 (using 1 tablespoon oil)
protein: excellent
iron, thiamin, niacin: good

Leg of Lamb with Mint Sauce

LEG OF LAMB WITH MINT SAUCE

Serves 6 to 8
Preparation time: 15 minutes
Cooking time: 2 hours and 10 minutes

An initial 30 minutes of roasting in a very hot oven seals in the juices and makes roast lamb moist and succulent. Serve piping hot with parsleyed potatoes and peas.

5 to 6 lb	**leg of lamb, thawed if frozen**
1	**clove garlic, thinly sliced**
1 Tb	**fresh rosemary leaves**
	salt and pepper to taste

MINT SAUCE:

½ cup	**water**
2 Tb	**sugar**
3 Tb	**chopped fresh mint**
⅓ cup	**white wine vinegar or cider vinegar**
	salt to taste

▪ For best results, have lamb at room temperature. Preheat oven to 400°F. ▪ With sharp knife, cut small incisions all over meaty portion of leg. Tuck garlic slices and rosemary into slits. Season with salt and pepper. ▪ Place lamb, fat side up, in roasting pan. Roast, uncovered, in 400°F oven for 30 minutes. ▪ Reduce heat to 350°F and roast another 30 minutes. ▪ Reduce heat to 300°F and roast another hour, or until lamb is cooked to desired doneness. ▪ For rare lamb, internal temperature will register 150°F; 160°F for medium; 170° to 180°F for well-done. ▪ Meanwhile prepare Mint Sauce. ▪ Make a syrup by heating water with sugar until sugar is dissolved. ▪ Let cool. ▪ Add chopped mint and vinegar and let stand 30 minutes before serving. ▪ Season with salt. ▪ Serve warm or at room temperature with roast lamb. Makes about ¾ cup.

calories/serving: 431 for 6 servings
323 for 8 servings
protein, niacin: excellent
iron, thiamin, riboflavin: good

IRISH STEW

Serves 6 to 8
Preparation time: 15 minutes
Cooking time: 1½ to 2 hours

A traditional one-pot dish from the Emerald Isle, the perfect winter warmer.

4 lbs	**mutton or lamb (use cheapest cut possible; neck will do)**
4 to 6	**small onions, sliced**
1	**leek, white stem and tender part of the green, well washed and sliced**
6	**medium potatoes, peeled and sliced**
1	**small turnip, sliced**
2	**carrots, sliced**
2	**parsnips, sliced**
	salt and pepper to taste
5 to 6 cups	**water or beef stock**

▪ Cut meat into large chunks and season with salt and pepper. ▪ Thoroughly butter a stewpan or oven-proof dish. ▪ Combine meat and vegetables with salt and pepper in dish. ▪ Add water to come half-way up sides of dish and cover with lid. ▪ Cook in preheated 350°F oven, or on top of the stove over a very low heat, for 1½ to 2 hours until lamb is tender.

calories/serving: 542 for 6 servings
409 for 8 servings
protein, iron, vitamin A, vitamin C, thiamin, niacin: excellent
riboflavin: good
fiber: high

PIQUANT HONEY LAMB

Serves 10
Preparation time: 10 minutes
Cooking time: 1 to 1¼ hours

This sweet-and-sour lamb stew is also delicious when made with pork.

½ cup	**cooking oil**
2½ lbs	**lean lamb shoulder or leg, cubed**
2	**onions, finely chopped**
2 Tb	**flour**
½ tsp	**ground cinnamon**
2 cups	**chicken or veal stock**
	salt and pepper to taste
½ cup	**honey**
	juice of 2 lemons
½ cup	**raisins**
1 can	**(14 oz/414 mL) apricot halves, drained**
½ cup	**sliced almonds, toasted**

▪ Heat oil in a large, heavy saucepan. ▪ Fry lamb quickly until brown. ▪ Add onions and cook just until tender, not colored. ▪ Add flour and cinnamon and cook 1 minute, stirring. ▪ Stir in stock and bring to boil. ▪ Season with salt and pepper. ▪ Add honey, lemon juice and raisins. ▪ Cover pan and cook slowly for 1 hour, or until lamb is tender. ▪ Remove lamb with slotted spoon and simmer pan juices until reduced and thickened. ▪ Return lamb to sauce and heat through. ▪ Serve over cooked rice, topped with apricot halves and almonds.

calories/serving: 437
protein, niacin: excellent
iron: good
vitamin C, thiamin, riboflavin: fair

LAMB PILAF

Serves 4
Preparation time: 15 minutes
Cooking time: 40 minutes

Rice pilaf made without the addition of cubed lamb is a flavorful accompaniment for roast lamb or grilled lamb chops.

1 cup	**long-grain rice (converted)**
2	**envelopes or cubes chicken bouillon**
1 tsp	**curry powder**
½ tsp	**salt**
¼ cup	**butter**
2	**stalks celery, thinly sliced**
1	**medium onion, chopped**
¼ cup	**chopped raisins**
¼ cup	**chopped toasted almonds**
¼ tsp	**ground cinnamon**
¼ tsp	**ground cardamom**
pinch	**grated nutmeg**
	black pepper to taste
1½ cups	**diced cooked lamb**
1	**banana, chopped, for garnish**
	chopped fresh parsley or chives, for garnish

▪ Boil 2½ cups water in a large saucepan. ▪ Stir in rice, chicken bouillon mix, curry powder and salt. ▪ Cover and simmer 20 minutes. ▪ Remove from heat and let stand 5 minutes. ▪ Fluff with fork. ▪ Heat butter in a skillet; add celery and onion. ▪ Sauté about 5 minutes, until onion is tender and celery limp. ▪ Stir in raisins, almonds, cinnamon, cardamom, nutmeg and pepper. ▪ Cook 1 minute. ▪ Add lamb and mix with cooked rice. ▪ Cook gently over medium heat, about 10 minutes, until heated through. ▪ Transfer to a heated platter or bowl. ▪ Garnish with banana and parsley.

calories/serving: 477
protein, niacin: excellent
iron, vitamin A, thiamin: good
vitamin C, riboflavin: fair

MUSTARDY RACK OF LAMB

Serves 8
Preparation time: 10 minutes
Cooking time: about 40 minutes

Rack of lamb is so delicately good it should be cooked in a simple way for a really elegant meal.

4	**racks of lamb**
2 tsp	**dried leaf oregano**
2 tsp	**dried leaf rosemary**
1 tsp	**paprika**
¼ tsp	**coarse cracked pepper**
¼ cup	**Dijon mustard**

▪ Thaw racks if necessary. ▪ Trim fat and meat off ends of rib bones, leaving about 1″ of bone exposed. ▪ Cover bone tips with foil and set lamb, meaty sides up, on a rack in a shallow roasting pan. ▪ Combine remaining ingredients and spread on meaty sides of racks. ▪ Roast in preheated 325°F oven about 40 minutes for slightly pink meat, about 50 minutes for well-done. ▪ Stand rack roasts up in pairs on a hot platter with exposed bones interlocking. ▪ Surround with boiled new potatoes and garnish with cooked artichoke bottoms filled with red currant jelly. ▪ Cut between the rib bones to serve.

calories/serving: 311 (assuming 4 racks at 1½ pounds each)
protein, niacin: excellent
iron, thiamin, riboflavin: good

BROILED LAMB CHOPS WITH LIME, MINT AND CHIVES

Serves 4
Preparation time: 5 minutes
Cooking time: 6 to 8 minutes

Fresh chives and mint make a simple but sensational garnish for lamb. Be sure to thaw chops if frozen.

8	**loin lamb chops, 1″ thick**
	juice of 1 lime or lemon
	salt and pepper to taste
3 Tb	**snipped fresh chives or chopped green onion tops**
3 Tb	**chopped fresh mint**

▪ Trim any excess fat from chops. ▪ Drizzle each chop with lime juice and sprinkle with salt and pepper. ▪ Preheat broiler to high. ▪ Place chops on rack of broiling pan set 4″ from heat. ▪ Broil 4 minutes; turn with tongs and broil on other side 2 to 4 minutes or until done. Inside flesh should be juicy and pink. ▪ Mix chives and mint together with a squeeze of lime juice. ▪ Place small amount of herbs on top of each chop; serve at once.

calories/serving: 330
protein, niacin: excellent
iron, thiamin, riboflavin: good

GRILLED LEG OF LAMB WITH AIOLI-MUSTARD MARINADE

Serves 8 to 10
Preparation time: 10 minutes
Marinating time: 1 hour to several hours
Cooking time: 40 to 50 minutes

Lamb is best barbecued only until rare; it will have a dark crust on the outside and will be deliciously juicy and pink inside.

1	**boneless butterflied leg of lamb, defrosted (about 4 lbs)**
1 cup	**mayonnaise**
4	**cloves garlic, crushed**
1 Tb	**lemon juice**
1 Tb	**Dijon mustard**
1 Tb	**minced ginger root**
½ tsp	**dried thyme**
¼ tsp	**black pepper**

▪ Make several slashes in thickest part of meat for more even cooking. ▪ Place lamb in a dish just large enough to hold it. ▪ Stir together mayonnaise, garlic, lemon juice, mustard, ginger, thyme and pepper in small bowl. ▪ Rub over all surfaces of lamb and let stand at room temperature for 1 hour or in refrigerator, covered, for several hours. ▪ If refrigerated, bring to room temperature 45 minutes to 1 hour before grilling. ▪ Place flat on oiled grill about 6″ over medium-hot coals or on medium-high setting for barbecue with controls. ▪ Basting often with any marinade left in dish and turning frequently, barbecue 20 to 25 minutes for rare. ▪ Internal temperature tested with a meat thermometer should be 140°F for rare, 150°F for medium and 160°F for well-done. ▪ Remove from barbecue when thermometer reads 5° to 10°F below desired temperature and let stand, loosely covered with foil, for 10 minutes before carving. ▪ Carve in thin diagonal slices and arrange on heated platter.

calories/serving: 489 for 8 servings
391 for 10 servings
protein, niacin, iron: excellent
thiamin, riboflavin: good

ROSEMARY AND GARLIC LAMB
Pierce the fat layer of the leg of lamb in a half-dozen places and slip slivers of garlic into each pocket. Then rub rosemary all over the leg. For medium-rare meat, roast in a preheated 325°F oven for 25 to 30 minutes per pound for bone-in lamb, 30 to 35 minutes per pound for boneless lamb, or until a meat thermometer registers 160°F.

Moussaka

MOUSSAKA

Serves 10
Preparation time: 1 hour
Cooking time: 1 hour

A delicious Greek one-dish meal that's perfect for feeding a crowd; serve with a green salad.

6 to 8	**small (*or* 3 medium) eggplants sliced lengthwise, ½″ thick**
⅓ cup	**olive oil**
2	**large onions, finely chopped**
2 Tb	**butter**
1½ lbs	**ground lamb or beef**
	salt and pepper to taste
1	**clove garlic, crushed**
4 to 6	**ripe tomatoes, peeled and chopped, *or* 1 can (28 oz/796 mL) Italian-style tomatoes**
1	**small bunch flat-leafed parsley chopped**
SAUCE:	
4 Tb	**unsalted butter**
4 Tb	**flour**
2 cups	**milk**
	grated nutmeg to taste
2	**eggs, beaten**
2 to 3 Tb	**grated Kefalotyri or Romano cheese**

▪ Sauté eggplant slices, a few at a time, in olive oil. ▪ Drain on paper towels and set aside. ▪ Sauté onions in butter until soft. ▪ Add meat, salt, pepper, garlic and tomatoes. ▪ Simmer, uncovered, until almost all liquid has evaporated, adding parsley for the last 5 minutes of cooking. ▪ Meanwhile to make sauce, melt butter in a saucepan. ▪ Add flour, stirring until blended. ▪ Gradually add milk, stirring constantly. ▪ Add nutmeg and stir until sauce is thickened. ▪ Remove from heat. ▪ Add a little sauce to the beaten eggs (to prevent them from curdling) and then add eggs to the sauce. ▪ Stir in cheese. ▪ Line bottom of oiled 9″ × 15″ pan or two 8″ pans with one layer of eggplant. ▪ Mix 3 tablespoons sauce into meat mixture. ▪ Spread half the meat mixture on eggplant. ▪ Add another layer of eggplant and another layer of meat. ▪ Pour sauce over all, smoothing with back of spoon. ▪ Bake in preheated 375°F oven for about 1 hour, or until top is golden. ▪ Cut into squares and serve with a green salad.

MICROWAVE DIRECTIONS: Sauté eggplant and onions on stove top. Set aside. Place meat, seasonings and tomatoes in a large casserole, cook on High 10 to 15 minutes. Drain excess liquid, add parsley, cook 1 minute. Place butter in 2-cup measure, cook on High 1 to 2 minutes. Whisk in flour, add milk, stir until smooth. Cook on High 3 to 4 minutes, stirring 2 or 3 times until sauce has thickened. Add nutmeg and stir. Proceed as above, using an unoiled dish. Sprinkle surface with paprika, cook on Medium 15 minutes or until heated through. Place under broiler to brown surface, if you wish.

calories/serving: 427
protein, vitamin C, niacin: excellent
iron, vitamin A, thiamin: good
calcium, riboflavin: fair
fiber: moderate

Poultry

CURRIED CHICKEN AND RICE CASSEROLE

Serves 8 to 10
Preparation time: 10 minutes
Baking time: about 1 hour

This delicious casserole is so easy it's great for family suppers. Accompany with little dishes of peanuts, shredded coconut, chutney and chopped cucumbers, if you wish.

1½ cups	raw rice
¼ cup	dried currants
2 tsp	shredded lemon peel
8 to 10	chicken breasts, skinned
	salt and pepper to taste
2 Tb	vegetable oil
2	unpeeled red apples, cored and thinly sliced
1	onion, chopped
2	cloves garlic, minced
1 to 2 Tb	good-quality curry powder or to taste
2 cups	chicken broth, preferably homemade
1 cup	heavy cream
	chopped fresh coriander or parsley for garnish

■ Place rice in a large shallow baking dish just big enough to hold chicken breasts in one layer. ■ Stir in currants and lemon peel. ■ Spread mixture evenly over bottom of pan. ■ Arrange chicken breasts, meat side up, in one layer on top of rice. ■ Sprinkle with salt and pepper. ■ Heat oil in a large skillet over medium heat and cook apples, onion and garlic, stirring often, for 5 minutes or until soft but not brown. ■ Stir in curry powder and cook, stirring, 2 minutes longer. ■ Stir in chicken broth and cream and bring to boil, scraping up any bits from bottom of pan. ■ Pour over chicken, cover tightly and bake in preheated 350°F oven for about 1 hour, or until chicken and rice are tender. ■ Garnish with chopped coriander or parsley to serve.

MICROWAVE DIRECTIONS: Precook rice. Cook remaining ingredients on High 3 to 4 minutes. Assemble casserole and cook on Medium about 25 minutes until chicken is tender.

calories/serving: 474 for 8 servings
380 for 10 servings
protein, niacin: excellent
iron, thiamin, vitamin A: fair

TURKEY CAKES

Serves 4
Preparation time: 10 minutes
Cooking time: 4 minutes

Moist, delicate and with lots of flavor, these cakes can be made with chicken, fish, seafood or even canned salmon. For a lighter patty, you can substitute plain yogurt for the heavy cream. Serve with cranberry sauce.

2 cups	finely chopped cooked turkey
2 Tb	butter
1	medium onion, finely chopped
1 cup	dry breadcrumbs
¼ cup	chopped fresh parsley
2	eggs, lightly beaten
1 Tb	Dijon mustard
1 tsp	Worcestershire sauce
¼ tsp	Tabasco sauce (optional)
	salt and pepper to taste
¼ cup (approx.)	heavy cream or plain yogurt
¼ cup	flour
¼ cup	vegetable oil
	lemon wedges for garnish

■ Heat butter until sizzling in a medium frying pan. ■ Add onion and sauté until softened, about 3 minutes. ■ Remove from heat and stir in breadcrumbs. ■ Combine turkey, breadcrumb mixture, parsley, eggs, Dijon mustard, Worcestershire sauce, Tabasco sauce, and salt and pepper in a large bowl. ■ Add enough cream to bind mixture together. ■ Using about ¼ cup mixture for each, form patties about 1″ thick. ■ Sprinkle flour on a plate and coat patties on both sides. ■ Heat oil in a large frying pan over medium heat. ■ Fry patties in batches until brown on both sides and heated through, about 2 minutes per side. ■ Serve garnished with lemon wedges.

calories/serving: 382 using heavy cream
367 using yogurt
protein, niacin: excellent
iron: good
vitamin A: fair

TURKEY LEFTOVERS

There are all sorts of quick and delicious ways to enjoy leftover turkey. For turkey schnitzel, dredge slices of cooked turkey in seasoned flour and fry quickly in butter until golden. Serve with sour cream. Spread leftover wings, drumsticks or thighs with a mixture of mustard, Worcestershire sauce and garlic powder. Broil until golden; serve hot or cold.

CHICKEN WITH BULGUR STUFFING

Serves 6 to 8
Preparation time: 30 minutes
Cooking time: 2 hours and 15 minutes

In the countries of the Middle East, chickens are usually stuffed with rice. However, because of cost, peasants substitute bulgur for rice; the bulgur stuffing turns out to be more tasty.

1 cup	coarse bulgur
5 to 6 lb	roasting chicken with giblets
½ cup	butter
½ cup	pine nuts
1	medium onion, chopped
1 cup	chicken stock
½ cup	finely chopped fresh coriander leaves or parsley and chives
2 tsp	salt
1 tsp	dried rosemary
½ tsp	pepper
½ tsp	allspice
1 tsp	ground cinnamon

- Soak bulgur in water for 5 minutes. - Drain in a sieve, pressing out excess water. - Wash chicken and cut giblets into small pieces, then set aside. - Melt butter in a frying pan and sauté pine nuts until golden brown. - Remove with a slotted spoon and set aside. - Add onion and chopped giblets to butter and stir-fry until onion is softened. - Stir in bulgur and stir-fry for 5 minutes. - Add remaining ingredients, except pine nuts and cinnamon, and stir-fry until stock is absorbed. - Remove from heat and allow to cool. - Add pine nuts and mix well. - Stuff chicken and sew or truss. - Place chicken in a roasting pan. - Brush with additional butter and cinnamon. - Cover with lid or foil and roast in preheated 350°F oven for 2 hours, basting chicken with its own juices every 15 minutes. - Uncover and cook for a further 15 minutes.

MICROWAVE DIRECTIONS: Stuffing can be cooked on stove top. Prepare chicken as in recipe, brushing with melted butter and cinnamon. Place on a microwave roasting rack, breast side down. Cook on High 10 minutes. Reduce power to Medium and cook 10 minutes more. Turn chicken over, baste well, cook further 30 to 40 minutes, depending on size of chicken. Alternately use meat probe or microwave thermometer and cook to an internal temperature of 190°F. Allow 10 to 12 minutes per pound cooking time.

calories/serving: 510 for 6 servings
382 for 8 servings
protein: excellent
riboflavin, niacin: fair

Barbecued Lemon Chicken

BARBECUED LEMON CHICKEN

Serves 4
Preparation time: 10 minutes
Marinating time: 20 minutes to 6 hours
Cooking time: 10 minutes

This simple way to cook chicken is sure to become a favorite.

4	boneless chicken breasts
	juice of 1 lemon
2 tsp	olive oil
1	clove garlic, minced
½ tsp	dried oregano *or* 1 Tb fresh
pinch	cayenne pepper

- Remove skin from chicken. - Arrange chicken in a shallow dish in single layer. - Combine lemon juice, oil, garlic, oregano and cayenne; mix well. - Pour over chicken and turn to coat both sides. - Let stand at room temperature for 20 minutes, or cover and refrigerate up to 6 hours. - Cook chicken over hot barbecue coals for 4 to 5 minutes on each side, or until meat is no longer pink inside.

calories/serving: 148
protein, niacin: excellent
low fat

Chicken in Spicy Yogurt

CHICKEN IN SPICY YOGURT

Serves 4 to 5
Preparation time: 10 minutes
Marinating time: 8 to 24 hours
Cooking time: 30 to 40 minutes

An Indian-style yogurt and spice marinade makes chicken moist and full of flavor. Serve with rice and sliced cucumber and tomatoes.

1	chicken, cut into pieces (about 2½ lbs)
1½ tsp	Dijon mustard
¼ cup	vegetable oil
¼ cup	plain yogurt
1½ tsp	peeled and minced ginger root
¼ tsp	cumin seeds
¼ tsp	coriander seeds
¼ tsp	ground turmeric
2 Tb	lemon juice
2 Tb	chopped, canned green chili or fresh green chili pepper, seeded and chopped

■ Place mustard in a mixing bowl or food processor. ■ Add oil, drop by drop, whisking or processing as if making mayonnaise, until well blended. ■ Stir in yogurt. ■ Using a mortar and pestle, minichop or coffee grinder, combine ginger, cumin, coriander and turmeric and pound or grind to form a paste. ■ Add lemon juice and mix. ■ Stir lemon mixture and chopped chili into yogurt mixture. ■ Remove skin from chicken pieces. ■ Using a knife, make very small cuts in chicken meat. ■ Arrange in a shallow dish or place in a plastic bag. ■ Pour yogurt-spice mixture over chicken and stir to coat all pieces. ■ Cover and refrigerate at least 8 hours or up to 24 hours. ■ Barbecue chicken on hot grill, 4″ to 6″ from hot coals, for 15 to 20 minutes on each side (15 minutes if cover is down on barbecue). ■ Watch carefully and turn frequently to prevent burning.

calories/serving: 343 for 4 servings
274 for 5 servings
protein, niacin: excellent
iron, riboflavin: fair

CHICKEN WITH CRABMEAT SAUCE

Serves 4
Preparation time: 15 minutes
Cooking time: 35 minutes

This instant sauce transforms simple baked chicken into something special.

4	chicken breasts, skinned and boned
	oil or melted butter
	salt and black pepper
½ cup	white wine or chicken stock
1 can	(4.23 oz/120 g) crabmeat, drained
⅓ cup	evaporated milk
⅓ cup	mayonnaise
½ cup	fresh parsley sprigs
1 Tb	tomato paste
	salt and a pinch cayenne pepper

■ Cut 4 squares of aluminum foil large enough to enclose chicken breasts. ■ Brush foil with oil or melted butter, place a chicken breast on each and sprinkle with salt and black pepper. ■ Turn up edges of foil and pour about 2 tablespoons of white wine or stock over each piece of chicken. ■ Draw foil up over chicken to enclose completely, sealing edges well. ■ Place foil parcels on a wire rack over a roasting pan of boiling water and bake in preheated 350°F oven for 30 to 35 minutes, until chicken breasts are tender. ■ While chicken is cooking, put all remaining ingredients in a food processor or blender and process until smooth. ■ When chicken is cooked, unwrap foil parcels and transfer chicken to a serving dish. ■ Serve hot with crabmeat sauce on the side or refrigerate chicken and serve cold, coated with sauce.

calories/serving: 422
protein, niacin: excellent
vitamin C: good
calcium, iron, vitamin A, riboflavin: fair

ROAST TURKEY WITH POTATO DRESSING

Serves 12
Preparation time: 45 minutes
Cooking time: 4 to 4½ hours

Humble mashed potatoes form the basis of an aromatic stuffing for roast turkey.

10 to 12 lb	turkey
3 cups	day-old fine breadcrumbs
1 Tb	summer savory
½ tsp	ground sage
	salt and pepper to taste
4 cups	hot mashed potatoes
½ cup	butter
1	egg, lightly beaten
½ cup	melted butter

■ Toss breadcrumbs with summer savory, sage, salt and pepper. ■ Combine mashed potatoes and ½ cup butter. ■ Add to seasoned breadcrumbs, along with beaten egg. ■ Stir dressing until evenly moistened. ■ Rinse turkey and pat dry inside and out with paper towelling. ■ Spoon some of stuffing into neck cavity and fasten with a skewer. ■ Place bird, breast side up, on a rack in a shallow roasting pan. ■ Brush with melted butter. ■ Roast in preheated 325°F oven, uncovered, for 4 to 4½ hours. ■ Baste several times during roasting with pan juices. ■ The turkey will be done when a meat thermometer inserted in the thigh registers 185°F, or the drumstick twists easily in the socket. ■ Let stand 15 minutes before carving.

calories/serving: 727
protein, iron, niacin: excellent
thiamin, riboflavin: good
calcium, vitamin A, vitamin C: fair

SKILLET ORANGE CHICKEN WITH GREEN BEANS

Serves 4 to 6
Preparation time: 15 minutes
Cooking time: 23 to 25 minutes

This is fine for family or guests. Use a 3-pound chicken, cut up, or whatever cuts of chicken your family prefers.

6 to 8	chicken pieces
	flour, salt and pepper
¼ cup	butter
1	onion, chopped
½ cup	frozen orange juice concentrate
¼ cup	white vermouth, wine or orange marmalade
¾ lb	fresh green beans
	orange slices and chopped fresh parsley for garnish

■ Lightly coat chicken with flour. ■ Sprinkle with salt and pepper. ■ Melt butter in a large heavy skillet. ■ Brown chicken on all sides; pour off fat. ■ Stir in onion, orange juice and wine or marmalade. ■ Cover and simmer for 10 minutes. ■ Slice green beans if they are too long and add to skillet. ■ Cover and cook for 8 to 10 minutes, or until beans are tender. ■ Spoon chicken and beans onto a hot platter. ■ If sauce is too thin, boil until it thickens; pour over chicken. ■ Garnish with orange slices and chopped parsley.

calories/serving: 645 for 4 servings
433 for 6 servings
protein, vitamin C, niacin: excellent
iron: good
vitamin A, thiamin, riboflavin: fair

CHICKEN WITH LIME AND GINGER

Serves 4
Preparation time: 20 minutes
Marinating time: at least 4 hours
Cooking time: 1 to 1½ hours

Lime juice acts as a tenderizer and ginger and soy sauce give an Oriental flavor to this succulent chicken casserole. When barbecue season comes around, omit the mushrooms and barbecue the chicken portions, basting with the marinade.

4	chicken portions, skinned
2	cloves garlic, chopped
	grated peel and juice of 2 limes
1 Tb	vegetable oil
1 Tb	honey
1 Tb	soy sauce
1	1″ piece ginger root, peeled and finely chopped
1 tsp	dried mint
	salt and pepper to taste
4 oz	mushrooms

■ Make slashes in chicken meat with a sharp knife and arrange portions in a single layer in a shallow oven-proof dish. ■ Mix together remaining ingredients, except mushrooms, and pour over chicken. ■ Cover and marinate for at least 4 hours, turning occasionally. ■ Add mushrooms to dish, re-cover and bake in preheated 350° F oven for 1 to 1½ hours until chicken is tender. ■ Serve with stir-fried vegetables and boiled rice.

calories/serving: 226
protein, niacin: excellent
iron, vitamin C, riboflavin: fair
low fat

Herbed Cornish Hens

HERBED CORNISH HENS

Serves 2
Preparation time: 10 minutes
Marinating time: 3 hours
Cooking time: 30 to 40 minutes

A delicious make-ahead dish for an intimate warm-weather dinner for two.

2	**Cornish hens**
1	**apple, cored and sliced**
2	**slices bacon**

MARINADE:

1 cup	**sweet white wine**
1	**onion, finely chopped**
1	**bay leaf, cracked into three**
3 Tb	**chopped fresh tarragon**
2 Tb	**chopped fresh rosemary**

▪ Combine ingredients for marinade in a shallow dish large enough to take Cornish hens. ▪ Marinate birds for 3 hours at room temperature, turning occasionally. ▪ Remove from marinade and pat dry. ▪ Strain marinade. ▪ Place birds in casserole just large enough to take them. ▪ Pour strained marinade over to make ½″ liquid in dish. ▪ Arrange apple slices over breasts of Cornish hens and cover with bacon strips. ▪ Cover and bake in preheated 325°F oven for 30 to 40 minutes, basting occasionally, until tender. ▪ Remove from oven, place on wire rack over plate to cool and drain. ▪ Refrigerate overnight in covered container. ▪ Serve with a crisp salad and fresh bread.

calories/serving: 475
protein, niacin: excellent
iron, riboflavin: good
vitamin C, thiamin: fair

CHICKEN BRAISED WITH APPLES

Serves 4
Preparation time: 20 minutes
Cooking time: 1 hour

Beautiful braised chicken, flavored with apples, cider and apple brandy.

3 Tb	butter
3½ lbs	chicken pieces
1	onion, minced
2	large apples, peeled, cored and diced
1 Tb	chopped fresh parsley
1 tsp	fresh thyme *or* ½ tsp dried
¼ cup	apple brandy
6 Tb	cider
6 Tb	heavy cream
	salt and pepper to taste

▪ Heat butter in a large skillet. ▪ Add chicken pieces and brown on all sides. ▪ Push chicken to one side and sauté onion, apples, parsley and thyme. ▪ Stir in brandy and cider. ▪ Stir ingredients together, reduce heat and simmer, covered, for 20 to 40 minutes or until tender. ▪ Remove chicken and spoon off excess fat. ▪ Add cream to pan and heat but do not boil. ▪ Season with salt and pepper. ▪ Return chicken to pan and baste with sauce. ▪ Serve immediately.

calories/serving: 675 with skin
570 without skin
protein, niacin: excellent
iron, vitamin A: good
vitamin C, thiamin, riboflavin: fair

HONEY GARLIC SESAME WINGS

Serves 3 to 4
Preparation time: 15 minutes
Marinating time: 1 hour or longer
Cooking time: 55 minutes

Always a favorite, these Oriental-flavored wings topped with toasted sesame seeds are almost addictive. Make lots.

3 lbs	chicken wings, trimmed and separated
⅓ cup	soy sauce
⅓ cup	white wine, chicken stock or water
⅓ cup	liquid honey
⅓ cup	brown sugar
1 Tb	sesame oil
3	large cloves garlic, minced
2 Tb	sesame seeds

▪ Mix soy sauce, wine, honey, sugar, sesame oil and garlic in a large bowl until sugar dissolves. ▪ Add wings. ▪ Stir and marinate at least 1 hour at room temperature. ▪ Meanwhile spread sesame seeds in single layer on a baking dish. ▪ Bake in preheated 400°F oven for 8 to 10 minutes or until golden. Set aside. ▪ Arrange wings in a single layer on a foil-lined baking sheet. ▪ Spoon on half the marinade. ▪ Bake, uncovered, in preheated 400°F oven for 30 minutes. ▪ Turn wings over and spoon on remaining marinade. ▪ Bake for 20 minutes longer, or until wings are brown and tender. ▪ Transfer to a serving platter. ▪ Pour marinade into saucepan and bring to boil. ▪ Cook for about 5 minutes or until sauce thickens slightly. ▪ Pour over wings and sprinkle with toasted sesame seeds.

calories/serving: 827 for 3 servings
620 for 4 servings
protein, niacin: excellent
iron: good
riboflavin: fair

CHICKEN RISOTTO

Serves 4
Preparation time: 5 minutes
Cooking time: 25 minutes

You can add all sorts of meat and vegetables to this simple risotto.

1 Tb	butter
1 lb	chicken meat, diced, or chicken livers, diced
2	slices bacon, finely chopped
1	small onion, finely chopped
1 cup	medium-grain rice
½ cup	dry white wine
2¼ cups	chicken stock
½ tsp	dried thyme
½ tsp	chili powder
½ tsp	ground turmeric
	salt and pepper to taste

▪ Melt butter in a large flame-proof casserole dish and fry chicken and bacon quickly over high heat until cooked. ▪ Remove with slotted spoon and keep warm. ▪ Add onion to dish and fry over medium heat until softened. ▪ Add rice and cook, stirring all the time, until rice looks transparent. ▪ Pour in wine, increase heat and boil rapidly until wine has reduced by half. ▪ Stir in stock, herbs and seasonings. ▪ Bring to boil, reduce heat to low, cover and simmer for 15 to 20 minutes, until rice is tender and liquid is absorbed. ▪ Stir in chicken and bacon and serve.

calories/serving: 466
protein, niacin: excellent
iron, thiamin: good
riboflavin: fair

Indonesian Chicken

HONEY MUSTARD CHICKEN WINGS

Serves 3 to 4
Preparation time: 15 minutes
Cooking time: 55 to 60 minutes

Wonderfully quick to prepare and delicious to eat, this honey mustard glaze is perfect for all chicken pieces.

3 lbs	chicken wings, trimmed and separated
½ cup	liquid honey
¼ cup	Dijon mustard
¼ cup	grainy mustard (Moutarde de Meaux)
1 tsp	curry powder

▪ Arrange wings in a single layer on a lightly greased, foil-lined baking sheet. ▪ Bake, uncovered, in preheated 375°F oven for 30 minutes. ▪ Drain off excess liquid and turn wings over. ▪ Mix honey, mustards and curry powder in a small bowl. ▪ Bake additional 25 to 30 minutes, or until wings are tender, basting once. ▪ Transfer to a platter and serve with sauce spooned over.

calories/serving: 717 for 3 servings
538 for 4 servings
protein, niacin: excellent
iron: good

INDONESIAN CHICKEN

Serves 4 to 6
Preparation time: 20 minutes
Marinating time: 2 hours
Cooking time: 40 to 45 minutes

In summer cook the chicken on the barbecue, 4″ to 6″ from coals, for 20 to 40 minutes, or until juices run clear when chicken is pierced with a skewer.

3 lb	broiler chicken
1 cup	sweet soy sauce (available in Oriental grocery stores)
2	cloves garlic, crushed
2 Tb	fresh lime juice
½ cup	melted unsalted butter
½ tsp	grated ginger root
1 tsp	Indonesian hot pepper sauce
	cornstarch (optional)
1 pkg	shrimp puffs (optional)
	fat or oil for deep frying

▪ Cut chicken into 8 pieces. Reserve carcass for stock. ▪ Blend remaining ingredients, except shrimp puffs and cornstarch, in a large bowl. ▪ Add chicken pieces and toss to coat. ▪ Marinate two hours at room temperature, stirring occasionally. ▪ Remove chicken from marinade, reserving marinade. ▪ Bake in preheated 400°F oven for 35 to 40 minutes or until done, basting with marinade as needed. If browning too quickly, cover with foil. ▪ Blend a little cornstarch with water. ▪ Combine with marinade and heat, stirring, until thickened. ▪ Deep-fry shrimp puffs in hot fat or oil (375°F on fat thermometer), draining at once on paper towels. The chips will puff up as soon as they hit the fat. Cook at the last minute. ▪ Serve chicken topped with sauce and with shrimp puffs on the side.

calories/serving: 497 not including shrimp puffs
protein, niacin: excellent
iron: good
riboflavin: fair

CHICKEN BREASTS WITH CURRIED CREAM SAUCE

Serves 4
Preparation time: 5 minutes
Cooking time: 40 minutes

Yogurt is an excellent light, low-calorie, low-fat base for a sauce; sour cream also works but is higher in calories and fat.

4	skinless chicken breasts
½ cup	plain yogurt
2 tsp	flour
2 tsp	curry powder or to taste
2 Tb	fine dry breadcrumbs
2 Tb	water

▪ Arrange chicken in a single layer in a baking dish. ▪ Combine yogurt, flour and curry powder in a small bowl. ▪ Spread over chicken. ▪ Sprinkle breadcrumbs over top. ▪ Add water to baking dish. ▪ Bake, uncovered, in preheated 350°F oven about 40 minutes, or until chicken is no longer pink inside.
MICROWAVE DIRECTIONS: Use a microwave-safe dish and cook on High uncovered about 12 minutes.

calories/servings: 210
protein, niacin: excellent
iron, riboflavin: fair

Honey Mustard Chicken Wings

Wild Rice and Sausage Stuffing

WILD RICE AND SAUSAGE STUFFING

Makes 10 cups (enough for 20 to 26 lb turkey)
Preparation time: 30 minutes
Cooking time: 45 to 55 minutes

Wild rice makes a wonderful stuffing for turkey, but if it's unavailable, substitute 4 cups coarse breadcrumbs made from stale bread and follow the recipe, starting with cooking the sausage.

1 cup	wild rice
2 cups	chicken stock
1 cup	water
1 lb	bulk sausage meat
2 Tb	butter
2	onions, chopped
2	apples, peeled, cored and diced
2 cups	chopped celery
½ tsp	each dried thyme and crumbled dried sage
pinch	sugar
	salt and pepper to taste

• Put rice in a fine sieve and rinse under cold water. • Combine rice, stock and water in a medium saucepan. • Bring to boil, reduce heat, partially cover and simmer 45 to 55 minutes, or until rice is tender. • Drain in sieve if necessary. • Meanwhile cook sausage meat in a large skillet, breaking up meat with spoon, over medium heat until no longer pink, 10 to 15 minutes. • With slotted spoon, transfer to a large bowl. • Drain off any fat from pan and melt butter over medium heat. • Cook onions and apples until soft, about 5 minutes. • Add celery and cook, covered, 5 minutes. • Add to sausage with cooked rice (or breadcrumbs), thyme, sage, sugar, salt and pepper. (If stuffing is refrigerated, bring to room temperature before using.)

calories/½ cup serving: 106

TURKEY FRITTERS

Serves 4
Preparation time: 15 minutes
Cooking time: 5 to 6 minutes

No one will believe these crisp, crunchy fritters are made with leftovers. Serve them with bacon strips and fried bananas for a Southern accent.

1½ cups	finely chopped cooked turkey
2 Tb	butter
½	green pepper, chopped
1	onion, chopped
	salt and pepper to taste
1 cup	flour
2	eggs, separated
½ cup	milk
1 tsp	baking powder
½ cup	vegetable oil

• Heat butter in a frying pan over medium heat. • Add green pepper and onion. • Cook, stirring, until softened, about 3 minutes. • Toss together with turkey. • Season with salt and pepper; set aside. • Combine flour, egg yolks, milk and baking powder in a medium bowl. Don't overmix. • Stir in turkey-vegetable mixture. • Beat egg whites until stiff in a large bowl. • Fold gently into turkey mixture. • Heat oil until hot in a frying pan. • Drop tablespoons of fritter batter into oil. • Fry until golden on one side, about 1 minute; turn over and fry second side until golden. • Remove and drain on paper towels. • Repeat with remaining mixture. • Serve with Piquant Sauce or chutney.

calories/serving: 394
protein, niacin: excellent
iron, vitamin C, thiamin: good
vitamin A, riboflavin: fair

PIQUANT SAUCE

Makes 1⅓ cups
Preparation time: 5 minutes

An excellent enhancement to any kind of fried food.

1 cup	mayonnaise
2 Tb	chopped dill pickles
1	clove garlic, chopped
2 Tb	chopped fresh parsley
2 Tb	chopped black olives
¼ tsp	Tabasco sauce or to taste
2 tsp	lemon juice
	salt and pepper to taste

• Combine all ingredients.

calories/tablespoon: about 50

Poached Salmon

POACHED SALMON

Serves 4
Preparation time: 30 minutes
Chilling time: 1 hour

This classic dish of poached salmon, served either hot with Wine Sauce or cold with Homemade Mayonnaise (see Savory Sauces), is bound to please.

5 lb	fresh whole salmon
10 cups	fish stock or water
1	medium onion
8	cloves
2	carrots, sliced
2 tsp	salt
2	bay leaves
½ cup	white wine vinegar
1 tsp	pickling spice
1 tsp	whole black peppercorns

▪ Bring all ingredients, except salmon, to boil in a pot large enough to hold salmon and simmer for 10 minutes. ▪ Wrap salmon in cheesecloth and lower into stock. ▪ Cover pot and simmer 20 minutes. ▪ Remove to platter. ▪ If serving cold, scrape away top layer of brown skin. ▪ Refrigerate. ▪ Decorate and serve with mayonnaise.

calories/serving: 493 for 4 servings
protein, niacin: excellent
iron, calcium, thiamin: good
vitamin A: fair

SHRIMP CURRY

Serves 4 to 6
Preparation time: 10 minutes
Cooking time: 5 to 10 minutes

Quick recipes are every cook's secret weapon, for lunch or Sunday brunch or supper.

2 lbs	cooked medium shrimp
¼ lb	butter
1 to 3 Tb	medium hot curry powder or to taste
1	medium onion
	freshly ground pepper to taste
¼ cup	Cognac
1 Tb	Worcestershire sauce
1½ cups	light cream
½ cup	dry sherry (optional)

▪ Heat shrimp with half the butter in top of a double boiler over simmering water. ▪ Melt remaining butter in a heavy frying pan. ▪ Add curry powder and stir over medium heat. ▪ Grate onion and add to curry, with its juice. ▪ Season with pepper. ▪ Remove from heat and add Cognac, Worcestershire sauce, cream and sherry. ▪ Pour over shrimp in double boiler and keep warm. Do not overcook. ▪ Serve with rice pilaf and chutney.

calories/serving: 696 for 4 servings
464 for 6 servings
protein, iron, niacin: excellent
calcium, vitamin A: good

Salmon Loaf

SALMON LOAF

Serves 4
Preparation time: 10 minutes
Cooking time: 40 minutes

When you think there's nothing in the house for supper, remember that a couple of cans of salmon from the cupboard make a quick nutritious loaf the whole family will like.

1½ cups	cracker crumbs (about 36 soda crackers)
½ cup	milk
2 cans	(each 7.5 oz/213 g) salmon
¼ cup	finely diced celery
2	eggs, lightly beaten
2 Tb	lemon juice
¼ tsp	each salt, pepper and paprika
pinch	cayenne pepper

▪ Place crumbs in a large bowl and soak in milk 5 minutes. ▪ Stir in salmon with its juice, mashing to crush bones and flake salmon. ▪ Stir in celery, eggs, lemon juice, salt, pepper, paprika and cayenne. ▪ Pack firmly into a greased 9" × 5" loaf pan. ▪ Set into a larger pan filled with hot water. ▪ Bake in preheated 350°F oven for 40 minutes or until golden on top. ▪ Let sit, covered loosely with foil, 5 minutes before cutting into slices.

calories/serving: 382
protein, niacin: excellent
iron, calcium: good
vitamin A, riboflavin: fair

GRILLED SHRIMP AND SCALLOP KEBABS WITH LEMON AND FENNEL

Serves 4 to 6
Preparation time: 20 minutes
Marinating time: 1 to 2 hours
Cooking time: 5 to 6 minutes

Kebabs of shellfish make a delightful change from grilled meats or poultry. They can be assembled in advance, covered and refrigerated after marinating with lemon, fennel and garlic.

1½ lbs	each medium shrimp and large scallops
	large, firm mushrooms (optional)
⅓ cup	fine dry breadcrumbs
	fresh fennel or dill sprigs and lemon wedges for garnish

MARINADE:	
1 cup	light oil (corn, sunflower)
½ cup	fresh lemon juice
¼ cup	chopped fresh fennel, dill or parsley

LEMON-FENNEL BUTTER SAUCE:	
¼ cup	melted unsalted butter
2 Tb	chopped fresh fennel or dill
	juice of 1 medium lemon
	freshly ground pepper
1	large clove garlic, finely chopped
2	green onions, chopped
	freshly ground pepper

▪ Shell shrimp, leaving small piece of shell on tail intact. ▪ Devein and rinse under cold water. ▪ Rinse scallops and set aside. ▪ Combine marinade ingredients in a mixing bowl. ▪ Add shellfish and stir to coat. ▪ Marinate 1 to 2 hours, stirring a few times. ▪ Meanwhile, if using bamboo skewers, soak in water. ▪ Lightly oil skewers; thread scallops and shrimp alternately. ▪ Reserve marinade for basting. If you wish, large, firm mushrooms can be added. ▪ Sprinkle shellfish kebabs with breadcrumbs. ▪ Cover with foil and refrigerate, several hours if you wish. ▪ Grill kebabs 4" or 5" over high heat, 4 to 5 minutes, turning often and brushing with reserved marinade. Don't overcook. ▪ Meanwhile, combine ingredients for Lemon-Fennel Butter Sauce and heat gently. ▪ Serve kebabs at once, garnished with fennel or dill sprigs and lemon wedges. ▪ Drizzle with sauce.

calories/serving: 785 for 4 servings
527 for 6 servings
protein, iron, niacin: excellent
calcium, vitamin C: good
thiamin: fair

Grilled Shrimp and Scallop Kebabs with Lemon and Fennel

Gratin of Scallops and Mushrooms

SALMON WITH GINGER LIME BUTTER

Serves 2
Preparation time: 10 minutes
Cooking time: 5 to 6 minutes

Salmon scallops are thin slices cut from a fillet. Because the scallops are thin, they do not need turning when broiled. If unavailable, use salmon steaks and broil 4 to 5 minutes on each side.

1 lb	salmon scallops
2 Tb	butter
1 tsp	ground ginger *or* 1 Tb finely chopped ginger root
	grated peel and juice of ½ lime
1 Tb	olive oil
	salt and pepper to taste

▪ In a food processor or by hand, cream butter, ginger, lime juice and peel. Reserve until needed. ▪ Line baking sheet with parchment paper or foil. ▪ Place salmon on top and brush with oil. ▪ Preheat broiler. ▪ Broil salmon 6″ from heat for 3 minutes on one side and 2 to 3 minutes on the other, or until white juices dot the salmon and it flakes when a fork is inserted. ▪ Sprinkle with salt and pepper. ▪ Top with ginger lime butter.
MICROWAVE DIRECTIONS: Place prepared salmon slices in microwave baking dish. Cover and cook on High 3 to 4 minutes. Rearrange slices halfway through cooking time; that is, move slices from center of dish to the outside to achieve even cooking. Continue as above.

calories/serving: 491
protein, niacin: excellent
calcium, iron, vitamin A, thiamin: good

FISH FILLETS WITH BASIL BUTTER

Serves 4
Preparation time: 5 minutes
Cooking time: 10 minutes

This is so simple and easy, yet it results in the best-tasting fish. If buying frozen fish, try to buy the kind that has been frozen in a single layer or individually wrapped fillets. If using the kind that has been frozen in a block, defrost the fish and separate into fillets before cooking. If buying fresh, choose whatever kind of fillets are freshest. About one tablespoon of any fresh herbs can be substituted for the basil – chopped fresh dill, thyme or tarragon.

1 lb	fish fillets
1 Tb	lemon juice
1 Tb	melted butter
½ tsp	dried basil
	salt and pepper to taste

▪ Arrange fillets in a single layer in a baking dish. ▪ Mix lemon juice, melted butter and basil together. ▪ Drizzle over fish. ▪ Sprinkle lightly with salt and pepper. ▪ Bake, uncovered, in preheated 450°F oven for 8 to 10 minutes (10 minutes per inch thickness for fresh fish), or until fish is opaque.
MICROWAVE DIRECTIONS: Prepare fish as above. Cover with plastic wrap and turn back corner to vent steam. Microwave on High 3½ to 4½ minutes.

calories/serving: 130
protein: excellent
low fat
low cal

GRATIN OF SCALLOPS AND MUSHROOMS

Serves 8
Preparation time: 30 minutes
Cooking time: 12 to 15 minutes

This is a delightfully light yet creamy way to prepare scallops. Instead of fresh scallops you can use two packages of frozen.

1 lb	scallops
½ cup	butter or margarine
1	green pepper, cut into short slivers
1	medium onion, finely chopped
½ lb	mushrooms, sliced
¼ cup	flour
	salt and white pepper to taste
2½ cups	light cream
2 Tb	grated Parmesan cheese
¼ tsp	paprika
pinch	grated nutmeg
⅓ cup	dry white wine
½ cup	fine dry breadcrumbs

▪ Butter 8 large scallop shells or individual baking dishes. ▪ Heat ¼ cup butter in a heavy saucepan and add green pepper and onion. ▪ Stir over medium-high heat 3 minutes. ▪ Turn heat to high and add mushrooms. ▪ Stir 3 minutes more, then add 2 tablespoons butter and sprinkle in flour, salt and pepper. ▪ Stir 2 minutes over low heat, then remove from heat and add cream, cheese, paprika and nutmeg, stirring to blend well. ▪ Return to medium-high heat and stir until sauce is just boiling. ▪ Reduce heat to low and stir until thick and smooth, about 5 minutes. ▪ Remove from heat and stir in scallops (cut large ones into halves) and wine and spoon mixture into prepared scallop shells or baking dishes. ▪ Sprinkle with mixture of breadcrumbs and 2 tablespoons melted butter. Refrigerate at this point if you wish. ▪ Bake in preheated 450°F oven 12 to 15 minutes or until lightly browned on top and bubbling well.

calories/serving: 307
protein, vitamin C, niacin: excellent
calcium, iron, vitamin A: good
thiamin, riboflavin: fair

BUYING MUSSELS

When buying mussels look for ones that are tightly closed; the shells should not move when pressed. When cleaning them make sure you pull or cut off the long "beard" attached to the shell.

Fresh Mussels Marinière

FRESH MUSSELS MARINIÈRE

Serves 4 to 6
Preparation time: 20 minutes
Cooking time: 5 minutes

Mussels are cheap. They are simple to do. Treat your guests.

4 lbs	fresh mussels
1 cup	dry white wine
4	shallots, chopped
1 cup	chopped fresh parsley
1	bay leaf
¼ tsp	dried thyme
	salt and pepper to taste

▪ Scrub mussels thoroughly with a very stiff brush under cold, running water. Be sure to remove sand and grit. ▪ Discard any mussels that remain open after being placed in cold water: they should close, indicating that the fish is alive. ▪ Place all ingredients in a large pot. ▪ Cover and steam over medium heat about four minutes, shaking the pot from time to time. ▪ Uncover and stir up to be sure all mussels are now open. If necessary, cook another minute or two. ▪ Any unopened mussels should be discarded. ▪ Transfer to a serving platter or soup tureen. ▪ Serve in wide soup bowls with crisp French bread. ▪ Each guest eats the mussels from the shells and drinks the broth, using a shell as a spoon. Forks and spoons are superfluous.

calories/serving: 202
protein, iron, niacin: excellent
calcium, vitamin C, thiamin: good
riboflavin: fair
low fat

Fillets of Salmon with Avocado and Tomato Relish

FILLETS OF SALMON WITH AVOCADO AND TOMATO RELISH

Serves 4
Preparation time: 10 minutes
Cooking time: 6 to 8 minutes

Chef Mark McEwan created this colorful dish, perfect for a fall barbecue entrée. The relish can be made up to an hour in advance. Boneless, skinless fillets are available at fish markets, or ask your fishmonger to cut them for you.

4	salmon fillets (about 6 oz each)
4 Tb	olive oil
	juice of 1 lemon
	salt and freshly ground pepper to taste
1	small red onion
2	small tomatoes
1	medium avocado
2 Tb	chopped fresh coriander or Italian parsley
1	clove garlic, minced
1 Tb	red wine vinegar

• Drizzle half the olive oil over the salmon. • Sprinkle with half the lemon juice and season with salt and pepper. • Set aside. • Peel and slice onion into matchstick strips. • Place in a mixing bowl. • Peel and seed tomatoes. • Cut into long slender pieces, using only the outer meat of the tomato. • Chop avocado into ½″ dice and add to bowl with tomatoes, chopped coriander and garlic. • Add remaining olive oil, red wine vinegar and remaining lemon juice. • Add salt and pepper and toss gently. • Grill salmon fillets over medium heat on gas or charcoal barbecue 3 or 4 minutes on each side. (Do not overcook or fish will become dry.) • Place salmon on center of dinner plate and put 3 tablespoons of relish directly over top of each serving. • Good served with boiled new potatoes or rice.

calories/serving: 454
protein, vitamin C, niacin: excellent
calcium, iron, thiamin: good
vitamin A: fair

SHRIMP IN GARLIC

Serves 4
Preparation time: 5 minutes
Cooking time: 12 minutes

Shrimp and garlic go well together, and in Spain they are often prepared in somewhat the same fashion as this dish.

1 lb	shelled fresh or frozen and thawed shrimp
4 Tb	butter
4	cloves garlic, crushed
1 Tb	finely chopped hot pepper
	salt and pepper to taste
2 Tb	lemon juice
4 Tb	finely chopped fresh parsley

• Melt butter in a medium frying pan. • Sauté garlic and hot pepper over medium heat for 5 minutes. • Add shrimp and sprinkle with salt and pepper. • Stir-fry for another 5 minutes. • Stir in lemon juice and parsley and stir-fry for another minute. • Serve sizzling hot, garnished with chopped parsley.

MICROWAVE DIRECTIONS: Preheat a microwave browning skillet according to manufacturer's instructions. Place butter in the skillet, add garlic and hot pepper and cook on High 1 minute. Add shrimp; do not sprinkle with salt as this will toughen them. Cook on High about 4 minutes, or until shrimp turn opaque. Season with lemon juice and parsley. Stir.

calories/serving: 189
protein, niacin: excellent
vitamin C: good
vitamin A, iron: fair
low cal

BARBECUED SALMON FILLETS

Serves 4
Preparation time: 5 minutes
Cooking time: 8 to 10 minutes

The barbecued flavor combined with this rich sauce is sublime.

4	salmon fillets
	oil
1	avocado, peeled
½ cup	mayonnaise
1 cup	sour cream
1 Tb	Worcestershire sauce
4 Tb	lemon juice
2 tsp	chopped fresh dill or to taste (optional)
	salt and pepper to taste

■ Dab the fillets with oil and barbecue 8 to 10 minutes, depending on thickness. ■ Blend remaining ingredients into a thick creamy sauce to serve on the side.

calories/serving: 674
protein, niacin: excellent
calcium, iron, vitamin C, thiamin: good

FILLET OF SOLE MONTMORENCY

Serves 4 to 6
Preparation time: 6 minutes
Cooking time: 25 minutes

Use sole or any firm white fish.

2 to 2½ lbs	sole fillets
2 to 4	shallots, peeled and chopped, or green onions, chopped
2 Tb	chopped fresh parsley
8	mushrooms, sliced
	salt and pepper to taste
½ cup	white wine, apple juice or vermouth
2 Tb	butter
3 Tb	heavy cream, heated
1 tsp	lemon juice

■ Butter a shallow baking dish that can go to the table. You may want to use two dishes, as fish should be cooked in a single layer. ■ Combine shallots and parsley and sprinkle over bottom of dish. ■ Lay fish fillets on top and sprinkle mushroom slices over fish. ■ Add salt and pepper. ■ Add wine and top with 1 tablespoon butter, cut into pieces. ■ Cut out a piece of parchment or brown paper to fit inside dish and lay on top of fish. Bake in preheated 500°F

oven for 15 minutes. ■ Pour off liquid and reduce in small, heavy pot over high heat. ■ When reduced to half, add hot cream, lemon juice and 1 tablespoon butter. ■ Stir and pour over fish. ■ Place in 550°F oven or under broiler until appetizingly browned. ■ Serve with small boiled potatoes.

calories/serving: 372 for 4 servings
248 for 6 servings
protein, niacin: excellent
iron, vitamin A, vitamin C, thiamin, riboflavin: fair
low fat

PAN-FRIED TURBOT WITH MUSHROOMS AND SHALLOTS

Serves 4
Preparation time: 5 minutes
Cooking time: 30 minutes

You can use sole or cod fillets for this dish; delicious with lemon rice.

1½ lbs	turbot fillets
	salt and pepper to taste
	flour
2 Tb	vegetable oil
	lemon wedges and dill sprigs for garnish (optional)
SAUCE:	
1 cup	dry white wine
2	shallots, chopped
pinch	dried thyme
¼ cup	heavy cream
4	mushrooms, sliced

■ To make sauce, heat wine, shallots and thyme in a heavy saucepan over high heat until reduced to ½ cup. ■ Add cream and mushrooms. ■ Lower heat to medium and cook another 8 to 10 minutes or until slightly thickened. ■ Meanwhile combine salt, pepper and flour and dust fish on both sides. Do not flour until just before panfrying or flour will become sticky. ■ Heat oil in a large heavy skillet over high heat until very hot. ■ Place fillets in pan and cook until light golden brown, turning once, about 4 to 5 minutes. Do not overcook. ■ Transfer to heated plates and garnish with lemon wedges and dill sprigs. ■ Spoon some of the sauce over fish and serve at once.

MICROWAVE DIRECTIONS: Place fish in one layer in a baking dish. Cover with mushrooms; sprinkle with shallots and thyme. Pour wine over top. Cover dish, cook on High 5 to 6 minutes. Remove fish to warm plate; keep warm. Mix 2 tablespoons flour into cream, stir into liquid from the fish. Cook on High 2 to 3 minutes, stirring each minute until sauce has thickened. Continue as above.

calories/serving: 471
protein, niacin: excellent
thiamin: good

Poached Arctic Char in Mornay Sauce

POACHED ARCTIC CHAR IN MORNAY SAUCE

Serves 6
Preparation time: 20 minutes
Cooking time: 8 to 15 minutes

This delicious fish lives in arctic waters. You can substitute another firm-fleshed fish, such as salmon, trout or pike.

2½ lbs	**arctic char fillets or salmon, trout or pike**
1½ Tb	**softened butter**
2 Tb	**finely minced shallots or scallions**
	salt and white pepper to taste
⅔ cup	**dry white vermouth or dry white wine**
2 cups (approx.)	**cool fish stock or diluted clam juice**

MORNAY SAUCE:

	fish-poaching liquid
3 Tb	**butter**
4 Tb	**flour**
1 cup (approx.)	**milk**
	salt and white pepper to taste
	lemon juice
½ cup	**grated Swiss or Parmesan cheese**

■ Smear half the butter in a baking dish about 12″ long and 1½″ deep. ■ Sprinkle in half the shallots. ■ Dry fish fillets on paper towels. ■ With a sharp knife, lightly score milky side of fillets to prevent curling. ■ Sprinkle both sides with salt and pepper. ■ Arrange fillets, slightly overlapping, in one layer in the baking dish. ■ Pour in wine and just enough fish stock to barely cover fish, and dot remaining butter on top. ■ Cut a piece of waxed or parchment paper the size of the baking dish and lay over fish. Set baking dish on asbestos pad or rack on top of the stove over moderate heat. Bring barely to the simmer, then place dish on bottom rack of preheated 400°F oven for 8 to 10 minutes. Fish is done when it is slightly resilient when pressed with a finger, but not squishy. ■ Remove fish to a warm platter and keep warm in 200°F oven. ■ Strain cooking liquid into a saucepan for sauce. ■ To make sauce, boil poaching liquid until reduced to about 1 cup. ■ Melt butter, blend in flour and cook slowly, stirring, for about 2 minutes. ■ Pour in hot poaching liquid and blend vigorously with a wire whisk. ■ Reduce heat and simmer, stirring constantly and gradually thinning out with milk. Sauce should be thick enough to coat a spoon fairly heavily. ■ Taste for seasoning, adding salt, white pepper and lemon juice to taste. ■ Remove from heat and stir in about ¼ cup cheese. ■ Pour sauce over fish and sprinkle remaining cheese on top. ■ Dot with 1 tablespoon butter and place under broiler for a moment to brown top lightly.

MICROWAVE DIRECTIONS: Arrange fish in casserole dish with thicker portions towards the outer edge of dish. Pour in wine and just enough stock to cover. Cover with lid or plastic wrap. Cook on High 6 to 8 minutes. To make sauce, put poaching liquid in a 2-cup oven-proof bowl. Boil on High to reduce. In another bowl, melt butter for 30 seconds; blend in flour. Add hot liquid and whisk to blend. Cook on High 2 minutes. Stir in milk to thin. Add cheese and seasonings. Cook 1 minute on High.

calories/serving: 493
potassium: good
protein: excellent

HOW TO FIX SAUCES

Don't toss a lumpy sauce into the garbage. It can be saved by rubbing it through a fine sieve into a clean saucepan. Thin an overly thick sauce, by adding extra liquid, one tablespoon at a time, until sauce is correct consistency. To thicken a runny sauce, blend equal quantities of cornstarch and cold milk or water. Stir into sauce and simmer, stirring, until thickened.

Cold Shrimp and Snow Peas

CRAB LEGS WITH HERB BUTTER

Serves 2
Preparation time: 20 minutes

This delectable dish requires no great skill but is utterly, voluptuously delicious.

4	king or snow crab legs
4 cups	boiling water
HERB BUTTER:	
½ cup	butter
1	clove garlic, minced
2 Tb	chopped fresh parsley
2 Tb	chopped fresh dill
3 Tb	dry sherry or white wine
	salt and pepper to taste

▪ Either break legs in two so they'll fit in a kettle of boiling water, or use a long roasting pan of water and boil legs until shells turn pink, about 5 minutes. ▪ Drain and serve with a bowl of Herb Butter for dipping. You can either peel the legs a section at a time by cracking the shell with a lobster cracker or nutcracker, or you can split the legs lengthwise with a sharp knife and pick the morsels out with a fork. ▪ To make Herb Butter, heat butter and sauté garlic, parsley and dill until garlic is soft. ▪ Add sherry or wine and sauté for another minute. Season to taste. ▪ Serve hot in a little chafing dish. ▪ Accompany crab legs with fluffy rice and a wedge of lemon.

calories/serving: 417
protein, vitamin A, niacin: excellent
thiamin: good
calcium, iron: fair

COLD SHRIMP AND SNOW PEAS

Serves 2 to 4
Preparation time: 10 minutes
Cooking time: 5 to 8 minutes
Chilling time: overnight

1 pkg	(8 oz/250 g) frozen cleaned shrimp
¼ lb	snow peas
2 tsp	sugar
¼ cup	red wine vinegar
few drops	sesame seed oil
¼ cup	vegetable oil
1	clove garlic, crushed
2 tsp	each bacon bits, fresh parsley and fresh chives

▪ Cook shrimp according to package instructions. ▪ Plunge into cold water to chill. ▪ Bring 2 cups water to boil. ▪ Trim stems and strings from snow peas and drop into boiling water. ▪ Remove when water has returned to boil, about 3 minutes. ▪ Plunge into cold water. ▪ Meanwhile mix remaining ingredients. ▪ Toss with shrimp and snow peas. ▪ Cover and refrigerate overnight.

calories/serving: 443 for 2 servings
222 for 4 servings
vitamin C: excellent
protein, niacin, iron: good

Whole Baked Fish with Dill

WHOLE BAKED FISH WITH DILL

Serves 4
Preparation time: 10 minutes
Cooking time: 20 to 30 minutes

A fishmonger can give advice on choosing fresh fish – salmon, trout, pickerel, perch. Fillets (sole, perch, haddock, turbot) may be substituted, but cooking time will be reduced.

3 lb	**whole fish, preferably fresh**
4	**shallots, peeled and minced**
8	**mushrooms, sliced**
6	**dill sprigs, fresh or frozen**
	salt, white pepper, lemon juice, butter to taste
1 cup	**clam juice (or fish stock) plus white wine**
½ cup	**heavy cream**
	whole dill sprigs and dilled lemon slices

BEURRE MANIÉ:

Blend 1 Tb unsalted butter with 1 Tb flour into a smooth ball

■ Have the fish dressed – scaled, eviscerated and fins removed. To behead or not is up to you. ■ Butter an oval baking dish large enough to hold fish. ■ Sprinkle a pan with half the shallots, mushrooms, and dill sprigs. ■ Lay fish on top. ■ Season with salt, pepper and lemon juice. ■ Place remaining shallots, mushrooms and dill sprigs on top of fish. ■ Dot with butter. ■ Combine clam juice or stock with white wine and pour around fish. ■ Loosely cover pan with foil and bake in preheated 450°F oven 20 to 30 minutes, until fish flakes when tested with a fork. ■ Remove fish to heated platter. If you or your dinner partner is handy with a deboning knife, show off those skills at the table while the other prepares the sauce. Otherwise, debone fish in kitchen and keep warm in low oven. ■ Strain pan juices into a heavy saucepan. ■ Discard dill sprigs but reserve shallots and mushrooms. ■ Add cream and boil over high heat to reduce sauce by one-third. ■ Whisk in beurre manié. Add more beurre manié if you like thicker sauce. ■ Season with salt, white pepper and lemon juice. ■ Add reserved shallots and mushrooms. ■ Pour some sauce over baked fish and serve remainder separately. ■ Garnish with whole dill sprigs and dilled lemon slices. ■ To make these, mince fresh dill and place on cutting board. ■ Gently fold a lemon slice in half and roll onto the minced dill to form a center band of dill. ■ Accompany with fluffy white rice seasoned with tiny leaves of fresh lemon thyme or chopped Italian parsley. Choose a colorful vegetable such as sautéed baby carrots or broiled tomato halves.

calories/serving: 628 (using fresh salmon)
protein, niacin: excellent
calcium, iron, vitamin A, thiamin: good
riboflavin: fair

BAKING FISH

The rule of thumb when baking fish is to bake it in a preheated 450°F oven, allowing 10 minutes per inch of thickness of fish, measured at its thickest point (20 minutes for frozen fish).

Meatless Dishes

MEATLESS CHILI

Serves 8
Preparation time: 25 minutes
Soaking time for beans: 1 hour
Cooking time: 1¼ hours

This filling and nutritious chili is rich in texture, fiber and color. Serve on rice or in heated bowls sprinkled with grated Monterey or Cheddar cheese. Garnish with sour cream and diced red onion. It's an ideal recipe to freeze in individual portions for future quick meals.

2½ cups	red kidney beans
	salt
1	small eggplant
2 Tb	vegetable oil
4	cloves garlic, minced
2	onions, coarsely chopped
1 can	(28 oz/796 mL) tomatoes
2	stalks celery, diced
2	carrots, diced
2	small green or yellow peppers, diced
¼ cup	chopped fresh parsley
2 Tb	tomato paste
2 Tb	lemon juice
2 Tb	chili powder
1 tsp	each dried cumin and oregano
dash	Tabasco sauce
	black pepper to taste
	grated cheese, sour cream, chopped red onion for garnish

▪ Pick over beans, discarding any stones or shrivelled beans. ▪ Rinse under cold running water. ▪ Place in a large kettle with 8 cups water and 2 teaspoons salt. ▪ Bring to boil and cook 3 minutes. ▪ Remove from heat, cover and let stand 1 hour. ▪ Cut eggplant into 1″ cubes, place in a sieve, sprinkle with salt and let stand 20 to 30 minutes. ▪ Drain and rinse beans. ▪ Return to pot with 5 cups fresh water and 1 teaspoon salt. ▪ Bring to boil, reduce heat to low, cover and simmer 30 minutes, stirring occasionally. ▪ Meanwhile heat oil and sauté garlic and onions in another saucepan for about 3 minutes or until soft. ▪ Add eggplant and sauté 5 minutes longer, stirring often. ▪ Stir in tomatoes with their liquid, celery, carrots, peppers, parsley, tomato paste, lemon juice, chili powder, cumin, oregano, Tabasco and

pepper to taste. ▪ Bring to boil, breaking up tomatoes as much as possible. ▪ Stir into beans after they have cooked 30 minutes. ▪ Cover, reduce heat to low and simmer together 30 minutes. ▪ Uncover and cook another 15 minutes, or until beans are tender and mixture is thick enough. ▪ Serve sprinkled with grated cheese.

MICROWAVE DIRECTIONS: Prepare and cook beans on stove top as per recipe. Prepare eggplant. In a 5-quart casserole combine garlic, onions, celery and carrots with can of chopped tomatoes. Cover, cook on High 5 to 6 minutes. Add green pepper, eggplant (well rinsed and drained), tomato paste and seasonings. Stir well and cook on High 6 to 7 minutes. Drain beans; stir well into vegetables. Cover and cook on High 15 to 20 minutes, stirring occasionally.

calories/serving: 296
vitamin C, niacin, iron, vegetable protein: excellent
fiber: high
vitamin A: good
low fat
low cal

SAVORY WEEKEND SCRAMBLED EGGS

Serves 4
Preparation time: 10 minutes
Cooking time: 5 to 10 minutes

It's fun to make something a little different on the weekend, but nothing too difficult.

1 Tb	butter
2	slices bacon, chopped
4	green onions, finely chopped
6	eggs
2 Tb	light cream
	salt and pepper to taste
½ cup	grated Cheddar cheese
1 Tb	chopped fresh parsley

▪ Heat butter in a frying pan. ▪ Add bacon and cook until just softened. ▪ Add green onions and continue cooking until bacon is just crisp. ▪ Drain off most of the fat from pan. ▪ Beat eggs gently with cream. ▪ Season with salt and pepper. ▪ Pour into pan. ▪ Stir gently until partially set. ▪ Fold in cheese and parsley and continue cooking until done. ▪ Adjust seasoning if necessary.

calories/serving: 239
protein: excellent
calcium, iron, vitamin A, niacin: good
vitamin C, riboflavin: fair

Tomato and Mushroom Omelet with Thyme

another 5 minutes or until juices evaporate. ▪ Quickly pour egg mixture over tomato mixture, rolling pan to evenly cover tomatoes. ▪ Sprinkle thyme over top. ▪ Cook over moderate heat 3 minutes, gently lifting sides with spatula to allow uncooked egg to run underneath. ▪ Gently fold omelet in half. ▪ Cook another 2 minutes, or until eggs are just set. Do not overcook. ▪ Serve on warm plates garnished with fresh thyme sprigs. To vary, sprinkle ¼ cup grated cheese (Cheddar, Fontina, Parmesan) over egg mixture in skillet and continue cooking as above.

calories/serving: 330
protein, vitamin A, vitamin C, niacin: excellent
iron, riboflavin: good
fiber: moderate

TOMATO AND MUSHROOM OMELET WITH THYME

Serves 2
Preparation time: 8 minutes
Cooking time: 10 to 12 minutes

This quick lunch or supper idea doubles easily for a weekend breakfast or brunch. Round out the meal with crusty French bread and a tossed salad with avocado.

4	large eggs, at room temperature
	salt and pepper to taste
1 tsp	water
2 Tb	butter
6	medium mushrooms, sliced
2	small, ripe tomatoes, peeled and chopped
1 tsp	chopped fresh thyme
	thyme sprigs for garnish (optional)

▪ Whisk eggs with salt, pepper and water in a small bowl. ▪ Set aside. ▪ Heat butter until bubbling in a medium non-stick skillet. ▪ Add mushrooms and cook over medium-high heat 2 minutes. ▪ Add chopped tomatoes and lower heat to medium. ▪ Cook

SPINACH AND CHEDDAR STRATA

Serves 4
Preparation time: 10 minutes
Standing time: 1 hour to overnight
Cooking time: 40 minutes

Cheese Strata is a simple, economical dish. This version is fancier, but it's still cheap and good.

8	slices whole wheat bread
2 Tb	butter
1 pkg	(10 oz/284 g) fresh spinach, lightly cooked and drained
1	small onion, chopped, *or* chopped chives to taste
1 cup	grated medium Cheddar cheese
3	eggs
1½ cups	milk
1 tsp	Worcestershire sauce
¼ tsp	cayenne pepper
¼ tsp	grated nutmeg
½ cup	grated Parmesan cheese
2 Tb	crushed dried parsley

▪ Butter a shallow baking dish just large enough to accommodate 4 slices of bread. ▪ Butter slices of bread as if you were going to make sandwiches and lay 4 of them in the dish, buttered side up. ▪ Chop cooked spinach. ▪ Mix with onion and Cheddar and spread mixture over bread. ▪ Cover with remaining bread slices, cut into triangles. ▪ Beat eggs with milk. ▪ Add Worcestershire sauce, cayenne and nutmeg. ▪ Pour over the bread. ▪ Cover and refrigerate at least 1 hour, or overnight. ▪ When ready to bake, preheat oven to 350°F. ▪ Mix Parmesan and parsley and sprinkle on top. ▪ Bake for about 40 minutes, until bubbly, set and golden.

calories/serving: 474
protein, calcium, iron, vitamin A, vitamin C, folate, niacin: excellent
thiamin, riboflavin: good

Baked Ratatouille

BAKED RATATOUILLE

Serves 8
Preparation time: 30 minutes
Cooking time: 1 hour

Ratatouille is a wonderful vegetable stew from the south of France. Rice would make a fine accompaniment.

1	**eggplant (about 1 lb)**
1 tsp	**salt**
½ cup	**olive oil**
2	**onions, sliced**
3	**cloves garlic, finely chopped**
2	**zucchini, sliced**
2	**sweet red peppers, sliced**
1 can	**(28 oz/796 mL) plum tomatoes**
	salt and pepper to taste
¼ tsp	**dried thyme**
1	**bay leaf**
¼ cup	**chopped fresh parsley**
½ cup	**black olives, preferably Kalamata**
3 Tb	**dry breadcrumbs**
1 cup	**grated Swiss cheese**
½ cup	**grated Parmesan cheese**

• Trim eggplant. • Slice crosswise into ½" slices. • Cut slices into halves. • Place in a colander, sprinkle with salt and allow to drain 15 minutes. • Meanwhile heat ¼ cup oil in a large skillet. • Add onions and garlic and cook until lightly browned. • Add zucchini and peppers. • Cook, stirring, about 5 minutes. • Add tomatoes, breaking them up with a spoon. • Add a little salt, pepper, thyme and bay leaf. • Cook 15 minutes, allowing some of the juice from the tomatoes to evaporate. • Taste and adjust seasoning if necessary. • Remove bay leaf. • Stir in parsley and olives. • Preheat broiler. • Pat eggplant slices dry. • Place eggplant in a single layer on a baking sheet. • Brush eggplant with some of the reserved oil. • Broil 4 to 5 minutes on each side until nicely browned. • Turn, brush again with oil and broil until browned. • Butter a 12" × 18" shallow casserole or baking dish. • Sprinkle with breadcrumbs. • Arrange eggplant in the bottom. • Spoon tomato-vegetable mixture on top. • Sprinkle with Swiss and then Parmesan cheese. This can all be done ahead. • Just before serving, bake in preheated 350°F oven for 30 to 40 minutes or until heated thoroughly.

calories/serving: 286
vitamin C: excellent
protein, calcium, vitamin A, niacin: good

Curried Fall Vegetables with Lentils

SWEET POTATO CASSEROLE

Serves 3 to 4 as main course
Preparation time: 30 minutes
Cooking time: 20 to 30 minutes

Inspired by northern Italian squash-stuffed ravioli and tortellini, this casserole mimics the wonderful taste while avoiding the sometimes fiddling work of stuffing small pasta.

2 cups	**cooked sweet potato, mashed (about 3 medium)**
4 Tb	**softened butter**
pinch	**grated nutmeg**
pinch	**ground cinnamon**
	salt and pepper to taste
2 Tb	**flour**
1½ cups	**milk**
¼ tsp	**salt**
1 cup	**freshly grated Parmesan cheese**
8 (approx.)	**broad lasagna noodles, cooked until just tender**
2 tsp	**firm butter in small pieces**

■ Butter a shallow 5-cup casserole or deep pie plate.
■ Combine mashed sweet potato, 2 tablespoons butter, nutmeg, cinnamon, salt and pepper. ■ Make sauce by melting 2 tablespoons butter, stirring in flour, cooking for 2 or 3 minutes, then whisking in milk and salt and continuing to cook until smooth and thickened. ■ Remove from heat and stir in half the grated Parmesan. ■ Spread one-quarter of the sauce on bottom of casserole, top with a single layer of lasagna, cut to fit, then sweet potatoes in one even layer. ■ Spread on another quarter of the sauce, then a second layer of lasagna, with rest of the sauce on top. ■ Finally sprinkle on rest of the Parmesan, dot with butter pieces and bake in preheated 350°F oven for about 20 minutes. ■ If top isn't golden enough at this point, slip dish under broiler for a minute. If your sweet potatoes were prepared ahead of time and chilled, you should add a few minutes to initial baking period. ■ Cut into squares or wedges to serve.

calories/serving: 671 for 3 servings
503 for 4 servings
protein, calcium, vitamin A, vitamin C, niacin: excellent
iron, thiamin, riboflavin: fair

CURRIED FALL VEGETABLES WITH LENTILS

Serves 4 to 6
Preparation time: 25 minutes
Cooking time: about 25 minutes

Lentils, which don't require the long soaking and cooking of dried beans and peas, form the low-cost, high-fiber, low-fat base for a quick and colorful curry. Served on rice, it provides protein equivalent to that of meat. Accompany with a favorite chutney and follow with a hot apple crisp or baked apples and yogurt.

1 cup	dried red lentils
¼ cup	vegetable oil
2	onions, chopped
2	cloves garlic, minced
1 Tb	ground cumin
1 Tb	ground coriander
2 tsp	turmeric
½ tsp	black pepper
¼ tsp	dried crushed chilies
2 Tb	lemon juice
2½ cups	chicken or vegetable stock
1	pepper squash or equivalent in other winter squash
1	small cauliflower
1	sweet red pepper
½ lb	green beans
1 tsp	salt or to taste
½ cup	peanuts

■ Pick over lentils for small stones or impurities. ■ Wash them in a sieve under cold running water. ■ Drain well and set aside. ■ Heat oil over medium heat in a large saucepan and sauté onions and garlic about 3 minutes or until softened. ■ Stir in cumin, coriander, turmeric, pepper and chilies. ■ Cook, stirring, 30 seconds. ■ Stir in lentils to coat well with oil. ■ Stir in lemon juice and stock. ■ Bring to boil. ■ Reduce heat, cover and simmer 5 minutes. ■ Meanwhile peel squash and cut into 1″ pieces. You should have about 4 cups. ■ Cut cauliflower into small florets, about 6 cups. ■ Cut red pepper into thin strips. ■ Trim beans and cut into halves. ■ Stir squash and cauliflower into lentil mixture. ■ Bring to boil again, reduce heat, cover and simmer another 5 minutes. ■ Stir in red pepper and beans and simmer 5 minutes longer. ■ Stir in salt and peanuts. ■ Cook, uncovered, about another 5 minutes, or until all vegetables are tender and lentils have formed a thick sauce. ■ Taste and adjust seasoning. ■ Serve on hot rice. The curry will thicken if made ahead of time and reheated. Add more stock or water if necessary. If you make it ahead, under-cook vegetables slightly.

MICROWAVE DIRECTIONS: Place onions, garlic and 2 tablespoons oil in a large casserole. Cook on High 2 minutes. Stir in seasonings, lentils, lemon juice and stock, mix well and cook 5 to 8 minutes on High, stirring once. Stir in cauliflower, squash and beans. Cover, cook on High 4 minutes, stir, continue cooking for further 5 minutes. Add red pepper, 1 cup more stock or water, peanuts and salt. Cover, cook on High 8 to 10 minutes, or until vegetables are tender.

calories/serving: 464 for 4 servings
309 for 6 servings
vegetable protein, vitamin A, niacin, vitamin C: excellent
fiber: high
iron, thiamin: good

BAKED VEGETABLE OMELET

Serves 6
Preparation time: 20 minutes
Cooking time: 30 minutes

A colorful oven dish for breakfast, brunch or supper.

1	small head romaine lettuce
1 cup	chopped fresh parsley
4	green onions, finely chopped
1	small onion, minced
8	eggs
2 Tb	flour
	salt to taste
5	fresh basil leaves, chopped, *or* 1 tsp dried basil
2 Tb	corn oil
2 Tb	grated Parmesan cheese

■ Chop lettuce and mix with parsley. ■ Add onions and mix well. All this can be done the day before and refrigerated, covered. ■ Beat eggs, adding flour, salt and basil. ■ Add to green vegetables and mix well. ■ Heat oil lightly in a round flat 8″ oven dish; add egg mixture and remove from heat. ■ Cover with aluminum foil and bake in preheated 350°F oven 30 minutes, or until omelet is almost firm. ■ Uncover, sprinkle omelet with cheese and broil for a few minutes. ■ Cut like a pie and serve with Tomato Coulis (see Savory Sauces) or your favorite relish.

calories/serving: 184
vitamin C: excellent
protein, iron, vitamin A, folate, niacin: good
calcium, thiamin, riboflavin: fair

Pasta

PASTA WITH QUICK TOMATO HERB SAUCE

Serves 4 to 6
Preparation time: 10 minutes
Cooking time: 20 to 25 minutes

Penne, rigatoni, spiral noodles or any other favorite dried pasta can be teamed with this spicy sauce. Use fresh herbs, if available.

6 cups	penne (quill-shaped noodles)

QUICK TOMATO HERB SAUCE:

2 Tb	vegetable oil
1	medium onion, chopped
1	large clove garlic, minced
1 can	(28 oz/796 mL) plum tomatoes
2 Tb	tomato paste
2 Tb	chopped fresh basil *or* 1 Tb dried
1 Tb	chopped fresh oregano *or* 1 tsp dried
1 tsp	crushed chili peppers, or to taste
1 Tb	red wine vinegar
dash	Tabasco sauce or to taste
	salt and pepper to taste
	chopped fresh basil or parsley for garnish
	grated Parmesan cheese (optional)

▪ Bring a large pot of salted water to rolling boil. ▪ Add penne noodles and cook, uncovered, about 8 to 10 minutes or until tender but firm to the fork. ▪ Meanwhile heat oil in large heavy saucepan. ▪ Add onion and garlic and cook, stirring, 2 or 3 minutes, to soften. ▪ Add tomatoes and tomato paste, basil, oregano, chili peppers and vinegar. ▪ Stir with wooden spoon to break up tomatoes. ▪ Simmer over medium heat 20 minutes or until slightly thickened. ▪ Taste sauce and add Tabasco for spicier sauce; add salt and pepper if needed. ▪ Keep warm while draining noodles. ▪ Add drained noodles to sauce. ▪ Toss to blend well and allow noodles to absorb sauce. ▪ Sprinkle with chopped fresh basil or parsley to garnish. ▪ Serve at once in heated bowls and pass Parmesan cheese separately.

calories/serving: 517
protein, iron, thiamin, riboflavin, niacin, vitamin C: excellent
calcium, vitamin A: good

FETTUCCINE WITH CLAM SAUCE

Serves 2
Preparation time: 15 minutes
Chilling time: several hours
Cooking time: 5 to 7 minutes

For those who adore pasta. The sauce can be white or, if you add a bit of tomato sauce, red.

18	cherrystone clams *or* 1 can (5 oz/142 g) clams
4 cups	water
	salt
½ lb	fettuccine
8 Tb	butter
1 Tb	finely chopped garlic
4 Tb	chopped fresh parsley
pinch	each thyme, basil and oregano
	salt and pepper to taste
½ cup	tomato sauce (optional)
1 cup	heavy cream
½ cup	grated Parmesan cheese

▪ If using fresh clams, chill for several hours in refrigerator or place briefly in freezer before opening: the muscle tends to relax when chilled. Then use a sharp clam knife to cut along the tender muscle that joins the two shells. Remove meat from shells. ▪ Chop clams. ▪ If using canned clams, drain and reserve liquid. ▪ Bring water and salt to boil and add liquid from canned clams. ▪ Add fettuccine. ▪ Cook until tender to the fork, 5 to 7 minutes. ▪ Meanwhile heat 6 tablespoons butter in a saucepan and add clams, garlic, parsley, thyme, basil, oregano, salt and pepper. ▪ Simmer 2 minutes. ▪ If you prefer a red clam sauce, blend in tomato sauce. ▪ Turn down heat and slowly stir in cream. ▪ When fettuccine is done, drain and place on a hot serving dish. ▪ Add sauce, remaining butter and cheese. ▪ Toss with a fork and spoon. ▪ Serve immediately.

calories/serving: 1,006
protein, calcium, vitamin A, niacin: excellent
iron, vitamin C: good
thiamin, riboflavin: fair

Creamy Cannelloni with Chicken and Almonds

CREAMY CANNELLONI WITH CHICKEN AND ALMONDS

Serves 8
Preparation time: 45 minutes
Cooking time: 60 to 70 minutes

This dish is ideal for no-fuss entertaining. You assemble it ahead of time, cover and refrigerate, then bake just before serving.

22	dried, precooked cannelloni shells
2	medium tomatoes, chopped
2 Tb	grated Parmesan cheese

SAUCE:

3 Tb	butter
1	medium onion, chopped
3 Tb	flour
1½ cups	chicken stock
1 cup	light cream
¼ tsp	salt
½ tsp	pepper
¾ cup	grated Swiss cheese

FILLING:

1½ cups	finely diced cooked chicken
1 pkg	(10 oz/300 g) frozen chopped spinach, thawed and well drained
¾ cup	Ricotta cheese
⅓ cup	sliced toasted almonds, chopped
¼ cup	grated Parmesan cheese
1	egg
¼ tsp	grated nutmeg

• To make sauce, melt butter in a medium saucepan over medium heat. • Sauté onion until tender, about 3 minutes. • Stir in flour and cook for 1 minute. • Add chicken stock, cream, salt and pepper. • Cook, stirring constantly, until sauce comes to boil and thickens, about 8 to 10 minutes. • Remove from heat and stir in Swiss cheese until melted. Set aside. • Cover surface of sauce with waxed paper to prevent skin from forming. • For filling, combine chicken, spinach, Ricotta, almonds, ¼ cup Parmesan cheese, egg and nutmeg in a medium bowl until well blended. • Stuff dried cannelloni shells with filling. • Pour thin layer of sauce over bottom of greased 13″ × 9″ baking pan. • Arrange stuffed cannelloni in single layer over sauce. • Sprinkle with chopped tomatoes, then pour remaining sauce evenly over pasta. • Sprinkle with 2 tablespoons Parmesan cheese. • Cover with aluminum foil. • Bake in preheated 350°F oven until tender, for 60 to 70 minutes, until pasta is soft and top is bubbling. If you stuff the cannelloni and assemble the dish the night before, storing it in the refrigerator, the cooking time can be cut to 35 minutes as the dried precooked cannelloni shells soften in the sauce. • Remove foil and place cannelloni under broiler, until golden, about 3 minutes.

MICROWAVE DIRECTIONS: To make sauce, combine butter and onion in a 4-cup glass measure. Microwave, uncovered, on High 2 to 3 minutes to soften onion. Stir in flour and microwave, uncovered, on High 40 to 60 seconds. Gradually stir in chicken stock, cream, salt and pepper. Microwave, uncovered, on High 5 to 7 minutes or until mixture comes to boil and thickens. Stir twice during cooking. Continue as above.

calories/serving: 386
protein, vitamin A, calcium, niacin: excellent
vitamin C, riboflavin: good
iron: fair
fiber: moderate

Pasta Sauce with Shrimp

PASTA SAUCE WITH SHRIMP

Serves 2
Preparation time: 10 minutes
Cooking time: 20 to 30 minutes

A great way to stretch expensive shellfish, especially as the recipe can be increased by doubling the other ingredients while using the same amount of shrimp. In Italy, as a rule, no grated cheese is served with seafood-based pasta sauces.

½ lb	medium shrimp, thawed (if frozen) and shelled
1	medium sweet red or green pepper, sliced thinly
	light olive or vegetable oil
1	large shallot, finely chopped
½	bay leaf
1	ripe tomato, peeled, seeded and roughly chopped, *or* 2 canned plum tomatoes
4 or 5	large mushrooms, sliced
	hot pepper flakes
	salt and pepper to taste
1	clove garlic, minced

▪ Sauté sweet pepper in a little oil in a saucepan until just tender, 2 to 3 minutes. ▪ Remove from pan. ▪ Add shallot, and more oil if necessary, and cook over low heat until limp and transparent, 4 to

5 minutes. ▪ Add bay leaf and tomato and simmer, stirring occasionally. ▪ When tomato mixture has cooked down to a saucelike consistency, 10 to 15 minutes, heat more oil in a skillet and sauté mushrooms 2 to 3 minutes, so they brown a little but don't begin to lose juice. ▪ Add mushrooms and reserved sweet pepper slivers to tomato, along with a shake or two of hot pepper flakes and salt and pepper to taste. ▪ Sauté garlic in skillet in more oil for 1 minute. ▪ Add shrimp, either whole or cut into two or three pieces, and cook about 2 minutes, stirring, until pink. ▪ Add to sauce. ▪ Remove bay leaf, adjust seasonings if necessary, then toss with spaghetti or fettuccine cooked al dente.

calories/serving: 285
protein, iron, vitamin C, niacin: excellent
calcium: good
vitamin A: fair

PASTA WITH SPICY TOMATO SAUCE

Serves 2
Preparation time: 5 minutes
Cooking time: 30 minutes

This spicy sauce needs a short dried pasta for best results. Penne is traditional, but spiral fusilli or other pastas work well. If pancetta (Italian cured bacon) is available, use it instead of regular bacon for a superb and different taste.

4	slices bacon
1 Tb	olive oil
1	small clove garlic, chopped
2 Tb	chopped onion
1 cup	canned plum tomatoes, drained and chopped
1 Tb	tomato paste
¼ tsp	hot pepper flakes or to taste
pinch	ground sage
	salt and pepper to taste
3 cups	penne or fusilli
¼ cup	grated Parmesan cheese

▪ Chop bacon coarsely. ▪ Heat olive oil in a skillet over medium heat. ▪ When hot, add bacon and sauté until crisp, about 5 minutes. ▪ Remove from skillet with slotted spoon. ▪ Set aside. ▪ Add garlic and onion to skillet and sauté until onion begins to color, about 5 minutes. ▪ Stir in tomatoes, tomato paste, hot pepper, sage, salt and pepper. ▪ Reduce heat to low. ▪ Cook gently for about 20 minutes, or until sauce is thick. ▪ Stir in bacon. ▪ Bring a large saucepan of salted water to boil. ▪ Add penne and cook until tender but firm to the fork, about 10 minutes. ▪ Drain. ▪ Combine pasta and sauce; stir together and cook 2 to 3 minutes. ▪ Serve cheese separately.

calories/serving: 547
protein, iron, thiamin, riboflavin, niacin, vitamin C: excellent
fiber: moderate

Skillet Pork and Pasta

SKILLET PORK AND PASTA

Serves 4 to 6
Preparation time: 10 minutes
Cooking time: 20 minutes

Vary this great family dinner by adding one or two of the following: chopped sweet red or green pepper, kernel corn, kidney beans, green beans, chopped carrot, fresh herbs and chopped parsley.

1 cup	uncooked tubular pasta: penne, macaroni or ziti
1 lb	ground pork
1	onion, chopped
1	clove garlic, minced
2	stalks celery, sliced
¼ lb	mushrooms, sliced (optional)
½ tsp	dried oregano
½ tsp	dried basil
1 can	(14 oz/398 mL) tomato sauce
1 pkg	(10 oz/284 g) frozen chopped spinach, thawed and thoroughly drained
1 cup	grated Cheddar or diced mozzarella cheese
	salt and pepper to taste
	chopped fresh Italian parsley for garnish

▪ Cook pasta in a large pot of boiling water until tender yet firm. ▪ Drain. ▪ Meanwhile cook pork in a large skillet or Dutch oven over medium heat for 3 to 4 minutes until browned. ▪ Pour off fat. ▪ Add onion and cook for 3 to 4 minutes until tender. ▪ Add garlic, celery, mushrooms, oregano and basil. ▪ Stir in tomato sauce. ▪ Simmer 10 minutes. ▪ Stir in spinach, pasta and ¾ cup cheese and cook until cheese melts. ▪ Add salt and pepper. ▪ Sprinkle remaining cheese on top. ▪ Garnish with chopped Italian parsley. This dish may be prepared in advance, spooned into baking dish, covered and reheated in preheated 350°F oven for 25 minutes.

calories/serving: 562 for 4 servings
375 for 6 servings
(using grated Cheddar cheese and enriched pasta)
protein, thiamin, niacin, vitamin A, vitamin C, potassium, iron: excellent
calcium, riboflavin: good

AL DENTE PASTA

Perfectly cooked pasta should be "al dente": tender but still with a "bite," and not at all mushy. Dried pasta will take 5 to 10 minutes, depending on shape; fresh will take 2 to 3 minutes. Test pasta halfway through cooking time by scooping out a piece and biting it. Keep testing until it's just right, then drain well.

CREAMY FETTUCCINE AND SMOKED SALMON

Serves 4
Preparation time: 10 minutes
Cooking time: 7 to 8 minutes

This creamy smoked salmon sauce is everything you ever wanted on fettuccine.

8 oz	smoked salmon, diced
4 Tb	butter
2 Tb	flour
pinch	each dried thyme, basil and oregano
6	sprigs fresh parsley, chopped
1	cube vegetable bouillon
1½ cups	heavy cream
	salt and pepper to taste
1 lb	fettuccine, cooked
1 small can	black lumpfish caviar or golden roe

■ Melt butter. ■ Add flour. ■ Blend and sauté for 2 to 3 minutes. ■ Add herbs and bouillon cube blended to a paste with a little water. ■ Add salmon and slowly blend in cream. ■ Heat through but do not boil. ■ Season to taste. ■ Pour sauce over cooked noodles and place caviar in the center.

calories/serving: 746
protein, vitamin A, niacin: excellent
thiamin, riboflavin: good
calcium, iron: fair

LINGUINE WITH OLIVES AND GARLIC

Serves 2
Preparation time: 5 minutes
Cooking time: 7 minutes

When it comes to pasta, simplest is often best. This makes a delicious main course for two, served with a salad and fresh bread, or will stretch to four as an appetizer.

½ lb	linguine
3 Tb	extra-virgin olive oil
2	cloves garlic, minced
12 (approx.)	ripe olives, pitted and roughly chopped
¼ cup	freshly grated Parmesan (plus more for the table)
	freshly ground black pepper
	fresh parsley, chopped

■ Cook linguine in a large saucepan of boiling, salted water for 5 to 7 minutes, until tender to the fork. ■ Meanwhile warm oil in a heavy pan. ■ Add garlic to oil and cook gently until it begins to color, but don't let it brown. ■ Stir in olives just to warm. ■ Drain cooked linguine, add to olive mixture, sprinkle cheese and pepper on top and toss well. ■ Sprinkle with parsley and pass more cheese at the table. ■ Use more garlic and fewer olives, if you prefer.

calories/serving: 449
protein, niacin: good
calcium: fair

PASTA SHELLS WITH SALMON AND BROCCOLI

Serves 4
Preparation time: 15 minutes
Cooking time: 25 minutes

The pasta shells can be cooked and the sauce mixed beforehand. Then at cooking time the assembly of this dinner-in-a-dish will be speedy.

1	bunch broccoli
2 cups	uncooked large pasta shells
1 can	(7.5 oz/213 g) red salmon
¾ cup	sour cream
2 Tb	sherry
2 tsp	lemon juice
2 tsp	Dijon mustard
1 tsp	Worcestershire sauce
1 tsp	chopped fresh dill or parsley
	salt and pepper to taste
pinch	grated nutmeg
½	sweet red pepper, coarsely chopped
¼ cup	grated Romano or Parmesan cheese

■ Wash and drain broccoli. ■ Cut into florets and cut tender stems into small pieces. ■ Cook in boiling water, or steam for 5 minutes. ■ Cool immediately under cold running water. This preserves the bright green color. ■ Cook pasta shells in boiling, salted water about 11 minutes until tender to the fork; drain. ■ Combine broccoli, pasta and undrained salmon in a shallow 6-cup casserole. ■ Make sauce by combining sour cream, sherry, lemon juice, mustard, Worcestershire sauce, dill, salt, pepper and nutmeg. ■ Pour over pasta mixture. ■ Sprinkle with red pepper. ■ Mix gently. ■ Sprinkle with cheese. ■ Cook in preheated 350°F oven 25 minutes until golden and bubbling. ■ Serve immediately.

calories/serving: 376
protein, calcium, vitamin C, niacin: excellent
iron, vitamin A: good
thiamin, riboflavin: fair
low fat

Creamy Fettuccine and Smoked Salmon

Vegetable Lasagna

AUTUMN FETTUCCINE

Serves 4
Preparation time: 20 minutes
Cooking time: about 5 minutes

Stir-fry a medley of harvest vegetables, while some pasta cooks, for a quick and colorful autumn supper.

2 Tb	**butter**
½ cup	**heavy cream**
1 cup	**Parmesan cheese**
2	**egg yolks**
¼ cup	**chopped fresh parsley**
½ tsp	**dried basil**
½ lb	**fettuccine**
	salt and black pepper to taste
2 Tb	**vegetable oil**
1 cup	**small broccoli florets**
1 cup	**small cauliflower florets**
1	**small zucchini, cut into thin slices**
1	**small red pepper, cut into strips**
1	**clove garlic, minced**
2 tbsp	**water**
½ cup	**coarsely chopped walnuts**
	additional Parmesan cheese

▪ Cream butter until light and fluffy. ▪ Gradually beat in cream. ▪ Stir in cheese, egg yolks, parsley and basil. ▪ Set aside. ▪ Cook fettuccine in a large pot of boiling, salted water until tender to the fork. ▪ Drain well and transfer to a large warm bowl. ▪ Stir in butter-cheese mixture to coat well. ▪ Add salt and pepper to taste and arrange on a large warm serving plate. ▪ While pasta cooks, heat oil in a wok or large skillet over medium-high heat. ▪ Stir-fry broccoli, cauliflower, zucchini, red pepper and garlic for 2 minutes. ▪ Stir in 2 tablespoons water, cover, reduce heat and steam 1 to 2 minutes, or until vegetables are tender but still firm. ▪ Arrange on top of sauced pasta and sprinkle with walnuts. ▪ Serve immediately with extra cheese.

calories/serving: 692
protein, calcium, iron, vitamin A, thiamin, riboflavin, niacin, vitamin C:
excellent
fiber: moderate

PASTA WITH SPICY SAUSAGE AND CREAM

Serves 4
Preparation time: 5 minutes
Cooking time: 10 to 15 minutes

Fresh pasta has the best flavor and cooks quickly – just 2 to 3 minutes – but dried pasta can be used with good results. Fish lovers can substitute two 7-oz cans drained tuna for the sausage.

12 oz	**fresh pasta *or* 8 oz dried (any shape)**
2 Tb	**butter**
1 cup	**sliced button mushrooms**
8 oz	**kolbassa or Polish sausage, cubed**
1 cup	**heavy cream**
2	**eggs, beaten**
2 Tb	**chopped fresh parsley**
½ tsp	**paprika**
¼ tsp	**grated nutmeg**
	salt and pepper to taste
	Parmesan cheese to taste

▪ Cook pasta in plenty of boiling salted water until tender but firm. ▪ Drain well. ▪ Meanwhile melt butter and sauté mushrooms for 2 to 3 minutes until soft. ▪ Add sausage and cook gently until heated through. ▪ Beat together remaining ingredients, except Parmesan cheese, in a small bowl. ▪ Add cream mixture, mushrooms and sausage to drained pasta and toss over gentle heat until sauce thickens slightly and pasta is well coated. ▪ Serve at once sprinkled with Parmesan cheese.

calories/serving: 762 with sausage
725 with tuna
protein, niacin: excellent
iron, vitamin A, thiamin: good
calcium, riboflavin: fair

VEGETABLE LASAGNA

Serves 10 to 12
Preparation time: 1 hour
Cooking time: 1 hour

This moist and hearty lasagna is perfect for a party because it's a do-ahead dish everyone will love. Or make it for your family and freeze the leftover portion for another time.

2 Tb	vegetable oil
2	onions, chopped
2	cloves garlic, minced
½ lb	mushrooms, sliced
1	green pepper, chopped
1 can	(28 oz/796 mL) plum tomatoes
1 can	(14 oz/398 mL) tomato sauce
2	carrots, shredded
¼ cup	chopped fresh parsley
1 tsp	each dried basil and oregano
	sugar and salt to taste
¼ tsp	black pepper
pinch	crushed dried chilies
1 pkg	(10 oz/284 g) spinach
9 to 15	lasagna noodles, depending on size
2	eggs
1 lb	low-fat Ricotta cheese
pinch	grated nutmeg
1 lb	partly skimmed mozzarella cheese, shredded
1 cup	grated Parmesan cheese

■ Heat oil in a medium saucepan over medium heat. ■ Add onions, garlic, mushrooms and pepper. ■ Cook, stirring often, for 5 minutes. ■ Add tomatoes and their juice, cutting up tomatoes as finely as possible. ■ Add tomato sauce, carrots, parsley, basil, oregano, sugar, salt, pepper and chilies. ■ Bring to boil, cover, reduce heat and simmer 30 minutes, stirring occasionally. ■ Meanwhile cook spinach in a covered heavy saucepan in just the water that clings to its leaves after washing. ■ Cook for 2 to 5 minutes or until just wilted. ■ Drain well in a sieve and when cool enough to handle, squeeze out any moisture with your hands. ■ Chop finely and set aside. ■ Cook noodles in a large pot of boiling, salted water according to package directions. ■ Drain, rinse with cold water, drain again and spread out on clean tea towels on a flat surface. ■ Blend eggs, Ricotta cheese, nutmeg and cooked spinach in a food processor until fairly smooth. ■ Spread one-quarter of tomato sauce in the bottom of a greased 13″ × 9″ baking dish. ■ Arrange single layer of noodles on top. ■ Spread with half of Ricotta mixture,

then one-quarter of tomato sauce, one-third of mozzarella and one-third of Parmesan. ■ Repeat these layers once. ■ Arrange remaining noodles on top, spread with remaining tomato sauce and sprinkle with remaining cheese. ■ The dish will be quite full but will accommodate everything. The recipe can be made ahead, covered and refrigerated up to 24 hours. ■ Bake, uncovered, in preheated 350°F oven for 30 minutes. ■ Cover with foil and bake another 10 to 15 minutes if previously refrigerated. ■ Let stand 10 minutes before cutting into squares to serve.

MICROWAVE DIRECTIONS: Cook noodles as per recipe directions. Cook spinach in a large casserole on High 3 to 4 minutes. Drain well and chop. Place onions, garlic, mushrooms and pepper in a 16-cup dish and cook on High 3 to 5 minutes. Drain tomatoes, add to onions with tomato sauce, remaining vegetables and seasonings. Cover; cook on High 10 minutes. Prepare spinach and egg mixture. Arrange lasagna layers in an ungreased dish, cover and cook for 5 minutes on High, then 15 to 20 minutes on Medium. Let stand 10 to 15 minutes.

FREEZING DIRECTIONS: If freezing baked lasagna, place in foil in baking dish same size as lasagna, or in individual servings or servings for 3 or 4. Seal foil tightly around lasagna and place in freezer until solid. Remove wrapped frozen food to store in freezer and return dish to your cupboard. Thawing isn't necessary; slip lasagna out of foil and back into baking dish. It will take about 1½ hours at 350°F, covered. If you want to thaw lasagna before reheating, defrost in refrigerator and reheat 20 to 25 minutes in preheated 350°F oven. If reheating in a microwave, shield edges by molding narrow strips of foil around sides of dish, overlapping top and bottom edges. Cover with waxed paper and defrost in microwave 20 minutes for 8″ square. Let stand 10 minutes; then cook on High 15 to 20 minutes. Let stand 10 minutes before serving. For an 8-oz serving, defrost 10 minutes; let stand 5 minutes and cook on Med/High 4 to 5 minutes. Let stand, covered, 5 minutes before serving with garlic bread and a green salad.

calories/serving: 427 for 10 servings
356 for 12 servings
protein, calcium, iron, vitamin A, niacin, vitamin C: excellent
thiamin, riboflavin: good

Savory Sauces

APRICOT DIPPING SAUCE

Makes 2 cups
Preparation time: 20 minutes
Cooking time: about 15 minutes

Serve this flavorful sauce with your favorite recipe for chicken wings or strips. It's also good for glazing barbecued chicken.

12	apricots
½ cup	water
1 Tb	butter
¼ cup	diced sweet red pepper
1	clove garlic, minced
¼ cup	brown sugar
1 Tb	lemon juice
1 tsp	each Dijon mustard and paprika
	salt and pepper to taste

■ Blanch apricots in boiling water for a few seconds; plunge into cold water. ■ Peel, cut into halves, remove pits and combine with ½ cup water in a small saucepan. ■ Bring to boil, reduce heat and simmer over low heat 5 to 10 minutes or until soft. ■ Purée, with liquid, in a blender or food processor. ■ Set aside. ■ Melt butter in a saucepan over medium-low heat and add red pepper and garlic. ■ Cook, stirring often, 5 minutes or until softened. ■ Do not let brown. ■ Stir in apricot purée, brown sugar, lemon juice, mustard, paprika, salt and pepper. ■ Turn heat to medium and cook, uncovered, 5 minutes or until thickened.

calories/tablespoon: 21
vitamin A: fair

APPLE MINT SAUCE

Serves 4
Cooking time: 5 minutes

This easy make-ahead sauce is best served warm.

¾ cup	apple jelly
2 Tb	crème de menthe
2 tsp	Dijon mustard

■ Combine apple jelly, crème de menthe and mustard in a small saucepan. ■ Warm gently, stirring, until jelly melts and mixes with other ingredients. Pour into small container. ■ Keeps in refrigerator for weeks. At serving time, warm again and pour into a small sauceboat.

calories/serving: about 110

CORIANDER BUTTER

Serves 4 to 6
Preparation time: 5 minutes
Refrigeration time: 20 minutes

For a special barbecue dinner, top grilled steaks or lamb chops with a pat of flavored butter. Instead of coriander you can use any fresh herb to taste.

½ tsp	coriander seeds
6	peppercorns
¼ cup	butter
1 tsp	minced chives or green onion
1 tsp	brandy
¼ tsp	Dijon mustard
1 Tb	minced fresh coriander or parsley

■ Grind coriander and pepper in a spice grinder, minichop or coffee grinder. ■ Combine ground spices, butter, chives, brandy, mustard and coriander in a small bowl or food processor. ■ Mix well. ■ Place on waxed paper and roll into cylindrical shape. ■ Refrigerate until firm. ■ Cut into rounds and serve on top of barbecued meats.

calories/serving: 87 for 4 servings
58 for 6 servings

CUCUMBER AND YOGURT SAUCE OR DIP

Makes 2 cups
Preparation time: 20 minutes

This is called Tzatziki in Greece, and it's a traditional sauce for fish or fried foods. It makes a wonderful salad or dip for raw vegetables too. It can be thin or thick, depending on the amount of cucumber.

1 or 2	cloves garlic to taste
pinch	salt
1 tsp	red wine vinegar
1 Tb	olive oil
1½ cups	thick plain yogurt
¼ to 1	English cucumber, unpeeled
1 tsp	chopped fresh dill (optional)

■ Mince garlic and mix thoroughly with salt, vinegar, oil and yogurt. ■ Refrigerate. ■ Half an hour before serving, seed and grate cucumber. ■ Squeeze out as much liquid from grated cucumber as possible. ■ Add to yogurt mixture. ■ Stir in dill, if you wish. ■ Chill.

calories/recipe: 400 (using 2% yogurt)
calcium, riboflavin: fair

BARBECUE BASTING SAUCE

Makes 2 cups
Preparation time: 10 minutes
Cooking time: 35 to 40 minutes

Use this versatile sauce to baste beef roasts, spare ribs, pork chops or burgers while they cook over the coals. Serve any remainder on the side, or reserve, refrigerated, for future barbecues.

¼ cup	butter
2 Tb	chopped onion
1	clove garlic, minced
2 cups	tomato juice
1 tsp	ground mustard
2 Tb	white wine vinegar
1 Tb	Worcestershire sauce
1 tsp	tomato paste
1 tsp	each chopped fresh basil, chopped fresh oregano, chopped fresh parsley, salt, black pepper, cayenne pepper and paprika or to taste

▪ Melt butter in a heavy saucepan. ▪ Add onion and cook over medium heat, stirring, until soft, about 3 minutes. ▪ Add garlic and cook 30 seconds. ▪ Add remaining ingredients, stir and let come to a boil. ▪ Turn heat to low and simmer 25 to 30 minutes or until slightly thickened. Sauce will thicken more after refrigeration. Keeps well in covered container in refrigerator up to 2 weeks.

calories/tablespoon: 18

MINT SAUCE

Makes 1 cup
Preparation time: 5 minutes
Cooking time: 5 minutes
Standing time: 15 to 20 minutes

This is especially good with lamb.

1 cup	wine vinegar or raspberry vinegar
½ cup	sugar or more to taste
1 cup	packed fresh mint sprigs, well washed
2 Tb	chopped fresh mint

▪ Bring vinegar and sugar to boil in a small saucepan, stirring until sugar is dissolved. ▪ Place mint in a bowl. ▪ Pour vinegar over mint and let stand to infuse with mint essence 15 to 20 minutes or until at room temperature. ▪ Strain through a sieve and add chopped mint. ▪ Serve warm or at room temperature. Keeps well, refrigerated, several weeks.

calories/tablespoon: 26

Mediterranean Sauce

MEDITERRANEAN SAUCE

Makes about 4 cups
Preparation time: 20 minutes
Cooking time: 45 minutes

A rich sauce to make when those large, fragrant tomatoes are cheap and plentiful. The sauce can be frozen, but if you plan to freeze it, omit the garlic and herbs and add them after thawing.

2 Tb	olive oil
2	onions, chopped
1	large clove garlic, crushed
3 lbs	ripe tomatoes, roughly chopped
2 Tb	tomato paste
2 tsp	sugar
2 tsp	red wine vinegar
1 tsp	dried oregano
1 tsp	dried basil
	salt and pepper to taste

▪ Heat oil in a large pan and fry onions and garlic over medium heat until onions are soft but not brown. ▪ Add remaining ingredients and bring to boil. ▪ Reduce heat, cover and simmer for 40 minutes, stirring occasionally. ▪ Remove from heat and leave to cool slightly. ▪ Process tomato mixture in a food processor or blender until smooth, then put through a food mill to remove seeds if you wish. ▪ Keeps for 1 week in refrigerator or up to 6 months in freezer.

calories/cup: 180
vitamin C: excellent
vitamin A: fair

Pizza Toppings

MUSTARD SAUCE

Makes 1⅔ cups
Preparation time: 5 minutes
Cooking time: 6 minutes

This piquant sauce keeps several weeks in the refrigerator. When you aren't spreading it on meat, use it to add zest to egg sandwiches or salad dressings.

2	eggs
⅔ cup	firmly packed brown sugar
⅓ cup	dry mustard
1 Tb	flour
¼ tsp	salt
⅔ cup	white vinegar
⅓ cup	water
2 Tb	butter

▪ Beat eggs until frothy in top of double boiler. ▪ Stir in brown sugar, mustard, flour and salt. ▪ Gradually stir in vinegar and water. ▪ Place over simmering water and cook, stirring constantly, until mixture thickens and bubbles, about 6 minutes. ▪ Remove from heat and stir in butter. ▪ Stir occasionally as sauce cools to prevent a skin from forming. ▪ When cool, store in covered jar in refrigerator.

MICROWAVE DIRECTIONS: Combine beaten eggs, dry ingredients, vinegar and water in an oven-proof bowl. Cook on High 3 to 4 minutes, stirring briskly after each minute. Stir in butter.

calories/tablespoon: about 40

PIZZA TOPPINGS

The ingredients listed below can be used in any combination. Spread them over tomato sauce on your favorite pizza crust. Many of these toppings can be prepared earlier in the day for quick assembly. The cheeses should always be on top of the pizza. Leftover pizza can be frozen for several weeks and reheated prior to serving.

2 cups	cooked shrimp
½ cup	thinly sliced pepperoni
4	anchovy fillets, finely chopped
2	large tomatoes, thinly sliced
1 cup	thinly sliced fresh mushrooms
2	green peppers, thinly sliced
½ cup	thinly sliced pitted green or black olives
1	small zucchini, thinly sliced
½ cup	grated Parmesan cheese
2 cups	grated mozzarella cheese
1 cup	grated Emmenthal or Gruyère cheese

Spread as many ingredients as you like over the pizza base and top with cheese. Bake in preheated 400°F oven for 20 to 30 minutes, until cheese is texture you like.

calories/slice: average of 261 for 8 servings (using Basic Pizza Dough and three toppings)
protein, calcium: excellent
vitamin A, vitamin C, niacin: good
iron, thiamin, riboflavin: fair

HOMEMADE MAYONNAISE

Makes 1½ cups
Preparation time: about 5 minutes

This quick blender method uses a whole egg. Make sure all ingredients are at room temperature.

1	egg
1 tsp	dry mustard
1 tsp	salt
1 tsp	sugar
pinch	cayenne pepper
¼ cup	olive or vegetable oil
1 cup	vegetable oil
3 Tb	lemon juice

▪ Put egg, mustard, salt, sugar, cayenne and ¼ cup olive oil in blender and blend at high speed. ▪ While blending, slowly add another ½ cup oil. ▪ Add lemon juice. ▪ Continue to blend and add remaining ½ cup oil. ▪ Blend until thick.

calories/tablespoon: 60

TOMATO SAUCE

Makes 3 cups
Preparation time: 15 minutes
Cooking time: 1 hour

Delicious spread on pizzas with toppings and cheese. Freeze unused sauce for later.

3 Tb	olive oil
1 cup	finely chopped onion
3 to 4	cloves garlic, finely chopped
1 can	(28 oz/796 mL) Italian plum tomatoes, coarsely chopped but not drained
1 can	(5.5 oz/156 mL) tomato paste
1 Tb	dried oregano, crumbled
1 Tb	finely chopped fresh basil *or* 1 tsp dried basil, crumbled
1	bay leaf
2 tsp	sugar
1 tsp	salt
	freshly ground black pepper to taste

▪ Heat oil in a large enamel or stainless steel saucepan and cook chopped onions, stirring frequently, until translucent but not brown, about 7 minutes. ▪ Add chopped garlic and cook for another 1 or 2 minutes, stirring constantly. ▪ Stir in coarsely chopped tomatoes and liquid, tomato paste, oregano, basil, bay leaf, sugar, salt and a few grindings of pepper. ▪ Bring sauce to boil and turn heat to low. ▪ Simmer, uncovered, stirring occasionally, for about 1 hour. When finished, sauce should be thick and fairly smooth. ▪ Remove bay leaf. ▪ Adjust seasonings, if necessary. If you want a smoother sauce, purée through a food mill or rub through a sieve with a wooden spoon.

MICROWAVE DIRECTIONS: Cook oil and onion in a large casserole on High 2 to 3 minutes or until soft. Stir in remaining ingredients. Cook, covered, on High until mixture boils. Remove lid, continue cooking on Medium for about 30 minutes, or until sauce has thickened.

calories/cup: 231
vitamin A: fair

HOW TO UNCURDLE MAYONNAISE

If your homemade mayonnaise curdles, toss an ice cube into the bowl and continue to beat the mixture; it will miraculously uncurdle.

TOMATO COULIS

Makes about ½ cup
Preparation time: 12 minutes
Cooking time: 15 minutes

Homemade tomato sauce can enliven soups or spaghetti sauces. It can be made a day ahead. Canned or frozen tomatoes may be used instead of fresh.

2	cloves garlic, minced
6 Tb	minced onion
2 Tb	olive oil
4 or 5	ripe tomatoes, stemmed
2 tsp	dried thyme
	salt and pepper to taste
	chicken or vegetable broth

▪ Heat garlic and onion in oil a few minutes, just enough to soften. ▪ Chop tomatoes into small pieces and add to onions. ▪ Add thyme and cook on low heat, 10 to 15 minutes or until mixture thickens. ▪ Remove from heat and purée in blender. ▪ Add salt and pepper. ▪ Put purée back in saucepan and heat again just before serving. ▪ If it is too thick, add 1 to 2 tablespoons of liquid (broth or water).

calories/½ cup: 65
vitamin C: excellent
vitamin A: fair

WINE SAUCE FOR POACHED SALMON

Serves 4
Preparation time: 5 minutes

If you decide to serve poached salmon hot, wine sauce is the perfect complement.

2 Tb	butter
2 Tb	flour
1	sprig fresh parsley, chopped
2 Tb	lemon juice
¼ cup	dry white wine
1 cup	fish stock, strained
1 cup	light cream
	salt and pepper to taste
	lemon wedges and parsley for garnish

▪ Add flour to butter in a heavy skillet and brown lightly. ▪ Add parsley, lemon juice, white wine and strained fish stock. ▪ Simmer for 4 to 5 minutes and slowly add cream. Don't let cream boil. ▪ Add salt and pepper. ▪ Pour over poached salmon. ▪ Garnish with lemon wedges and parsley.

calories/serving: 161

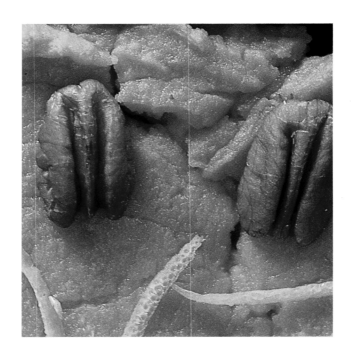

VEGETABLES AND SIDE DISHES

What do you suppose would happen if we told children vegetables were *bad* for them? Do children just naturally hate vegetables or do we teach them this reaction by our own behavior?

"Eat up your vegetables or you don't get any dessert!"

"Eat up your vegetables. They're good for you."

How many of us grew up with those dreaded words ringing in our ears? And how many of us continued to resist vegetables all our lives as a result? And how many of us pass our anti-vegetable attitudes on to our children?

To add to our prejudice, the vegetables of our childhood were often watery canned peas, turned gray from sitting on the stove too long. Besides being presented as a penance for the reward of dessert, vegetables were frequently overcooked. My mother's generation believed they were indigestible unless soft, and they often overshot soft and achieved mush.

In winter we rarely saw any but root vegetables where I grew up. Carrots, potatoes, turnip, squash, beets and parsnips were the everyday fare, usually supplemented with canned peas, beans or corn. There was nothing wrong with these wholesome vegetables, and we were frequently told we should be grateful to have

them when "the children in Africa (or China or wherever the current famine was occurring) would be glad to get them."

We knew all this was true and we felt vaguely guilty about it but would gladly have mailed all the vegetables on our plate to India if it meant we could get immediately to the pie or cake.

When I look back on those buttery mounds of mashed turnip, those fluffy baked potatoes topped with melting butter or thick cream, those carrot and parsnip slices glazed in brown sugar, I don't believe I could possibly have disliked them. Was it all a pose to pretend I didn't want to eat them so I could improve my bargaining position regarding dessert? Is it somehow one of the unspoken agreements among children that you must never let grown-ups know you actually *like* vegetables? I remember liking squash — especially dry, mealy Hubbard squash whipped (again with butter) and baked in the oven. I even liked spinach, though it's doubtful if slivers under my fingernails would have made me admit it to the other kids. Is one of the qualifications for fitting into the society of children that you exclaim "Ugh" whenever vegetables are mentioned?

Today, fast trains and trucks with climate-controlled

storage cars speed all manner of exotic and out-of-season vegetables and fruits from warmer regions or sun-trapping greenhouses to our markets. There's almost no limit to the varieties we can buy, at least in the large centers of population, if we're able to pay the price. We take it for granted now that we can have eggplant and zucchini, green beans, kohlrabi, cucumbers, tomatoes (pink and hard though they be) and an array of crunchy greens all winter.

With the fashion for vegetables cooked only until the edge is taken off the crunch, we've discovered just how beautiful they can be on a plate. A couple of crisp snow peas, a spear of barely steamed carrot, a spray of green onion, a fan of broccoli or cauliflower florets can be arranged on a plate to resemble a painter's still life. Some plates of vegetative arrangements I've been served were so lovely to look at that my urge was to lacquer them and hang them on the wall.

Restaurant reviewers frequently judge the quality of a meal and the skill of a chef by the tastiness of the vegetables they're served. It's not a bad way to assess, since attention to detail and a commitment to bringing out the best in ingredients is what makes a good cook. Usually, the cook who treats vegetables tenderly so that they arrive at the table with a little of their crunch still intact will be equally considerate of the other courses.

One of the signs of adulthood may be the capacity to enjoy vegetables openly and aboveboard, as they deserve. The fashion for overcooking is waning; now the hazard is more likely to be a vegetable so undercooked that you can't pick it up with a fork. Raw vegetables, of course, are a fine and tasty thing when you *expect* them — but a little unnerving when you assume they're cooked only to find your knife bounces instead of cuts.

Vegetables present the cook with an infinite richness of raw material from which to create simple, beautiful and nourishing main dishes or side dishes for any meal. We hope the delicious recipes in the following section may even persuade your children to like vegetables. But don't count on it; they have their reputations to protect. What would the other kids say?!

POTATO CROQUETTE CASSEROLE

Serves 8
Preparation time: 20 minutes
Cooking time: 45 minutes

This is a make-ahead version of an all-time favorite potato dish.

2 lbs	potatoes (6 to 8 medium)
¼ cup	butter
1	onion, chopped
2	cloves garlic, chopped
⅓ cup	heavy cream
1 cup	grated Cheddar cheese
	salt and pepper to taste
pinch	grated nutmeg
TOPPING:	
1 cup	dry breadcrumbs
1 cup	sliced almonds
¼ cup	butter, melted

■ Peel potatoes and cut into 2″ pieces. ■ Cook in boiling, salted water for 20 to 25 minutes or until tender. ■ Meanwhile melt ¼ cup butter and cook onion and garlic until tender and very fragrant. ■ Drain potatoes thoroughly. ■ Mash potatoes and beat in onion-garlic mixture, cream, cheese, salt, pepper and nutmeg. ■ Combine breadcrumbs with almonds and butter for topping. ■ Butter an 8″ square casserole. ■ Sprinkle about ½ of crumb mixture on the bottom and sides. ■ Spoon in potato mixture. ■ Sprinkle remaining crumbs on top. ■ Just before serving, bake in 350°F oven for 20 to 30 minutes or until heated thoroughly. ■ If you wish, place under broiler for a minute to brown slightly.

calories/serving: 408
protein, calcium, iron, niacin, vitamin C: good
vitamin A, riboflavin: fair

ZUCCHINI AND TOMATO SAUTÉ

Serves 4
Preparation time: 5 minutes
Cooking time: 8 to 10 minutes

4	small to medium zucchini
	salt
1 Tb	vegetable oil
1 tsp	butter
1	clove garlic, minced
2	green onions, chopped
½ cup	tomato sauce
	salt and pepper to taste

■ Wash zucchini; trim and slice into ¼″ rounds. ■ Sprinkle with salt and let stand in a colander while preparing other ingredients. ■ Heat oil with butter in a skillet. ■ Over medium heat, cook garlic and onions, stirring to soften, 1 minute. ■ Rinse zucchini under cold running water (to rinse off bitter juices). ■ Squeeze or pat very dry. If zucchini is very fresh and young, this step can be eliminated. ■ Add zucchini to skillet and cook, stirring, 3 to 4 minutes. ■ Stir in tomato sauce, salt and pepper, and continue cooking another 3 to 5 minutes, or until zucchini is tender. ■ Serve at once, or keep warm over low heat.

MICROWAVE DIRECTIONS: Prepare zucchini. Microwave garlic, green onions and butter for 2 minutes on High in casserole. Add zucchini and tomato sauce and cook on High 4 to 5 minutes.

calories/serving: 74
vitamin C: good

POTATO CASSEROLE WITH PARSLEY CRUMB TOPPING

Serves 8
Preparation time: 20 minutes
Cooking time: 30 minutes
Reheating time: 30 minutes

This make-ahead potato dish is ideal for entertaining.

8	potatoes
¼ cup	butter
1 pkg	(8 oz/250 g) cream cheese, cut into small cubes
¾ cup	sour cream
	salt and pepper to taste
¼ cup	each fine fresh breadcrumbs and chopped fresh parsley

■ Peel and cook potatoes in boiling salted water in a covered saucepan for about 30 minutes or until tender. ■ Drain well and return to heat briefly to dry. ■ Mash potatoes with half the butter. ■ Add cream cheese, sour cream, salt and pepper. ■ With electric hand mixer, beat until creamy. ■ Spoon into a greased 8-cup casserole. ■ Melt remaining butter and stir together with breadcrumbs and parsley. ■ Sprinkle evenly over top of potato mixture. ■ If you wish, let cool, cover and refrigerate overnight. ■ Bring to room temperature 30 minutes before reheating. ■ Bake in preheated 350°F oven, covered, 20 minutes. ■ Uncover and continue to bake about 10 minutes longer or until hot throughout.

calories/serving: 311
vitamin A, vitamin C, niacin: good

PEAS SAUTÉED WITH LETTUCE

Serves 8
Preparation time: 10 minutes
Cooking time: 4 to 5 minutes

Simple green peas are lifted to company style and buttery goodness in this quick and easy dish. Be sure lettuce and onions are dry before sautéing.

¼ cup	butter
1 pkg	(10 oz/284 g) frozen green peas
6	green onions, sliced
2 Tb	chicken stock
1 tsp	sugar
1	small head Boston lettuce, finely shredded
	salt and pepper to taste

▪ Melt butter in a large skillet over medium heat. ▪ Add frozen peas and onions. ▪ Cook, stirring, 2 minutes. ▪ Stir in chicken stock and sugar. ▪ Cook 1 more minute. ▪ Turn heat to high. ▪ Add lettuce and cook, tossing, until wilted and much of the liquid has evaporated, 1 to 2 minutes. ▪ Peas should still be bright green and crisp, lettuce should still have some bite. ▪ Season with salt and pepper and serve immediately.

calories/serving: 84
vitamin C: good

CELERY AMANDINE

Serves 6 to 8
Preparation time: 15 minutes
Cooking time: 10 minutes

Almonds can be browned ahead of time and celery sliced and stored in a plastic bag in the refrigerator.

¼ cup	butter or margarine
⅔ cup	slivered blanched almonds
2	chicken bouillon cubes
8 cups	diagonally sliced celery
2 Tb	grated onion
1 tsp	sugar
¼ tsp	black pepper
¼ tsp	garlic powder
¼ tsp	ground ginger

▪ Heat butter or margarine in a large heavy skillet. ▪ Add almonds and cook gently, stirring until lightly browned. ▪ Crumble bouillon cubes into mixture and add all remaining ingredients, stirring to blend. ▪ Cover and cook, stirring occasionally, until celery is tender-crisp, about 7 minutes. ▪ Serve immediately.

calories/serving: 155 for 6 servings
116 for 8 servings
vitamin C: good
niacin: fair
fiber: moderate

Buttered Green Beans with Almonds

BUTTERED GREEN BEANS WITH ALMONDS

Serves 8
Preparation time: 15 minutes
Cooking time: 15 to 20 minutes

These beans have a wonderful flavor from the butter that has been cooked to a nutty brown stage. Use unsalted butter as it is less likely to burn.

2 lbs	green beans
3 Tb	unsalted butter
⅓ cup	sliced almonds
1 Tb	lemon juice
	salt to taste

▪ Trim beans so that they are all the same length. ▪ Bring a large pot of water to boil and cook beans 3 minutes or until bright green but still very crunchy. ▪ Drain. ▪ Chill in ice water and then pat dry. ▪ Arrange in a buttered oven-proof dish. ▪ Melt butter in a medium skillet and add almonds. ▪ Allow nuts to brown very slowly until golden. ▪ Add lemon juice and salt. ▪ Spread butter-almond mixture over beans and reheat for 10 to 15 minutes in preheated 350°F oven.

calories/serving: 96
vitamin C: good
fiber: moderate
vitamin A: fair

Grilled Zucchini with Tomatoes, Savory and Thyme

GRILLED ZUCCHINI WITH TOMATOES, SAVORY AND THYME

Serves 4
Preparation time: 20 minutes
Cooking time: 10 minutes

This simple dish is good with grilled lamb or veal chops, or barbecued chicken.

2½ cups	sliced, unpeeled zucchini (¼" rounds)
1 tsp	chopped fresh savory
1 tsp	chopped fresh thyme
1 cup	coarsely chopped tomatoes
	salt and pepper to taste

▪ Place zucchini in a square of heavy foil. ▪ Sprinkle with savory and thyme. ▪ Place tomatoes on top and add salt and pepper. ▪ Seal edges tightly, then twist ends. ▪ Barbecue on grill 4" to 5" from coals for 10 minutes, turning often.

calories/serving: 32
vitamin C: excellent
fiber: moderate
low fat
low cal

SHREDDED RUTABAGA TURNIP

Serves 12
Preparation time: 30 minutes (10 minutes using a food processor)
Cooking time: 35 minutes

Grating and sautéeing the humble rutabaga turnip transforms it into a completely different vegetable. The sharp cabbage flavor disappears in favor of a sweet squashlike taste.

2	rutabaga turnips
½ cup	butter
	salt and freshly ground pepper
	ground cinnamon (optional)

▪ Peel and grate turnips. ▪ Melt butter in a Dutch oven or large skillet. ▪ Add grated turnip and stir over medium heat until it starts to wilt and is reduced in volume. ▪ Continue frying over medium-low heat, stirring occasionally, until soft. You may serve it at this stage, or continue cooking until slightly crisp and caramelized. ▪ Season to taste with salt and pepper. ▪ Sprinkle with cinnamon if you wish.

calories/serving: 107
vitamin C: excellent
fiber: moderate

GREEN BEANS WITH BACON AND PARMESAN CHEESE

Serves 4
Preparation time: 5 minutes
Cooking time: 8 to 10 minutes

If beans are large, cut them diagonally in half; otherwise, leave whole.

1 lb	**green beans**
4	**slices bacon or ham**
2 Tb	**butter**
	black pepper to taste
⅓ cup	**grated Parmesan cheese**

▪ Wash beans, remove tip ends if you wish. ▪ Bring lightly salted water to rolling boil in a saucepan. ▪ Add beans and cook, uncovered, 8 to 10 minutes until slightly tender but crisp. ▪ Meanwhile, chop bacon or ham into small pieces. ▪ Fry in skillet until crisp. ▪ Drain well and set aside. ▪ Drain beans and toss with butter and pepper. ▪ Sprinkle with Parmesan cheese and bacon pieces. Serve at once.
MICROWAVE DIRECTIONS: Prepare beans. Place 1 cup water in casserole; bring to boil on High 1 to 1½ minutes. Add beans, cover and cook on High 5 to 6 minutes. Cook bacon on High about 4 minutes. Chop or crumble. Continue as above.

calories/serving: 152
riboflavin: excellent
vitamin C: good
vitamin A: fair
fiber: moderate

POTATOES WITH CORIANDER

Serves 6 to 8
Preparation time: 20 minutes
Cooking time: 25 minutes

These tasty potatoes have that special Middle Eastern touch.

4 Tb	**olive oil**
5	**large potatoes, peeled and diced into ¼″ cubes**
4 Tb	**finely chopped fresh coriander leaves *or* chopped fresh parsley and chives**
2	**cloves garlic, crushed**
	salt and pepper to taste

▪ Heat oil in a large frying pan, add diced potatoes and cover. ▪ Simmer over medium heat for 15 minutes, stirring occasionally. ▪ Uncover and stir in remaining ingredients. ▪ Stir-fry for 10 minutes, or until potatoes turn limp.

calories/serving: 150 for 6 servings
113 for 8 servings
vitamin C: good to excellent

Stir-Fried Mixed Vegetables

STIR-FRIED MIXED VEGETABLES

Serves 4 or 5
Preparation time: 10 minutes
Cooking time: 5 minutes

This is a lovely vegetable dish for any occasion. If it is part of a meatless meal, add tofu for added protein. Other vegetables you have on hand can be substituted for these.

3 Tb	**vegetable oil**
1	**onion, halved then sliced**
3	**cloves garlic, minced**
½	**sweet green or red pepper, sliced**
¼ lb	**snow peas *or* 4 stalks celery, sliced**
2	**green onions, chopped**
1 cup	**sliced mushrooms**
2 cups	**bean sprouts**
½ tsp	**sugar**
2 Tb	**soy sauce**
2 Tb	**water**
4 oz	**tofu, cut into cubes (optional)**

▪ Heat oil in a wok or heavy skillet over medium-high heat. ▪ When hot, add onion and garlic and stir-fry for 2 minutes. ▪ Add pepper, snow peas, green onions and mushrooms and stir-fry for 1 minute. ▪ Add bean sprouts, sugar, soy sauce and water and stir-fry until vegetables are tender-crisp. ▪ Stir in tofu. ▪ Heat through and serve with rice or noodles.

calories/serving: 166 for 4 servings
132 for 5 servings
vitamin C: excellent
niacin: good
fiber: moderate
iron: fair

MINTED PEAS AND CARROTS IN BASKETS

Serves 8
Preparation time: 20 minutes
Cooking time: 10 minutes

Here's an attractive way to serve small vegetables. Fresh mint sparks up the delicate flavor of the young peas and carrots.

4 cups	**sliced fresh or frozen baby carrots**
	several large outside leaves iceberg lettuce
2 pkgs	**(each 10 oz/350 g) tiny frozen peas**
3 Tb	**finely chopped fresh mint**
1 Tb	**lemon juice**
1 Tb	**finely chopped green onion**
2 Tb	**butter**
8	**individual pastry shells, cooked**
8	**fresh mint sprigs for garnish**

▪ Cook sliced carrots in a little boiling water until just tender. ▪ Set aside. ▪ Line the bottom of a large heavy skillet with lettuce leaves and add peas, breaking up any that are frozen together. ▪ Sprinkle with chopped mint, lemon juice and onion and dot with butter. ▪ Cover tightly and cook 2 minutes over high heat, until peas are almost tender. ▪ Add carrots and continue steaming over medium heat until everything is hot, about 3 minutes more. ▪ Pull out and discard lettuce. ▪ Keep vegetables hot in the top of a double boiler over simmering water if necessary. ▪ Spoon into pastry shells at serving time and garnish with mint sprigs.

calories/serving: 255
vitamin A: excellent
iron, vitamin C, thiamin, niacin: good
fiber: high

PARSNIP CURRANT PUFFS

Serves 8
Preparation time: 15 minutes
Cooking time: 30 minutes

These little individual puffs with a dab of red currant jelly hidden in the center will be a hit with even those who say parsnips are not on their list of favorites.

2 lbs	**parsnips**
2	**eggs, separated**
½ tsp	**ground ginger**
	salt and pepper to taste
3 Tb	**red currant jelly**

▪ Peel parsnips and cut into about 6 pieces each. ▪ Cook, covered, in a small amount of boiling, salted water for 10 minutes or until soft. ▪ Drain well.

▪ Place in a food processor, in batches if necessary, and purée. ▪ Add egg yolks, ginger, salt and pepper. ▪ Process until light and fluffy. Recipe can be prepared ahead to this point, covered and refrigerated up to 1 day. Bring to room temperature before proceeding. ▪ Whip egg whites in a medium bowl until stiff but still moist. ▪ Fold into parsnip mixture. ▪ Divide most of the mixture among 8 buttered 6-oz custard cups or individual soufflé dishes. ▪ Make a well in each, spoon in one-eighth of the jelly and cover with remaining parsnip mixture, smoothing the top. ▪ Place filled dishes in a shallow pan with boiling water halfway up the sides of dishes. ▪ Bake in preheated 325°F oven about 20 minutes or until slightly puffed and set on top. ▪ Serve immediately.

calories/serving: 126
vitamin C, folate: good
fiber: moderate

SWEET POTATO FLAN

Serves 8 to 10
Preparation time: 15 minutes
Cooking time: 25 minutes
Reheating time: 30 minutes

A smooth, flavorful purée is garnished with slices of the vegetable itself.

3½ lbs	**sweet potatoes**
¼ cup	**heavy cream**
¼ cup	**butter**
2 Tb	**honey**
½ tsp	**grated nutmeg**
	salt and pepper to taste

▪ Scrub potatoes, but do not peel. ▪ Cook sweet potatoes in boiling, salted water, covered, for 25 minutes or until tender. ▪ Do not let them become mushy. ▪ Drain, peel and thinly slice. ▪ Set aside enough slices to go around the inside (overlapping) rim of a deep 9″ pie plate or similar baking dish. ▪ Purée remainder in a food processor or blender, with cream, half the butter, honey, nutmeg, salt and pepper, until smooth and fluffy. ▪ Taste and adjust seasoning if necessary. ▪ Spoon purée into greased dish and arrange slices overlapping slightly around the inside rim. ▪ Dot with remaining butter. ▪ Cover with foil. ▪ This dish can be refrigerated up to 3 days. ▪ Remove from refrigerator at least 30 minutes before reheating. ▪ Reheat, covered, in preheated 325°F oven for 30 minutes or until hot throughout.
MICROWAVE DIRECTIONS: Pierce sweet potatoes and bake on High 12 to 15 minutes. Follow regular recipe. To reheat, cover flan with plastic wrap and heat on Med/High 4 to 5 minutes.

calories/serving: 264 for 8 servings
216 for 10 servings
vitamin A, vitamin C: excellent
riboflavin, niacin: fair
fiber: moderate

RUTABAGA AND CARROT PUFF

Serves 8
Preparation time: 25 minutes
Cooking time: 45 minutes
Reheating time: 30 minutes

Rutabaga – yellow turnip – has long been a Canadian favorite as a side dish with roast turkey. Here carrots add their own special sweetness. This dish can be made ahead of time and reheated.

1	**rutabaga turnip**
4	**carrots**
½	**onion, chopped**
1½ cups	**chicken stock**
¼ cup	**butter**
1 Tb	**brown sugar**
pinch	**grated nutmeg**
2	**eggs, lightly beaten**
2 Tb	**flour**
1 tsp	**baking powder**
	salt and pepper to taste
¼ cup	**finely chopped pecans or hazelnuts**

▪ Trim and peel rutabaga and carrots; cut into ½" chunks. ▪ Combine rutabaga, carrots, onion, stock, 3 tablespoons of the butter, sugar and nutmeg in a large saucepan. ▪ Bring to boil. ▪ Reduce heat and cook, partially covered, about 45 minutes, or until vegetables are very tender, stirring occasionally. ▪ With slotted spoon, transfer vegetables to a food processor or blender. ▪ Set pan over high heat and boil remaining liquid, stirring constantly, 2 to 3 minutes or until reduced to about 1 tablespoon. ▪ Add to processor and purée until very smooth. ▪ Transfer to mixing bowl and cool to room temperature. ▪ Stir in eggs, flour, baking powder, salt and pepper. ▪ Transfer to buttered 6-cup casserole or soufflé dish. ▪ Melt remaining butter and stir together with nuts. ▪ Sprinkle evenly around edge of casserole to make border. ▪ If you wish, cover and refrigerate overnight. ▪ Bring to room temperature 30 minutes before reheating. ▪ Bake, uncovered, in preheated 350°F oven about 30 minutes or until puffed, firm and golden brown.

calories/serving: 150
vitamin A, vitamin C, niacin: excellent
fiber: moderate

Rutabaga and Carrot Puff

SPICY BAKED BEETS

Serves 4
Preparation time: 10 minutes
Cooking time: 30 minutes

Beets are often neglected, but they can be very appealing in this easy, yet flavorful side dish. Pop it in the oven with a roast of beef.

5	**medium beets**
1	**small onion**
1	**small potato**
2 Tb	**vegetable oil**
2 Tb	**white vinegar**
2 Tb	**brown sugar**
1 Tb	**water**
½ tsp	**salt**
¼ tsp	**each black pepper, celery seed, ground cloves**

▪ Peel beets and shred coarsely. You should have about 3 cups. ▪ Place in a greased 1-quart casserole. ▪ Peel and grate onion and potato and stir into beets. ▪ Stir together oil, vinegar, sugar, water, salt, pepper, celery seed and cloves. ▪ Stir into vegetable mixture, cover tightly and bake in preheated 350°F oven for 30 minutes. ▪ Stir once or twice.
MICROWAVE DIRECTIONS: Place vegetables in an ungreased casserole dish. Mix oil, vinegar, sugar, water and seasonings as directed, stir into mixture, cover dish and cook on High 8 minutes or until tender.

calories/serving: 148
vitamin C, folate, fiber: good

Stuffed Tomatoes with Shallots and Basil

STUFFED TOMATOES WITH SHALLOTS AND BASIL

Serves 4
Preparation time: 20 minutes
Cooking time: 12 to 15 minutes

If basil is not available, substitute your favorite herb – oregano, parsley, dill, chives – in this stuffing. Lovely for dinner with roast lamb or pork.

4	medium-large firm tomatoes
1 Tb	butter
¼ cup	finely chopped shallots
1	small clove garlic, finely chopped
2 Tb	chopped fresh basil or to taste
½ cup	packed, torn stale bread
	salt and pepper to taste

TOPPING:	
3 Tb	fine dry breadcrumbs
3 Tb	grated Parmesan cheese
1 tsp	butter

▪ Core and cut top inch off each tomato. ▪ Carefully scoop out pulp with spoon, trying not to break through tomato skin, leaving a sturdy shell ¼″ thick. ▪ Chop pulp and reserve. ▪ Drain tomato shells upside down on paper towels. ▪ Heat butter in a skillet. ▪ Add shallots and gently cook 2 minutes, stirring. ▪ Add garlic and reserved tomato pulp and cook 5 to 7 minutes, or until most of the juice has evaporated. ▪ Remove from heat and blend in basil, bread, salt and pepper. ▪ Divide mixture evenly into tomato shells; pat down gently to flatten. ▪ Combine topping crumbs and cheese and carefully sprinkle on top. ▪ Top with a small dab of butter. ▪ Bake in preheated 350°F oven 10 to 15 minutes. ▪ Broil 1 to 2 minutes to brown tops. ▪ Serve at once.

calories/serving: 102
vitamin C: excellent
vitamin A: good
low cal

CREAMED POTATO CASSEROLE

Serves 12
Preparation time: 30 minutes
Cooking time: 40 minutes

Here's a simple potato dish that is a nice complement to a rich main dish. It can be prepared ahead of time and refrigerated.

24	medium potatoes
¾ cup	butter or margarine
½ cup	flour
4 cups	chicken stock
4 cups	light cream
6	egg yolks, lightly beaten
	salt and black pepper to taste
½ tsp	cayenne pepper
1 cup	chopped fresh parsley
1 cup	fine dry breadcrumbs

▪ Peel potatoes and boil in lightly salted water until just tender. ▪ Drain. ▪ Heat ½ cup butter in a large saucepan over medium heat. ▪ Sprinkle in flour and stir to blend. ▪ Remove from heat and stir in chicken stock and cream all at once. ▪ Return to medium heat and stir until boiling, thickened and smooth. ▪ Gradually add about 1 cup of this hot mixture to the egg yolks, then stir back into the hot sauce along with salt, pepper, cayenne and parsley. ▪ Remove from heat. ▪ Butter two 2½-quart casseroles. ▪ Put a layer of sauce in each casserole, add a layer of sliced potatoes, then another layer of sauce, and repeat until all is used, ending with a layer of sauce. ▪ Mix fine dry breadcrumbs and ¼ cup butter and sprinkle half over the top of each casserole. ▪ Bake in preheated 400°F oven 40 minutes or until bubbling and very hot.

calories/serving: 373
vitamin C, niacin: excellent
protein, vitamin A, thiamin: good
calcium, iron, riboflavin: fair

ZUCCHINI SPAGHETTI WITH BASIL

Serves 2
Preparation time: 5 minutes
Cooking time: 5 minutes

Do not peel zucchini when grating; the skin adds a touch of color. Try for long shreds to make the zucchini look like spaghetti.

2 Tb	olive oil
3	medium zucchini, grated
1 tsp	dried basil *or* 1 Tb fresh
	salt and pepper to taste

▪ Heat oil in skillet over high heat. ▪ Add zucchini and sauté until softened, 4 to 5 minutes. ▪ Sprinkle on basil, salt and pepper. ▪ Stir together and serve. **MICROWAVE DIRECTIONS:** Place zucchini and oil in a baking dish. Cook on High 3 to 4 minutes, stirring 2 or 3 times during cooking. Sprinkle with basil, salt and pepper. Stir and serve.

calories/serving: 162
vitamin C: good
fiber: moderate

APPLE TURNIP CASSEROLE

Serves 10 to 12
Preparation time: 35 minutes
Cooking time: 30 to 40 minutes

1	large turnip
1½ cups	water
⅓ cup	butter
1	large onion, chopped
3	large apples, cored and shredded
¼ cup	flour
1 cup	chicken stock
1 cup	light cream or milk
¾ tsp	salt
¼ tsp	grated nutmeg
	pepper to taste
½ cup	cracker or dry breadcrumbs
2 Tb	melted butter

▪ Cut turnip into thick slices and peel. ▪ Shred turnip into a large saucepan, add water and bring to boil. ▪ Reduce heat, cover and cook until turnip is barely tender, about 5 minutes. ▪ Drain well. ▪ Melt butter in a large saucepan and cook chopped onion until tender. ▪ Stir in shredded apples and cook over medium-high heat until apples are tender, stirring constantly. ▪ Sprinkle in flour and stir until well blended. ▪ Add chicken stock, cream, salt, nutmeg and pepper. ▪ Cook, stirring constantly, 2 or 3 minutes, until sauce comes to boil and thickens. ▪ Remove from heat and stir in cooked turnip. ▪ Mix cracker crumbs and melted butter. ▪ Lightly grease a 9″ × 13″ shallow casserole or baking dish. ▪ Pour in apple-turnip mixture and spread evenly. ▪ Sprinkle with buttered crumbs. ▪ This dish can be prepared beforehand and refrigerated. ▪ Before serving, bake in preheated 350°F oven for 30 minutes or until hot and bubbly. Allow an additional 10 minutes if previously refrigerated.

calories/serving: 140 using 2% milk
vitamin C: good
fiber: moderate

BROCCOLI WITH CREAMY DRESSING

Serves 4
Preparation time: 5 minutes
Cooking time: 5 to 10 minutes

Use the creamy dressing to add sparkle to other vegetables – it's especially delicious with hot baked potatoes.

8 oz	broccoli florets (fresh or frozen)
1 Tb	lemon juice
1 Tb	wine vinegar
2 Tb	salad oil
½ cup	plain yogurt or sour cream
2 Tb	mayonnaise
1	small clove garlic, crushed
1 tsp	dry mustard
2 Tb	chopped fresh chives
	salt and pepper to taste

■ Steam or boil broccoli until tender-crisp. ■ Meanwhile whisk together remaining ingredients in a small bowl. ■ Drain cooked broccoli, toss in the dressing and serve hot.

calories/serving: 151 using yogurt
vitamin C: excellent
calcium, vitamin A: fair
fiber: moderate

PURÉE OF FALL ROOT VEGETABLES

Serves 4 to 6
Preparation time: 10 minutes
Cooking time: 20 to 30 minutes

This creamy purée is simple to make and especially delicious with roast meat or chicken.

4	carrots
3	parsnips
½	small rutabaga turnip
2 cups	water
1 Tb	brown sugar
	salt and pepper to taste
¼ cup	butter
2 tsp	fresh lemon juice
	buttered breadcrumbs or chopped nuts (optional)

■ Peel vegetables and cut into 1″ pieces or lengths. ■ Combine vegetables with water, brown sugar, salt and pepper. ■ Bring to boil, reduce heat to medium and cook, uncovered, until water has evaporated and vegetables are very tender, for 20 to 30 minutes, stirring occasionally. ■ Cool slightly, then purée in a food processor or blender with butter and lemon juice. ■ Taste and adjust seasoning if necessary.

■ Purée can be served immediately or made beforehand and reheated in the top of a double boiler or in a microwave oven. Or place in a greased baking dish, sprinkle with buttered breadcrumbs or chopped nuts and reheat, uncovered, in preheated 350°F oven for 20 to 30 minutes.

MICROWAVE DIRECTIONS: Place vegetables in a casserole with sugar and pepper. Dissolve salt in ½ cup of water; pour over vegetables. Cover dish, cook on High 8 to 10 minutes or until tender. Continue as above.

calories/serving: 105 for 6 servings
*   160 for 4 servings*
vitamin A: excellent
vitamin C, fiber: good
potassium: fair

SWEET POTATO AND PECAN PURÉE

Serves 12
Preparation time: 15 minutes
Cooking time: 60 to 75 minutes

A delicious and colorful addition to a buffet table. This can be made ahead of time and refrigerated, then baked before serving. Just increase cooking time by 5 to 10 minutes.

6	large sweet potatoes
	salt
1 cup	light cream
2	eggs
4 Tb	butter
1 Tb	grated orange peel
1 tsp	salt
½ tsp	each grated nutmeg and freshly ground black pepper
½ cup	pecan halves

■ Peel and quarter sweet potatoes. ■ Place in a large saucepan and cover with water. ■ Salt lightly. ■ Cover and bring to boil. ■ Reduce heat and cook until potatoes are fork tender, about 20 to 25 minutes. ■ Drain sweet potatoes and transfer to a large bowl. ■ Mash until smooth, then beat in cream with an electric mixer. ■ Beat in eggs, 3 tablespoons butter, orange peel and seasonings. ■ Spoon into a well-buttered 8-cup casserole. ■ Arrange pecan halves around edge of dish. ■ Dot with remaining butter and bake in preheated 350°F oven until hot, 35 to 45 minutes.

calories/serving: 161
vitamin A: excellent
vitamin C: good

STORING ROOT VEGETABLES

Root vegetables will keep for three or four weeks in a cool, dark place, such as the vegetable crisper of your refrigerator or a cold basement.

Sweet Potato and Pecan Purée and Broccoli with Creamy Dressing

Spiced Spinach

SPICED SPINACH

Serves 2
Preparation time: 5 minutes
Cooking time: 8 to 10 minutes

The slightly tangy taste and the dark green color of the spinach are a natural combination to enhance any fish.

1 pkg	(10 oz/284 g) spinach
1 Tb	butter
2	cloves garlic, finely chopped
2	green onions, finely chopped
1 tsp	Dijon mustard
1 tsp	ground cumin
pinch	cayenne pepper
¼ cup	yogurt
	salt and pepper to taste

▪ Remove stems from spinach and wash thoroughly. ▪ Place spinach in a heavy saucepan with just the water that clings to its leaves. ▪ Steam, covered, on medium heat until leaves wilt, about 5 minutes, shaking pan occasionally. ▪ Drain and rinse with cold water to stop cooking. ▪ Drain well. ▪ Heat butter until sizzling in a medium skillet. ▪ Add garlic, green onions and mustard and sauté until green onions have softened, about 2 minutes. ▪ Stir in spinach, cumin and cayenne. ▪ Sauté about 1 minute, until spinach is hot. ▪ Remove from heat. ▪ Stir in yogurt. ▪ Season with salt and pepper.

MICROWAVE DIRECTIONS: Cook prepared spinach in covered casserole on High 2 to 3 minutes. Drain, rinse and squeeze dry. Cook butter, garlic, green onions and mustard in a separate dish for 2 minutes. Add spinach and seasonings. Cook on High 2 minutes; add yogurt and cook on Medium 2 to 3 minutes, or until heated through.

calories/serving: 104
iron, vitamin A, folate, vitamin C: excellent
calcium: good
fiber: moderate

BAKED BROWN RICE

Serves 6
Preparation time: 10 minutes
Cooking time: 1 hour and 20 minutes

Use chicken stock if you are serving this with fowl, veal or fish; beef stock if it's to go with red meat. All ingredients except stock can be assembled ahead of time and refrigerated.

2 Tb	butter or margarine
1 cup	finely chopped onion
1 cup	finely chopped celery
1 cup	brown rice
2½ cups	stock (chicken or beef)
⅛ tsp	dried thyme
⅛ tsp	dried marjoram
	salt and pepper to taste

▪ Butter a 1½-quart casserole. ▪ Heat butter in a large saucepan. ▪ Add onion and celery and stir over medium heat 5 minutes. ▪ Remove from heat, stir in remaining ingredients and pour into prepared casserole. ▪ Cover and bake in preheated 350°F oven 1 hour. ▪ Uncover, stir with a fork and bake about 15 minutes, until rice is tender and moisture has nearly all been absorbed.

calories/serving: 190
niacin: good
iron, thiamin: fair
fiber: moderate

WHICH RICE TO CHOOSE?

Long-grain is good as an accompaniment, for use in Oriental dishes, in casseroles or stuffings. Brown rice is simply unpolished long-grain. It contains more fiber, is more nutritious than regular long-grain rice and takes longer to cook. Short-grain rice cooks to a creamier consistency and is the best choice for desserts.

INDONESIAN FRIED RICE

Serves 6
Preparation time: 15 minutes
Cooking time: 25 minutes

A great way to use up leftovers from the weekend roast. To save time, boil the rice and chop the vegetables ahead of time. Indonesian sweet soy sauce and hot pepper sauce (Sambal Oelek) will give a more authentic taste to the dish and are available at Oriental grocery stores.

2 cups	**long-grain rice**
3 cups	**water or chicken stock**
1 Tb	**cooking oil**
1	**medium onion, chopped**
1	**stalk celery, chopped**
2	**cloves garlic, chopped**
¼ tsp	**grated ginger root**
1 Tb	**hot pepper sauce**
1 tsp	**curry powder**
1 Tb	**sweet soy sauce**
2	**green peppers, diced**
1 cup	**shredded cabbage or diced carrots**
6	**large, fresh shrimp, peeled and deveined, cut into quarters (optional)**
1 cup	**diced, cooked chicken, ham, pork or lamb**
	salt to taste

▪ Cook rice in boiling water or chicken stock about 10 minutes until slightly underdone. ▪ Refresh under cold running water, drain well and pat dry. ▪ Heat oil in large heavy saucepan or wok and sauté onion until soft, stirring constantly. ▪ Add celery, garlic, ginger, hot pepper sauce, curry powder and sweet soy sauce and sauté 2 minutes. ▪ Add green peppers and cabbage or carrots and sauté 3 minutes. ▪ Add shrimp and diced, cooked meat and sauté 2 minutes. ▪ Add rice and sauté until light brown. Adjust seasoning and serve hot.

calories/serving: 335
protein, vitamin C, niacin: excellent
iron, thiamin: good
low fat

LEMON SPRING RICE

Serves 4
Preparation time: 5 minutes
Cooking time: 30 to 35 minutes

This rice accompaniment bakes to fluffy perfection without requiring any extra attention, and gives the cook time to attend to other dishes.

1 cup	**long-grain rice**
2 cups	**chicken stock *or* 1 chicken bouillon cube dissolved in 2 cups boiling water**
1	**green onion, chopped**
1 Tb	**lemon juice**
	salt and pepper to taste

▪ Place rice in lightly buttered 6-cup baking dish with lid. ▪ Heat stock, or bouillon cube and water, and pour over top. ▪ Blend in green onion, lemon juice, salt and pepper. ▪ Cover tightly and bake in preheated 350°F oven 30 to 35 minutes or until fluffy. ▪ Stir quickly during last 10 minutes of cooking. ▪ Re-cover and continue cooking. Leftover rice keeps well for future sautés or rice salads.

calories/serving: 142
thiamin: good

RICE PILAF

Serves 4 to 6
Preparation time: 10 minutes
Cooking time: 30 to 40 minutes

Frozen peas can be added to the pilaf if you wish; the peas will cook in the heat of the rice.

4 Tb	**butter**
1	**medium onion, chopped**
2 cups	**long-grain rice**
4 cups	**hot chicken broth**
	salt and pepper to taste

▪ Melt butter in a heavy frying pan. ▪ Add onion and stir. ▪ Add rice and stir until rice is glistening and coated with butter. ▪ Add broth slowly and season to taste. ▪ Transfer to buttered baking dish and bake in preheated 350°F oven 30 minutes. ▪ Stir, and if rice is still too wet, bake another 10 minutes.

calories/serving: 513 for 4 servings
345 for 6 servings
niacin: excellent
protein, iron, thiamin: good

BREADS AND QUICK BREADS

*B*read has been both my downfall and my blessing. My downfall because most of the extra padding I carry on my hips can be blamed on bread. But bread's a great blessing nevertheless. If I were to be marooned on that hypothetical desert island with only two foods, hefty crusty homemade bread would be one of them. (Cheese might very well be the other.) Coming home from school to find the house fragrant with the seductive aroma of fresh bread was one of the peak experiences of childhood. Sawing off a jagged slice (warm bread doesn't cut neatly) and deciding whether to add peanut butter to the chunks of cold butter already sinking in, or to save that delight for the second slice, was worth all the warnings I had to listen to about spoiling my dinner and warm bread being indigestible.

Even today I choose restaurants largely on the basis of the bread they serve. More often than not, good bread means the rest of the food will be decently treated.

Looking back, I can see that my career as a food writer/editor started with bread. I left home and became a newspaper reporter, writing about bank holdups, traffic accidents and teachers' conventions. But then I got married and had children and began looking for real bread to feed them. I couldn't find any. We all know that sliced bread was greeted as the greatest invention since the wheel, and in the early '50s it was everywhere. Housewives had stopped baking; even bakers had stopped baking (except for a few diehards who never plied their sainted trade near me). The only trouble with this new convenient sliced bread in its pristine cellophane packages (no, plastic hadn't hit the market yet) was that I thought it tasted much like steamrollered facial tissue.

So I got a recipe and tried my hand at bread. To my amazement, not only was it easy to make, it offered a chance to knead and pummel, to whack and pound, to shape and smooth, to a person who had always longed to sculpt in clay but never had either the nerve or the opportunity. And you almost *had* to meditate while your hands were busy mixing and whacking. During the hours the loaves were plumping themselves up in the warm cocoon you provided, they filled the house with delicious yeasty smells. When they came out of the oven all golden and crusty and swollen, even if they were lopsided they were just about the most beautiful sight known to mankind.

So I became hooked on bread baking, and didn't

even warn my kids when they came home from school about spoiled dinners and ruined digestions.

Then I discovered there was yet another payoff to bread baking. My friends began to notice and to draw the conclusion that anyone who baked bread was a GOOD COOK. I could serve them the same old pork chop-and-applesauce I'd served them before, but because homemade bread went with it, they sang my praises. So I wrote a piece for the *Star Weekly* about how anyone could win an instant reputation as a superlative cook just by filling the house with the smell of fresh bread. (I'm told that real-estate agents believe that the smell of fresh-baked bread can sell a house.)

Bread led to the heady realm of cinnamon buns, to banana breads and date loaves, to muffins and Yorkshire pudding. The bread success destroyed forever the myth that baking was a mysterious and difficult art. Before our marriage I had baked my husband a cherry pie that he had to cut with a knife and fork. (Oh, the humiliation of it!) Now, with the help of my mother's foolproof pastry recipe, pies became child's play, buns could be whipped up before breakfast, cookies streamed out of my oven and into the cookie jar every day or so. I WAS A COOK.

Since I had always talked a lot about food as an eater, my emphasis shifted only a little as far as I could tell. But editors began to ask me to write about food, as though enthusiasm was the same thing as expertise. And so a career as a food writer began to run a parallel course beside my other writing. My reason for baking bread has vanished: you can buy good bread and good muffins on almost every city street corner today. But if you'd like to have the fun and ego-gratification of making your own, take it from me, *you can do it, too*.

BASIC WHITE BREAD

Makes six 20-oz loaves
Preparation time: 40 minutes
Rising time: 2 to 2½ hours
Cooking time: 40 to 45 minutes

Make sure the water used to dissolve the yeast is around 110°F – it should feel just barely warm to your wrist or elbow. If too hot, it will kill the yeast; too cold and the yeast won't be activated.

⅓ cup plus 1 tsp	sugar
6 cups	warm water
2 Tb	dry active yeast (2 envelopes)
¾ cup	skim milk powder
5 tsp	salt
½ cup	softened shortening
14 cups (approx.)	flour

▪ Dissolve 1 teaspoon sugar in ½ cup warm water and sprinkle yeast over. Let stand 10 minutes until bubbling. ▪ Mix together ⅓ cup sugar, skim milk powder and salt in a large bowl. ▪ Stir in yeast mixture, shortening, 5½ cups warm water and 4 cups flour. ▪ Beat well until smooth. ▪ Stir in about 8 cups flour until dough leaves sides of bowl. ▪ Turn out onto floured surface and knead in flour until dough is smooth and elastic and forms stiff, not sticky, dough, about 10 minutes. ▪ Grease bowl lightly and return dough, turning it to grease top. ▪ Cover with a damp cloth and let rise in a warm draft-free place until doubled in size, about 1½ hours. ▪ Punch dough down, divide into 6 pieces and form loaves. ▪ Place in non-stick or greased 9″ × 5″ × 2½″ loaf pans and let rise, covered, until doubled in size, 30 minutes to 1 hour. ▪ Bake in preheated 400°F oven for 20 minutes. Reduce heat to 350°F and bake until loaves sound hollow when tapped with your knuckle, another 20 to 25 minutes. Remove from pans to rack and brush tops with melted butter if a soft crust is desired.

calories/slice: 80
low fat

SCOTTISH SCONE

Serves 6
Preparation time: 10 minutes
Cooking time: 15 to 18 minutes

Your favorite jam will make a lovely spread for this quick bread. It's also good served with berries and ice cream.

2 cups	flour
1½ Tb	baking powder
1 tsp	sugar
½ tsp	salt
¼ cup	unsalted butter, cut into cubes
2	eggs
⅔ cup	sour milk or buttermilk

▪ Sift flour, baking powder, sugar and salt into a large bowl. ▪ With pastry cutter, 2 knives or fingertips, work in butter until crumbly. ▪ Whisk eggs lightly with milk in a small bowl. ▪ Pour into center of dry ingredients and blend quickly with a spatula. ▪ Turn out onto greased cookie sheet. ▪ With floured hands, pat into a circle about 8″ in diameter. ▪ Score top into a cross with a knife. ▪ Bake in preheated 400°F oven for 15 to 18 minutes, or until toothpick inserted in center comes out clean. ▪ Serve warm, cut into pie-shaped wedges, with jam.

calories/serving: 265
thiamin, niacin: good
iron: fair

CORN BREAD

Makes 1 small loaf
Preparation time: 10 minutes
Cooking time: 15 to 20 minutes

¾ cup	flour
¾ cup	yellow cornmeal
1 Tb	sugar
2 tsp	baking powder
½ tsp	salt
1	egg, lightly beaten
½ cup	milk
2 Tb	vegetable oil

▪ Grease a 9″ × 5″ loaf pan. ▪ Combine flour, cornmeal, sugar, baking powder and salt in a medium bowl. ▪ Combine egg, milk and oil in a small bowl or measuring cup. ▪ Stir egg mixture into dry mixture all at once and mix just until blended. ▪ Spoon into prepared pan and bake in a preheated 350°F oven for 15 to 20 minutes, or until toothpick inserted in center comes out clean. ▪ Run knife around edges of pan. ▪ Remove to a rack and let cool completely in pan.

calories/½″ piece: 64
low fat

Whole Wheat Bread

WHOLE WHEAT BREAD

Makes 4 loaves
Preparation time: 40 minutes
Rising time: 3 hours
Cooking time: 35 to 40 minutes

Whole wheat and rye flours are heavier than white, so a third rising results in a lighter, firmer textured bread.

3 Tb	dry active yeast (3 envelopes)
4 cups	warm water
¼ cup plus 1 Tb	sugar
½ cup	milk powder
4 tsp	salt
½ cup	oil or melted shortening
11 to 12 cups (approx.)	whole wheat flour

▪ Dissolve 1 tablespoon sugar in ¾ cup of the warm water and sprinkle yeast over. ▪ Let stand 10 minutes until bubbling well. ▪ Combine 3¼ cups warm water, milk powder, ¼ cup sugar, salt and oil. ▪ Add yeast mixture. ▪ Stir in 6 cups flour and beat well. ▪ Stir in more flour until a dough ball is formed. ▪ Turn out onto floured board and knead about 10 minutes, adding more flour as necessary to make a smooth, elastic dough. ▪ Place in greased bowl, turning to grease top, and cover with a damp cloth. Let rise about 1½ hours or until doubled in volume. ▪ Punch down, fold edges towards center and let rise again until doubled, about 1 hour. ▪ Form into 4 loaves and place in greased 9″ × 5″ × 2½″ loaf pans. ▪ Cover and let rise until doubled in size, about ½ hour. ▪ Bake in preheated 375°F oven 35 to 40 minutes, or until loaves are a little loose in pans.

Honey-Bran Variation: *Reduce water to 3 cups and substitute ½ cup honey for sugar. Add 1 cup natural bran to flour.*

calories/slice: 83 (20 slices/loaf)
thiamin, niacin: fair
fiber: moderate
Honey-Bran Variation – calories/slice: 88

Strawberry Rhubarb Muffins

STRAWBERRY RHUBARB MUFFINS

Makes 1 dozen medium
Preparation time: 10 minutes
Cooking time: 20 minutes

The flavors of strawberries and rhubarb marry perfectly in these fruit-full muffins.

1 cup	rolled oats
1 cup	strawberry yogurt
½ cup	vegetable oil
¾ cup	brown sugar
1	egg
1 cup	flour
1 tsp	salt
½ tsp	baking soda
1 tsp	baking powder
1 tsp	ground cinnamon
1 cup	natural bran
¾ cup	chopped rhubarb
¼ cup	sugar
½ cup	sliced strawberries

▪ Soak rolled oats in strawberry yogurt just to moisten. ▪ Add oil, brown sugar and egg. ▪ Beat well. ▪ Sift in flour, salt, baking soda, baking powder, cinnamon and bran. ▪ Toss rhubarb in sugar. ▪ Add rhubarb and strawberries to flour mixture and stir just to combine. Do not overmix. ▪ Fill muffin cups three-quarters full. ▪ Bake in preheated 400°F oven for 20 minutes, or until toothpick inserted in center comes out clean.

MICROWAVE DIRECTIONS: Prepare as per recipe. Chop rhubarb and strawberries into small pieces and stir well into mixture. Use two paper liners in microwave muffin pan. Fill two-thirds full and cook on High 3 to 3½ minutes.

calories/muffin: 264
iron, vitamin C, thiamin, niacin: fair
fiber: moderate

LEMON LOAF

Makes 1 loaf
Preparation time: 15 minutes
Cooking time: 1 hour

A tangy glaze tops this lemon and walnut tea bread.

2 Tb	shortening
1 cup	sugar
2	eggs
1½ cups	flour
1½ tsp	baking powder
pinch	salt
½ cup	finely chopped walnuts
1 tsp	grated lemon peel
½ cup	milk
TOPPING:	
⅓ cup	sugar
3 Tb	lemon juice
1 tsp	grated lemon peel

▪ Blend shortening and 1 cup sugar. ▪ Add eggs one at a time, beating well after each addition. ▪ Sift together dry ingredients and toss with chopped nuts and grated lemon peel. ▪ Add to egg mixture alternately with milk. ▪ Pour into a greased 9″ × 5″ × 2½″ loaf pan. ▪ Bake in preheated 325°F oven for 1 hour, or until a toothpick inserted in the center comes out clean. ▪ Remove to a plate and cool 5 minutes. ▪ Prick top of loaf in several places with a fork. ▪ To make topping, mix sugar, lemon juice and lemon peel and pour over hot loaf. ▪ Finish cooling and serve at room temperature, sliced and buttered.

calories/½″ slice: 151
low fat

JUICING LEMONS
Citrus fruits will yield more juice if you warm them first, either for a few minutes in a medium oven or by microwaving for a few seconds. Alternatively, roll the fruit firmly for a few seconds on a hard surface with the palm of your hand.

ORANGE DATE LOAF

Makes 1 loaf
Preparation time: 15 minutes
Cooking time: 1 hour

This tea bread is quick to make and tastes wonderful sliced and spread with butter.

2 cups	chopped dates
⅓ cup	shortening
1 cup	boiling water
4 Tb	cold water or orange juice
1 Tb	orange juice
1 tsp	baking soda
¾ cup	brown sugar
1 tsp	vanilla
1 tsp	grated orange peel
1	egg, lightly beaten
2 cups	flour
1 tsp	baking powder
1 tsp	salt

▪ Put dates and shortening into a mixing bowl and pour boiling water over them. ▪ Beat until shortening breaks into small lumps. ▪ Add cold water and orange juice. ▪ Stir in baking soda, brown sugar, vanilla, orange peel and egg. ▪ Add flour, baking powder and salt. ▪ Beat until well blended. ▪ Pour batter into greased 9″ × 5″ × 2½″ loaf pan. ▪ Bake in preheated 350°F oven for about 1 hour, or until toothpick inserted in center comes out clean.

MICROWAVE DIRECTIONS: Prepare as per recipe. Use glass or microwave loaf pan, or a ring mold. Line bottom of dish with waxed or parchment paper. Do not grease. Cook on Medium 8 minutes, then on High 3 to 5 minutes. Let stand in dish on countertop for 10 minutes.

calories/½″ slice: 180
vitamin C, iron: fair
low fat

Orange Date Loaf

PUMPKIN BISCUITS

Makes 3 dozen
Preparation time: 25 minutes
Rising time: 1 hour and 35 minutes
Cooking time: 10 to 12 minutes

These yeast-raised pumpkin biscuits are light, moist and golden. You can substitute winter squash, if you like.

½ cup	hot milk
2 Tb	butter
3 Tb	sugar
½ cup	puréed pumpkin or winter squash
1 tsp	salt
3¼ cups	flour
1 Tb	dry active yeast (1 envelope)
¼ cup	warm water

▪ Combine hot milk, butter, sugar, pumpkin, salt and ¼ cup of the flour in a large bowl. ▪ Stir yeast into ¼ cup warm water and let it stand for 5 minutes or until bubbly. ▪ Add yeast to the first mixture and beat vigorously. ▪ Cover and leave in a warm place to rise for 30 minutes or until light. ▪ Add remaining 3 cups of flour and mix well. ▪ Cover and let rise again for 45 minutes or until double in bulk. ▪ Turn out onto a lightly floured board. ▪ Pat dough until it is ¼″ thick, and cut into 2″ rounds. Place rounds about 1″ apart on a greased baking sheet. ▪ Cover and let rise for 20 minutes or until almost double. ▪ Bake in preheated 400°F oven for 10 to 12 minutes or until golden brown.

calories/biscuit: 59
low fat

Apple Bran Streusel Muffins

APPLE BRAN STREUSEL MUFFINS

Makes 18
Preparation time: 20 to 25 minutes
Cooking time: 25 to 30 minutes

Moist and delicious, these nutritious muffins make tasty treats for breakfast, snacks and brown bag lunches. They freeze well but taste best when reheated just before serving.

2 cups	flour
1 cup	natural bran
¾ cup	lightly packed brown sugar
1 Tb	baking powder
½ tsp	baking soda
1 tsp	ground cinnamon
1 tsp	salt
2	large unpeeled apples, cored and chopped
1 cup	milk
½ cup	vegetable oil
2	eggs

STREUSEL TOPPING:

¼ cup	flour
¼ cup	packed brown sugar
½ tsp	ground cinnamon
2 Tb	cold butter

▪ To make streusel topping, stir together flour, sugar and cinnamon. ▪ Cut in butter until mixture is like coarse meal. ▪ Set aside. ▪ Stir together flour, bran, sugar, baking powder, baking soda, cinnamon and salt in a large bowl. ▪ Stir in chopped apples. ▪ Beat milk, oil and eggs together. ▪ Pour into dry ingredients and stir just until blended. Do not overmix. ▪ Fill muffin cups three-quarters full. ▪ Sprinkle each muffin with a heaping teaspoon of streusel. ▪ Bake in preheated 400°F oven for 25 to 30 minutes, or until toothpick inserted in center comes out clean.
calories/muffin: 202
fiber: moderate

OLD-FASHIONED OATCAKES

Makes 4 to 5 dozen
Preparation time: 20 minutes
Cooking time: 10 to 15 minutes

Warm or cold, with or without butter, honey or jam, oatcakes are as addictive as salted peanuts. You can use old-fashioned oatmeal or quick-cooking (not instant) rolled oats.

2 cups	flour
1½ cups	rolled oats
1 tsp	sugar
1 tsp	salt
½ tsp	baking soda
¾ cup	shortening or lard
½ cup	water

▪ Mix together dry ingredients in a large bowl. ▪ Cut in shortening with a pastry blender or two knives until mixture resembles coarse meal. ▪ Stir in water with a fork. Dough should just cling together. ▪ Divide dough into three portions. ▪ On a lightly floured surface, roll out each portion as thin as possible. ▪ Cut into triangles. ▪ Place 1″ apart on an ungreased cookie sheet and bake in preheated 375°F oven for 10 to 15 minutes. Oatcakes should not brown but be still quite blonde when done.
MICROWAVE DIRECTIONS: Place triangles on a glass pie plate. Cook on High: 6 triangles will take 3 minutes. These cakes will be softer when first cooked. Remove from dish with a spatula and place on a wire rack to dry.
calories/oatcake: 64 for 4 dozen
52 for 5 dozen
niacin, thiamin: good
iron: fair
fiber: moderate

BROWN SUGAR SCONES

Makes about 18
Preparation time: 10 minutes
Cooking time: 15 minutes
These scones are rich and irresistible.

3 cups	flour
2 tsp	baking powder
1 cup	golden (not dark) brown sugar
1 cup	butter or margarine
1 cup	raisins
1 cup	milk

▪ Stir together flour, baking powder and sugar in a mixing bowl. ▪ Cut in butter until mixture is like coarse meal. ▪ Mix raisins evenly through dry ingredients. ▪ Add milk and stir until sticky dough forms. ▪ On a floured surface, and with a floured rolling pin, roll dough into a long rectangle about ¾″ thick. ▪ With a sharp knife, cut dough into triangles. ▪ Place on ungreased cookie sheets in preheated 375°F oven and bake until golden brown and a toothpick inserted in center comes out clean.
calories/scone: 250

LEMON OATMEAL MUFFINS

Makes 1 dozen medium
Preparation time: 10 minutes
Cooking time: 15 to 20 minutes
A spicy topping makes these lemony muffins extra special.

1 cup	rolled oats
1½ cups	lemon or plain yogurt
2 cups	flour
¾ cup plus 1 Tb	sugar
1 Tb	baking powder
1 tsp	salt
½ cup	melted butter
½ cup	lemon juice
	grated peel of 1 lemon
2	eggs, lightly beaten
½ tsp	ground cinnamon

▪ Soak rolled oats in lemon yogurt just to moisten. ▪ Combine flour, ¾ cup of the sugar, baking powder and salt. ▪ Add melted butter, lemon juice, lemon peel and eggs to oatmeal mixture. ▪ Add oatmeal mixture to dry ingredients and stir just to combine. Do not overmix. ▪ Fill muffin cups three-quarters full. ▪ Sprinkle tops with mixture of 1 tablespoon of sugar and cinnamon. ▪ Bake in preheated 400°F oven for 15 to 20 minutes, or until toothpick inserted in center comes out clean.
calories/muffin: 251
vitamin C, niacin: fair

Orange Streusel Coffee Cake

ORANGE STREUSEL COFFEE CAKE

Makes one 9″ square cake
Preparation time: 15 minutes
Cooking time: about 30 minutes
You'll really wow them when you make this: be prepared to hand out the recipe.

2 cups	sifted flour
½ cup	sugar
2½ tsp	baking powder
½ tsp	salt
	grated peel of 1 orange
1	egg, lightly beaten
½ cup	milk
½ cup	orange juice
⅓ cup	vegetable oil
STREUSEL TOPPING:	
¼ cup	flour
¼ cup	sugar
2 Tb	grated orange peel
2 Tb	butter or margarine

▪ Sift together flour, sugar, baking powder and salt. ▪ Stir in grated orange peel. ▪ Make a well and mix in egg, milk, orange juice and oil just enough to moisten flour – the batter should be lumpy. ▪ Pour into a greased 9″ square pan, or an angel food pan. ▪ Blend together streusel ingredients until crumbly. ▪ Sprinkle on top of cake and bake in preheated 350°F oven for about 30 minutes or until golden.
calories/serving: 339 for 10 servings

Bran Muffins

BRAN MUFFINS

Makes 1 dozen
Preparation time: 10 to 15 minutes
Cooking time: 17 to 25 minutes

From one basic recipe you can make up to five different varieties – all of them tasty and good for you, too.

1	egg
¼ cup	liquid honey
1 cup	milk
¼ cup	vegetable oil
1 cup	natural bran
1½ cups	flour
3 tsp	baking powder
¼ tsp	baking soda
½ tsp	salt

▪ Beat egg in a mixing bowl and stir in honey, milk, oil and bran. ▪ Sift remaining ingredients together into honey mixture and stir just to combine. Do not overmix. ▪ Spoon into greased large muffin cups, filling about two-thirds full. Bake in preheated 400°F oven 17 to 20 minutes. Serve warm.

Fig-Orange:
Add ½ cup chopped dried figs and ½ cup well-drained small pieces of orange to honey mixture.

Apple-Carrot:
Add ½ cup grated unpeeled apple and ½ cup finely grated carrot to honey mixture and ½ teaspoon ground nutmeg to dry ingredients. Bake 20 to 25 minutes.

Molasses:
Replace honey with molasses, and milk with 1¼ cups buttermilk.

Spice-Date:
Make as for molasses, except add ½ cup chopped dates to molasses mixture and ½ teaspoon ground cinnamon, ¼ teaspoon ground nutmeg and ¼ teaspoon ground cloves to dry ingredients. Top each muffin with a date half.

calories/muffin: 143
niacin: good
iron, thiamin: fair
dietary fiber: moderate
low fat
Fig-Orange – calories/muffin: 165
Apple-Carrot – calories/muffin: 148
(these muffins are also a fair source of vitamin A)
Molasses – calories/muffin: 136
(with molasses replacing honey, these muffins are a good source of iron)
Spice-Date – calories/muffin: 168

CRANBERRY LOAF

Makes 1 loaf
Preparation time: 10 minutes
Cooking time: 35 minutes

Spice and cranberries give a festive flavor to this quick bread.

	grated peel from ½ orange
¾ cup	sugar
¾ cup	orange juice
1	egg
3 Tb	vegetable oil
1¾ cups	flour
¾ cup	natural bran
3 tsp	baking powder
1 tsp	ground cinnamon
½ tsp	salt
1 cup	cranberries

▪ Combine orange peel, sugar, orange juice, egg and oil. ▪ Beat well. ▪ Combine flour, bran, baking powder, cinnamon and salt. ▪ Stir into batter just to blend. ▪ Stir in cranberries. ▪ Turn into a greased and floured 9″ × 5″ × 2½″ loaf pan. ▪ Bake in pre-heated 350°F oven for 35 minutes, or until toothpick inserted in center comes out clean. ▪ Cool 5 minutes, then invert and cool thoroughly on wire rack.

calories/½″ slice: 55
vitamin C: fair
low fat

BASIC PIZZA DOUGH

Makes four 12″ pizzas
Preparation time: 20 minutes
Rising time: 1 hour
Cooking time: about 20 minutes

Metal pizza pans can be bought in hardware stores, but aluminum pie plates, rectangular baking dishes or cookie sheets make fine small pizza pans. After all, pizza doesn't have to be round to taste good. This dough can be made ahead of time and frozen.

1 Tb	dry active yeast (1 envelope)
2 cups	warm water
2	eggs
2 Tb	sugar
4 Tb	oil
1 tsp	salt
6 cups	flour
	cornmeal

▪ Stir yeast into warm water and let sit for 5 minutes. ▪ Combine yeast with eggs, sugar, oil and salt in a large bowl. ▪ Whisk until mixture foams. ▪ Add 3 cups of the flour and stir until liquid is absorbed.

▪ Work the remaining flour in gently with your hands until dough is soft and smooth. ▪ Divide into 4 parts and shape each into a patty. ▪ Brush with oil and cover with a towel and let rise in a warm place 1 hour or until doubled in bulk. ▪ Punch down. ▪ Roll each patty out on a floured surface to fit a 12″ pan which has been oiled and sprinkled lightly with cornmeal. ▪ Place dough on pan, pushing it out to fit with your fingertips. ▪ Make a lip around the edge by squeezing the dough between your thumb and fingers. Use immediately or freeze for later. ▪ Cover with Tomato Sauce and Pizza Toppings (see Main Dishes: Savory Sauces) and bake 15 to 20 minutes in preheated 400°F oven until cheese is texture you like.

calories/whole pizza crust: 678
niacin: good

WHOLE WHEAT OATMEAL PIZZA CRUST

Makes one 12″ pizza
Preparation time: 20 minutes
Rising time: 1 hour
Cooking time: 12 to 15 minutes

This is a hearty, nutritious crust.

1 cup	quick-cooking rolled oats
1 tsp	sugar
½ tsp	salt
1 Tb	dry active yeast (1 envelope)
2 Tb	vegetable oil
½ cup plus 2 Tb	warm water
½ to ¾ cup	whole wheat flour
½ cup	all-purpose flour

▪ Process oats in a blender or food processor until oats resemble flour. ▪ Combine oat flour, sugar, salt and yeast in a large mixing bowl. ▪ Add oil and warm water, mixing well. ▪ Add ½ cup whole wheat flour. ▪ Beat with an electric mixer at medium speed for 1 minute. ▪ Add enough remaining flours to make a stiff dough. ▪ Turn dough out on floured surface and knead until smooth and elastic, about 5 minutes. ▪ Place in a large lightly oiled bowl, turning to coat top. ▪ Cover and let rise in a warm place about 1 hour or until doubled in bulk. ▪ Punch dough down and turn out onto lightly floured surface. ▪ Roll to a 14″ circle. ▪ Place on a lightly oiled 12″ pan. ▪ Turn extra dough under at edge to form a rim. ▪ Cover with Tomato Sauce and Pizza Toppings (see Main Dishes: Savory Sauces) and bake in preheated 400°F oven 12 to 15 minutes or until cheese is texture you like.

calories/whole pizza crust: 1,069
fiber: moderate
iron, thiamin, niacin: good

Apple Cranberry Muffins

APPLE CRANBERRY MUFFINS

Makes 1 dozen medium
Preparation time: 10 minutes
Cooking time: 20 minutes
A delicious way to start the day.

1 cup	rolled oats
1 cup	orange or plain yogurt
½ cup	vegetable oil
¾ cup	brown sugar
1	egg
1 cup	flour
1 tsp	salt
½ tsp	baking soda
1 tsp	baking powder
2 tsp	grated orange peel
¾ cup	cranberries, chopped
⅛ cup	sugar
	unpeeled tart apple, cored and chopped

▪ Soak rolled oats in yogurt just to moisten. ▪ Add oil, brown sugar and egg. ▪ Beat well. ▪ Sift in flour, salt, baking soda, baking powder and orange peel. ▪ Toss cranberries in sugar. ▪ Add cranberries and apple to flour mixture and stir just to combine. Do not overmix. ▪ Fill muffin cups three-quarters full. ▪ Bake in preheated 400°F oven for 20 minutes, or until toothpick inserted in center comes out clean.

calories/muffin: 235
thiamin, niacin: fair

PUMPKIN BREAD

Makes 2 loaves
Preparation time: 10 minutes
Cooking time: 1 hour
A good way to use up leftover pumpkin after Thanksgiving or Halloween. Serve this tea bread still warm from the oven, sliced and spread with butter.

1¼ cups	brown sugar
½ cup	vegetable oil
1⅔ cups	cooked or canned pumpkin
2	eggs
2½ cups	flour
3 tsp	baking powder
½ tsp	each salt, ground ginger and ground cloves
1¼ tsp	ground cinnamon

▪ Beat together 1 cup of the sugar, oil, pumpkin and eggs in a bowl. ▪ Mix together flour, baking powder, salt, ginger, cloves and 1 teaspoon of the cinnamon in another bowl. ▪ Combine pumpkin mixture with dry ingredients just enough to moisten all ingredients. ▪ Spoon into 2 lightly greased loaf pans. ▪ Mix together remaining ¼ cup sugar and ¼ teaspoon cinnamon. ▪ Sprinkle over unbaked loaves. ▪ Bake in preheated 350°F oven for 1 hour, or until toothpick inserted in center comes out clean. ▪ Cool slightly and remove from pans.

calories/½" slice: 101
vitamin A: good

CHEESY BEER BREAD

Makes 1 loaf
Preparation time: 10 minutes
Cooking time: 45 minutes
Cheese gives a savory taste and beer a moist lightness to this quickly prepared bread.

3 cups	flour
4 tsp	baking powder
2 tsp	salt
1½ cups	grated Cheddar cheese
½ cup	grated Parmesan cheese
1 Tb	dried parsley
1 cup	beer
1 Tb	liquid honey

▪ Combine flour, baking powder, salt, grated cheeses and parsley. ▪ Stir in beer and honey until well mixed. ▪ Spread into greased 9" × 5" × 2½" loaf pan. ▪ Bake in preheated 350°F oven for 45 minutes, or until browned and a toothpick inserted in center comes out clean. ▪ Turn out on rack to cool.

calories/½" slice: 130
calcium, niacin: fair
low fat

REFRIGERATOR ROLLS

Makes 3 dozen
Preparation time: 40 minutes
Rising time: 24 hours in refrigerator, or 3 to 4 hours at room temperature
Cooking time: 15 minutes

Few cooks have time for regular breadmaking, but this recipe allows you to have fresh hot rolls any time you want them.

½ cup	sugar
2½ cups	warm water
2 Tb	dry active yeast (2 envelopes)
2	eggs, beaten
1 Tb	salt
8 cups	all purpose flour
¼ cup	melted shortening

- Dissolve 1 tablespoon of the sugar in ½ cup of the lukewarm water in a 2-cup measure. - Sprinkle yeast on top and let stand 10 minutes. - Meanwhile pour remaining water into a large warm bowl and stir in remaining sugar, eggs and salt. - Stir yeast mixture vigorously with a fork and add to egg mixture. - Beat in half the flour. - Add shortening. - Gradually add only enough of the remaining 4 cups flour to make a soft dough you can handle. Do not add any more flour than necessary to keep dough from sticking. - On a lightly floured surface, knead until smooth and elastic, about 8 minutes. - Shape into a ball. Place in a clean, very large, well-greased bowl and turn to grease the top. - Cover with greased waxed paper and a damp tea towel until double in volume, 24 hours in refrigerator, or 3 to 4 hours at room temperature. The dough will keep up to one week in the refrigerator. - During the first day, punch down; after that, once every couple of days should be enough. - When needed, cut off amount of dough required and let rest, covered, at room temperature about 2 hours. - Shape into rolls. - Place on greased baking sheet, grease tops well and let sit, covered with a piece of greased waxed paper, in a warm place, until doubled in volume, about 1¼ hours. - Bake in preheated 400°F oven about 15 minutes, or until light brown and hollow-sounding when tapped on the bottom. - Cool on racks or serve hot.

calories/roll: 117
niacin: good
thiamin: fair
low fat

Marmalade Muffins

MARMALADE MUFFINS

Makes 1 dozen medium
Preparation time: 20 minutes
Cooking time: 20 minutes

These moist, light muffins have surprise centers. Bake them the day before and serve at room temperature, or bake, cool and freeze for up to 2 months. If you wish, you may add ¼ cup finely chopped almonds to oatmeal-buttermilk mixture and substitute ⅓ cup raspberry jam for the marmalade.

1 cup	rolled oats
1 cup	buttermilk
1 cup	flour
¼ cup	sugar
1 tsp	baking powder
½ tsp	each baking soda and salt
1	egg, lightly beaten
¼ cup	melted butter
1 tsp	vanilla
⅓ cup	marmalade

- Stir together rolled oats and buttermilk in a small bowl. - Add almonds, if you wish. Let stand 10 minutes. - Meanwhile stir together flour, sugar, baking powder, baking soda and salt in a large bowl. - Stir in egg, butter and vanilla. - Mix in oat mixture just to combine. Do not overmix. - Spoon small amount of batter into each greased muffin-cup. - Place about 1 teaspoon marmalade in center of each and spoon in remaining batter. Cups should be about three-quarters full. - Bake in preheated 400°F oven about 20 minutes, or until tops are golden brown and slightly firm to the touch.

calories/muffin: 154
niacin: fair
low fat

PANCAKES AND CRÊPES

*P*ancakes were not a breakfast meal in our family when I was growing up, but we had pancakes frequently for supper at six o'clock (dinner was the main meal and was served at noon). We would have had them more often still, if I'd had more influence than I did: my mother judged them to be too starchy and, by the time we'd slathered them in syrup, too sweet to be entirely good for us.

Our pancakes were simple unembellished affairs — made with white flour, butter, eggs and either plain whole milk, sour milk or buttermilk, depending on what was most plentiful. To my recollection Mother never dabbled in blueberry pancakes or waffles: these wonders later came to represent to me the astonishing sophistication of big city restaurants, and they played a larger part in my diet for a time than either my mother or any sane nutritionist would have approved.

But our pancakes were nevertheless fine things. They puffed up sometimes to become tender and fluffy in the middle, with a golden crisp surface. At other times they were thin, quite flat, dark brown to almost black on the outside and presented a bit of resistance to the teeth. I could never decide which version I liked best, though Mother always said the second version was a

mistake, that she'd added too much milk and the stove was too hot.

Since I felt we didn't have pancakes often enough (though we *never* missed a Shrove Tuesday), when Mother went to Winnipeg to visit her sisters, I applied a combination of nagging and flattery to get the hired girl to make pancakes. My father grumbled that D____, the current boss over our meals, couldn't make pancakes "like your mother." He was right, and for a while we had a series of disappointing pancakes that looked all right but were runny in the middle.

My father must have felt this was a domestic crisis requiring firm action because suddenly Mother gave a lesson in pancake making. The secret D____ and I needed to know about cooking pancakes is that after you pour (or spoon) the batter onto a hot griddle, you wait until bubbles appear on the top surface and the surface appears *almost* dry, with a satiny sheen, before you flip the pancake over to brown on the other side. Voilà! No runny middles.

Our pancakes were always drenched in maple syrup. Every spring a tall gallon tin with our name on it arrived by train from Quebec. It was doled out, a pitcher at a time, for our pancake suppers and poured over the

butter that had come from the creamery across the road in five-pound lots. I don't know what the maple syrup cost, but the butter I was sent to bring home was five pounds for a dollar.

When I discovered in Toronto that pancakes were available in restaurants all day long and into the night, I went on a year-long binge and gained more weight than was becoming. I found blueberry pancakes, and blueberry syrup. I was astonished at waffles and advanced swiftly to the further delights of waffles with cinnamon, ice cream *and* maple syrup. When my husband and I were ''courting'' (that's the only word I can think of — which certainly dates me), I worked nights at *The Globe and Mail* and he worked days at *The Toronto Star*. Most of our dance of advance and retreat was conducted at 2 A.M. in an all-night restaurant over plates of waffles (for me) and apple pie (for him).

Later still, when I in turn became the stern guardian of my children's nutrition, I began to make pancakes with whole wheat and sometimes buckwheat flour. I found that adding blueberries made pancakes purple. I didn't know that if you dredged the berries in flour before adding them to the batter, they ''bled'' less, but I did discover that leftover pancake batter would keep agreeably in the fridge for a couple of days.

My sister-in-law impressed me enormously by making Crêpes Suzette for Christmas Day breakfast: I'd never seen food *deliberately* set on fire before, though I'd accomplished it once by accident when a brown bag I was heating buns in burst into flames. Crêpes seemed an enchanting idea, with most of the advantages of pancakes and the added challenge of filling them with all the other things you like best. I still can't decide whether I prefer sweet crêpes filled with fruit and dusted with icing sugar or praline, or savory crêpes bulging with shrimp and crab. In a certain devil-may-care mood I've been known to order both in a crêperie.

My mother died without ever knowing the crêpe. I wonder what she'd have thought of them. The prairie cooking of the Depression years didn't permit such high-flown fancies. But there's no reason you and I shouldn't enjoy them while we may. They'll never supplant the old-fashioned pancake for a simple common-sense breakfast or supper, but you'll find some delectable recipes for both in the following pages.

Basic Pancakes

BASIC PANCAKE BATTER

Makes about 1 dozen 4" pancakes
Preparation time: 5 minutes
Cooking time: about 2 minutes per pancake

These pancakes are wonderful with maple syrup or fruit syrups. Batter can stand overnight in the refrigerator if you wish.

1¼ cups	sifted flour
2½ tsp	baking powder
¾ tsp	salt
¾ cups	milk (or more, if you like moister pancakes)
1	egg, beaten
3 Tb	melted butter, margarine or shortening

▪ Measure flour into a bowl with baking powder and salt. Add milk, egg and melted butter and beat a little with wooden spoon; batter should be a little lumpy. ▪ Pour onto medium-hot, non-stick or well-seasoned cast-iron griddle. ▪ When bubbles begin to form on top, flip over and brown on other side.
calories/pancake: about 100

CRÊPE BATTERS

Makes 18 crêpes
Preparation time: 10 minutes

Crêpes are wonderful envelopes for all kinds of fillings.

BASIC CRÊPES:

3	eggs
1½ cups	flour
1½ cups	milk
2 Tb	vegetable oil
	salt to taste

▪ Beat eggs well at medium speed in a large bowl. ▪ Gradually add dry ingredients alternately with milk and oil. ▪ Beat until smooth. Batter may be cooked immediately or refrigerated in a covered container for up to 3 days. ▪ Brush a 10″ frying pan lightly with oil and heat over medium-high heat. ▪ Pour 2 to 3 tablespoons of batter into pan while holding it just above the heating unit. ▪ Immediately tilt pan in all directions, swirling the batter so it covers the bottom of the pan in a very thin layer. This must be done quickly before the batter cooks too much. ▪ Replace pan on heating unit and continue to cook over medium-high heat. ▪ As crêpes cook, they lose their glossy appearance and the edges and top become slightly dry. The finished crêpe will be slightly browned on the underside. ▪ Loosen crêpe with a spatula and turn over; cook other side for a few seconds. ▪ Remove from pan with a spatula. ▪ To store prepared crêpes, stack with waxed paper between layers in a plastic container. Prepared crêpes may be refrigerated for 3 to 5 days or frozen for several months. Thaw frozen crêpes for at least one hour before using as the crêpes become brittle and fragile when frozen.

Parmesan Herb Crêpes:
Add to ingredients of Basic Crêpes:

½ cup	grated Parmesan cheese
1 Tb	dried parsley
1 tsp	dried thyme

Chocolate Dessert Crêpes:
Add to ingredients of Basic Crêpes:

¼ cup	sugar
1 tsp	coffee liqueur
2 Tb	sifted cocoa powder

Basic Dessert Crêpes:
Decrease quantity of milk in Basic Crêpes to 1⅓ cups and add the following ingredients:

1 Tb	sugar
1 tsp	rum

Basic Crêpes – calories/crêpe: 79
Parmesan Herb Crêpes – calories/crêpe: 90
Chocolate Dessert Crêpes – calories/crêpe: 90
Basic Dessert Crêpes – calories/crêpe: 82

CRÊPES SUZETTE

Serves 4
Preparation time: 10 minutes
Standing time: 2 hours
Cooking time: less than 1 minute per crêpe

The French make nearly transparent circles, pour a Grand Marnier-based syrup over them and flame them with liqueurs and brandy to create the well-known dessert, Crêpes Suzette. You'll need clarified butter for these.

CRÊPES:

3	eggs
2	egg yolks
½ cup	milk
½ cup	cold water
½ cup	unsalted clarified butter
2 Tb	brandy
1 cup	flour
½ tsp	salt
2 Tb	sugar
1 tsp	orange extract (optional)

SAUCE:

½ cup	unsalted butter
½ cup	icing sugar
	grated peel and juice of 1 large orange
12 Tb	Grand Marnier, Curaçao or Cointreau
½ cup	brandy
1 Tb	sugar

Crêpes Suzette

- Put all crêpe ingredients (use only 2 tablespoons of the clarified butter) into a blender. - Whirl until smooth. - Let batter stand two hours at room temperature. - Heat an 8″ non-stick skillet until very hot. - Brush with clarified butter. - Add 2 to 3 tablespoons of batter. - Quickly turn and tip skillet so that batter forms a thin, even film. It will cook almost immediately – 10 seconds at most. - Turn. - Cook another few seconds. - Slide out onto a warm plate. - Repeat procedure, adding butter as necessary, until all batter is used. You will have about 24 crêpes. - To make sauce, cream together butter and icing sugar. - Add grated orange peel to the butter-sugar mixture. - Stir in orange juice and 6 tablespoons of the liqueur. - Put mixture into a chafing dish or electric skillet. - Heat until mixture bubbles. - Using a fork, dip each crêpe into the hot mixture, fold into quarters and leave in the skillet. - When all crêpes have been added, sprinkle on 1 tablespoon sugar. - Add the remaining 6 tablespoons liqueur and the brandy. - Stand back and light the liquid with a match. - Spoon flaming liquid over crêpes. - Serve as soon as the flames subside.

calories/serving: 951

CRANBERRY HONEY SAUCE

Serves 6 to 8
Preparation time: 15 minutes
Cooking time: 10 minutes

Serve this delicious sauce over pancakes or hot breakfast cereal.

2 cups	cranberry sauce
⅓ cup	fresh orange juice
¼ cup	honey
½ tsp	grated orange peel

- Combine all ingredients in a small saucepan. - Stir over medium heat until blended and hot, about 10 minutes.

calories/serving: 160 for 6 servings
120 for 8 servings

CLARIFIED BUTTER

Butter contains salt, milk solids and impurities that tend to burn when heated to high temperatures. One way to prevent this is to use clarified butter for sautéeing or frying. To clarify butter, cut it into small pieces and place in a saucepan over moderate heat. When the butter has melted, skim off the foam and strain the clear, yellow liquid into a bowl, leaving behind the milky residue. The residue can be used to enrich sauces or soups.

Crêpe Quiche

CHICKEN OR TURKEY CRÊPES

Serves 8 to 10
Preparation time: 25 to 30 minutes
Cooking time: 25 minutes

A tasty way to use leftover chicken or turkey.

8 to 10	prepared Parmesan Herb Crêpes
¼ cup	butter
⅓ cup	flour
	salt and pepper to taste
1 Tb	finely chopped fresh parsley
1½ cups	milk
1½ cups	grated Cheddar cheese
1 cup	leftover sage and onion bread stuffing
1 cup	cooked chicken or turkey chunks

■ Melt butter in a medium saucepan. ■ Add flour, salt, pepper and parsley. ■ Gradually stir in milk. ■ Add cheese. ■ Cook and stir until thick. ■ Mix 1 cup of sauce with leftover bread stuffing and chicken or turkey. ■ Fill center strip of each crêpe with stuffing mixture and fold 2 sides over filling. ■ Place crêpes, folded side down, in a buttered baking pan. ■ Cover with remaining sauce. ■ Bake in preheated 325°F oven for 25 minutes, or until filling is bubbling.

calories/serving: 357 for 8 servings
305 for 10 servings
protein, niacin: excellent
calcium: good
iron, vitamin A, thiamin, riboflavin: fair

CRÊPE QUICHE

Serves 6 to 8
Preparation time: 20 minutes
Cooking time: 15 to 20 minutes

An easy but elegant brunch dish.

6 to 8	prepared Basic Crêpes
1 cup	diced cooked ham
½ cup	grated Cheddar cheese
½ cup	grated Emmenthal cheese
1 Tb	mustard
1	green onion, chopped
2 cups	milk
4	eggs
	salt and pepper to taste

■ Line individual greased 4″ custard cups with cooked crêpes. ■ Combine ham, cheeses, mustard and green onion. ■ Arrange in prepared crêpe cups. ■ Beat together milk, eggs, salt and pepper. ■ Pour over the filling. ■ Bake in preheated 350°F oven for 15 to 20 minutes or until firm. ■ Cool slightly before removing from custard cups. ■ Serve hot.

calories/serving: 355 for 6 servings
284 for 8 servings
protein, niacin: excellent
calcium, iron, vitamin A, thiamin, riboflavin: good

POTATO PANCAKES

Serves 8 to 10
Preparation time: 15 minutes
Cooking time: 1 to 2 minutes per pancake

Middle European families sit down to pancakes made from potatoes or potato flour. In Jewish families Passover meals usually include matzo meal latkes, potato pancakes made from pulverized wheat crackers.

2	eggs
3 cups	grated, drained raw potatoes (measure after draining)
¼ cup	grated onion
1 tsp	salt
½ tsp	pepper
2 Tb	flour
½ cup	butter or chicken fat

■ Beat eggs. ■ Add potatoes, onion, salt, pepper and flour. ■ Stir until smooth. ■ Heat ¼ cup of the fat in a large non-stick skillet. ■ Drop batter by heaping tablespoons onto hot fat. ■ Fry until browned on both sides and crisp. Repeat with remaining fat and batter. ■ Serve with sour cream or applesauce.

calories/serving: 186 for 8 servings
149 for 10 servings
vitamin C: excellent
vitamin A, niacin: fair

BUCKWHEAT PANCAKES

Serves 8
Preparation time: 10 minutes
Standing time: at least 1 hour
Cooking time: 1 to 2 minutes per pancake

Russian "blinis" are made with buckwheat flour for a hearty meal.

2 cups	buckwheat flour
1 cup	unsifted all-purpose flour
1 tsp	sugar
2 tsp	salt
1 Tb	dry active yeast (1 envelope)
1 cup plus 1 Tb	warm water
2 cups	milk
¼ cup	melted butter
½ tsp	baking soda

▪ Combine flours with sugar and salt. ▪ Sprinkle yeast onto warm water and let stand 5 minutes; stir. ▪ Add milk and butter. ▪ Combine flour and liquid mixtures; beat until smooth. ▪ Allow to rise in a warm place at least 1 hour, or overnight. ▪ Stir in baking soda dissolved in 1 tablespoon warm water. ▪ Mix well. ▪ Cook on a hot, greased, non-stick griddle, using 3 tablespoons batter per pancake. ▪ Serve with syrup or sour cream and caviar, if your budget will allow.

calories/serving: 234
niacin: good
protein, calcium, thiamin, riboflavin: fair
fiber: moderate

CHEDDAR SALMON CRÊPES

Serves 8 to 10
Preparation time: 25 to 30 minutes
Cooking time: 25 minutes

A delicious, nourishing combination for supper, buffet table or brunch.

8 to 10	prepared Parmesan Herb Crêpes
5 Tb	butter or margarine
½ cup	chopped green onions
1 cup	sliced mushrooms
⅓ cup	flour
	salt and pepper to taste
1 Tb	finely chopped fresh parsley
1¼ cups	milk
3 cups	grated Cheddar cheese
2 Tb	sherry
1 can	(7.5 oz/213 g) salmon, drained, boned and flaked

▪ Melt 1 tablespoon of the butter in a large skillet and sauté onions and mushrooms. ▪ Add remaining butter, flour, salt, pepper and parsley. ▪ Gradually stir in milk. ▪ Add 1½ cups of the cheese and sherry. ▪ Cook and stir until thick. ▪ Mix in salmon. ▪ Fill strip along center of each crêpe with salmon mixture and fold up 2 sides. ▪ Place crêpes, folded side down, in a buttered baking pan. ▪ Sprinkle with remaining cheese. ▪ Bake in preheated 325°F oven for 25 minutes.

calories/serving: 429 for 8 servings
364 for 10 servings
protein, calcium, niacin: excellent
vitamin A, riboflavin: good
iron, thiamin: fair

CRÊPES MANICOTTI

Serves 8
Preparation time: 10 minutes
Cooking time: 20 to 30 minutes

This would be an attractive dish for a buffet table.

8	prepared Parmesan Herb Crêpes
1 cup	cottage cheese
1 pkg	(4 oz/125 g) cream cheese, softened
2 Tb	softened butter or block margarine
3 Tb	finely chopped fresh parsley
1 Tb	finely chopped fresh chives
1	egg, beaten
	salt to taste
1 can	(5½ oz/156 mL) tomato paste
½ cup	water
2 tsp	garlic salt
½ tsp	dried thyme
¾ cup	grated Parmesan cheese

▪ Mix together cottage cheese, cream cheese, butter, 2 tablespoons of the parsley, chives, egg and salt. ▪ Spoon 2 tablespoons of cheese mixture along center strip of each crêpe and fold over two sides. ▪ Place, folded side down, in a shallow buttered baking pan. ▪ Stir together tomato paste, water, remaining parsley, garlic salt, thyme and ¼ cup of the Parmesan cheese in a small bowl. ▪ Spread tomato mixture over crêpes. ▪ Sprinkle with remaining Parmesan cheese. ▪ Bake in preheated 350°F oven for 20 to 30 minutes.

calories/serving: 259
protein, niacin: excellent
calcium, vitamin A: good
iron, vitamin C, thiamin, riboflavin: fair

DESSERTS

One of the many shocks I endured when I left home was to discover there was no homemade dessert in the *Globe and Mail* cafeteria. I grew up surrounded by chocolate cakes, oatmeal cookies, fruit pies, custards and puddings smothered in whipped cream.

We lived in a farming community, and every Saturday night a farmer's wife dropped off a quart-sealer of thick yellow cream at our door. When I could surprise my mother in an indulgent mood on Sunday morning, I would make something I called Chocolate Mousse. I pirated about two cups of the cream, whipped it into soft peaks and folded in enough cocoa to make it the color of milk chocolate. Then I froze it in the top of the fridge. My father and I ate it from large soup bowls. Ambrosia. (Mercifully we'd never heard of cholesterol: I don't think it had been invented yet.)

My father said he could eat sawdust with whipped cream. If he picked a horse in the Irish Sweepstakes, he told us, he would buy a Jersey cow and a strawberry patch on Vancouver Island. When I was small, I thought we needed the horse to get us there and formed an alarming mental picture of me, as the smallest, bumping over the mountains on the furthest back end of the

horse, clinging to its tail. I doubted that even all the strawberries and whipped cream you could eat would be worth it.

We took our sweets seriously and without guilt. My girlfriend and I made devastating batches of chocolate fudge; my sister's specialty was green and pink Divinity Fudge. I once incurred her terrifying wrath by accidentally sitting on a batch she had set out to cool.

One Sunday on their ''Sunday Drive'' my parents were invited to stay for dinner at a neighboring farm. Mother phoned to tell my oldest brother (then about 16) that he was in charge of dinner and that there was a chocolate cake *in the suitcase under my father's bed*. I remember my brother telling her we'd already found the cake, but I don't recall whether we'd eaten it or just admired it.

After I left home, my first attempt at making an honest-to-goodness dessert was a cherry pie, a sturdy affair, as it turned out, that I could have rolled to the table without doing it serious damage. I served it to the man I was dating at the time, on a card table in the grotty little bed-sitting room I shared with another girl.

The pie was meant to instill confidence in the young man that when he married me he'd be well fed. (We

Lemon Lime Cheesecake and Navel Orange Slices in Spiced Red Wine

thought like that in those days.) He struggled with his fork for a few minutes before taking up his knife to gain access to the filling. It was one of the low moments of my 18-year-old life.

Perhaps it was the candlelight, or the slinky black dress I'd taken the precaution of wearing, but shortly after the pie he became my fiancé. (The word seems almost quaint now, but that's the word we used.)

I reluctantly took the pie problem to my mother, who provided me with a foolproof pastry recipe (you'll find it in this book) and the admonition to handle pastry ''with a light touch.'' So charmed was I by future successes, and so eager to become the apple-pie-cooling-on-the-windowsill kind of wife presented as the ideal by all the women's magazines, that pies became standard fare at my table.

Cookie making, that other compulsory set-piece of the 1950s repertoire, was not difficult, but it took *so much time*. Children seemed equipped with the ability to eat four dozen cookies a day. Conventional wisdom decreed that only sloths fed their children store-bought cookies.

So I learned to trick myself into making cookies while pretending I wasn't. Early in the morning I'd plunk a chunk of butter or shortening into a large mixing bowl, lay a cookie recipe beside it and go about my laundry. Later, when the shortening was soft, I'd beat in some sugar. Later still I'd sidle up to the recipe and see what came next and toss it into the bowl. By late afternoon I'd painted myself into a corner where I either had to make cookies or throw the whole mess out. Money was scarce and waste unthinkable, so I'd sigh and get on with the job. By the time the kids came home from school, cookies would be cooling all over the kitchen counters and I could award myself the Good Housekeeping seal of approval. Cookies alone were enough to make me enlist in the women's liberation movement when it arrived.

''What's for dessert?'' is still the question most often heard from my grandchildren. And the yearning for the yummy desserts of childhood may be the spur that goads many reluctant cooks to don an apron. We think the desserts you find here will be well worth your efforts. They may even get woven into your family's memories.

Cookies, Squares and Candies

BROWN SUGAR COOKIES

Makes 5 to 6 dozen
Preparation time: 20 minutes
Chilling time: 1 hour or overnight
Cooking time: 8 to 9 minutes

Spiceless but not spineless gingerbread men or Santas can be cut from this brown sugar cookie dough. Add spices – ground cinnamon, ginger, grated nutmeg – if you wish.

½ cup	softened butter or margarine
1 cup	dark brown sugar
1	egg
¾ tsp	vanilla
2 cups	flour
1¼ tsp	baking powder
¼ tsp	salt
2 tsp	milk

SUGAR ICING:

¼ cup	softened butter
4½ cups	sifted icing sugar
1 Tb	vanilla
4 to 5 Tb	milk or light cream
	food coloring (optional)

▪ Cream butter or margarine with sugar. ▪ Add egg and vanilla and beat until mixture is light and fluffy. ▪ Sift together flour, baking powder and salt and mix in alternately with milk. ▪ Chill dough until it is stiff enough to handle, 1 hour or overnight. ▪ Roll dough to ⅛″ thickness on a lightly floured board or pastry cloth. ▪ Cut out cookies in rounds or using a gingerbread man cutter and place on greased cookie sheets. ▪ Bake in preheated 400°F oven 8 to 9 minutes, or until delicately brown. ▪ Remove from cookie sheets and let cool on wire racks. ▪ To make sugar icing, cream butter until fluffy. ▪ Gradually stir in icing sugar. ▪ Add vanilla and a little milk or cream and continue stirring until you have a smooth consistency. Make icing stiff if you're piping with a pastry tube. Thin with a few drops of hot water if you're spreading icing with a spatula. ▪ Separate icing into small bowls and tint each bowlful with a different food coloring. ▪ Keep covered with a damp cloth to prevent drying out. Icing will keep covered in the refrigerator for several days.

calories/cookie: 91 for 5 dozen
76 for 6 dozen

MARZIPAN

Makes about 1¾ cups
Preparation time: 20 minutes
Standing time: 1 week
Cooking time: about 10 minutes

It's important to store the almond paste in an airtight jar for at least a week until it ripens into a soft mass.

½ lb	blanched almonds
1 cup	sugar
½ cup	water
	icing sugar
few drops	almond extract, vanilla extract or rose water

▪ Grind almonds through fine blade of food chopper 3 or 4 times until very fine, or whirl in food processor. ▪ Bring sugar and water to boil in a medium saucepan, stirring until sugar dissolves. ▪ Boil hard for about 10 minutes, until syrup registers 238°F on a candy thermometer or syrup forms a soft ball when dropped into cold water. ▪ Add almonds and stir until creamy. ▪ Sprinkle a large platter with icing sugar, then spread almond mixture on the platter and cool. ▪ Take crumbly mixture off the platter and pack it into a jar with a tight-fitting lid. ▪ Cover tightly and let stand 1 week to mellow. ▪ Gather almond mixture into a ball and knead on a board sprinkled with icing sugar, until smooth and pliable. Knead in a few drops of desired flavoring.

calories/tablespoon: about 80

SHORTBREAD STARS AND BELLS

Makes about 4 dozen
Preparation time: 15 minutes
Chilling time: 30 minutes
Cooking time: 12 to 15 minutes

There are only three ingredients to measure for this buttery shortbread, which can be cut into stars, bells and trees, or shaped into melt-in-your-mouth bars.

1 cup	softened butter
½ cup	light brown sugar
2½ cups (scant)	flour

▪ Cream butter until fluffy. ▪ Gradually add sugar, then flour. ▪ Work with your hands until mixture forms a ball. If necessary, chill until dough is stiff enough to handle, about 30 minutes. ▪ Pat out and roll to ½″ thickness on a lightly floured board or pastry cloth. ▪ Cut into stars, bells and other shapes. ▪ Place them on ungreased cookie sheets and bake in preheated 325°F oven 12 to 15 minutes or until light golden brown. ▪ Let cool on cookie sheets before removing to wire racks.

calories/cookie: 71

PRALINES

Makes about 2 dozen
Preparation time: 10 minutes
Cooking time: 15 minutes

Even if you don't usually like candy, you'll fall for these.

1¾ cups	sugar
1 cup	boiling water
pinch	salt
1 Tb	butter
½ tsp	vanilla
1 cup	pecan halves

▪ Stir ½ cup of the sugar in a medium saucepan over medium heat until it melts into a pale yellow syrup. ▪ Remove from heat and carefully add boiling water. ▪ Return to heat and stir until lumps dissolve. ▪ Stir in salt, butter and remaining 1¼ cups sugar and boil hard, stirring constantly, until candy thermometer registers 238°F, or syrup forms a soft ball when dropped into cold water. ▪ Remove from heat and let stand 5 minutes. ▪ Add vanilla and pecans and stir 3 to 5 minutes until creamy, then quickly drop by large spoonfuls onto waxed paper. ▪ Let stand until set.

calories/piece: 96

STUFFED DRIED FRUITS

Preparation time: 15 minutes

What could be nicer than dried fruit to top off a wonderful meal? Here are some suggestions to make special treats from apricots, dates and prunes.

dried apricots
marzipan
blanched toasted almonds
dates
walnut pieces
sugar
pitted prunes

▪ Stuff apricots with marzipan, using either 1 large apricot half folded around the marzipan filling, or 2 small halves sandwiched around the marzipan. ▪ Press an almond into the top of each. ▪ Stuff dates with walnut pieces and roll them in sugar. ▪ Stuff prunes with either marzipan or walnut pieces and roll in sugar. ▪ Set into individual paper candy cases. ▪ Place in a dish and cover tightly with plastic wrap until serving time.

calories/marzipan-stuffed apricot: 36
calories/walnut-stuffed date: 42
calories/marzipan-stuffed prune: 48
calories/walnut-stuffed prune: 39

Pralines

APPLE SHORTBREAD WEDGES

Serves 8
Preparation time: 30 minutes
Cooking time: 25 minutes

Imagine a combination of buttery shortbread and spicy cooked apples.

SHORTBREAD BASE:

1 cup	butter, at room temperature
½ cup	brown sugar
2 cups	flour
1 tsp	vanilla

TOPPING:

3 cups	diced, peeled apples
½ cup	brown sugar
¼ tsp	ground cinnamon
1 Tb	flour
	whipped cream or ice cream
	ground cinnamon for decoration

▪ Mix together ingredients for shortbread, and knead into a firm ball. ▪ Roll dough into a 10″ circle, ¼″ thick. ▪ Place in 10″ springform cake pan or pie plate and turn up the edges to form a rim. ▪ For topping, mix apples, brown sugar, cinnamon and flour in a bowl. ▪ Spread on top of shortbread, leaving a 1″ border. ▪ Bake in preheated 375°F oven for 25 minutes. ▪ Make sure that the center is thoroughly baked. ▪ While still hot from the oven, cut carefully into eight wedges. ▪ Serve hot or cold with whipped cream or ice cream, dusted with cinnamon.

calories/serving: about 340

HERMITS

Preparation time: 30 minutes
Cooking time: 8 to 10 minutes

Who knows why these are called Hermits, but they always are. Whole wheat flour can be used, if you prefer, and the sugar can be reduced to 1 cup.

1 cup	**softened butter or margarine**
1½ cups	**brown sugar**
2	**eggs**
1 cup	**raisins**
1 cup	**pitted, chopped dates**
⅓ cup	**walnut pieces**
½ tsp	**baking soda**
2 Tb	**boiling water**
2¼ cups (approx.)	**flour**
1 tsp	**salt**
1 tsp	**ground cinnamon or to taste**
½ tsp	**grated nutmeg or to taste**
pinch	**ground cloves**

▪ Beat butter or margarine until light. ▪ Beat in sugar and eggs thoroughly. ▪ Mix in raisins, dates and walnuts. ▪ Dissolve baking soda in boiling water and add, mixing thoroughly. ▪ Sift flour with spices and add gradually to butter mixture until you have a firm dough. ▪ Drop by tablespoons onto greased cookie sheets and bake in preheated 375°F oven until firm, about 8 to 10 minutes. ▪ Let cool on a wire rack.

calories/cookie: 105

PUMPKIN CHOCOLATE CHIP COOKIES

Makes about 4 dozen
Preparation time: 15 minutes
Cooking time: 8 to 10 minutes

Pumpkin gives a new and delicious twist to an old favorite.

1 cup	**sugar**
1 cup	**cooked or canned pumpkin**
½ cup	**shortening**
1 Tb	**grated orange peel**
2 cups	**flour**
1 tsp	**baking powder**
1 tsp	**baking soda**
1 tsp	**ground cinnamon**
¼ tsp	**salt**
1 cup	**semi-sweet chocolate chips**

▪ Mix sugar, pumpkin, shortening and orange peel with an electric mixer until well blended. ▪ Sift dry ingredients, except chocolate chips, and stir into blended mixture. ▪ Add chocolate chips. ▪ Drop by teaspoonfuls onto an ungreased cookie sheet. ▪ Bake in preheated 375°F oven until light brown, about 8 to 10 minutes. ▪ Remove from cookie sheet and let cool on rack.

calories/cookie: 70

APPLE OATMEAL SQUARES

Makes 16
Preparation time: 30 minutes
Cooking time: 30 minutes

These versatile squares make a nice dessert when served warm with a dollop of whipped cream or ice cream. For speed of preparation and added nutrition, use unpeeled apples.

½ cup	**butter**
1 cup	**packed brown sugar**
1 cup	**rolled oats**
1 cup	**flour**
½ tsp	**baking soda**
½ tsp	**salt**
½ cup	**chopped walnuts, hazelnuts, pecans or almonds**

APPLE FILLING:	
½ cup	**packed brown sugar**
2 Tb	**flour**
1 tsp	**ground cinnamon**
½ cup	**raisins, currants or chopped dates**
1	**egg, beaten**
3	**large apples, unpeeled, cored and chopped**

▪ Using an electric mixer, cream butter and 1 cup sugar together. ▪ Add rolled oats and mix to blend. ▪ Combine 1 cup flour, baking soda and salt. ▪ Add to oatmeal mixture. ▪ Blend well until mixture is crumbly. ▪ Set aside 1 cup of the mixture and stir in chopped nuts. This will be used later for topping. ▪ Press remaining mixture into a buttered 9″ square baking dish. ▪ Bake in preheated 350°F oven for 15 minutes. ▪ To make apple filling, stir together sugar, flour, cinnamon and raisins. ▪ Blend in egg. ▪ Add chopped apples and stir until blended. ▪ Pour over baked crust and spread evenly. ▪ Sprinkle with reserved crumb-nut mixture. ▪ Bake in 350°F oven for additional 30 minutes, or until apples are tender. ▪ Cool to lukewarm in pan before cutting.

calories/square: 246
fiber: moderate

Hermits, Pumpkin Chocolate Chip Cookies and
Apple Oatmeal Squares

Old-Fashioned Butterscotch Patties, Peanut Clusters and Peppermint Bark

PEPPERMINT BARK

Makes about ½ lb
Preparation time: 10 minutes
Setting time: several hours

This easy treat uses the holiday season's bright candy canes.

½ lb	white or dark chocolate
⅓ cup	crushed candy canes

▪ Break up chocolate slightly and place in heat-proof bowl over hot, not boiling, water. ▪ Stir chocolate occasionally until it melts. ▪ Remove from heat and stir in crushed candy canes. ▪ Spread in thin layer on waxed paper. ▪ When cool, lift paper and candy into an airtight container to set. ▪ Break into chunks to serve.

calories/recipe: 796

OLD-FASHIONED BUTTERSCOTCH PATTIES

Makes about 7 dozen
Preparation time: about 45 minutes
Cooking time: about 35 minutes

These bright golden-brown gems will remind you of your favorite childhood candy store. They're really quite easy to make at home, if you have a candy thermometer.

2 cups	sugar
¾ cup	corn syrup
¼ cup	water
¼ cup	light cream
½ cup	unsalted butter

▪ Combine sugar, corn syrup, water and cream in an oiled or non-stick saucepan. ▪ Bring to boil over medium heat, stirring constantly. ▪ Cook, stirring often, until mixture registers 260°F on a candy thermometer or it forms a hard ball when dropped into cold water. ▪ Add butter. ▪ Cook, stirring often, until mixture registers 280°F on thermometer. (A teaspoon of syrup will separate into threads that are hard but not brittle.) ▪ Remove from heat. ▪ Let cool 3 minutes. ▪ Drop from tip of teaspoon onto 3 large lightly buttered cookie sheets to form 1″ round patties. If mixture gets too stiff to drop, reheat gently over simmering water. ▪ When patties are cool, gently loosen with a metal spatula. ▪ Store in airtight container.

calories/candy: 39

PEANUT CLUSTERS

Makes about 4 dozen
Preparation time: 15 minutes
Setting time: 3 hours

It is worth buying good quality chocolate and very fresh peanuts for this candy. It's super easy to make and sure to be a hit.

13 oz	bittersweet (or semi-sweet) chocolate or milk chocolate
3 cups	unsalted dry roast peanuts

▪ Break up chocolate slightly and place in a large heat-proof bowl. ▪ Fill medium saucepan half full of water and bring to boil. ▪ Remove from heat and when rapid boiling stops, set bowl on top of, but not in, water. ▪ Stir chocolate occasionally until it melts, placing saucepan back on low heat if chocolate doesn't completely melt. Be sure not to let water come to boil again. ▪ Stir in peanuts until evenly coated. ▪ Place by heaping teaspoonfuls on waxed paper and leave, uncovered, at room temperature until cool and set, at least 3 hours. ▪ Store in cool place.

calories/piece: 94

TRIPLE DECKER SQUARES

Makes 117 1-inch squares
Preparation time: 15 minutes
Cooking time: 32 minutes

A quick-to-make treat that the kids will love.

2 cups	**flour**
¼ cup	**sugar**
1 cup	**butter**
FILLING:	
1 cup	**butter**
1 cup	**packed brown sugar**
¼ cup	**corn syrup**
1 can	**(14 oz/300 mL) sweetened condensed milk, not evaporated**
1 tsp	**vanilla**
2 cups	**semi-sweet chocolate chips**

▪ Stir together flour and sugar in a large bowl. ▪ Cut in 1 cup butter until mixture resembles crumbs. ▪ Press evenly into greased 13″ × 9″ baking pan. ▪ Bake in preheated 350°F oven about 25 minutes or until lightly colored. ▪ Meanwhile prepare filling. Stir together 1 cup butter, brown sugar, syrup and milk in a medium heavy saucepan over low heat until sugar is dissolved. ▪ Bring to boil over medium heat, stirring constantly. ▪ Boil gently 7 minutes. ▪ Remove from heat, add vanilla and beat well. ▪ Pour over warm base and spread to cover evenly. ▪ Cool in pan on rack. ▪ Melt chocolate chips in top of double boiler, over simmering water, and spread over cooled filling. ▪ Refrigerate to set chocolate. ▪ Cut into squares with a sharp knife.

calories/1″ square: 76

PECAN PIE FINGERS

Makes 32
Preparation time: 15 minutes
Cooking time: 40 to 55 minutes

Everyone loves pecan pie, but no one ever admits to eating a whole piece. The solution: cutting this classic dessert into fingers. Toasting the pecans is an easy step, and gives much more depth of flavor.

1½ cups	**coarsely chopped pecans**
1 cup	**packed brown sugar**
½ cup plus 2 Tb	**butter**
1 cup	**flour**
½ cup	**corn syrup**
3	**eggs, lightly beaten**
1 tsp	**vanilla**
¼ tsp	**salt**

▪ Spread pecans out on large baking sheet and toast in preheated 350°F oven for 5 to 10 minutes or until golden and fragrant. ▪ Set aside to cool. ▪ Cream together ¼ cup of the sugar and ½ cup butter in a large bowl. ▪ Stir in flour until mixture resembles coarse crumbs. ▪ Pat into ungreased 9″ square pan. ▪ Bake in preheated 350°F oven for 10 to 15 minutes or until slightly brown around edges. ▪ Meanwhile melt remaining 2 tablespoons butter in a small saucepan over medium heat. ▪ Stir in remaining ¾ cup brown sugar. ▪ Remove from heat and stir in corn syrup, eggs, vanilla and salt. ▪ Stir in pecans and spread over hot crust. ▪ Bake about 25 to 30 minutes or until set. ▪ Run knife around outside edge to loosen. Cool and cut into thin fingers or, while slightly warm, cut into larger pieces to serve with ice cream as a wonderful family dessert.

calories/finger: 150

MELTING CHOCOLATE

Chocolate should be melted in a double boiler, or in a bowl placed over hot, *not* boiling, water. Make sure the inside of the pot or bowl is completely dry before putting in chocolate. Adding 1 to 2 tablespoons vegetable oil (not butter) will aid the melting process. Chocolate may also be melted in liquid, but there should be no more than 6 oz chocolate to each ¼ cup liquid. When adding liquid to melted chocolate, add at least 2 tablespoons at a time.

MELTING CHOCOLATE IN THE MICROWAVE

Microwave 1 to 3 squares at a time, on Medium or Low for 2 to 3 minutes per square. When chocolate starts to soften, stir to finish melting process.

CHOCOLATE SUBSTITUTION

Unsweetened cocoa powder can be used as a substitute for chocolate in many recipes: 3 tablespoons cocoa plus 1 tablespoon shortening is the equivalent of 1 oz (1 square) unsweetened chocolate.

CRANBERRY OAT SQUARES

Serves 8
Preparation time: 20 minutes
Cooking time: 35 to 40 minutes
Try these for dessert, topped with ice cream.

1 cup	**flour**
½ tsp	**baking soda**
1 cup	**butter**
1 cup	**lightly packed brown sugar**
2 cups	**rolled oats**
1½ to 2 cups cranberry sauce	

▪ Sift flour and baking soda into a large bowl. ▪ Cut in butter until mixture resembles fine breadcrumbs. ▪ Add sugar and oats and stir until evenly mixed. ▪ Press half mixture into a buttered 8″ square baking dish. ▪ Spread cranberry sauce evenly over oat mixture. ▪ Cover with remaining oat mixture and pat lightly to smooth. ▪ Bake in preheated 325°F oven for 35 to 40 minutes or until golden brown. Cool in pan before cutting into squares.

calories/serving: 535

APRICOT CITRUS BARS

Makes 40 bars
Preparation time: 30 minutes
Cooking time: 25 to 30 minutes
The tartness of apricot is a pleasant surprise in these thin cake-like bars.

1 cup	**dried apricots**
1½ cups	**flour**
1 tsp	**baking powder**
½ tsp	**salt**
½ cup	**butter, at room temperature**
1¾ cups	**packed brown sugar**
2	**eggs**
1 Tb	**orange or apricot brandy**
1 tsp	**grated orange peel**
ICING:	
1½ cups	**icing sugar**
2 Tb	**fresh orange juice**
1 Tb	**fresh lemon juice**
4 tsp	**softened butter**
1 tsp	**grated orange peel**

▪ Place apricots in a medium bowl and cover with boiling water. ▪ Let soak 15 minutes. ▪ Drain well; chop and stir together with ½ cup of the flour. ▪ Set aside. ▪ Stir together remaining flour, baking powder and salt. ▪ Set aside in a large bowl. ▪ Cream butter and brown sugar until light and fluffy. ▪ Beat in eggs, one at a time. ▪ Stir in brandy and 1 teaspoon orange peel. ▪ Blend in flour mixture only until combined. ▪ Fold in floured apricots and turn mixture into greased 15″ × 10″ jelly roll pan, spreading evenly. ▪ Bake in preheated 350°F oven for 25 to 30 minutes, or until toothpick inserted in center comes out clean. ▪ For icing, combine icing sugar, orange juice, lemon juice, butter and 1 teaspoon orange peel in a small bowl until smooth. ▪ Remove pan from oven and let cool on wire rack 10 minutes. ▪ Run knife around outside edge to loosen. ▪ Spread icing evenly over top. ▪ Cool completely in pan before slicing.

calories/bar: 73

COMMY'S OATMEAL COOKIES

Makes 5 dozen
Preparation time: 30 minutes
Cooking time: 10 to 12 minutes
A great way to fill the cookie jar; children love these.

1 cup	**softened shortening or block margarine**
1 cup	**sugar**
2 cups	**flour**
1 tsp	**salt**
1 tsp	**baking powder**
2 cups	**rolled oats**
½ cup	**warm water**
1 tsp	**vanilla**
1 tsp	**baking soda**
DATE FILLING:	
2 cups	**chopped, pitted dates**
⅓ cup	**brown sugar**
1¼ cups	**water**
1 Tb	**flour**
1 tsp	**vanilla**

▪ Beat shortening or margarine until soft and creamy. ▪ Add sugar and beat until somewhat fluffy. ▪ Mix together flour, salt, baking powder and rolled oats in another bowl. ▪ Stir vanilla and baking soda into warm water. ▪ Gradually add oats mixture and liquid alternately to the shortening. Use your hands, if necessary, to get a good mix. ▪ If dough is too soft to roll, chill for a little while. ▪ Roll out to ⅛″ thickness and cut out cookies with the top of a 2″ water glass. Save scraps and roll again. ▪ Bake on greased cookie sheets in preheated 375°F oven until slightly brown. ▪ Lift from cookie sheets and cool on brown paper or paper towels. ▪ To make date filling, combine all ingredients in a saucepan and boil, stirring, until thickened but not stiff. ▪ Cool. ▪ If you like, put some cooled cookies together like sandwiches with date filling.

calories/cookie: 86

UNCOOKED CHOCOLATE FUDGE

Makes about 2 dozen squares
Preparation time: 15 minutes
Chilling time: 1 hour

Beating old-fashioned cooked fudge is hard work. This uncooked fudge is creamy and good and you can beat everything with an electric mixer.

1	egg
1¾ to 2 cups	sifted icing sugar
4 oz	semi-sweet chocolate
2 Tb	butter
3 Tb	peanut butter

▪ Beat egg well in a large bowl. ▪ Beat in 1¾ cups icing sugar. ▪ Melt chocolate with butter in top of a double boiler. ▪ Stir in peanut butter. ▪ Stir into egg mixture, adding an additional ¼ cup icing sugar if mixture is not stiff enough. ▪ Press into buttered 8″ square pan. ▪ Chill until firm, about 1 hour. ▪ Cut into squares and store in airtight container in refrigerator.

calories/square: 89

LANGUES DE CHAT

Makes about 4½ dozen
Preparation time: 25 minutes
Cooking time: 7 to 8 minutes

The name, meaning cat tongues, describes the shape of these dainty, crisp sweets.

⅓ cup	softened butter
⅔ cup	sugar
¼ tsp	almond extract
2	egg whites
½ cup	sifted flour
	sugar

▪ Cream butter, ⅔ cup sugar and almond extract until light and fluffy. ▪ Beat egg whites until stiff and fold into creamed mixture. ▪ Fold in flour. ▪ Fit a pastry bag or cookie press with a tip with a plain round hole about ¼″ in diameter. ▪ Fill with cookie mixture. ▪ Squeeze onto greased and floured cookie sheets as evenly as possible in strips about pencil width and 2″ to 3″ long. ▪ Leave space between for spreading and try to avoid any thin spots. ▪ Sprinkle each strip with sugar. ▪ Have oven rack just above the center of the oven. Bake cookies in preheated 350°F oven for 7 to 8 minutes, or until browned on the bottom but only lightly browned on top. ▪ Loosen from pan while hot, lift off carefully and cool on racks.

calories/cookie: 27

Uncooked Chocolate Fudge and Sour Cream Fudge

SOUR CREAM FUDGE

Makes about 2 dozen squares
Preparation time: 15 minutes
Cooking time: 15 to 20 minutes

If you're not keen on overly sweet candy, this easy fudge is for you. Toast the pecans until brown and fragrant in a 350°F oven for even more flavor.

2 cups	sugar
1 cup	sour cream
½ tsp	salt
2 Tb	unsalted butter
1 tsp	vanilla
½ cup	chopped pecans
1 oz	semi-sweet chocolate

▪ Combine sugar, sour cream and salt in an oiled or non-stick saucepan. ▪ Bring to boil over medium-high heat and boil until syrup registers 238°F on a candy thermometer or syrup forms a soft ball when dropped into cold water, about 15 minutes. ▪ Immediately remove from heat. ▪ Add butter and vanilla. ▪ Cool to lukewarm without stirring. ▪ Beat vigorously until mixture starts to thicken. ▪ Stir in nuts and pour into well-buttered 8″ square pan. ▪ When cool, melt chocolate in microwave or in a bowl over a pot of simmering water and drizzle over fudge. ▪ Cut into squares and store in airtight container in refrigerator.

calories/square: 117

Easy Chocolate Almond Truffles

PEANUT DATE LOGS

Makes 4 dozen
Preparation time: 10 minutes
Cooking time: 35 to 40 minutes

The combination of peanuts and dates gives these log-shaped cookies a delicious flavor; substitute walnuts for peanuts, if you prefer.

1 cup	sugar
¾ cup	flour
1 tsp	baking powder
¼ tsp	salt
1 cup	finely chopped pitted dates
1 cup	finely chopped unsalted peanuts
3	eggs
1 tsp	vanilla
	fruit sugar or granulated sugar

• Stir together sugar, flour, baking powder and salt in a large bowl. • Blend in dates and nuts. • Beat eggs in a small bowl until thick and lemon colored. • Blend into dry ingredients and stir in vanilla. • Spread in a greased 9″ square pan and bake in preheated 325°F oven 35 to 40 minutes, or until golden brown and a dent is left when you touch the top lightly with a fingertip. • Run knife around outside edge to loosen. • While still warm, cut into 2″ × ½″ bars. • Roll each warm bar between palms of hands into log-shaped cookies. • Roll in fruit sugar (or fine granulated sugar pulverized in a blender) until coated on all sides.

calories/log: 66

EASY CHOCOLATE ALMOND TRUFFLES

Makes about 2½ dozen
Preparation time: 15 minutes
Setting time: about 2 hours

For special gifts, pop these creamy truffles into tiny gold foil cups.

½ cup	heavy cream
6 oz	bittersweet or semi-sweet chocolate, chopped
2 Tb	butter
2 Tb	almond liqueur
⅓ cup	ground almonds
1 cup	icing sugar
	cocoa powder or finely chopped almonds

• Heat cream in a small saucepan until it boils. • Remove from heat and stir in chocolate until it melts. • Stir in butter, almond liqueur, almonds and icing sugar. • Refrigerate about 2 hours or overnight, until chocolate is firm enough to roll. • Form into 1″ balls. • Roll balls in cocoa powder or chopped almonds. • Store in airtight container in refrigerator.

calories/truffle: 87

Swedish Nuts

NO-BAKE MOCHA SQUARES

Makes 2 dozen
Preparation time: 10 minutes
Cooking time: 1 minute

These easy squares are not overly sweet.

1 cup	packed brown sugar
½ cup	butter or block margarine
2 Tb	cocoa powder
2 Tb	milk
1 Tb	instant coffee powder
2	eggs, beaten
3 cups	chocolate graham cracker crumbs
¾ cup	chopped walnuts, pecans or hazelnuts
ICING:	
1 tsp	instant coffee powder
3 Tb	boiling water
2 cups	icing sugar

■ Stir together brown sugar, butter, cocoa, milk, coffee powder and eggs in a small saucepan. ■ Bring to boil, stirring, and boil 1 minute, stirring constantly. ■ Remove from heat; immediately stir in crumbs and nuts. ■ Press into greased 9″ square pan. ■ Cool. ■ To make icing, dissolve coffee powder in boiling water in a cup. ■ Blend hot liquid into icing sugar in a small bowl and stir until smooth. ■ Spread immediately over chocolate base. ■ Let set and cut into squares.

calories/square: 197

SWEDISH NUTS

Makes about 3½ cups
Preparation time: 15 minutes
Cooking time: 45 minutes

These sweet-coated treats are so good they are addictive.

½ lb	blanched almonds (about 1½ cups)
½ lb	pecan halves (about 2 cups)
	salt
2	egg whites
1 cup	sugar
½ cup	butter

■ Toast almonds and pecans in preheated 350°F oven until almonds are golden. ■ Watch pecans carefully or they will get too dark. ■ Sprinkle pecans lightly with salt and let all nuts cool. ■ Beat egg whites and pinch of salt until foamy, then add sugar gradually, beating well after each addition and continuing beating until stiff. ■ Add nuts and fold until they are coated with meringue. ■ Reduce oven temperature to 325°F. ■ Put butter on a large shallow pan with sides (a jelly roll pan is best) and set in oven until butter melts. Add nut mixture to melted butter and stir to blend a little. It will look messy and wrong, but as it bakes, a slightly crisp, sweet coating forms on the nuts. ■ Bake for about 45 minutes, stirring every 10 minutes, until golden brown. ■ Cool and store in a tight container.

calories/¼ cup serving: about 280

Cakes and Tortes

CRANBERRY ORANGE CHEESECAKE

Serves 12 to 16
Preparation time: 40 minutes
Cooking time: 1 hour and 10 minutes

During cranberry season it's nice to use them often. This orange-flavored cheesecake is topped with a fresh cranberry glaze.

1 cup	fine rusk crumbs (8 rusks)
3 Tb	melted butter
2 cups plus 3 Tb	sugar
2 cartons	(each 1 lb/500 g) cream-style cottage cheese
5	eggs
½ cup	sifted flour
2 Tb	grated orange peel
4 Tb	orange juice
	orange food coloring (optional)
1 cup	whipping cream
2 cups	cranberries
¾ cup	water
1½ tsp	unflavored gelatine
½ cup	coarsely chopped walnuts

▪ Combine rusk crumbs, melted butter and 3 tablespoons sugar. ▪ Press mixture evenly in the bottom of buttered 9″ springform pan. ▪ Bake in preheated 350°F oven for 10 minutes. ▪ Cool. ▪ Press cottage cheese through a sieve into a bowl. ▪ Add eggs, one at a time, and beat well after each addition. Or, whirl cottage cheese and eggs in a food processor until smooth and creamy. ▪ Mix flour and 1 cup sugar and beat into the cheese mixture. ▪ Stir in orange peel and 2 tablespoons of the orange juice. ▪ Add a few drops food coloring to tint a delicate orange if you wish. ▪ Whip cream until soft peaks form and fold in, then pour over the crust in the springform pan. ▪ Bake in 350°F oven about 1 hour and 10 minutes or until set. ▪ Cool in pan, then chill. ▪ Cook cranberries, water and remaining 1 cup sugar 5 minutes or until the berries pop. ▪ Soak gelatine in remaining 2 tablespoons orange juice 5 minutes, then stir into the hot berries. ▪ Chill until it begins to thicken, then stir in nuts. ▪ Remove sides from springform pan and slip cheesecake onto a serving plate. Spread with cranberry mixture and chill until shortly before serving time.

calories/serving: 453 for 12 servings
338 for 16 servings
protein, niacin: good
vitamin A, riboflavin: fair

BERRY-FILLED CAKE ROLL

Serves 8
Preparation time: 30 minutes
Cooking time: 17 to 20 minutes
Chilling time: several hours

This jelly roll is best served the day it's made.

3	large eggs
1 cup	sugar
5 Tb	water
1 tsp	vanilla
1 cup	sifted flour
1 tsp	baking powder
¼ tsp	salt
1 tsp	grated lemon peel
	icing sugar

LEMON CREAM FILLING:

1 Tb	cornstarch
½ cup	sugar
¼ cup	lemon juice
¼ cup	water
1 tsp	grated lemon peel
2	egg yolks
1 Tb	butter or margarine
½ cup	whipping cream
1½ cups	blueberries, blackberries or raspberries

▪ Grease sides of a 15″ × 10″ × 1″ jelly roll pan and line bottom with waxed or heavy brown paper. Grease paper. ▪ Beat eggs in a small bowl until thick and fluffy. ▪ Add sugar gradually and beat well after each addition. ▪ Stir in water and vanilla. ▪ Sift flour, baking powder and salt into egg mixture and beat until smooth. ▪ Stir in lemon peel. ▪ Pour into prepared pan and spread evenly. ▪ Bake in preheated 375°F oven 12 to 15 minutes, or until top springs back when touched lightly in the center. ▪ Sift icing sugar over top of cake and turn it out on a towel. ▪ Roll cake and towel up together loosely from one narrow end and let stand on wire rack until cool. ▪ For filling, combine cornstarch and sugar thoroughly in a small saucepan. ▪ Stir in lemon juice, water and lemon peel. ▪ Cook, stirring constantly, over medium-high heat until boiling, thickened and clear. ▪ Beat egg yolks lightly with a fork and add at least half of the hot mixture to them gradually, stirring well. ▪ Return mixture to saucepan and stir over medium heat 1 minute. ▪ Remove from heat and stir in butter or margarine. ▪ Cool. ▪ Whip cream until soft peaks form and fold in. ▪ Unroll cake and spread with filling mixture. ▪ Sprinkle with berries and roll cake up again. ▪ Put on serving plate and cover loosely with transparent wrap. ▪ Chill several hours before serving.

calories/serving: 377

Maple Pecan Torte

MAPLE PECAN TORTE

Serves 8
Preparation time: 45 minutes
Cooking time: about 45 minutes
Chilling time: 1 hour or up to 3 or 4 days
A perfect dessert when maple syrup is abundant.

4 cups	chopped pecans
⅔ cup	sugar
6	eggs, separated
⅔ cup	maple syrup
1 tsp	instant coffee powder
1 cup	unsalted butter, at room temperature
1 cup	icing sugar
8	pecan halves

▪ Spread chopped pecans out on a large cookie sheet.
▪ Toast in preheated 350°F oven, stirring occasionally, until lightly browned, about 10 to 15 minutes.
▪ Set aside to cool. ▪ Butter a 9″ springform pan and line bottom with circle of waxed paper. ▪ Butter waxed paper and dust entire inside of pan and paper with flour. ▪ Set aside. ▪ In two batches, place toasted pecans in food processor with 1 tablespoon of the sugar in each batch. ▪ Process until ground, being careful not to overprocess until gummy. ▪ Set aside.
▪ Beat egg yolks with 2 tablespoons of the maple syrup and all but 1 tablespoon of the remaining sugar. ▪ Beat about 6 minutes or until doubled in volume and very thick. ▪ Beat egg whites with clean beaters in another large bowl until soft peaks form.
▪ Add remaining 1 tablespoon sugar and beat until stiff but not dry. ▪ Fold ground pecans into egg yolks. ▪ Stir in one-quarter of egg whites, then gently fold in remaining egg whites. ▪ Transfer batter to prepared pan and bake in preheated 350°F oven about 45 minutes, or until a toothpick inserted in center of torte comes out clean. ▪ Remove from oven and immediately run a long sharp knife all around inside of pan. ▪ Cool in pan on rack 15 minutes. ▪ Remove sides of pan and let cool completely. The torte will shrink on cooling. ▪ Meanwhile dissolve instant coffee in 1 teaspoon boiling water. Combine with remaining maple syrup in a small saucepan. ▪ Bring to boil. ▪ Reduce heat to medium-low and boil 5 minutes to thicken slightly, stirring only if necessary. ▪ Set aside to cool. ▪ Beat butter with electric mixer in a large bowl until pale and fluffy. ▪ Gradually add icing sugar and continue beating until creamy. ▪ Gradually beat in maple syrup and coffee mixture. ▪ Invert cooled torte onto large flat serving plate. ▪ Remove base of pan and waxed paper, using long metal spatula. ▪ Spread maple icing over sides and top and decorate by running a decorating comb over surface, if you wish. ▪ Place 8 pecan halves around top edge of torte. ▪ Refrigerate, loosely covered with waxed paper, at least 1 hour and up to 3 or 4 days before serving.
calories/serving: 851

Black Forest Cake

BLACK FOREST CAKE

Serves 12
Preparation time: 30 minutes
Cooking time: 40 to 45 minutes

Many Black Forest cake recipes are complicated, but not this deliciously simple version.

CHOCOLATE SPONGE CAKE:

6	egg whites, at room temperature
¾ tsp	cream of tartar
1½ cups	sugar
6	egg yolks
1½ cups	flour
⅓ cup	cocoa powder
1 tsp	baking powder
½ tsp	salt
½ cup	fruit juice or water
1 Tb	grated orange peel (optional)
1 tsp	vanilla or rum flavoring
½ cup	cherry liqueur

CHERRY FILLING:

½ cup	softened butter
3½ cups (approx.)	icing sugar
2 tsp	strong coffee
3 to 4 cups	pitted sour cherries, frozen, or canned and drained

ICING:

2 cups	whipping cream
¼ cup	sugar
1 tsp	vanilla
	chocolate curls

▪ Add cream of tartar to egg whites and beat at high speed until foamy. ▪ Gradually add ¾ cup of the sugar, continuing to beat until stiff peaks form. ▪ Beat remaining ¾ cup sugar together with egg yolks. ▪ Sift together dry ingredients. ▪ Add to egg yolk mixture alternately with fruit juice or water, orange peel and flavoring. ▪ Mix until blended and beat 1 minute. Batter will be stiff. ▪ Fold in egg whites gently. ▪ Pour batter into an ungreased tube pan and bake in preheated 350°F oven for 40 to 45 minutes, or until toothpick inserted in center comes out clean. ▪ Cool in pan and slice horizontally to make 4 layers altogether. ▪ Sprinkle each layer with cherry liqueur. ▪ For filling, blend butter, icing sugar and coffee until creamy and spreadable. ▪ Spread one-third over bottom layer of cake. ▪ Press one-third of the cherries into this filling. Repeat with next two layers. ▪ Put fourth layer on top. ▪ Whip the cream. ▪ Add ¼ cup sugar and vanilla. ▪ Slather whipped cream on top and sides of cake. ▪ Decorate with remaining cherries and the chocolate curls.

calories/serving: about 620

SPONGE CAKE

Makes 2 layers
Preparation time: 20 minutes
Cooking time: 25 minutes

This easy, light cake can be made up to two days ahead and kept in a dry place, or frozen up to two months in an airtight container. Before serving, fill the layers with jam, or fruit, and cream, or your favorite icing.

6	eggs
½ cup	sugar
1 tsp	vanilla
1 cup	flour
pinch	salt

▪ Butter two 8″ round cake pans and line bottoms with waxed paper or parchment paper. ▪ Butter paper and flour inside of pans. ▪ With electric hand mixer, beat eggs in a large bowl until broken up. ▪ Gradually beat in sugar. ▪ Set bowl over pan of hot, not boiling, water and beat about 10 minutes, or until mixture is light in color and tripled in volume. ▪ Remove bowl from heat, add vanilla and continue beating until mixture is cool. ▪ Sift flour and salt over batter in 3 batches, folding in each batch with a rubber spatula. ▪ Blend until combined. ▪ Immediately pour into prepared pans and bake in preheated 350°F oven about 25 minutes, or until toothpick inserted in center comes out clean. ▪ Run a knife around inside of pans and turn out cakes onto racks. ▪ Carefully remove paper and let cool.

calories/layer: 690

CHOCOLATE TORTE

Serves 12
Preparation time: 1 hour
Cooking time: 12 to 15 minutes
Chilling time: several hours

Three thin chocolate cake layers, drizzled with coffee liqueur and filled with liqueur-flavored pastry cream, are topped with vanilla icing and more chocolate.

CHOCOLATE SPONGE LAYERS:

5	eggs
¾ cup plus 2 Tb	sugar
1 tsp	vanilla
2	squares unsweetened chocolate
¼ cup	cool water
¼ tsp	baking soda
¾ cup	sifted cake flour
½ tsp	baking powder
¼ tsp	salt
4½ Tb	coffee liqueur

COFFEE LIQUEUR CREAM:

⅓ cup	water
½ cup	sugar
5	egg yolks
1 cup	softened unsalted butter
1 Tb	coffee liqueur
¼ tsp	vanilla

VANILLA ICING:

1 cup	icing sugar
2 Tb	softened butter
1 Tb (approx.)	light cream
½ tsp	vanilla

GARNISH:

1	square semi-sweet chocolate
1 tsp	shortening

Chocolate Torte

- Grease three 8″ layer cake pans and line bottoms with waxed paper. ▪ To make chocolate sponge layers, beat eggs until thick and light colored, about 5 minutes at high speed on the mixer. ▪ Gradually beat in the ¾ cup sugar. ▪ Stir in vanilla. ▪ Meanwhile heat 2 squares chocolate in a small bowl over a saucepan of simmering water. ▪ When almost melted, remove from heat and stir until completely melted. ▪ Stir in cool water, baking soda and the 2 tablespoons sugar, blending well. ▪ Sift flour, baking powder and salt into egg mixture and fold quickly but lightly with a rubber scraper. ▪ Add melted chocolate and stir quickly to blend. ▪ Turn batter into prepared pans and bake in preheated 350°F oven 12 to 15 minutes, or until tops spring back when touched lightly in the center. ▪ Let cool about 5 minutes and turn out on racks to cool. ▪ Strip off paper carefully while cakes are still warm. ▪ Sprinkle each layer with 1½ tablespoons coffee liqueur. ▪ For coffee liqueur cream, combine water and sugar in a small saucepan. ▪ Heat, stirring until sugar dissolves. Bring to boil and boil, without stirring, until syrup registers 238°F on a candy thermometer or until the syrup spins a 6″ thread when dropped from the tines of a fork. ▪ Beat egg yolks in a small bowl until thick and lemon colored, about 5 minutes at high speed on the mixer. ▪ Add sugar syrup gradually, beating constantly, and continue beating until lukewarm. ▪ Add butter in small pieces, beating to blend after each addition. ▪ Beat in coffee liqueur and vanilla. ▪ If very soft, chill for a few minutes. ▪ Spread about ⅔ of coffee liqueur cream on top of two cakes. ▪ Stack the three cakes on top of each other, with the plain one on top. ▪ Spread remaining coffee liqueur cream around sides of torte. ▪ For vanilla icing, blend all ingredients, adding enough cream to make an icing that is easy to spread. ▪ Spread evenly on top of torte. ▪ For garnish, melt 1 square of semi-sweet chocolate and 1 teaspoon shortening in a small bowl over a saucepan of simmering water until the chocolate is almost melted. ▪ Remove and stir until melted and blended. ▪ Using a teaspoon, either drip this mixture around the top edge of the cake, letting the chocolate run down the sides in uneven lines, or drizzle it in concentric circles ½″ apart on top of the cake, then pull a knife from the center to the outside edge, through the chocolate and icing, making 12 wedge shapes and forming an attractive web design. ▪ Chill several hours. ▪ This cake will keep in the refrigerator for several days.

calories/serving: 417

RICH DARK FRUIT CAKE

Makes 13½ lbs
Preparation time: 45 minutes
Soaking time: overnight
Cooking time: about 3 hours (depending on size of pans)

This Christmas cake gets better as it ripens. Make it at least two or three weeks before Christmas – longer if you can. And it's best to prepare the fruit the day before you intend to bake. After the cake is stored (well wrapped in a cool, dark place), open it up every week or so and drizzle a little rum or brandy over the top before cake is iced.

½ lb	blanched almonds, slivered
	juice of 1 orange
3 lbs	washed seedless raisins
1 lb	washed sultana raisins
1 lb	candied pineapple, cut
1 lb	candied red cherries, cut or whole
1 lb	candied green cherries, cut or whole
1 lb	candied citron peel, finely cut
1 cup	grape juice *or* ½ cup each grape juice and rum
4 cups	flour
1 lb	butter
2 cups	sugar
12	medium eggs, separated
1 jar	(6 oz) grape jelly
1 oz	unsweetened chocolate, melted
1 tsp	baking powder
1 lb	pecans, halved

▪ If almonds are whole in their skins, pour boiling water over them, drain and slip off skins. ▪ Toast lightly in preheated 250°F oven. ▪ Slice. ▪ Soak overnight in orange juice. ▪ Prepare fruit. ▪ Soak overnight in grape juice or grape juice and rum. ▪ Next day, sprinkle a little flour over fruit. ▪ Cream butter at room temperature (not too soft; until like whipped cream). ▪ Add sugar gradually, creaming until no grains remain. ▪ Beat egg yolks together and thoroughly beat into butter mixture. (All steps must be followed as given to prevent butter oozing out of cake during baking.) ▪ Stir in jelly and melted chocolate. ▪ Blend in remaining flour and baking powder. ▪ Add fruit, a small amount at a time, mixing thoroughly (a wooden spoon is best). ▪ Add almonds and pecans. ▪ Stiffly beat egg whites and fold into batter. ▪ Line pans (you can use small loaf tins, regular cake pans, clean coffee tins – whatever shapes you like) with 3 layers of greased brown paper (or grease pans and line with parchment pa-per) and spread batter in pans. ▪ Bake in preheated 275°F oven together with a small pan of water, until cakes spring back when pressed in middle. A 4″ × 4″ cake will take about 1½ hours; 6″ × 6″, 3 hours; 8″ × 8″, about 4½ hours. ▪ Ice cake a few days before Christmas, if you wish.

calories/1-ounce slice: about 120

CHOCOLATE MARBLE CHEESECAKE

Serves 12
Preparation time: 25 minutes
Cooking time: 45 minutes to 1 hour
Cooling time: 30 minutes
Chilling time: 3 to 4 hours

This is a spectacular cheesecake with decorative swirls of chocolate and vanilla. The cheesecake itself is very rich and dense.

1½ cups	chocolate wafer crumbs
4 Tb	melted butter
1 cup plus 2 Tb	sugar
1 lb	cream cheese
2	eggs
1 tsp	vanilla
1 Tb	orange liqueur or rum (optional)
2 cups	sour cream
1 Tb	grated lemon peel
¼ cup	lemon juice
4 oz	semi-sweet or unsweetened chocolate, melted

▪ Combine wafer crumbs, butter and 2 tablespoons sugar and spread and pat over the bottom of a greased springform pan. ▪ Chill for 5 minutes, then bake in preheated 350°F oven for 10 minutes. This will give a crispier crust. ▪ Cream together cheese and 1 cup sugar in a large bowl. ▪ Beat in eggs and stir in vanilla and liqueur. ▪ Measure 3 cups of this cheese-egg mixture into a separate bowl and beat in 1½ cups of the sour cream, grated lemon peel and lemon juice. ▪ Pour onto prepared crust in pan. ▪ Beat chocolate gradually into remaining sour cream. ▪ Add to remaining cheese-egg mixture and mix well. ▪ Spoon on top of the lemon cheesecake and swirl together with a knife to give a marbled effect. ▪ Bake in preheated 350°F oven for 45 minutes to 1 hour. ▪ The sides will have risen, but the center will still be wobbly. Turn oven off and let cheesecake cool in oven for 30 minutes. ▪ Remove to rack and cool to room temperature. Refrigerate 3 to 4 hours before serving.

calories/serving: 452

Chocolate Marble Cheesecake

Birthday Chocolate Layer Cake

BIRTHDAY CHOCOLATE LAYER CAKE

Serves 12 to 18
Preparation time: 20 minutes
Cooking time: 25 minutes

Birthdays wouldn't be complete without a special cake, and this one certainly fits the bill.

½ cup	softened shortening or margarine
2 cups	brown sugar
2	eggs
1½ cups (generous)	sifted flour
½ cup	cocoa powder
1 tsp	baking powder
⅔ tsp	salt
1 tsp	baking soda
½ cup	boiling water
½ cup	sour milk or fresh milk with a few drops of vinegar added

BUTTER-MOCHA ICING:

3 Tb	softened butter
1½ Tb	cocoa powder
2 to 3 cups	icing sugar
2 to 3 Tb	strong coffee

■ Beat together shortening, sugar and eggs until light and fluffy. ■ Sift together flour, cocoa powder, baking powder and salt. ■ Mix baking soda and boiling water. ■ Add dry ingredients to shortening mixture alternately with hot water and sour milk, beating to keep mixture smooth. ■ Pour into two oiled 9″ cake pans and bake in preheated 350°F oven for 25 minutes, or until a toothpick inserted in the center comes out clean. ■ Cool on racks. ■ For the icing, cream butter and cocoa together. ■ Start adding icing sugar alternately with coffee and beat until you get the quantity of icing and consistency to spread. ■ Sandwich cakes together with icing and spread rest of icing over top and sides.

calories/serving: 416 for 12 servings
277 for 18 servings

RHUBARB STRUDEL

Serves 12
Preparation time: 40 minutes
Cooking time: 30 to 35 minutes

This recipe makes two strudels: one for now and one for freezing.

2 cups	**chopped fresh or frozen rhubarb**
½ cup	**firmly packed light brown sugar**
½ tsp	**ground cinnamon**
½ tsp	**grated nutmeg**
¾ cup	**finely chopped walnuts**
½ cup	**golden raisins**
1 Tb	**grated orange peel**
¾ cup	**unsalted butter, melted**
1 pkg	**(1 lb/500 g) phyllo pastry**
¾ cup	**crushed gingersnap cookies**
	icing sugar or vanilla icing for garnish
	whipped cream

▪ If using fresh rhubarb, cover with boiling water, let stand 30 seconds, then drain thoroughly. For frozen rhubarb, thaw fruit in a colander and pat dry with paper towel. ▪ Combine sugar, cinnamon, nutmeg, walnuts, raisins and orange peel in a medium bowl. ▪ Add rhubarb and stir just enough to mix all ingredients. ▪ Prepare two 15″ × 10″ cookie sheets by brushing them liberally with melted, unsalted butter. ▪ Stack 10 of the phyllo sheets between 2 slightly damp tea towels. ▪ Remove 1 sheet, recovering the rest, place it on a prepared cookie sheet and brush with melted butter. ▪ Sprinkle 1 to 2 tablespoons crushed gingersnaps evenly over phyllo sheet. ▪ Top with second phyllo sheet and repeat process with butter and gingersnaps. ▪ Repeat with 3 more sheets, brushing each with melted butter and sprinkling each with crushed gingersnaps; 5 sheets makes 1 strudel. ▪ Spread half of the rhubarb mixture in a 2″ strip along the edge of one of the long sides of layered phyllo sheets. ▪ Roll up pastry (all 5 layers) just enough to cover rhubarb mixture. ▪ If edge has dried out a bit, brush with small amount of melted butter to make pastry more flexible. ▪ To keep filling in place, make a 1″ fold along the top, bottom and remaining side of pastry. ▪ Continue rolling up strudel and arrange, seam side down, on cookie sheet. ▪ Cover with a slightly damp cloth while making second strudel. ▪ Repeat entire procedure with second strudel. ▪ Prick 4 holes along top of each strudel. ▪ Bake strudels in preheated 375°F oven for 30 to 35 minutes or until crisp and evenly brown. ▪ Transfer to a wire rack and cool. ▪ While strudel is warm, not hot, sprinkle with icing sugar, or once strudel has cooled, drizzle your favorite vanilla icing over each roll. ▪ Serve warm or cold with whipped cream.

calories/serving: 446

APPLE STRUDEL

Serves 6
Preparation time: 30 minutes
Cooking time: 40 minutes

This traditional filling for strudel dough can be substituted for the rhubarb filling in Rhubarb Strudel.

4 to 5 cups	**peeled, cored and sliced apples**
1 cup	**brown sugar**
½ cup	**raisins**
½ cup	**chopped nuts**
½ tsp	**ground cinnamon**
	grated peel of 1 lemon (optional)
5	**sheets phyllo pastry**
½ cup	**melted butter**
	icing sugar for decoration

▪ Combine all ingredients, except phyllo, butter and icing sugar. ▪ Stack 5 sheets phyllo pastry as described in Rhubarb Strudel recipe, brushing with most of the melted butter, but omitting crushed gingersnaps. ▪ Spread apple mixture in 2″ strip and roll up as described. ▪ Bake in preheated 450°F oven for 10 minutes. ▪ Reduce heat to 350°F and bake about 30 minutes longer, brushing with melted butter once or twice during baking. ▪ Dust baked strudel with icing sugar, let it cool, then cut into 2″ slices.

calories/serving: 455

PHYLLO PASTRY

Ready-made phyllo pastry is the perfect substitute for strudel pastry. It's available in frozen food departments of most grocery stores. Let the pastry thaw at room temperature before unwrapping. Remove only the number of sheets required for the recipe. Keep these sheets covered with a damp tea towel until you need them. Rewrap and refreeze the remainder for use in another recipe.

COCONUT ALMOND CAKE

Makes two 9″ round or 10″ × 6″ cakes
Preparation time: 30 minutes
Cooking time: 1 hour and 45 minutes

This cake will stay fresh tasting for a couple of weeks if it's stored in an airtight tin or plastic bag in a cool place.

1 cup	softened butter
2 cups	sugar
1½ lbs	shredded coconut
1 cup	milk
5	egg whites
1 lb	blanched almonds, finely sliced
3½ cups	sifted flour
2 tsp	baking powder
1 lb	citron peel, chopped

■ Line base and sides of two 9″ springform pans or 10″ × 6″ loaf pans with heavy brown paper or good quality parchment paper. Grease the paper. ■ Cream butter and sugar together in a very large bowl until light and fluffy. ■ Add coconut alternately with milk. ■ Beat whites in a separate bowl until soft peaks form. ■ Fold egg whites and almonds into creamed mixture. ■ Gently mix in flour and baking powder. ■ Gently stir in citron peel. ■ Spoon batter into prepared pans. Bake in preheated 300°F oven, together with a small pan of water, for 1 hour and 45 minutes, until a toothpick inserted in center of cakes comes out clean.

calories/serving: about 140 for 80 servings

CHOCOLATE CLEMENTINE MOUSSE CAKE

Serves 10
Preparation time: 45 minutes
Cooking time: 25 minutes
Chilling time: 4 hours or overnight

Mousse cakes, combining simple fruit mousses and crumb crusts, are especially appealing. They are so elegantly creamy, and almost best of all, they can be made ahead of time.

CHOCOLATE HAZELNUT CRUST:

½ cup	shelled hazelnuts
1 cup	chocolate wafer crumbs (about 18 wafers)
¼ cup	butter, melted
1 tsp	coarsely grated orange peel
1½ oz	bittersweet (or semi-sweet) chocolate, grated (optional)

CLEMENTINE MOUSSE:

1½ envelopes unflavored gelatine	
⅓ cup	water
4 tsp	finely grated clementine peel
1¼ cups	strained clementine juice
½ cup	sugar
2 Tb	lemon juice
1½ cups	whipping cream
1 Tb	mandarin or orange liqueur

CHOCOLATE GLAZE:

3 Tb	heavy cream
3 oz	bittersweet (or semi-sweet) chocolate, grated

■ Toast hazelnuts for about 10 minutes in preheated 350°F oven, or until skins begin to crack to reveal golden-brown nuts. ■ Transfer to a kitchen towel and rub off as much of the skins as possible. ■ Chop nuts finely and combine with wafer crumbs, butter and orange peel. ■ Press into the bottom of an 8″ springform pan. ■ Bake in preheated 300°F oven for 15 minutes or until firm. ■ If using chocolate, immediately sprinkle over hot crust. ■ Let melt and smooth gently with the back of a spoon. ■ Let crust cool completely. ■ To make mousse, sprinkle gelatine over water in a small saucepan and stir. ■ Set aside to let gelatine soften evenly. ■ Combine clementine peel, juice, sugar and lemon juice in a large saucepan. ■ Set over low heat and warm, stirring until sugar dissolves. ■ Remove from heat. ■ Warm gelatine over low heat until syrupy and blend into clementine mixture. ■ Transfer to a large bowl and chill in refrigerator until thickened to the consistency of raw eggs, stirring if necessary to keep the thickening even. ■ Whip cream until it holds soft peaks. ■ Fold into gelatine mixture with liqueur. ■ Pour over crust, smooth top and refrigerate until firm, about 4 hours, or overnight. ■ Add glaze as soon as mousse is firm, but no earlier than 1 hour before serving. ■ For glaze, bring 3 tablespoons cream to boil in a small saucepan. ■ Remove from heat and immediately stir in chocolate to make a satiny smooth blend. ■ Spoon evenly over chilled mousse. ■ Smooth or swirl into an attractive pattern. ■ Return to refrigerator to firm. ■ Remove pan sides carefully, running a knife around edge if needed. ■ Center mousse cake on a serving plate.

calories/serving: 390

Pumpkin Cheesecake

PUMPKIN CHEESECAKE

Serves 16
Preparation time: 25 minutes
Cooking time: 1½ to 1¾ hours
Cooling time: 1 hour
Chilling time: several hours or overnight

Queen Elizabeth reportedly ate three-quarters of her portion of this dessert when it was served to her at Winnipeg's Dubrovnik Restaurant in 1984 – apparently a sure sign of success, since the Queen has a small appetite.

1 cup	crushed gingersnap cookies
3 Tb	melted butter
1 tsp	ground cinnamon
2 Tb	brown sugar
2 lbs	cream cheese, softened
1½ cups	sugar
5	eggs
¼ cup	flour
2 tsp	pumpkin pie spice or to taste
1 can	(14 oz/398 mL) pumpkin
2 Tb	light rum
1 cup	whipping cream, whipped

▪ Combine crushed gingersnaps, butter, cinnamon and brown sugar. ▪ Press into base of a lightly greased 9″ springform cake pan. Pat firmly and chill. ▪ Beat softened cream cheese with electric or rotary beater until fluffy. ▪ Slowly beat in sugar. ▪ Add eggs one at a time, beating well after each addition. ▪ Gradually beat in flour, pumpkin pie spice, pumpkin and rum. ▪ Pour batter over crust. ▪ Bake in preheated 325°F oven for 1½ to 1¾ hours, or until filling is set. ▪ Cool cheesecake in pan on a wire rack for 1 hour. ▪ Refrigerate several hours or overnight. ▪ Remove from pan, top with whipped cream and serve.

MICROWAVE DIRECTIONS: For better results in the microwave, make two 9″ cakes. Use two round oven-proof glass baking dishes such as deep pie plates. Use half the ingredients for each cake, but use 3 eggs per cake. Microwave butter in baking dish for 1 minute. Stir in crust ingredients, mix and press firmly in bottom of dish. Cool. Add cheesecake mixture. Microwave on Medium 20 to 25 minutes, or until center is almost set. If you have difficulty with centers of cakes not cooking, elevate dish on microwave-safe rack, or use another cake pan inverted, on bottom of your oven. Continue as above.

calories/serving: 419

Apple Walnut Bundt Cake

APPLE WALNUT BUNDT CAKE

Serves 12
Preparation time: 30 minutes
Cooking time: 1 hour
A good old-fashioned spice and apple cake.

½ cup	sugar
1 cup	vegetable oil
3	eggs
1 tsp	vanilla
2 cups	flour
1 tsp	baking soda
1 tsp	grated nutmeg
1 tsp	allspice
1 tsp	ground cinnamon
1 cup	buttermilk
1 cup	finely chopped walnuts
2 cups	diced, peeled apples

GLAZE:

½ cup	sugar
½ tsp	vanilla
¼ cup	buttermilk
4 Tb	butter
1 Tb	corn syrup
pinch	baking soda

■ Beat together sugar and vegetable oil. ■ Add eggs and vanilla and mix thoroughly. ■ Sift together flour, baking soda and spices. ■ Alternately add dry ingredients and buttermilk to the first mixture. ■ Mix well, but do not beat. ■ Stir in walnuts and apples. ■ Pour into a buttered and lightly floured 12-cup Bundt pan. ■ Bake in preheated 350°F oven for 1 hour. ■ Fifteen minutes before the cake is to come out of the oven, blend together in a saucepan all the glaze ingredients. ■ Stir over medium heat until sugar dissolves and mixture is frothy. ■ Remove from heat. ■ When cake is done, remove from oven and let sit for 10 minutes. ■ Invert cake onto a cooling rack and brush warm glaze over cake. ■ When cake is cool, transfer to a plate to serve.
calories/serving: about 450

BUTTERMILK SUBSTITUTION
In place of buttermilk, you can use milk soured by adding a few drops of lemon juice or white vinegar. For a less tart flavor, add a spoonful of yogurt to milk.

ANGEL FEATHER ICING

*Makes enough for top and sides of 9" × 13" cake
or middle, top and sides of 8" layer cake*
Preparation time: 15 minutes

There's nothing better for an angel cake or a layer
cake than this almost fool-proof and luscious icing;
it doesn't dissolve, run away or get crusty. It stays
fluffy for days if anyone lets it last that long.

2	egg whites
¾ cup	sugar
⅓ cup	corn syrup
2 Tb	water
¼ tsp	cream of tartar
¼ tsp	salt
1 tsp	vanilla or almond extract

▪ Put everything but the vanilla into the top of a
double boiler with fast-boiling water below. ▪ Start
beating immediately with a rotary beater or electric
mixer until the mixture stands in stiff peaks. ▪ Remove from heat, add vanilla and keep on beating
until it is thick enough to spread easily.

ALMOND SPONGE CAKE

Serves 16
Makes one 10" tube cake
Preparation time: 20 minutes
Cooking time: 1 hour

This cake batter produces an ultra-light tube cake
with a delicate almond flavor.

1⅓ cups	cake flour
⅓ cup	lightly toasted ground almonds
½ tsp	baking powder
¼ tsp	salt
5	eggs, separated
½ cup	ice-cold water
1½ cups	sugar
½ tsp	almond extract
1 tsp	vanilla
¾ tsp	cream of tartar

▪ Mix together flour, almonds, baking powder and
salt. ▪ Beat egg yolks in a separate bowl until thick
and lemony. ▪ Beat in ice-cold water until pale and
foamy. ▪ Add sugar and beat until very light and
sugar is dissolved, about 10 minutes with an electric
beater. ▪ Add almond extract and vanilla. ▪ Fold
flour into yolks in three batches. ▪ Beat egg whites
with cream of tartar until soft peaks form and fold
into batter. ▪ Gently turn batter into ungreased 10"
tube pan and bake in preheated 325°F oven for 1
hour. ▪ Invert pan over funnel or bottle to cool before removing cake from pan.

calories/serving: 157

Coconut Cloud Cake

COCONUT CLOUD CAKE

Makes one 9" × 13" cake or two 8" round cakes
Preparation time: 15 minutes
Cooking time: 30 to 45 minutes

This versatile cake can be made into a glamorous
layer cake or baked in a big pan to serve 20 people.

¾ cup	softened butter or shortening or margarine
1½ cups	sugar
3	eggs, separated (keep one white apart)
3 cups	sifted flour
4½ tsp	baking powder
¾ tsp	salt
1 cup	desiccated coconut
2 cups	milk
1 tsp	vanilla
1 tsp	almond extract
	shredded coconut

▪ Cream butter, add sugar and beaten egg yolks and
1 egg white (set aside remaining egg whites for
Angel Feather Icing); continue beating until fluffy.
▪ Sift flour with baking powder and salt, mix with
coconut and add alternately with milk and flavor-
ings to butter mixture. ▪ When smooth pour into a
greased 9" × 13" pan or into two greased 8" round
cake pans and bake in preheated 350°F oven – the
flat pan for about 45 minutes, the layers about 30
minutes, but test both and don't overbake. ▪ Cake
is done when a toothpick inserted in center comes
out clean. ▪ Cool; remove layers from pans to a
rack and ice with Angel Feather Icing. Place one
layer on top of other and sprinkle shredded coconut
generously on top and sides. ▪ Spread the big, flat
cake with Angel Feather Icing.

*calories/serving: 307 for 20 servings
255 for 24 servings*

LEMON LIME CHEESECAKE

Serves 10 to 12
Preparation time: 25 minutes
Cooking time: 35 minutes

This cheesecake is in three layers: a toasted coconut crust, a creamy rich filling and a gloss of tangy lemon and lime curd over the top.

TOASTED COCONUT CRUST:

2 cups	**shredded coconut**
2 Tb	**sugar**
2 Tb	**butter, melted**
½ tsp	**grated lemon peel**

CREAM CHEESE FILLING:

1½ lbs	**cream cheese**
1 cup	**sugar**
4	**eggs**
1 tsp	**grated lemon peel**
2 Tb	**lemon juice**
1 Tb	**lime juice**
pinch	**salt**

LEMON LIME CURD TOPPING:

2	**eggs**
¾ cup	**sugar**
1½ tsp	**each coarsely grated lemon and lime peel**
¼ cup	**lemon juice**
2 Tb	**lime juice**
2 Tb	**butter**
	shredded coconut or strips of candied lemon or lime peel for garnish

▪ To make crust, toss together coconut, sugar, butter and peel. ▪ Spread evenly in a lightly greased 10″ springform pan, patting down lightly. ▪ Bake in preheated 350°F oven for 10 to 12 minutes or until lightly toasted around the edges. ▪ For filling, work cheese in a food processor, or in a bowl with electric mixer, until fluffy and smooth. ▪ Blend in sugar, then eggs, one at a time. ▪ Add peel, juices and salt. ▪ Pour over toasted coconut crust, smoothing the top. ▪ Return to 350°F oven and continue baking for 35 minutes or until firm almost to the center. ▪ Remove from oven. ▪ Run a knife around the cheesecake filling. This step releases the cake from the edges of the pan and helps prevent the cake from cracking. ▪ Set pan on a rack to cool completely. ▪ Just before serving, remove cheesecake from pan and set on a serving plate. ▪ To make topping, whisk eggs until foamy. ▪ Combine with sugar, grated peel, juices and butter in a heavy, non-aluminum saucepan. ▪ Cook over low heat, stirring frequently, or whisking if necessary, until smooth, honey-like and thickened, about 6 to 8 minutes. ▪ Remove from heat to cool. ▪ If making ahead, store in airtight container in the refrigerator. ▪ Just before serving, spread in an even layer over cheesecake. ▪ Garnish with coconut or strips of candied lemon or lime peel.

calories/serving: 600 for 10
500 for 12

MATRIMONY CAKE

Serves 16
Preparation time: 15 minutes
Cooking time: 25 minutes

Kids will love this special cake.

1 cup	**flour**
1 tsp	**baking soda**
1 cup	**brown sugar**
2 cups	**rolled oats**
¾ cup	**softened butter or margarine**

FILLING:

2 cups	**pitted and chopped dates**
⅓ cup	**brown sugar**
1¼ cups	**water**
1 Tb	**flour**
1 tsp	**vanilla**

▪ Combine flour, baking soda, 1 cup brown sugar, rolled oats and butter in a medium mixing bowl. ▪ Rub together with fingers until it resembles coarse meal. ▪ Combine filling ingredients in a saucepan and simmer, stirring constantly, until slightly thickened. ▪ Press half the flour mixture into the bottom of a greased 9″ × 9″ cake pan. ▪ Spoon filling on top and smooth with the back of a spoon. ▪ Sprinkle remaining flour mixture evenly on top. ▪ Bake in preheated 375°F oven for about 25 minutes, until top is slightly browned. ▪ Cool in pan and cut into squares.

calories/servings: 289

Chocolate Yule Log

CHOCOLATE YULE LOG

Serves 8 to 10
Preparation time: 30 minutes
Cooking time: 12 to 15 minutes
A decadent dessert, but easy to make. Refrigerate until serving time. An alternative garnish could be a red bow.

1 cup	flour
¼ cup	cocoa powder
1 tsp	baking powder
¼ tsp	salt
3	eggs
1 cup	sugar
⅓ cup	water
1 tsp	vanilla
ICING:	
2 cups	icing sugar
½ cup	cocoa powder
1 cup	butter, at room temperature
1½ tsp	vanilla
6	egg yolks
GARNISH:	
	sugar
4	green gumdrops
6	red cinnamon candies

▪ Line a greased 15″ × 10″ jelly roll pan with parchment or waxed paper; grease and lightly dust with flour. ▪ Set aside. ▪ Combine flour, cocoa, baking powder and salt. ▪ Beat eggs with an electric mixer in a medium bowl until thick and light colored, about 5 minutes. ▪ Add sugar gradually and continue beating until light and fluffy. ▪ Stir in water and vanilla. ▪ Blend in dry ingredients at lowest speed on mixer. ▪ Spread batter into prepared pan. ▪ Bake in preheated 375°F oven for 12 to 15 minutes, or until top springs back when lightly touched. ▪ Immediately loosen edges and invert cake onto a tea towel dusted with cocoa powder; peel off paper. ▪ Roll up cake and towel together, starting at short end. ▪ Cool on wire rack, seam side down. ▪ Meanwhile, to make icing, sift icing sugar and cocoa together. ▪ Cream butter until light; beat in icing sugar-cocoa mixture and vanilla. ▪ Add egg yolks, one at a time, beating well after each addition. ▪ Unroll cooled cake and spread with about half the icing. Roll up cake again and cover outside with remaining icing. ▪ Decorate as a yule log by making ridges in icing with a metal spatula to resemble bark. ▪ To make holly and berry garnish, sprinkle a little granulated sugar on a cutting board. ▪ Place one green gumdrop at a time on sugared board; sprinkle with more sugar. ▪ With a rolling pin, flatten into an oval. ▪ Firmly press the tip of a teaspoon around outside edge of gumdrop, cutting away tiny pieces to make scalloped edges of a holly leaf. ▪ Repeat with remaining gumdrops. ▪ Near each end of log, press 2 leaves and 3 cinnamon candies gently into icing. ▪ Refrigerate until serving time.

calories/serving: 616 for 8 servings
493 for 10 servings

Pies and Tarts

NEVER-FAIL PASTRY

Makes enough for 2 double-crust pies
Preparation time: 10 minutes

This is one of those invaluable recipes that gets passed on from mother to daughter, generation after generation, because it works. It will keep about a week in the refrigerator – months in the freezer. Or you can make pie shells and freeze them. You can even make this pastry in a food processor if you don't overmix. Even re-rolled scraps aren't tough.

5 cups (scant)	sifted all-purpose flour
1 lb	cold lard
2 tsp	salt
1	egg
1½ Tb	vinegar
	cold water

▪ Mix together slightly less than 5 cups of flour together with salt in a large mixing bowl. (You'll use some flour to flour your rolling pin and board.) ▪ Cut in lard with two knives or pastry cutter until lard is in small pieces throughout the flour. ▪ Mix with fingertips until mixture is like coarse meal. ▪ Beat egg in the bottom of an 8-ounce measuring cup. ▪ Add vinegar and beat again. ▪ Add cold water to fill cup and beat to mix thoroughly. ▪ Make a well in the flour mixture and add liquid. ▪ Mix with a fork until pastry holds together. It may be sticky. ▪ Gently press dough into a ball. ▪ Wrap and chill before rolling. ▪ Cut off the amount you need and refrigerate or freeze the rest.

MAKE-AHEAD PASTRY

Makes enough for 3 double-crust pies, plus tarts
Preparation time: 15 minutes
Chilling time: 15 minutes

This pastry rolls out easily. Covered with heavy plastic wrap, it keeps up to a week in the refrigerator and freezes well for up to two months.

7 cups	cake and pastry flour (stir before measuring)
2 tsp	salt
1 lb	cold shortening
⅔ cup	ice-cold water
⅓ cup	cold milk

▪ Combine flour and salt in a very large mixing bowl. ▪ Cut shortening into 2″ chunks. ▪ Cut shortening into flour with pastry blender until mixture resembles very coarse meal with some larger pieces about the size of peas. ▪ Combine water and milk. ▪ While stirring flour mixture with a fork, using swift, light, broad strokes, sprinkle just enough liquid over the mixture so that dough clings together but is not wet. ▪ Gather into a ball, cover and let rest 15 minutes in refrigerator. ▪ Shape into a fat log and cut crosswise into six even pieces. ▪ To use immediately, roll out on floured board. ▪ To store in refrigerator or freezer, wrap tightly in plastic wrap or place individual portions in small plastic bags. To roll out, let stand at room temperature until pliable, about 15 minutes, longer if frozen.

NO-ROLL PASTRY

Makes one 9″ pie shell
Preparation time: 10 minutes
Chilling time: 25-30 minutes
Cooking time: 15 minutes

Use this pastry when you don't want to fuss with a rolling pin to make a single pie shell. It's crisp and light, but not as flaky as regular pastry.

⅓ cup	shortening or lard
1	egg yolk
1 Tb	cold water
1 tsp	vinegar
½ tsp	sugar
pinch	salt
1 cup	cake and pastry flour

▪ Melt shortening in a medium heat-proof bowl over small saucepan half-filled with simmering water. ▪ Remove to wire rack and let cool until opaque but still liquid. ▪ Combine egg yolk, water, vinegar, sugar and salt. ▪ Stir into shortening. ▪ Add flour all at once and, using a fork, mix with a few light strokes just until all the flour is moistened. ▪ Refrigerate 5 to 10 minutes (dough should be pliable). ▪ With fingertips, press dough on bottom and sides of 9″ pie plate. ▪ Do not try to get surface as smooth as rolled crust. ▪ Prick all over with fork. ▪ Chill 20 minutes. ▪ Line with parchment or foil. ▪ Fill with pie weights or uncooked rice. ▪ Bake in pre-heated 400°F oven for 8 minutes. ▪ Remove liner and weights and bake 6 to 8 minutes more or until golden brown.

Harvest Fruit Pie

HARVEST FRUIT PIE

Serves 8 to 10
Preparation time: 1 hour
Cooking time: 1 hour

The three fruits in this pie combine perfectly in taste and texture. Serve the pie warm with a slice of old Cheddar cheese or ice cream.

PASTRY:

1¾ cup	flour
2 Tb	sugar
½ tsp	salt
¾ cup	cold unsalted butter
5 Tb	ice-cold water or more

FILLING:

3	ripe pears, preferably Bartlett
3	apples
¾ cup	dried apricots
⅔ cup	sugar
3 Tb	flour
2 Tb	lemon juice
1 Tb	ground cinnamon
pinch	grated nutmeg
3 Tb	unsalted butter, cut into cubes

GLAZE:

1	egg
1 tsp	sugar

▪ To make pastry, combine flour with sugar and salt. ▪ Cut in butter until mixture resembles coarse crumbs. ▪ Sprinkle with water and gather dough together into a ball. ▪ Divide dough into two pieces – one slightly larger than the other. ▪ Chill for 30 minutes. ▪ Roll larger piece to fit a 10″ pie plate. ▪ Roll out second piece and reserve for the top. ▪ For the filling, peel, halve and core pears and apples. ▪ Slice into a bowl. ▪ Cut apricots with scissors and add to other fruit. ▪ Combine fruit with sugar, flour, lemon juice, spices and butter. ▪ Spoon into crust. ▪ Top pie with round of dough. ▪ Crimp edges. ▪ Cut steam slit in top. ▪ Combine egg with sugar and brush on to glaze pastry. ▪ Bake in preheated 425°F oven for 15 minutes. ▪ Reduce heat to 350°F and bake 45 minutes longer, or until fruit is tender and nicely browned. ▪ Check pie after 30 minutes; if it is browning too much, cover loosely with foil. ▪ Cool at least 30 minutes before serving.

calories/serving: 470 for 8 servings
377 for 10 servings

PREBAKED PIE SHELLS

To bake a pie shell "blind" before adding a filling, line the shell with foil or waxed paper and fill with raw rice, dried beans or ceramic baking beans. This weighs down the pastry and stops it from distorting during cooking. Bake in preheated 375°F oven for 10 minutes. Remove foil or paper and rice or beans and bake a further 5 minutes, until pastry is set and lightly browned.

Baklava

BAKLAVA

Makes 35 to 40 pieces
Preparation time: 40 minutes
Cooking time: 35 to 50 minutes

Baklava, the king of Arab pastry, is always found at sumptuous Middle Eastern feasts. In that part of the world it used to be said that no young lady would make a good wife unless she knew how to make baklava dough – that was before the commercially produced dough or phyllo pastry of our times.

2 cups	walnuts, chopped
1 cup	sugar
2 cups	melted butter
2 tsp	ground cinnamon
1 Tb	orange blossom water (available at drugstores or health stores)
1 pkg	(1 lb/500 g) phyllo pastry
SYRUP:	
2 cups	sugar
1 cup	water
2 Tb	lemon juice
2 tsp	orange blossom water

■ Combine walnuts, sugar, ¼ cup of the butter, cinnamon and orange blossom water and set aside. ■ Butter a 10″ × 15″ baking pan and set aside. ■ Remove pastry from package and spread on a slightly damp tea towel. ■ Cover with second damp tea towel. ■ Remove one sheet of pastry and place on the baking pan. ■ Brush with butter. Repeat procedure, layering the sheets one on top of the other, until half the package is used. ■ Spread walnut mixture evenly over the top. ■ Spread a sheet of pastry over the walnut mixture and brush with butter. ■ Continue buttering and layering until the remainder of the pastry is used up. ■ Trim the edges. ■ Heat remaining butter and pour evenly over the top. ■ With a sharp knife carefully cut into 2″ squares. ■ Bake in preheated 400°F oven for 5 minutes. ■ Lower heat to 300°F and bake for 30 to 45 minutes, or until the sides are a light shade of brown. ■ While the baklava is baking, prepare syrup. ■ Boil sugar and water over medium heat, stirring constantly, for 10 minutes. ■ Remove from heat and stir in lemon juice and orange blossom water. ■ Cool. ■ Place baked baklava tray under the broiler and turn the pan around until the top is evenly golden brown. ■ Remove from oven and allow to cool for 15 minutes. ■ Spoon syrup over each square. ■ Allow to cool and serve.

calories/serving: 272 for 35
238 for 40

Blueberry and Raspberry Pie

BLUEBERRY AND RASPBERRY PIE

Serves 6
Preparation time: 20 minutes
Cooking time: 42 to 50 minutes

When winter deepens into biting cold, use berries from the freezer to bring a touch of summer to supper menus.

	pastry for 8″ double-crust pie
1 pkg	(12 oz/300 g) unsweetened frozen raspberries
1 pkg	(12 oz/300 g) unsweetened frozen blueberries
⅔ cup	sugar
3 Tb	cornstarch

▪ Thaw raspberries sufficiently to separate easily. ▪ Combine in a medium bowl with blueberries. ▪ In another bowl stir together sugar and cornstarch. ▪ Toss gently into berries. ▪ Set aside. ▪ On floured work surface, roll out just over half the pastry and fit into 8″ pie plate. ▪ Spoon in fruit mixture. ▪ Roll out remaining pastry. ▪ Moisten rim of bottom crust with cold water. ▪ Top with pastry. ▪ Seal, trim and flute edges. ▪ Cut steam vent in center. ▪ Bake in preheated 450°F oven for 12 to 15 minutes, or until rim is lightly golden. ▪ Reduce temperature to 375°F 30 to 35 minutes longer, or until golden brown and filling is bubbly. ▪ Serve warm or at room temperature.

calories/serving: 425

CHOCOLATE PECAN PIE

Makes one 9″ pie
Preparation time: 20 minutes for filling
Cooking time: 30 to 40 minutes
Chilling time: 2 to 3 hours

This is a luscious decadent chocolate dessert.

1	9″ pastry shell, partially baked
¼ cup	butter
¾ cup	brown sugar
3	eggs
¾ cup	golden corn syrup
¼ tsp	salt
1 tsp	vanilla
1 Tb	rum (optional)
2 oz	semi-sweet chocolate, melted
1 cup	pecans
	whipped cream or vanilla ice cream

▪ Cream together butter and sugar in a large bowl. ▪ Gradually beat in eggs, corn syrup and salt. ▪ Add vanilla, rum and melted chocolate and mix well. ▪ Stir in pecans. ▪ Pour into prepared shell and bake in preheated 350°F oven for approximately 35 minutes. The center will still be soft to the touch but will continue cooking when removed from the oven. ▪ Let cool to room temperature, then refrigerate for 2 to 3 hours before serving. ▪ Serve with mounds of whipped cream or scoops of vanilla ice cream.

calories/serving: 536 for 8 servings
429 for 10 servings

MANDARIN ALMOND TARTE

Serves 8
Preparation time: 45 minutes
Chilling time: 30 minutes
Cooking time: 25 to 30 minutes

A buttery almond filling with mandarin highlights makes this French-inspired pastry a hit for afternoon tea or as a finale to a holiday dinner.

PASTRY:

1 cup	flour
1 Tb	sugar
pinch	salt
½ tsp	grated mandarin peel
⅓ cup	cold unsalted butter
2 Tb	shortening
1	egg yolk
2 Tb	mandarin juice

FILLING:

½ cup	unsalted butter
½ cup	sugar
2	eggs
1 Tb	coarsely grated mandarin peel
2 Tb	mandarin juice
1 cup	finely ground almonds
1 Tb	flour
pinch	salt

GARNISH:

1	mandarin
¼ cup	water
2 Tb	sugar
1 cup	whipping cream

▪ Stir flour, sugar, salt and peel together in a large bowl. ▪ Cut in butter and shortening, using a pastry blender or 2 knives, until mixture is crumbly. ▪ Stir together egg yolk and juice. ▪ Drizzle over dry ingredients and with a fork toss to blend ingredients. ▪ Press into a ball, flatten into a disk, wrap and chill for 30 minutes or up to 4 days. Allow to soften to room temperature before rolling. ▪ Roll out to fit a shallow 10″ tart tin. ▪ Trim edges neatly and line with foil. ▪ Fill with pie weights or dried beans. ▪ Bake in preheated 375°F oven for 15 minutes. ▪ Remove weights and continue baking for 2 to 5 minutes or until light gold and partially baked. ▪ To make filling, cream butter with sugar in a large bowl or in a food processor. ▪ When fluffy, add eggs, one at a time. ▪ Blend in peel and juice. ▪ Combine almonds with flour and salt. ▪ Mix in quickly. ▪ Pour into partially baked crust. ▪ Bake at 350°F for 25 to 30 minutes, or until firm and golden brown, and a skewer inserted in the center comes out clean.

▪ Let cool on a rack. ▪ To garnish, pare off thin outer peel from mandarin. ▪ Cut into 16 strips, each about 2″ long and as wide as a matchstick. ▪ Simmer in water in a small covered saucepan until tender and translucent, about 10 minutes. ▪ Sprinkle on sugar and continue cooking, still covered, for about 5 minutes. ▪ Uncover to thicken syrup slightly. ▪ Remove strips and let cool, separated, on waxed paper. ▪ Before serving, brush any syrup over tarte. ▪ Whip cream and spoon or pipe on rosettes at equal intervals around the tarte. ▪ Cross 2 strips of peel over each rosette. ▪ Serve immediately.

calories/serving: 588

CLASSIC PUMPKIN PIE

Serves 6 to 8
Preparation time: 10 minutes (longer if making pastry)
Cooking time: 55 to 60 minutes

This traditional pumpkin pie has a smooth texture and nice spicing.

1	9″ unbaked pie shell
2	eggs
¾ cup	firmly packed brown sugar
1½ cups	canned or cooked, strained pumpkin
1 tsp	ground cinnamon
½ tsp	salt
¼ tsp	ground cloves or to taste
¼ tsp	ground ginger or to taste
¼ tsp	grated nutmeg
1 cup	milk
½ cup	light cream

GARNISH:

1 cup	whipping cream
1 Tb	sugar
1 tsp	vanilla

▪ Beat eggs in a medium bowl. ▪ Add sugar, pumpkin, seasonings, milk and light cream, mixing well after each addition. ▪ Pour into pie shell and bake in preheated 450°F oven for 10 minutes, then reduce temperature to 350°F for 45 to 50 minutes, or until a knife inserted in the center comes out almost clean. Don't overcook, as filling will set as it cools. ▪ Cool before serving. ▪ Just before serving, whip cream. ▪ Stir in sugar and vanilla and serve with pie.

calories/serving: 506 for 6 servings
379 for 8 servings
vitamin A: excellent

Mandarin Almond Tarte

Burwick House Mincemeat

BURWICK HOUSE MINCEMEAT

Makes 11 cups
Preparation time: 15 minutes

With this traditional mincemeat recipe you can make pies and tarts for a crowd and freeze them; they reheat nicely.

8	medium apples
	grated peel and juice of 3 lemons
4 cups	firmly packed brown sugar
2½ cups	currants
2½ cups	seedless raisins
2 cups	finely grated suet
½ cup	chopped mixed candied peel
1 tsp	grated nutmeg
½ tsp	ground cinnamon
¼ tsp	ground cloves
¼ tsp	salt
2 Tb	brandy
	apple cider or apple juice

▪ Peel, core and grate apples coarsely to make 8 cups. ▪ Mix together all ingredients except apple cider. At this stage the mincemeat is quite runny, but within 2 days the dried fruit will have absorbed most of the liquid. ▪ Store mincemeat in a covered plastic container in the refrigerator for 2 weeks. The 1860s cook would have ripened it in a crock in the cold cellar. If you want to keep it longer, freeze it. ▪ If the mincemeat is too dry when you want to use it, add a little apple cider or apple juice; if it's too moist, add a little more dried fruit.

calories/cup: 982

APRICOT PEACH PIE

Serves 6 to 8
Soaking time: 1 hour
Preparation time: 45 minutes
Cooking time: 15 to 20 minutes

Although the filling is made from dried and canned fruits, this pie has a really fresh fruit taste.

1	unbaked 9″ pie shell
1 cup	packed dried apricots, cut into halves
1 can	(19 oz/540 mL) sliced peaches
1 Tb	lemon juice
1 tsp	grated lemon peel
¼ cup	sugar
2 Tb	cornstarch
STREUSEL TOPPING:	
½ cup	sliced almonds
¼ cup	sugar
¼ cup	flour
2 Tb	butter

▪ Cover apricots with boiling water in a small saucepan and let stand 1 hour. ▪ Meanwhile prick pastry shell all over with a fork. ▪ Line with parchment or foil and fill with pie weights or dry rice. ▪ Bake in preheated 425°F oven for 8 minutes. ▪ Remove liner and weights; bake 7 minutes longer or until bottom is dry and firm. ▪ Let cool on rack while you prepare filling. ▪ Drain apricots well and discard liquid. ▪ Pour liquid from peaches over apricots; set peaches aside. ▪ Add lemon juice and peel to apricots and bring to boil. ▪ Reduce heat to medium-low, cover and simmer until apricots are very tender and liquid is reduced by about one-third, about 20 minutes. ▪ Stir together sugar and cornstarch. ▪ Blend into apricots and cook, stirring gently over medium heat until liquid is thickened and translucent. ▪ Gently stir in peaches. ▪ Cool 5 minutes, then spoon into baked pie shell. ▪ To make streusel topping, stir together almonds, sugar and flour. ▪ Blend in butter with a fork until mixture is crumbly. ▪ Sprinkle with streusel topping. ▪ Bake in preheated 425°F oven for 15 to 20 minutes, or until filling is bubbly and topping is golden brown.

calories/serving: 425 for 6 servings
317 for 8 servings

PASTRY TIP

When you line a pie plate with rolled pastry, be careful not to stretch the pastry, because it will shrink during cooking. Let the pie shell rest before trimming the edges, then chill for 30 minutes before baking.

STRAWBERRY RHUBARB TART

Serves 6 to 8
Preparation time: 20 minutes
Chilling time: 1 hour
Cooking time: 40 to 50 minutes

Rhubarb used to be nicknamed "pieplant" because it tasted so good in pies. Here is a recipe for a particularly delicious variation of rhubarb pie.

PASTRY:

1½ cups	flour
pinch	salt
½ cup	softened butter
¼ cup	fruit sugar
	grated peel and juice from 1 medium orange (about ¼ cup juice)

FILLING:

⅔ cup	fruit sugar
¼ cup plus 1 Tb	flour
3 Tb	cornstarch
2 cups	chopped fresh or frozen rhubarb
2 cups	sliced fresh strawberries

TOPPING:

⅓ cup	flour
⅓ cup	brown sugar
2 Tb	butter

■ To make pastry, sift flour and salt into a bowl and rub in softened butter until mixture resembles breadcrumbs. ■ Add sugar and orange peel and stir in sufficient orange juice to give a soft but not sticky ball of dough. ■ Wrap dough in plastic wrap and chill 1 hour. ■ To make filling, mix together sugar, flour and cornstarch. ■ Combine with rhubarb and strawberries. ■ On a floured surface roll out pastry to fit a 9″ tart or flan dish. ■ Line dish with pastry and fill evenly with strawberry-rhubarb mixture. ■ To make topping, combine flour and sugar, then cut in butter until mixture has a crumbly texture. ■ Sprinkle over top of tart. ■ Place tart on a cookie sheet (to catch drips) before placing in preheated 400°F oven. ■ Bake for 40 to 50 minutes, or until pastry is golden brown and filling is bubbly.

calories/serving: 493 for 6 servings
370 for 8 servings

Rum Pecan Pumpkin Pie

RUM PECAN PUMPKIN PIE

Makes one 9″ pie
Preparation time: 10 minutes
Cooking time: 45 to 55 minutes

A sumptuous pie for a special occasion.

1	unbaked 9″ pie shell
½ cup	pecan halves
1½ cups	cooked or canned pumpkin (if using homemade, add 1 Tb cornstarch)
⅔ cup	firmly packed brown sugar
1¼ tsp	ground cinnamon
½ tsp	ground ginger
pinch	grated nutmeg
¼ tsp	salt
1 cup	milk
¼ cup	dark rum
3	eggs, lightly beaten

■ Sprinkle pecan halves into unbaked pie shell. ■ Mix pumpkin and sugar until sugar dissolves. ■ Add remaining ingredients, stirring well to blend. ■ Pour filling into pie shell. ■ Bake in preheated 450°F oven for 10 minutes. ■ Reduce heat to 350°F and bake 35 to 45 minutes longer, until inserted knife comes out almost clean. ■ Serve warm or at room temperature, with whipped cream or ice cream.

calories/serving: 410 for 6 servings

Puddings, Ices and Fruit

LEMON PUDDING

Serves 6 to 8
Preparation time: 10 minutes
Cooking time: 45 minutes

This is a light airy pudding, good warm or cold. If you like your lemon flavor really sharp, add more grated lemon peel.

2 Tb	butter
1 cup	sugar
2	eggs, separated
	grated peel and juice of 1 lemon
2 Tb	flour
1 cup	milk

▪ Beat butter and sugar together in a mixing bowl until fluffy. ▪ Add egg yolks, lemon juice and peel and beat until well combined. ▪ Add flour and milk and beat again. ▪ In another bowl beat egg whites until stiff. ▪ Fold egg whites gently into milk mixture. ▪ Turn batter out into a greased pudding dish or 9″ square cake pan. ▪ Set pudding dish in a shallow pan of water, making sure water is not deep enough to boil over into the pudding. ▪ Bake in preheated 350°F oven for about 45 minutes, or until a toothpick inserted in center comes out clean. ▪ Serve plain or with whipped cream.

calories/serving: 229 for 6 servings
172 for 8 servings

LEMON CREAM

Serves 4 to 6
Preparation time: 15 minutes
Freezing time: 6 to 8 hours

A refreshing dessert to serve after a rich main course.

4 cups	heavy cream
1 cup	milk
1½ cups	sugar
	juice of 4 large lemons

▪ Mix cream, milk and sugar until mixture is thin and sugar is dissolved. ▪ Place bowl in freezer and when mixture has begun to solidify, remove and whip, adding lemon juice. ▪ Return to freezer to solidify again. ▪ Remove and whip again. Mixture will be smooth and firming up. ▪ Return to freezer in a metal mold, which hastens the freezing. The time it takes to freeze depends on the temperature of your freezer. ▪ Serve with slightly thawed frozen raspberries.

calories/serving: 1,200 for 4 servings
800 for 6 servings

CHOCOLATE FONDUE

Serves 6
Preparation time: 10 minutes
Cooking time: 5 minutes

This makes a terrific dessert for company. Kids love it, too, if you leave out the liqueur.

2 Tb	honey
½ cup	heavy cream
8 oz	semi-sweet chocolate
1 tsp	vanilla
1 Tb	orange or coffee liqueur
	fruits of your choice

▪ Combine honey, cream and chocolate in a small saucepan. ▪ Heat slowly over medium-low heat until chocolate has melted and ingredients are well blended. ▪ Stir in vanilla and liqueur. ▪ Cut fruits such as bananas (peeled and drizzled with lemon juice), canned or fresh pineapple, strawberries, apples (peeled, cored and drizzled with lemon juice), kiwifruit and melon into bite-size chunks. Arrange on a large platter. ▪ Pour melted chocolate into a small fondue pot or into a small oven-proof dish set over a candle. ▪ Use fondue forks to dip fruit into chocolate.

calories/serving: 257 without fruit

CRÈME BRÛLÉE

Serves 4 or 5
Preparation time: 10 minutes
Cooking time: 45 to 50 minutes

A French classic that's sure to become a family and company favorite.

2 cups	light cream
5	egg yolks
¼ cup	sugar
2 tsp	vanilla
pinch	salt
⅓ cup	soft brown sugar

▪ Scald cream in a heavy saucepan or in top of a double boiler. ▪ Beat together egg yolks, sugar, vanilla and salt in a large bowl. ▪ Gradually stir in hot cream. ▪ Pour into a buttered 4- to 5-cup deep casserole. ▪ Place dish in a pan containing 1″ water. ▪ Bake in preheated 325°F oven for 45 to 50 minutes, or until custard is barely set. Do not overbake. ▪ Cool. ▪ Sieve brown sugar over top. ▪ Broil until sugar is melted, watching closely in case sugar burns. ▪ Serve warm or cold.

calories/serving: 415 for 4 servings
335 for 5 servings

Chocolate Fondue

Citrus Mincemeat Trifle

CITRUS MINCEMEAT TRIFLE

Serves 8 to 10
Preparation time: 20 minutes
Chilling time (for filling): at least 3 hours
Cooking time: 10 to 12 minutes
Chilling time (for trifle): overnight

Sensational in appearance and taste, this dessert is simple to make, especially if done in stages. Use a purchased sponge cake, if you wish, or make your own favorite sponge cake. If an 8" cake is not available, or you don't have an 8" bowl, cut the cake into strips to fit into bowl.

½ cup	coarsely chopped walnuts
3 cups	milk
5	egg yolks
⅓ cup	sugar
3 Tb	cornstarch
1 tsp	vanilla
2	8" layers sponge cake
¼ cup	orange brandy, brandy or dry sherry
4	tangerines or clementines
2 cups	mincemeat
1 cup	whipping cream
2 Tb	icing sugar
	candied fruit for garnish

■ Spread walnuts out on a baking sheet and toast in preheated 350°F oven 5 minutes. ■ Set aside to cool. ■ Heat milk in a small saucepan until bubbles start to appear around edge. ■ Beat egg yolks in a medium saucepan until combined. ■ Beat in sugar and cornstarch until smooth. ■ Stir in milk in slow stream. ■ Stir constantly over medium heat until thickened, 3 to 5 minutes. ■ Reduce heat to low and simmer, stirring, 1 minute. ■ Remove from heat and stir in vanilla. ■ Press a piece of buttered waxed paper onto surface and refrigerate at least 3 hours or up to 2 days. ■ Cut each cake layer in half horizontally to provide 4 layers. If your cake is not the same size as bowl, cut it into strips, dividing them into 4 portions and arranging each portion as a layer of cake. ■ Lay cake out on waxed paper, cut side up, and drizzle each layer equally with some of the brandy. ■ Peel tangerines and, with sharp knife, cut in between membranes to remove segments. ■ Place segments in a medium bowl as you work, and stir in mincemeat and walnuts. ■ In 8" straight-sided trifle bowl or other glass bowl, spread a thin layer of custard sauce. ■ Place one cake layer on top and spread with one-quarter mincemeat mixture, being sure it goes right to edges. ■ Pour on ½ cup custard and repeat layers until cake, mincemeat and custard are used up. ■ Cover and refrigerate overnight. ■ To finish, whip cream with icing sugar until stiff and spread half on top of trifle. ■ Using pastry bag with decorative tip, pipe remaining cream in rosettes around edge. ■ Or, apply in decorative swirls with spoon. ■ Garnish top with bits of candied fruit.

calories/serving: 610 for 8 servings
488 for 10 servings

ZABAGLIONE TRIFLE

Serves 8
Preparation time: 30 minutes
Cooking time: 10 to 15 minutes
Chilling time: overnight

A traditional Italian dessert has a new twist when combined with cake and strawberries.

6	egg yolks
½ cup plus 3 Tb	sugar
1 cup	dry Marsala
⅓ cup	Cognac or brandy
2 cups	whipping cream
1 qt	fresh strawberries
3 Tb	rum
8 oz	sponge cake or pound cake
2 oz	bittersweet or semi-sweet chocolate, grated

■ Beat egg yolks with ½ cup sugar in the top of a double boiler or in a bowl that will fit snugly over a pot of simmering water. ■ Beat in Marsala and Cognac. ■ Set over simmering water and stir constantly until custard thickens, 10 to 15 minutes. ■ Cool to room temperature. ■ Whip cream until soft peaks form and fold into cooled custard. Mixture should be quite creamy in texture. ■ While custard is cooling, dice berries and combine with 3 tablespoons sugar and the rum. ■ Allow to marinate about 30 minutes or until juicy. ■ Cut cake into cubes and place half in the bottom of a glass serving bowl. ■ Spoon over half of the berries. ■ Spoon over half of the custard. ■ Layer the remaining cake and berries and cover with remaining custard. ■ Sprinkle with chocolate. ■ Cover with plastic wrap and refrigerate overnight.

calories/serving: 610

HOW TO SEPARATE EGGS

There's a less messy – and foolproof way – to separate eggs that saves you juggling with eggshell halves. Break the egg onto a saucer or small plate. Carefully invert an egg cup over the yolk and, holding it firmly to the saucer, simply pour off the white.

Apple Crisp

APPLE CRISP

Serves 6
Preparation time: 15 minutes
Cooking time: 30 minutes

Apple pie is good, but apple crisp is faster and easier to make, has fewer calories (no pastry) and is every bit as tasty – perhaps even better.

6 to 8	apples, cored and sliced
2 Tb	lemon juice
½ cup	brown sugar
1 Tb	flour
½ to 1 tsp	ground cinnamon
¼ tsp	salt
TOPPING:	
¾ cup	rolled oats *or* ¼ cup flour plus ½ cup rolled oats
¾ cup	brown sugar
¼ cup	melted butter
½ cup	chopped nuts (optional)

■ Combine apples, lemon juice, sugar, flour, cinnamon and salt. ■ Put mixture into a greased baking dish or 9″ square cake pan. ■ Blend topping ingredients to make a crumbly mixture. ■ Sprinkle over the apple mixture. ■ Bake in preheated 350°F oven for about 30 minutes or until apples are soft and topping is golden. ■ Serve hot or cold, with whipped cream or ice cream, if you wish.

calories/serving: 451
fiber: moderate

Baked Fudge Pudding

BAKED FUDGE PUDDING

Serves 6 to 8
Preparation time: 15 minutes
Cooking time: 25 minutes

Puddings that make their own sauce while they cook always look more complicated than they really are.

¼ cup	block margarine
¾ cup	sugar
1½ cups	flour
2½ tsp	baking powder
½ tsp	salt
¾ cup	milk
¾ cup	chopped nuts
TOPPING:	
¼ cup	cocoa powder
¾ cup	brown sugar
¼ tsp	salt
1 cup	boiling water

■ Cream together margarine and sugar until fluffy. ■ Sift together flour, baking powder and salt. ■ Add to margarine mixture alternately with milk. ■ Stir in nuts. ■ Spoon batter into a greased pudding dish or 9″ square cake pan. ■ Combine cocoa, brown sugar and salt. ■ Sprinkle cocoa mixture over pudding batter. ■ Gently pour boiling water over top. ■ Bake in preheated 375°F oven for about 25 minutes, or until toothpick inserted in center comes out clean. ■ Serve warm.

calories/serving: 528 for 6 servings
396 for 8 servings

PORT JELLY

Serves 4
Preparation time: 10 minutes
Chilling time: 2 to 3 hours

This flavorful jelly can be prepared a day ahead.

3 Tb	lemon juice
1	envelope unflavored gelatine
1½ cups	port
3 Tb	sherry
1 Tb	red currant jelly
3 Tb	sugar
4 Tb	water

■ Put lemon juice in a big bowl and sprinkle with gelatine; let soak for 10 minutes. ■ Put all other ingredients in a saucepan and heat until boiling. ■ Pour boiling liquid on gelatine and stir to dissolve it completely. ■ Rinse a pretty mold with cold water and fill with jelly. ■ Refrigerate 2 to 3 hours, unmold and serve.

calories/serving: 160
low cal
low fat

HALF-HOUR PUDDING

Serves 6 to 8
Preparation time: 10 minutes
Cooking time: 30 minutes

As this warm, comforting pudding cooks, the lovely caramelly sauce sinks to the bottom.

⅓ cup	brown sugar
1 cup	flour
2 tsp	baking powder
¼ tsp	salt
½ cup	raisins
¾ cup	milk
SAUCE:	
2 cups	boiling water
¾ cup	brown sugar
1 Tb	butter
¼ tsp	grated nutmeg

■ Combine ⅓ cup brown sugar, flour, baking powder, salt and raisins in a medium bowl. ■ Beat in milk. ■ Put batter into greased pudding dish or 9″ square cake pan. ■ To make sauce, combine boiling water, brown sugar, butter and nutmeg. ■ Pour over batter and bake in preheated 350°F oven for 30 minutes, or until batter has set and a toothpick inserted in center comes out clean. ■ Serve warm. For a special treat, serve with unsweetened whipped cream or vanilla ice cream.

calories/serving: 303 for 6 servings
227 for 8 servings

Orange Chocolate Mousse

INSTANT MOCHA MOUSSE

Serves 2
Preparation time: 15 minutes
Cooking time: 3 to 5 minutes

An instant mousse that keeps for up to three days in the refrigerator. For a stronger coffee taste, use espresso. For total decadence try the mousse as a filling for chocolate layer cake.

3 oz	semi-sweet chocolate
¼ cup	strong coffee
1 cup	whipping cream
2 Tb	icing sugar

▪ Melt the chocolate in the coffee in a small heavy saucepan or in a double boiler over gently simmering water. ▪ Stir until smooth. ▪ Remove from heat and pour into a cold metal bowl for faster cooling. ▪ Whip cream in a separate bowl, gradually adding sugar until cream is thick and light. ▪ Fold in cooled chocolate mixture and beat again if cream becomes too soft. ▪ Pile into glass serving dishes and refrigerate until serving time.

calories/serving: 662

ORANGE CHOCOLATE MOUSSE

Serves 2 to 4
Preparation time: 10 minutes
Chilling time: 30 minutes

This quick and easy chocolate mousse is guaranteed to be sensational.

4 oz	semi-sweet chocolate, chopped
3	eggs, separated
6 Tb	softened butter
1 Tb	orange liqueur
½ tsp	vanilla
	sprigs fresh mint for garnish

▪ Place chocolate in a saucepan and set saucepan in hot, almost boiling water and cover. ▪ Let melt over low heat. ▪ Remove pan from heat and beat in egg yolks one by one until sauce thickens slightly. ▪ Beat in butter, orange liqueur and vanilla. ▪ Leave to cool slightly. ▪ Beat egg whites until stiff peaks form. ▪ Stir one-quarter of the egg whites into chocolate mixture, then gently fold this mixture into remaining egg whites. ▪ Spoon into individual glass dishes and chill. ▪ Garnish with sprigs of mint.

calories/serving: 734 for 2 servings
367 for 4 servings

WINTER FRUIT SALAD WITH CITRUS YOGURT SAUCE

Serves 8
Preparation time: 25 minutes
Cooking time: 10 minutes
Chilling time: overnight

This refreshing fruit salad and creamy sauce both benefit from being made ahead of time.

3	oranges
1	lemon
¾ cup	water
½ cup	sugar
2 Tb	orange liqueur (optional)
1	pink grapefruit
2	kiwifruit
2	winter pears
2	red Delicious apples
2 cups	seedless grapes

CITRUS YOGURT SAUCE:

1 cup	plain yogurt
2 Tb	sour cream
2 Tb	brown sugar
1 tsp	finely grated orange peel
½ tsp	vanilla

■ Grate 1 teaspoon peel from 1 orange and set aside for sauce. ■ Squeeze juice from this orange and the lemon into a small saucepan. ■ Add water and sugar and stir over medium heat until sugar dissolves. ■ Bring to boil; reduce heat to medium-low and simmer 10 minutes. ■ Cool. ■ Add liqueur. ■ Peel remaining oranges and grapefruit, removing outside membrane. ■ Holding fruit over a large bowl, remove segments between connecting membrane with a sharp knife. ■ Place fruit in bowl and squeeze membranes to extract all juice. ■ Remove pits. ■ Peel and slice kiwifruit, unpeeled pears and unpeeled apples into bowl. ■ Cut grapes into halves and add. ■ Pour syrup over top and toss fruit gently together to mix. ■ Cover and refrigerate fruit overnight, tossing together once or twice. ■ Stir together yogurt, sour cream, brown sugar, orange peel and vanilla in a small bowl. ■ Cover and refrigerate until serving time – up to 5 days.

calories/serving: 191
vitamin C: excellent
fiber: moderate
low fat

CHOCOLATE MINT MOUSSE

Serves 4
Preparation time: 25 minutes
Setting time: several hours
Chilling time: overnight

This mousse requires a little more effort in preparation than some, but the texture is airy and the flavor marvelous.

1	envelope unflavored gelatine
¼ cup	water
3	eggs, separated
½ cup plus 1 Tb	sugar
2 tsp	cornstarch
1 cup	milk
½ cup	chocolate mint chips, melted
1 tsp	grated orange peel
½ cup	whipping cream
	chocolate rose leaves or whipped cream and strawberries for garnish

■ Soften and dissolve gelatine in water as directed on package. ■ Set aside. ■ Combine egg yolks, ½ cup sugar and cornstarch in a small bowl. ■ Beat until smooth. ■ Heat milk over hot water in a double boiler. ■ Gradually add hot milk to egg mixture, mixing well. ■ Return to double boiler and cook over hot water, whisking constantly until slightly thickened. ■ Stir in melted chocolate mint chips, grated orange peel and dissolved gelatine. ■ Set aside, or cover and refrigerate, to cool to room temperature. ■ Beat egg whites with 1 tablespoon sugar until stiff and fold into chocolate mixture. ■ Refrigerate mixture until partially set. ■ Beat cream until stiff and fold into mousse mixture. ■ Spoon into a glass serving bowl and refrigerate, preferably overnight, until well set. ■ Decorate with chocolate rose leaves or whipped cream and strawberries.

calories/serving: 427

CHOCOLATE ROSE LEAVES

For a simple but effective way to decorate desserts of all kinds, melt some semi-sweet chocolate and, using a small paint brush, cover the backs of real, washed rose leaves with even layer of chocolate. Let cool until chocolate hardens, then carefully peel off and discard the rose leaves.

Commy's Suet Pudding

COMMY'S SUET PUDDING

Serves 20
Preparation time: 45 minutes
Cooking time: 3 hours

Great for entertaining, this pudding can be made a week or so ahead of time and steamed again just to heat through.

1 cup	finely chopped suet
1 cup	raisins
1 cup	currants or other dried fruit or grated carrot
1 cup	brown sugar
2 cups	flour
2 tsp	baking powder
½ tsp	each ground cloves, ground cinnamon, allspice and grated nutmeg
¼ cup	candied mixed peel
pinch	salt
1 tsp	baking soda
1 cup	sour milk
1 tsp	vanilla
1 tsp	lemon extract

WINE AND BRANDY SAUCE:

1 cup	brown sugar
3 Tb	flour
½ cup	cold water
½ cup	dry white wine
3 Tb	light cream or combination cream and brandy
1 Tb	butter
½ tsp	vanilla
pinch	salt
⅓ cup	chopped, toasted almonds (optional)

▪ Mix together suet, raisins, currants, brown sugar, flour, baking powder, spices, peel and salt. ▪ Dissolve baking soda in sour milk. ▪ Add milk, vanilla and lemon extract to other ingredients, mixing well to form slightly flattened ball. ▪ Wrap snugly but not too tightly in two layers of cheesecloth and tie top with string. ▪ Put on rack in a steamer or above (not in) boiling water in a large kettle. ▪ Cover and steam for about 3 hours. ▪ For sauce, blend together brown sugar and flour. ▪ Add water and wine and cook over medium heat until mixture is thick, stirring constantly. ▪ Add cream or cream and brandy, butter, vanilla, salt and almonds. ▪ Heat through. ▪ Unwrap pudding and place on a serving plate. ▪ Pour the sauce into a sauce boat and serve separately.

calories/serving: 314

Steamed Cranberry Pudding

STEAMED CRANBERRY PUDDING

Serves 12
Preparation time: 45 minutes
Cooking time: 45 minutes to 2½ hours,
depending on size of molds

A rich and delicious pudding chock full of cranberries.

2 cups	flour
4 tsp	baking soda
½ tsp	salt
1 cup	molasses
⅔ cup	boiling water
4 cups	cranberries, halved
1 cup	chopped pecans or raisins

SWEET BUTTER SAUCE:

¾ cup	butter
¾ cup	light cream
1½ cups	sugar
1 tsp	vanilla

- Combine flour, baking soda and salt in a large bowl. ■ Mix molasses and boiling water. ■ Add to flour and stir until evenly moistened. ■ Stir in cranberries and pecans. ■ Pour batter into 2 buttered 6-cup ceramic or metal molds, or 12 buttered individual molds. ■ Cover molds with heavy foil and tie to rim with cotton string. ■ Place on a rack in two large pots. ■ Pour boiling water to a depth of 1″ in the pot. ■ Cover and steam over medium-low heat for 1½ to 2½ hours for the large molds and 45 minutes for the individual molds. When done, an inserted skewer should come out clean. ■ For sauce, combine butter, cream and sugar in a medium saucepan. ■ Stir over medium-high heat until sauce comes to boil. ■ Reduce heat and simmer for 20 minutes. ■ Stir occasionally. ■ Add vanilla. ■ When puddings are done, remove molds from pot and let stand 10 minutes. ■ Unmold onto a serving plate and serve warm with the hot sauce.

calories/serving: 449
iron: excellent
calcium, thiamin, niacin: good

BRANDY HARD SAUCE

Serves 8
Preparation time: 10 minutes

The perfect accompaniment to hot Christmas pudding, this sauce may be garnished with nut meats, sliced candied cherries or grated nutmeg. If preferred, rum may be substituted for brandy.

½ cup	softened unsalted butter
1½ cups	sifted icing sugar
2 to 3 Tb	brandy
1	egg yolk

- Cream butter in a bowl. ■ Gradually add sugar and beat until fluffy. ■ Add brandy and stir. ■ Add egg yolk and beat until sauce becomes very light. ■ Spoon sauce into a serving dish and refrigerate until firm.

calories/serving: 217

CITRUS FRUIT DISHES

Hollow out citrus fruits, such as lemons, oranges and grapefruit, and freeze the shells to make pretty "dishes" for ice-creams and sorbets.

TANGERINE ICE CREAM WITH CHOCOLATE-TANGERINE FUDGE SAUCE

Serves 6 to 8
Preparation time: 20 minutes
Freezing time: 15 minutes (using an ice-cream maker)
Cooking time: 15 minutes

Nothing could be simpler than this citrusy ice cream. Even without an ice-cream maker, the recipe yields a smooth frozen treat but will take longer to freeze.

TANGERINE ICE CREAM:

2 cups	whipping cream
¾ cup	sugar
⅓ cup	strained lemon juice
2 tsp	finely grated tangerine peel
½ cup	strained tangerine juice

CHOCOLATE-TANGERINE FUDGE SAUCE:

¾ cup	sugar
⅔ cup	water
2 oz	unsweetened chocolate
1 oz	semi-sweet chocolate
¼ cup	softened unsalted butter
½ tsp	vanilla
½ tsp	finely grated tangerine peel
1 Tb	orange or tangerine liqueur (optional but recommended)

■ Combine cream and ¾ cup sugar in a large bowl, stirring to dissolve granules. ■ Blend in lemon juice, 2 teaspoons tangerine peel and the tangerine juice. ■ Freeze in an ice-cream maker according to manufacturer's instructions and pack into airtight containers for storage in the freezer. Or freeze in flat cake pan until firm, whiz until smooth in food processor or blender and pack into airtight containers to store in freezer. ■ To make sauce, combine ¾ cup sugar and the water in a small heavy saucepan. ■ Bring to boil, reduce heat and simmer gently for 5 minutes. ■ Chop chocolate coarsely. ■ Add to syrup and bring back to a simmer. ■ Cook gently, whisking almost constantly, for 5 to 8 minutes or until silky and thickened. ■ Remove from heat before stirring in butter, vanilla, ½ teaspoon tangerine peel and liqueur. Sauce can be made ahead of time and refrigerated. Reheat gently, whisking to prevent separation. ■ Pour chocolate sauce over scoops of tangerine ice cream.

calories/serving: 264 (ice cream only)
calories/serving: 516 with fudge sauce

Cranberry Bavarian

CRANBERRY BAVARIAN

Serves 6
Preparation time: 15 minutes
Chilling time: 2 hours

For festive occasions, garnish this delicate pink dessert with whipped cream and cranberry sauce.

¼ cup	water
2	envelopes unflavored gelatine
¾ cup	undiluted cranberry juice concentrate
½ cup	cranberry sauce
¼ cup	sugar
2	eggs
1¼ cups	crushed ice
1 cup	heavy cream
2 Tb	orange liqueur (optional)

■ Pour water into blender and sprinkle with gelatine. ■ Let soften for 5 minutes. ■ Meanwhile heat cranberry juice concentrate to simmering. ■ Pour over gelatine, cover and process for 40 seconds. ■ Add cranberry sauce, sugar and eggs. ■ Cover and process for 20 seconds. ■ Add crushed ice, cream and liqueur. ■ Cover and process for 20 seconds, or until ice has dissolved. ■ Pour mixture into an oiled 4-cup mold or spoon into serving dishes. ■ Chill at least 2 hours before serving.

calories/serving: 325

MARQUISES GLACÉES WITH STRAWBERRIES

Serves 8
Preparation time: 20 minutes
Cooking time: 5 minutes
Freezing time: about 2½ hours

Marquises are desserts made from a frozen mixture (like an ice) enriched with whipped cream. The ice gives the dessert a slightly granular texture.

1½ cups	water
¾ cup	sugar
1 Tb	lightly grated orange peel
2 Tb	lemon juice
2¼ cups	sparkling rosé wine
3 Tb	orange liqueur
6 cups	sliced fresh strawberries
2 cups	whipping cream
8	whole strawberries for garnish

■ Boil water and sugar hard for 5 minutes. ■ Add orange peel and lemon juice and cool. ■ Stir in 2 cups rosé wine and 2 tablespoons of the orange liqueur. ■ Strain into a metal pan and freeze until firm but not hard, about 2½ hours. ■ While wine mixture is freezing, add remaining wine and liqueur to sliced strawberries. ■ Let stand at room temperature 30 minutes, stirring occasionally, then spoon into tall glasses, filling about half full. ■ Chill. ■ Stir frozen mixture with a fork at serving time. ■ Whip cream and fold the two mixtures together. ■ Spoon over berries and serve immediately, topped with a whole berry.

calories/serving: 382
vitamin C: excellent
vitamin A: good

RHUBARB AND APPLE COMPOTE

Serves 4 or 5
Preparation time: 5 to 10 minutes
Cooking time: 10 to 15 minutes

This recipe combines rhubarb, the first fruit of spring, with the winter staples of orange and apple. For variety, add a handful of raisins or other dried or fresh fruit you may have on hand.

1 lb	fresh or frozen rhubarb
1	large apple
	grated peel and juice of 1 orange
¼ cup (approx.)	sugar
	plain yogurt
	brown sugar

■ Cut rhubarb into 1″ lengths. ■ Peel, core and thinly slice apple. ■ Combine orange peel and juice, rhubarb, apple and sugar in a saucepan. ■ Cover and bring to boil. ■ Reduce heat and simmer for 10 minutes or until fruit is soft, stirring occasionally. ■ Taste and add more sugar if necessary. ■ Serve warm or cold. ■ Top each serving with a spoonful of yogurt and sprinkle with brown sugar.

calories/serving: 158
potassium: excellent
vitamin C: good
low cal

POACHED PEARS IN RASPBERRY SAUCE

Serves 6
Preparation time: 20 minutes
Cooking time: 30 to 35 minutes

An elegant ending to a meal. Both the pears and the sauce can be made earlier in the day and chilled until serving time.

3 cups	water
1 cup	sugar
	grated peel and juice of 1 lemon
½	vanilla bean *or* 1 tsp vanilla (optional)
6	firm, ripe pears

RASPBERRY SAUCE:

2 pkgs	(each 12 oz/300 g) frozen, unsweetened raspberries, thawed and drained
2 Tb	orange liqueur

■ Combine water, sugar, lemon peel, juice and vanilla bean, if using, in a large saucepan. ■ Bring to boil, reduce heat and simmer 5 minutes. ■ Meanwhile peel pears, keeping stems intact. ■ Add pears to poaching liquid, arranging so that pears are covered in liquid. ■ Simmer gently until pears are tender when tested with a fork, 25 to 30 minutes. ■ Remove from heat and cool in liquid. ■ When cool, remove from liquid and pare thin slice from bottom so pears will sit upright. Place in individual serving dishes. ■ To make sauce, purée raspberries in a food processor or blender, then strain through a sieve to remove seeds. ■ Stir in liqueur. ■ Spoon raspberry sauce over pears.

MICROWAVE DIRECTIONS: Microwave poaching liquid on High 2 minutes, until sugar is dissolved. Add pears with thickest end towards outside of dish. Microwave, covered, on High 6 minutes. Baste and turn pears over. Microwave 6 to 8 minutes or until tender. Continue as above.

calories/serving: 270
vitamin C: excellent
fiber: moderate
low fat

Poached Pears in Raspberry Sauce

Raspberry Sorbet

RASPBERRY SORBET

Serves 6
Preparation time: 15 minutes
Freezing time: about 3 hours

What could be more refreshing on a hot summer day than icy cold fruit sorbet? This one has a minimum of sugar (you'll find it melts faster than those with more sugar) and no cooking, to give the freshest possible fruit flavor. Use the same method for strawberry, blueberry, peach, nectarine or plum sorbet, adding slightly more sugar for plums and slightly less for peaches and nectarines.

4 cups	red or black raspberries
1 cup (approx.)	instant dissolving sugar
1 Tb	lemon juice

▪ Purée raspberries in a food processor or blender. ▪ Strain through fine nylon sieve into a stainless steel bowl, pressing firmly with a spatula and scraping off the bottom of sieve to get all the juice and pulp. ▪ Discard seeds. ▪ Stir in sugar and lemon juice until sugar dissolves. ▪ Taste and add more sugar if necessary. ▪ Freeze until solidified around outside but still soft in the center, 2 to 3 hours. ▪ Break into chunks and beat with wooden spoon or place in food processor, returning bowl to freezer. ▪ Beat chunks until smooth but be careful not to melt. ▪ Return to cold bowl and freeze another 30 minutes or until firm. ▪ Serve. Freezing times depend a great deal on freezer used and can only be approximate. If desired, you can keep the sorbet, covered, several days in the freezer. You might like to process it 15 minutes before serving and return it to the freezer. Again be careful not to melt. If you have an ice-cream maker, follow manufacturer's instructions.

calories/serving: 179
vitamin C: excellent
low fat
low cal

SHERRIED GRAPEFRUIT SORBET

Serves 6
Preparation time: 40 minutes
Cooking time: 15 minutes
Freezing time: several hours

The tang of citrus is perfect for flavoring refreshing sorbets, and this grapefruit one is particularly good. Its soft consistency makes it easy to scoop straight from the freezer.

3	pink or white grapefruit
⅔ cup	sugar
1½ cups	water
6 Tb	sweet sherry
2	egg whites
	fresh mint leaves for garnish

▪ Halve fruit and, using a sharp knife, scoop out flesh into a bowl, taking care not to damage outer skins. ▪ Discard any membrane, pith or seeds and set aside flesh. ▪ Wash empty fruit shells, scraping insides clean with a teaspoon. ▪ Place in freezer. ▪ Dissolve sugar in water in a small pan over low heat. ▪ Bring to boil, boil for 10 minutes, then remove from heat and leave to cool. ▪ Purée grapefruit flesh in a food processor or blender. ▪ Measure 2 cups, making up quantity with water if necessary, and add to cool sugar syrup with sherry. ▪ Pour into shallow, freezer-proof container and freeze until slushy, 1 to 2 hours. ▪ Whisk egg whites until stiff. ▪ Transfer grapefruit slush into a bowl and fold in egg whites. ▪ Pour back into container and return to freezer until firm. ▪ To serve, scoop into frozen grapefruit shells and garnish with mint leaves.

calories/serving: 145
vitamin C: excellent
low fat
low cal

CHERRIES WITH SOUR CREAM DIP

Serves 2
Preparation time: 5 minutes

Although pitting cherries is extra work, it's worth the effort. If you love cheese, serve with a slice of ripe oozing Brie instead of the dip.

½ lb	cherries
½ cup	sour cream
2 Tb	brown sugar
¼ tsp	almond extract

▪ Wash and pit cherries and place on individual serving plates. ▪ Combine sour cream, brown sugar and almond extract. ▪ Spoon into 2 small bowls. Serve cherries with dip.

calories/serving: 198
low cal

NAVEL ORANGE SLICES IN SPICED RED WINE

Serves 6
Preparation time: 30 minutes
Cooking time: 20 minutes
Chilling time: 2 hours to overnight

Red wine syrup, spiced with cloves and cinnamon, gives a fragrant, colorful touch to a bowl of cool orange slices. Serve with lightly whipped cream.

6	large navel oranges
1 cup	water
1 cup	dry red wine
½ cup	sugar
2 Tb	lemon juice
1	1″ cinnamon stick, crushed
4	whole cloves
pinch	grated nutmeg

▪ Pare thin outer peel from 3 oranges. ▪ Cut into toothpick-sized strips. ▪ Bring strips and water to a boil in a small saucepan. ▪ Reduce heat, cover and simmer until strips are tender, about 10 minutes. ▪ Remove strips and set aside. ▪ Add wine, sugar, lemon juice, cinnamon stick, cloves and nutmeg to liquid. ▪ Bring back to boil, reduce heat and simmer for 10 minutes. ▪ Let cool. ▪ Remove cloves and cinnamon stick. ▪ Meanwhile peel oranges and, with a sharp paring knife, cut off outer membrane. ▪ Cut crosswise into ¼″ slices, removing any seeds. ▪ Arrange in a pretty glass bowl. ▪ Sprinkle orange peel strips over, and drizzle on the wine sauce. ▪ Cover and let stand 2 hours, or overnight, in the refrigerator. ▪ Good served cold or at room temperature.

calories/serving: 168
low cal

BASIC FRUIT SHERBET

Makes about 2 quarts
Preparation time: 30 minutes
Cooking time: 10 minutes
Freezing time: 4 to 5 hours

The possibilities of this recipe are endless. Try it with other fruits such as cherries or papayas, or mix fruits to come up with your own delightful flavors.

1	envelope unflavored gelatine
¼ cup	cold water
¾ cup	sugar
1 cup	water
2	egg whites
3 cups	fruit purée
	flavoring (see variations)

▪ Soak gelatine in cold water for 5 minutes. ▪ Boil ½ cup of the sugar and 1 cup water over high heat in a small saucepan for 10 minutes. ▪ Remove from heat and stir in soaked gelatine. ▪ Beat egg whites until foamy while syrup is cooking. ▪ Gradually add remaining sugar to egg whites and beat until stiff and glossy. ▪ Add hot sugar syrup in a thin stream, beating constantly. ▪ Cool but do not chill, then stir in fruit purée and flavoring. ▪ Pour into a metal pan and freeze 2 hours or until almost frozen. ▪ Chill a large mixer bowl and beaters while sherbet is freezing. ▪ Turn sherbet into cold bowl and beat until smooth and fluffy. ▪ Work quickly so mixture doesn't melt. ▪ Pour back into metal pan, cover and freeze until firm, 2 to 3 hours. ▪ If you aren't serving the sherbet immediately, pack it into plastic cartons and press some transparent wrap down on top of it to expel the air before putting on lid, then freeze until needed.

Peach or Apricot: *Use about 4 cups sliced fruit to make purée. Add 1 teaspoon grated orange peel and ½ teaspoon almond extract or 2 tablespoons almond-flavored liqueur.*

Strawberry: *Use about 4 cups whole berries to make purée. Replace water in sugar syrup with ½ cup orange juice and ½ cup water. Add 1 tablespoon grated orange peel or 1 tablespoon orange-flavored liqueur.*

Raspberry: *Use about 5 cups berries to make purée. Add ½ teaspoon vanilla, 1 teaspoon grated lemon peel and 2 tablespoons orange-flavored liqueur.*

Blackberry: *Use about 5 cups berries to make purée. Add 1 teaspoon vanilla.*

Rhubarb: *Cook 4 cups cut-up rhubarb with ⅓ cup water until tender, then purée with half a small orange. Purée 1½ cups strawberries and add to rhubarb. This will give you 3 cups purée.*

Pear: *Use about 6 large ripe pears for purée. Replace water in sugar syrup with red wine. Add 2 tablespoons Cognac.*

Peach or Apricot – calories/serving: 125 for 8 servings
Strawberry – calories/serving: 120 for 8 servings
Raspberry – calories/serving: 140 for 8 servings
Blackberry – calories/serving: 135 for 8 servings
Rhubarb – calories/serving: 100 for 8 servings
Pear – calories/serving: 165 for 8 servings

Melon with Ginger Sauce

BANANAS WITH CHOCOLATE FUDGE SAUCE

Serves 4
Preparation time: 5 minutes
Cooking time: 10 minutes

This recipe is such a cheat it's embarrassing. The bananas take just minutes to sauté, and though the rich, chocolatey sauce is impressive, it really couldn't be simpler. A dash of brandy or liqueur added to the sauce makes it even better.

4	bananas, peeled
1 Tb	butter
2 Tb	lemon juice
1	large Caramilk chocolate bar
2 Tb	cream or milk
4	scoops vanilla ice cream

▪ Sauté bananas in butter. ▪ Sprinkle with lemon juice. ▪ Break chocolate bar into pieces and place, with the cream, in a small bowl set over a pan of hot water, stirring occasionally until melted. ▪ Beat well with a wooden spoon until smooth. ▪ Place bananas in individual dishes, top each with a scoop of ice cream, then drizzle chocolate sauce on top.

calories/serving: 425
vitamin C: good
calcium, riboflavin: fair
fiber: moderate

MELON WITH GINGER SAUCE

Serves 4
Preparation time: 5 minutes
Cooking time: 10 minutes

Cool melon is a popular choice for a summer dessert. Served with a quick ginger sauce, it takes on a new flavor.

1 cup	soft brown sugar
2 Tb	butter
2 Tb	maple syrup
4 Tb	heavy cream or evaporated milk
¼ cup	finely chopped preserved ginger
½ tsp	vanilla
1	small ripe melon

▪ Put sugar, butter, syrup and cream or evaporated milk in a small, heavy saucepan. ▪ Bring to boil, stirring occasionally, and simmer for 5 minutes. ▪ Stir in ginger and vanilla and keep sauce warm. ▪ Just before serving, cut melon into 4 wedges and remove seeds. ▪ Put melon on individual plates and spoon on sauce.

calories/serving: 357
vitamin C: excellent

BAKED APPLES WITH GINGER

Serves 6
Preparation time: 20 minutes
Cooking time: 30 minutes

The apple takes on new glamor in this very simple dish.

6	medium apples (McIntosh or Delicious)
4 Tb	sugar
2 Tb	butter
	juice of 2 lemons
	candied ginger

▪ Core and peel apples. ▪ Cut into thin slices, not wedges, and arrange in a buttered shallow baking dish, edges overlapping, starting on the outside and working towards the middle. ▪ Sprinkle with sugar, dot with butter and repeat layers until dish is filled. ▪ Sprinkle with lemon juice and bake in preheated 375°F oven for 30 minutes, until apples are tender but not mushy. Watch during baking and do not overcook. ▪ Remove from oven and sprinkle with slivers of candied ginger. ▪ Serve at room temperature. Serve these apples the day they are cooked.

calories/serving: 169
vitamin C: good
fiber: moderate
low cal

Strawberry Shortcake

STRAWBERRY SHORTCAKE

Serves 6
Preparation time: 20 minutes
Cooking time: 12 to 15 minutes

Throughout the decades, strawberry shortcake has been the focus of many festivals and summer suppers: a dessert everyone must have at least once in strawberry season. Use the old-fashioned shortcake base given here for peach, blueberry or raspberry shortcakes, too. Just sweeten the fruit to taste.

2 cups	flour
3 Tb	sugar
1 Tb	baking powder
½ tsp	salt
½ cup	butter
⅔ cup	light cream
1	egg
1 cup	whipping cream
4 cups	strawberries
⅓ cup	icing sugar
1 tsp	vanilla
	softened butter

■ Sift or stir together flour, 2 tablespoons of the sugar, baking powder and salt in a large bowl. ■ Cut in butter until it resembles fine crumbs. ■ Beat light cream and egg together in a measuring cup. ■ Quickly stir all at once into dry ingredients to moisten. ■ Form into ball and pat into ungreased 8″ square cake pan. ■ Brush with 2 teaspoons of the whipping cream and sprinkle on remaining tablespoon sugar. ■ Bake in preheated 450°F oven for 12 to 15 minutes or until golden brown on top. ■ Remove shortcake from pan and place on rack to cool for about 30 minutes. The shortcake is best served slightly warm. ■ While the shortcake bakes, rinse and hull strawberries. ■ Set aside 6 whole berries for garnish and slice or chop remainder. ■ Place sliced berries in a medium bowl and sprinkle with all but 1 tablespoon of the icing sugar. ■ Set aside until serving time. ■ In a chilled bowl, beat remaining whipping cream with reserved icing sugar and vanilla until stiff peaks form. ■ Cut shortcake into 6 pieces and slice each piece horizontally. ■ Set bottom half on individual serving plates, cut side up. ■ Butter both cut sides. ■ Spoon on sliced berries and their juices. Place top half on berries. ■ Spread with whipped cream and garnish each with a whole berry.

calories/serving: 694
vitamin C: excellent
iron, vitamin A, thiamin, niacin: good
fiber: moderate

Fruit in Cherry Liqueur

FRUIT IN CHERRY LIQUEUR

Serves 2 to 4
Preparation time: 10 minutes
Chilling time: overnight
A quick and delicious fruit salad to make ahead.

1 cup	**fresh strawberries**
½ cup	**fresh blueberries**
2	**plums**
1	**peach**
1	**apple**
1	**orange, peeled and segmented**
½ cup	**cherry liqueur**

▪ Wash and hull strawberries. ▪ Wash blueberries.
▪ Pit plums and peach, core apple and cut into chunks.
▪ Toss all fruit together in a serving bowl and pour cherry liqueur over the fruit. ▪ Refrigerate overnight. ▪ Toss again before serving.

calories/serving: 189
vitamin C: excellent
fiber: high
low fat
low cal

MAPLE ORANGES

Serves 4
Preparation time: 5 minutes
Cooking time: 5 minutes
For a family dessert, omit the alcohol and serve to the kids.

4	**large juicy oranges**
2 Tb	**gin or orange-flavored liqueur**
½ cup	**maple syrup**

▪ Thinly peel 1 orange, cut peel into fine strips and set aside. ▪ Using a very sharp knife and holding oranges over a bowl to catch any juice, remove peel and pith from all four. ▪ Thinly slice peeled oranges and arrange slices in a shallow serving dish. ▪ Sprinkle with gin or liqueur. ▪ Put reserved peel in a small saucepan with water to cover. ▪ Bring to boil, strain and discard water. ▪ Return peel to saucepan and add maple syrup. ▪ Heat gently until boiling, then simmer for 1 to 2 minutes. ▪ Pour hot syrup over oranges. ▪ Leave to cool slightly, then chill in the refrigerator until ready to serve. ▪ Serve with cream or ice cream.

calories/serving: 190

SAUTÉED BANANAS

Serves 4
Preparation time: 5 minutes
Cooking time: 5 to 7 minutes

For added flair, heat a little rum or liqueur such as Poire Williams or Grand Marnier, pour over bananas at the table and ignite – voilà, flambéed bananas.

2 Tb	butter
4	medium-ripe bananas
¼ cup	brown sugar
1 Tb	lemon juice
2 Tb	rum or liqueur (optional)
	ground cinnamon (optional)

▪ Melt butter in a large skillet over medium heat. ▪ Peel and cut bananas lengthwise into halves. ▪ Arrange bananas in skillet and sprinkle with sugar. ▪ Drizzle lemon juice over top. ▪ Cook over medium to low heat, turning bananas once, until fruit is heated through, 5 to 7 minutes. ▪ To flambé, heat rum or liqueur over low heat. ▪ Bring sautéed bananas in skillet to table. ▪ Pour rum or liqueur over top and carefully ignite with match. ▪ Just before serving, sprinkle with cinnamon, if you wish.
MICROWAVE DIRECTIONS: Melt butter in baking dish 1 minute on High. Arrange bananas in single layer, sprinkle with sugar and drizzle lemon juice over top. Cook on High 3 minutes. Pour rum over top, heat 15 seconds on High. Take to table, ignite and serve.

calories/serving: 216
vitamin C: good

STRAWBERRIES DIPPED IN CHOCOLATE

Serves 2
Preparation time: 10 minutes
Cooking time: 3 to 5 minutes

A luscious way to serve fresh, ripe strawberries, the chocolate-dipped fruit are great with coffee after dinner.

4 oz	semi-sweet chocolate or a mixture of sweet and unsweetened chocolate
12	whole, fresh strawberries, unhulled

▪ Chop each chocolate square into 4 pieces. ▪ Partially melt chocolate in a bowl placed over hot water. About one-third of the chocolate should be unmelted, and there should still be small pieces. ▪ Remove from heat and continue stirring until completely smooth. ▪ Set chocolate over a pan of lukewarm water and dip the strawberries. ▪ Place berries on waxed paper and refrigerate to set.

calories/serving: 319
vitamin C: excellent

Melon with Blueberries

MELON WITH BLUEBERRIES

Serves 6
Preparation time: 30 minutes

A quick-to-make, refreshing dessert. Or try it as a first course or breakfast treat. Peaches, grapes, kiwifruit or other fresh fruit in season can be used instead of blueberries. If serving as a first course, omit the honey, arrange wedges of melon on individual salad plates, drizzle with lemon juice mixed with liqueur or lime juice, and garnish with blueberries.

½	cantaloupe
½	honeydew melon
2 cups	watermelon cubes
1 cup	blueberries
2 Tb	honey
2 Tb	lemon juice
2 Tb	melon or orange liqueur or sherry (optional)
	fresh mint leaves for garnish

▪ Cut cantaloupe and honeydew melon into cubes or balls. ▪ In a glass serving bowl, combine cantaloupe, honeydew, watermelon and blueberries. ▪ Combine honey and lemon juice. ▪ Blend in liqueur, if using. ▪ Pour over melons; toss to mix. ▪ Cover and refrigerate. ▪ Bring to room temperature before serving. ▪ Spoon into stemmed glasses, garnish with mint and serve.

calories/serving: 122
Vitamins A and C, fiber: excellent

Cherry Clafouti

CHERRY CLAFOUTI

Serves 8
Preparation time: 10 minutes
Cooking time: 45 to 50 minutes

A kind of custard or thick fruit pancake from Limousin, France, clafouti is delicious made with sour red cherries. As the season progresses, make it with other fruits, varying the liqueurs to complement the fruit – pear liqueur with pears, Amaretto with peaches and so on – and varying the amount of sugar according to the fruit's sweetness.

4 cups	pitted cherries
2 Tb	Kirsch or Cognac
5 Tb	sugar
2 cups	light cream
3	eggs
¼ cup	flour
pinch	salt
1 tsp	vanilla
	icing sugar

▪ Toss cherries with Kirsch and set aside. ▪ Butter a 2-quart shallow baking dish and sprinkle evenly with 2 tablespoons of the sugar. ▪ In a blender or food processor, blend cream, eggs, flour and salt for 2 minutes. ▪ Add remaining sugar and vanilla; blend a few seconds longer. ▪ Distribute cherries and their juice over bottom of prepared dish. ▪ Pour egg mixture over fruit. ▪ Bake in preheated 375°F oven for 45 to 50 minutes or until well puffed and golden. ▪ Serve barely warm, sprinkled with icing sugar just before serving.

calories/serving: 231
vitamin A, iron: good

STRAWBERRY BRÛLÉE

Serves 2
Preparation time: 5 minutes
Chilling time: 30 minutes
Cooking time: 5 minutes

Typical crème brûlée is a thick egg custard with a heavy caramel topping. This is an easier, lighter version of the classic.

1 pint	strawberries
1 cup	whipping cream
1 Tb	lemon juice
2 Tb	sherry
2 Tb	sugar
¼ cup	brown sugar

▪ Slice strawberries thickly and arrange on bottom of a small, shallow, oven-proof dish. ▪ Beat cream until it holds its shape. ▪ Beat in lemon juice, sherry and sugar. ▪ Continue beating until thick and light. ▪ Spread mixture on top of berries and chill for 30 minutes. ▪ Just before serving, sprinkle brown sugar over cream. ▪ Preheat broiler and broil until sugar melts and caramelizes. ▪ Serve at once.

calories/serving: 613
vitamin A, vitamin C: excellent
fiber: moderate

HIGHLAND CREAM

Makes 1 cup
Preparation time: 10 minutes

An instant topping for fruit to whip up when you are in a hurry. The ingredients are Scottish, but you could make Caribbean Cream by using rum, ginger marmalade and crushed gingersnaps.

½ cup	whipping cream
2 Tb (approx.)	Scotch whisky
3 Tb	orange marmalade
2 Tb	brown sugar
1 tsp	lemon juice
2	shortbread cookies, crushed

▪ Whip cream until it holds soft peaks. ▪ Beat together whisky, marmalade, sugar and lemon juice in a small bowl. ▪ Gradually fold marmalade mixture into whipped cream. ▪ Stir in shortbread crumbs. ▪ Refrigerate until ready to serve.

calories/tablespoon: 60

PEARS IN RED WINE

Serves 4 to 6
Preparation time: 10 minutes
Cooking time: 30 to 40 minutes

With a bowl of these in the refrigerator, you are well on the way to a great dinner party.

½ cup	red wine
1 cup	sugar
1	small cinnamon stick
1	generous strip of lemon peel
6	large fresh pears

▪ Bring first four ingredients to boil in a large saucepan. ▪ Peel pears (slightly under-ripe pears can be used but will need longer cooking). Cut lengthwise into halves and remove core. ▪ Place in syrup and simmer gently until pears are tender. ▪ Remove to glass bowl. ▪ Discard cinnamon and peel and boil syrup to reduce by half. ▪ Pour over pears. ▪ Serve warm or cold.

calories/serving: 372 for 4 servings
248 for 6 servings
vitamin C: fair
fiber: moderate
low fat

PEACHES CATHERINE

Serves 12
Preparation time: 15 minutes
Chilling time: overnight
Cooking time: 2 minutes

During peach season, this is a wonderful dessert for large buffet parties. On top of all its other recommendations, it's one of the easiest recipes you'll ever make.

15	ripe peaches
2 Tb	lemon juice
2 cups	whipping cream
¾ cup	packed brown sugar

▪ Peel, slice and arrange peaches in 12-cup shallow baking dish. ▪ Sprinkle with lemon juice as you work. ▪ Whip cream until very stiff and spread all over top of peaches. ▪ Sprinkle cream evenly with brown sugar by putting sugar through a fine sieve. ▪ Cover well with plastic wrap and refrigerate overnight. (This is a necessary step.) ▪ Just before serving, heat broiler and broil peaches about 4″ from heat about 2 minutes or until crispy golden on top.

calories/serving: 269
vitamin A, vitamin C: good

RHUBARB MOUSSE

Serves 10
Preparation time: 15 minutes
Cooking time: 15 minutes
Chilling time: at least 3 hours

Tasty, nutritious rhubarb becomes a pretty company dessert in this creamy mousse. The brighter the rhubarb in color, the prettier the results.

1 cup	sugar
½ cup	cold water
2 lbs	rhubarb, fresh or frozen and thawed, cut into ½″ pieces
1	envelope unflavored gelatine
4	egg whites
pinch	salt
2 cups	whipping cream
½ tsp	vanilla
	whipped cream and fresh mint sprigs for garnish

▪ Combine half the sugar and half the water in a heavy saucepan. ▪ Bring to boil, add rhubarb, bring to boil again. ▪ Reduce heat, cover and simmer until very tender, about 12 minutes, stirring occasionally. ▪ Purée in a food processor or blender. ▪ Transfer back to cooking pan or a large bowl. ▪ Dissolve gelatine in remaining ¼ cup cold water. ▪ Add to hot puréed rhubarb and stir until completely dissolved. ▪ Cool mixture to room temperature, but do not refrigerate. ▪ Beat egg whites with salt until soft peaks form. ▪ Gradually beat in remaining ½ cup sugar. ▪ Set aside while you whip cream. ▪ Without washing beaters, whip cream until soft peaks form. ▪ Stir vanilla into cream. ▪ Carefully fold whipped cream, then beaten egg whites, into cooled rhubarb mixture. ▪ Pour into an 8-cup glass or crystal serving dish, cover and chill at least 3 hours, or overnight. ▪ Garnish with whipped cream rosettes or a swirl of whipped cream, and fresh mint.

calories/serving: about 270

RELISHES AND PRESERVES

I n this rich world of smells, I have two all-time favorites — the delicate, achingly sweet fragrance of lilacs and the pungent, vigorous aroma of pickles cooking. Both evoke a nostalgic yearning for the innocence of childhood, along with a jubilant conviction that the world is not entirely lost as long as such delicious smells still occasionally drift on the air. Even if driven to the wall, I'd be incapable of choosing which of these two smells should permeate Heaven: both, perhaps, on alternate days.

We humans can't duplicate the true essence of lilacs (though lilac incense has been worth buying in some of the Januarys of my life), but with a little sugar and vinegar, pickle spices and onion, cucumbers, tomatoes and other tempting stuff, we could, if we wished, keep the house eternally full of pickle smells. But we don't, and perhaps if we did, the aroma would lose its charm.

No, just as lilacs are for spring, pickles belong to fall. The steamy vats, bubbling and filling the air with sharp, vinegary fumes with overtones of cinnamon or cloves or mustard create a veritable banquet of smells. Such an olfactory feast would justify our work even if we couldn't eat the result, but then comes the feast for the taste buds: crunchy mustard relish on a roast beef

sandwich, tart dills that send delicious wakeup signals up the taste buds to where the ears begin, rich, sweet gingery chutneys beside the roast, thick tomatoey chili sauces on the hot dogs and hamburgers! Bliss.

My mother, aunts and neighbors embarked on veritable preserving frenzies in the fall. Everything that couldn't survive the winter in its natural state, in a cool basement or root cellar, was boiled or blanched, whole or cut up, and drenched in a sugar syrup (for fruit) or vinegary brine (for vegetables) and crammed into sterilized glass sealers which would eventually repose in neat, sparkling rows on the fruit-cellar shelves. It was a common custom for visitors in late fall to be shown the fruit cellar before they were served tea.

"Got your peaches put away yet?" was an invitation to disclose just what you *had* been thrifty enough to "lay by" and the only way to let your interrogator know for sure, was to show them — just as you'd show a quilt you'd finished or a sweater you'd knit. And the audience conducted down the steep cellar stairs was sure to be a sympathetic one: all those gleaming, carefully labelled jars made a fine sight and reassured everyone that there'd be good meals on the table, come winter. The champion preserver in our clan was Great

Aunt Maggie, an enormous woman, who lived on a farm, and served three kinds of pie, at least two cakes, homemade bread, and a staggering array of preserved fruits and pickles at every Sunday dinner. And then she sent you home with a basket of preserves sneaked into the trunk of your car.

And the jams and jellies! Living where we did in southern Saskatchewan, we were surrounded in summer by chokecherry bushes; nothing as sweet and tender as a blueberry or wild strawberry survived in our drought-ridden, blistering summers. But the chokecherry grew profusely in large clumps on tall bushes and you could pick a honey pailful in an hour. My mother made jelly from it and a tart syrup we added to water to make refreshing summer drinks. Some people, it was whispered, even fermented chokecherries and made wine. The chokecherry, raw, jelled or in syrup, was a main feature of my summer diet. Because an old wives' tale, generally accepted in our town, had it that if you ate chokecherries before drinking milk you would curdle up and die, I would have a handful before every meal, announce it, and stick out my wine-colored tongue to prove it: at that stage of my life I despised milk.

You won't find any chokecherry recipes in this sec-

tion since neither markets nor farmers' fruit stands seem to have heard of them. Perhaps you're not missing anything. They were very tart, almost bitter, and each berry had a nasty pit in the center that lodged between the teeth. But when the juice was squeezed out and the pits entrapped in a cheesecloth drip bag, they did make lovely jelly.

Undoubtedly they're glorified in my memory by the sunny, happy haze that hangs over childhood and honey pails dangling from the belt — and escape from milk. In the next pages you will find recipes to fill your house with delectable smells, to steam up your windows and to gladden your meals.

Mum's Green Tomato Chutney

MUM'S GREEN TOMATO CHUTNEY

Makes 6 pints
Preparation time: 30 to 40 minutes
Cooking time: 40 minutes

This is a mild chutney. Hot dogs and hamburgers are more delicious with this special chutney, and it's an ideal accent with cold meats.

3 lbs	green tomatoes (10 to 12 medium)
1¼ lbs	red apples (4 medium)
3	medium sweet red peppers
4	medium onions
1½ Tb	salt
1½ tsp	pepper
1½ tsp	ground cinnamon
¾ tsp	ground cloves
2½ cups	sugar
2 cups	apple cider vinegar

▪ Wash tomatoes, apples and peppers thoroughly. ▪ Trim and quarter tomatoes. ▪ Core and quarter apples. ▪ Seed and slice peppers. ▪ Peel and quarter onions. ▪ Put vegetables and fruit through the coarse blade of a food grinder or process in small batches in a food processor. ▪ As each batch of fruit-vegetable mixture is processed into medium chunks, place it in a large Dutch oven or roasting pan. ▪ Add all remaining ingredients to the pot and stir with a wooden spoon to blend thoroughly. ▪ Bring mixture to slow boil over medium heat, then simmer, uncovered, stirring frequently to prevent scorching, for 30 minutes. ▪ Remove from heat. ▪ Immediately pour hot relish into 6 sterilized pint jars. ▪ Fill to within ½ inch of the top and seal at once. ▪ Cool before storing.

calories/tablespoon: 15

SPICY CRANBERRY SAUCE

Makes 2 cups
Preparation time: 5 minutes
Cooking time: 15 to 20 minutes

Make lots of this sauce to share with family and friends. It will keep in the refrigerator for 2 weeks. For longer storage, pour into hot, sterilized jars and seal. Process in boiling water bath for 5 minutes.

⅔ cup	white vinegar
⅓ cup	water
2 cups	sugar
2 tsp	cinnamon
½ tsp	ground cloves
4 cups	cranberries

▪ Combine vinegar, water, sugar and spices in a large saucepan or Dutch oven. ▪ Bring to boil over medium-high heat. ▪ Add cranberries, reduce heat and simmer, uncovered, for 15 to 20 minutes, stirring occasionally. Sauce is done when berries have popped and mixture has thickened. ▪ Pour into clean jars and seal.

calories/serving: 185 for 10 servings
150 for 12 servings

FRESH CRANBERRY ORANGE RELISH

Makes 2½ cups
Preparation time: 20 minutes
Standing time: overnight

Raw cranberries are very refreshing with roast poultry.

½ cup	coarsely chopped walnuts
2 cups	cranberries, fresh or frozen
1	seedless orange
1 cup	sugar
¼ cup	dried currants

▪ Spread walnuts out on cookie sheet and toast in preheated 350°F oven 5 minutes or until fragrant. ▪ Set aside to cool. ▪ Rinse cranberries in a sieve and grind finely in a food processor or meat grinder. ▪ Transfer to a medium bowl. ▪ With a small sharp knife, remove outer peel from orange without the white pith underneath. ▪ Put peel in processor. ▪ Remove and discard pith and membrane around orange and cut orange into quarters, add to processor and chop finely. ▪ Add to cranberries with sugar, walnuts and currants and stir until sugar dissolves. ▪ Cover and refrigerate overnight or up to 2 weeks; or freeze in airtight container several months.

calories/tablespoon: 34

NECTARINE AND GOLDEN RAISIN CONSERVE

Makes about eleven 8-ounce jars
Preparation time: 45 minutes (chopping by hand)
Cooking time: 1 hour

Serve with hot muffins or tea biscuits for weekend breakfasts. From Monday to Friday, spread some over toast. For special occasions, spread thinly over crêpes or thin with brandy for ice-cream sauce.

2	oranges
½	lemon
1 cup	cold water
11 cups	chopped, unpeeled, pitted nectarines (3½ lbs)
8 cups	sugar
1½ cups	golden raisins
1 cup	slivered almonds

▪ Squeeze juice from oranges and lemon. ▪ Strain juice into a large heavy saucepan. ▪ Chop orange and lemon peel, using a food processor or fine blade of a food grinder. ▪ Combine peel and water in a small heavy saucepan. ▪ Cover, bring to boil, reduce heat and simmer until tender, about 30 minutes. ▪ Add softened peel and liquid, nectarines, sugar and raisins to the contents of the large pan. ▪ Bring to boil over high heat and, stirring con-

Fresh Cranberry Orange Relish

stantly, boil conserve for about 25 minutes. ▪ Add almonds and continue boiling until a few drops, drizzled on a cold plate, set. To test, run your fingertip through the cold conserve; if the surface wrinkles, the conserve is set. ▪ Skim off foam. ▪ Ladle into hot sterilized jars and seal.

calories/tablespoon: 52

PUMPKIN APRICOT MARMALADE

Makes 6 to 8 cups
Preparation time: 10 minutes
Cooking time: 1 to 1½ hours

An unusual combination makes a delicious preserve.

2	medium oranges, rinsed
2	lemons, rinsed
8 cups	sugar
2 cups	dried apricots, cut into strips
½ tsp	ground cinnamon
¼ tsp	allspice
¼ tsp	grated nutmeg
4 cups	cooked or canned pumpkin
¼ cup	brandy

▪ Slice unpeeled citrus fruit very thinly. ▪ Remove seeds. ▪ Add fruit, sugar, dried apricots and spices to pumpkin in a large saucepan. ▪ Bring mixture to boil. ▪ Reduce heat and simmer, stirring occasionally, for 1 to 1½ hours or until thick. ▪ Stir in brandy. ▪ Pour into hot sterilized jars and seal with melted paraffin wax.

calories/tablespoon: 70

Bread and Butter Pickles, Old-Fashioned Pepper and Cucumber Relish, Corn Chow Chow and Red Tomato and Apple Chutney

BREAD AND BUTTER PICKLES

Makes about 6 pints
Preparation time: 1 hour (chopping by hand)
Standing time: 4 hours
Cooking time: 30 minutes

Most pickles and relishes start out with a brining step. Here sliced cucumbers are layered with ice cubes and salt and left for 3 to 4 hours.

10 cups	sliced small cucumbers (about 2½ lbs)
5 cups	sliced white onions
1	large sweet red pepper, seeded and sliced into strips
½ cup	pickling salt
4	trays ice cubes
2¼ cups	white vinegar
4 cups	sugar
1 Tb	yellow mustard seed
2 tsp	celery seed
1 tsp	freshly and coarsely ground pepper

▪ Layer cucumbers, onions, pepper strips, salt and ice cubes in a large glass bowl or crock. ▪ Cover with a clean tea towel and let stand 4 hours, or overnight if convenient. ▪ Drain thoroughly and rinse in cold water. ▪ Drain again. ▪ Combine vinegar, sugar, mustard and celery seed with pepper in a large saucepan. ▪ Bring to boil. ▪ Add vegetables and bring back to boil. ▪ Cook, uncovered, at a simmer until vegetables are tender-crisp, 2 to 3 minutes. ▪ Pack immediately into hot sterilized canning jars and seal.
calories/¹/₄ cup: 76

RED TOMATO AND APPLE CHUTNEY

Makes about eight 8-ounce jars
Preparation time: 1 hour (chopping by hand)
Cooking time: 2 hours

Serve a bowl of spicy tomato and apple chutney with cold turkey or pork, or serve with cream cheese and crackers as a snack or quick and easy hors d'œuvre.

11 cups	coarsely chopped peeled tomatoes (5 lbs)
5 cups	sliced tart apples (5 large)
1½ cups	finely chopped onions
1 cup	slivered dried apricots
1 cup	golden raisins
½ cup	currants
½ cup	slivered candied ginger
2	cloves garlic, minced
1½ cups	sugar
1½ cups	cider vinegar
2 tsp	pickling salt
1 tsp	ground cinnamon
1 tsp	curry powder
pinch	cayenne pepper

▪ Combine all ingredients in a large heavy saucepan. ▪ Bring to boil, stirring frequently. ▪ Reduce heat to simmer and cook, stirring often, until chutney is thick and a rich red. ▪ Taste, adjust seasoning and add more sugar, if you wish. ▪ Pack into hot sterilized jars and seal with paraffin wax.
calories/tablespoon: 26

CORN CHOW CHOW

Makes about eight 8-ounce jars
Preparation time: 1½ hours (chopping by hand)
Standing time: 1 hour
Cooking time: 1 hour

Sausages for supper, or cold meat for lunch? Try them with this tangy crunchy golden relish.

4 cups	**finely shredded green cabbage**
4 cups	**finely chopped cauliflower**
4 cups	**fresh corn kernels (5 large ears)**
1¼ cups	**finely chopped sweet red pepper (1 large)**
1¼ cups	**finely chopped sweet green pepper**
1 cup	**finely chopped onions**
2 Tb	**pickling salt**
	boiling water
1¾ cups	**sugar**
1 Tb	**dry mustard**
2 tsp	**turmeric**
4 tsp	**yellow mustard seed**
4 tsp	**celery seed**
3 cups	**cider vinegar**
3 Tb	**cornstarch**
¼ cup	**cold water**

▪ Combine cabbage, cauliflower, corn, red and green peppers and onions in a large glass or ceramic bowl. ▪ Sprinkle on salt and cover with boiling water. ▪ Let stand for 1 hour. ▪ Drain thoroughly and rinse. ▪ Drain again and place in a large heavy saucepan. ▪ Blend together sugar, mustard and turmeric. ▪ Stir in mustard and celery seed and vinegar. ▪ Pour over vegetables. ▪ Bring to boil, stirring often. ▪ Reduce heat and simmer for 30 minutes, uncovered, until vegetables are tender and liquid has reduced. ▪ Blend cornstarch into cold water. ▪ Stir into relish mixture. ▪ Cook for 2 to 3 minutes, or until relish liquid clears and thickens. ▪ Taste, adding more sugar for a sweeter relish, and a touch of salt if you wish. ▪ Pack immediately into hot sterilized canning jars and seal.

calories/tablespoon: 20

OLD-FASHIONED PEPPER AND CUCUMBER RELISH

Makes about five 8-ounce jars
Preparation time: 1 hour (chopping by hand)
Standing time: 3 to 4 hours
Cooking time: 20 minutes

Think hot dogs and hamburgers when you think this relish. Use a food processor, if you have one, to chop all the vegetables. Wash and trim cucumbers and celery, wash and core peppers, and peel onions before chopping.

4 cups	**finely chopped cucumbers (1¼ lbs)**
2½ cups	**finely chopped sweet green pepper (2 large)**
1¼ cups	**finely chopped sweet red pepper (1 large)**
1¼ cups	**finely chopped sweet yellow pepper (1 large)**
1½ cups	**finely chopped onions (2 medium)**
1 cup	**finely chopped celery (2 stalks)**
2 Tb	**finely chopped hot banana pepper (optional)**
¼ cup	**pickling salt**
	cold water
2 cups	**white vinegar**
3½ cups	**sugar**
1 Tb	**each yellow mustard seed and celery seed**

▪ Combine cucumbers, sweet peppers, onions, celery and hot pepper, if you wish, in a large glass or ceramic bowl. ▪ Sprinkle on salt and cover with cold water. ▪ Let stand for 3 to 4 hours at room temperature. ▪ Drain. ▪ Rinse well in two changes of cold water. ▪ Drain and firmly press out as much moisture as possible. ▪ Combine vinegar, sugar and seeds in a large heavy saucepan. ▪ Bring to boil, uncovered. ▪ Add drained vegetables. ▪ Bring back to boil and boil for 10 to 15 minutes, stirring frequently. The relish is done when the vegetables turn translucent and mixture has thickened. ▪ Pack immediately into hot sterilized canning jars and seal.

calories/tablespoon: 39

METRIC EQUIVALENTS

Please note that recipes with Imperial measures cannot be directly converted to Metric measures. The equivalencies below are approximate.

Oven Temperatures

300°F – 150°C
325°F – 160°C
350°F – 180°C
375°F – 190°C
400°F – 200°C
425°F – 220°C
450°F – 230°C

Volume Measures

1/4 tsp   – 1 mL
1/2 tsp   – 2 mL
1 tsp   – 5 mL
1 Tb   – 15 mL
2 Tb   – 25 mL
3 Tb   – 50 mL

1/4 cup   – 50 mL
1/3 cup   – 75 mL
1/2 cup   – 125 mL
2/3 cup   – 150 mL
3/4 cup   – 175 mL
1 cup   – 250 mL
2 cups   – 500 mL
3 cups   – 750 mL
4 cups   – 1 L
5 cups   – 1.2 L
6 cups   – 1.5 L
12 cups   – 3 L
16 cups   – 4 L

Bakeware

Baking pans
8″ × 11″ – 20 cm × 28 cm
9″ × 9″   – 23 cm × 23 cm
9″ × 15″ – 23 cm × 37.5 cm
10″ × 15″ – 25 cm × 37.5 cm

Cake pans
8″ round – 20 cm
8″ × 8″   – 20 cm × 20 cm
9″ round – 23 cm
9″ × 9″   – 23 cm × 23 cm

Loaf pans
8″ × 4″   – 20 cm × 10 cm
9″ × 5″   – 23 cm × 13 cm
10″ × 6″ – 25 cm × 15 cm

Pie plates   Springform pans
8″ – 20 cm   8″ – 20 cm
9″ – 23 cm   9″ – 23 cm
10″ – 25 cm   10″ – 25 cm

Jelly Roll Pan
10″ × 15″ – 25 cm × 37.5 cm

Bundt pan
12-cup – 3 L

Casserole dishes
1 qt – 1 L
2.5 qt – 2.5 L
5 qt – 3 L
5 cup – 1.2 L
6 cup – 1.5 L

INDEX AND RECIPE CREDITS

Note: In this index, each recipe title is followed by its author's initials in parentheses. To find out the author's full name, refer to the following key:

AL	Anne Lindsay
BH	Barb Holland
BJW	Betty Jane Wylie
BM	Beth Moffatt
BS	Bonnie Stern
CA	Carroll Allen
EB	Elizabeth Baird
EF	Elizabeth Falkner
EJO	Emily-Jane Orford
ES	Edna Staebler
GV	Gloria Varley
HG	Helen Gougeon
HS	Habeeb Salloum
IR	Iris Raven
JA	Julia Aitken
JC	Judith Comfort
JP	Jean Patterson
JR	Jane Rodmell
JW	Jean Waterworth
KB	Kate Bush
KC	Kathy Chute
KS	Kay Spicer
LF	Lili Fournier
LLL	Louise Lambert-Lagacé
LW	Lucy Waverman
MO	Margo Oliver
NE	Nancy Enright
NS	Nancy Smallwood
RD	Rollande DesBois
RM	Rose Murray
WA	Wendy Affleck

G

H

I

J

K

L

THE CONTRIBUTORS

Wendy Affleck is a Vancouver home economist, teacher and avid entertainer. She has written for *Homemaker's/Recipes Only* and edited *Let's Cook International*, a cookbook for the Red Cross.

Julia Aitken is a regular contributor to *Homemaker's/Recipes Only* and has written for *Images, à la carte, Canadian Living* and *Table D'Haute* magazines. Her first book – *Baker's Secret Quick and Easy Baking* – was published in 1986.

Elizabeth Baird is the author of *Classic Canadian Cooking, Apples, Peaches & Pears, Summer Berries,* and *Elizabeth Baird's Favourites*. She is the food editor of *Canadian Living* magazine and her column, "Come on over," appears weekly in the *Toronto Sun*.

Kate Bush is *Homemaker's/Recipes Only*'s food stylist. She is a regular contributor to *Toronto Life* magazine and co-author of *The Getaway Chef*.

Kathy Chute is co-author of *Apples, Apples, Apples*. She developed and tasted recipes for *Cynthia Wine's Hot and Spicy Cooking* and *Across the Table*. Kathy is a freelance food stylist.

Judith Comfort is a freelance food writer. She is the author of *Some Good!, Spuds! Dulse! Fiddleheads!, Some Good City Food* and *Judith Comfort's Christmas Cookbook* and co-author of *Apples, Apples, Apples*.

Rollande DesBois studied at the Cordon Bleu Cookery School and teaches at L'Institut de tourisme et d'hôtellerie du Québec and at L'Institut national des viandes in Montreal. She is author of *La fine cuisine québécoise*.

Nancy Enright is the author of *Nancy Enright's Canadian Herb Cookbook* and a contributor to *A Basket Full of Favourites*. Nancy wrote regularly for the *Globe and Mail* "Shopping Basket" for seven years where she created the "Spice Rack" column.

Elizabeth Falkner lives in Venice, Florida, where she frequently indulges her passion for stone crabs, coquina broth, boniatos, swamp cabbage and cherimoyas.

Lili Fournier, formerly a lifestyle columnist for the *Toronto Sun*, operated Lili's Gourmet Delights, Toronto's first gourmet shop to feature foods of the world.

Helen Gougeon is a longtime reporter, editor and broadcaster whose writing has appeared in many newspapers and magazines, including *The Ottawa Journal, The Ottawa Citizen, The Toronto Star Saturday Magazine, Weekend, The Canadian* and *Canadian Living*.

Barb Holland is a freelance home economist, microwave specialist and food writer. Her weekly column, "Making Microwaves" appears in the *Calgary Sun* and *Toronto Sun*. Barb has written features for *Chatelaine, Homemaker's/Recipes Only, Canadian Living* and *You/Verve* magazines. She is also co-author of *Microwave Cooking with Style*.

Louise Lambert-Lagacé is a consulting dietician and author of two books: *Feeding Your Child* and *The Nutrition Challenge for Women*. She lectures in nutrition at the University of Montreal.

Anne Lindsay is a freelance home economist, food writer and consultant. She is a regular contributor to *Homemaker's/Recipes Only*, *Canadian Living* and *Canadian Living Food* magazines. Anne is the author of the best-selling cookbooks *Smart Cooking* and *The Lighthearted Cookbook*.

Beth Moffatt is a freelance food writer and food stylist. In 1981 she set up the *Canadian Living* magazine test kitchen and was test kitchen manager. A graduate home economist, Beth has written for *Homemaker's/Recipes Only* and *Canadian Living* magazines.

Rose Murray is a freelance food writer and food consultant. She is the author of three books, *The Christmas Cookbook*, *Rose Murray's Vegetable Cookbook* and *Secrets of the Sea* and has contributed to several other major Canadian cookbooks.

Margo Oliver is the author of six cookbooks, the latest of which is *Margo Oliver's Cookbook for Seniors*. She wrote food columns for *Weekend*, *The Canadian* and *Today* magazines from 1959 to 1982 and a syndicated column of menus and recipes for the following two years.

Emily-Jane Orford is a freelance writer and photographer. She is a regular contributor to *Profile Kingston* and *Western People* magazines and the co-editor of the *B.C. Diocesan Post*.

Jean Patterson is the senior home economist for Canada Packers Inc. and one of her functions is to develop and test recipes using company products.

Iris Raven is a food writer and home economist and has written for *Canadian Living* magazine, among others. She specializes in recipe development and believes most recipes could do with a lighter touch.

Jane Rodmell's culinary career began when she found herself Head Cook in a boy's prep school in Buckinghamshire. She contributes food articles regularly to several Canadian magazines, she is co-author of *The Getaway Chef* and a partner in a specialty food shop, "All the Best Breads and Cheese."

Habeeb Salloum worked for Canada Customs for 36 years, the latter years also working as a part-time writer. Now retired, he is a full-time freelance writer, specializing in travel, history and the foods of the Middle-East, North Africa, Spain, and Central and South America.

Nancy Smallwood is an Ottawa home economist and food writer with a love of cooking and entertaining. She has written cookbooks for the Canadian Egg Marketing Agency and food columns on a freelance basis for many Canadian publications.

Kay Spicer is a home economist, food consultant and journalist. She writes articles for newspapers and magazines across Canada and is the author of the bestselling cookbooks *Light and Easy Choices*, *Light and Easy Choice Desserts* and the forthcoming book *From Mom With Love – Real Home Cooking*.

Edna Staebler, who lives in Ontario's Mennonite region, is the author of *Sauerkraut and Enterprise*, *Cape Breton Harbour* and *Whatever Happened to Maggie*. Her cookbooks *Food That Really Schmecks*, *More Food That Really Schmecks* and *Schmecks Appeal* are bestsellers.

Bonnie Stern opened her own cooking school in 1973. She is a regular on several radio and television shows and is the author of five cookbooks, the most recent of which is *Desserts*. Bonnie has a weekly column in *The Toronto Star* called "Quick Cuisine."

Gloria Varley is a contributing editor to *Toronto Life* and writes regular columns and features on food history for *Rotunda*, the magazine for the Royal Ontario Museum.

Jean Waterworth has contributed to *Homemaker's/Recipes Only*. For nine years Jean was the cookery class instructor and held cooking demonstrations for the Micro Cooking Centre.

Lucy Waverman is a food writer, consultant, teacher and author of *Lucy Waverman's Cooking School Cookbook* and *Lucy Waverman's The Seasonal Canadian Kitchen*. She is on the Board of Directors of the International Association of Cooking Professionals and a weekly columnist for the *Toronto Sun*.

Betty Jane Wylie is a writer who cooks, not a cook who writes. A playwright, she writes practical non-fiction books to make a living.

PHOTOGRAPHY CREDITS

Masao Abe   86, 119, 194

Bert Bell   52, 59, 132, 138, 166, 172, 213, 231

Clive Champion   58, 81, 97, 153

Peter Croydon   37, 103, 110, 128, 134, 142, 201, 219, 221

Michael Day   93, 123, 137, 152, 205, 225

Skip Dean   114, 170, 173

Adrien Duey   24, 38, 70, 91, 168, 181, 195, 202, 222, 255

Pat LaCroix   56, 82, 100, 145, 146, 169, 223, 238

Brad Ruelens   51

George Simhoni   2, 41, 65, 74, 77, 149, 175, 176, 177, 228, 235, 236

Carl Valiquet   79

Mike Visser   18, 21, 63

Michael Waring   226, 229, 232

Gary White   21, 47, 48, 62, 85, 92, 94–95, 98, 107, 122, 126, 133, 139, 151, 178, 193, 207, 208, 216, 237

Robert Wigington   19, 31, 33, 34–35, 36, 39, 44, 45, 61, 66, 69, 73, 83, 99, 104, 109, 112, 115, 116, 121, 124, 125, 129, 130, 141, 155, 156, 159, 160, 163, 165, 167, 183, 185, 186, 189, 190, 191, 197, 198, 203, 209, 211, 212, 215, 217, 218, 230

Doug Workman   43, 55, 88

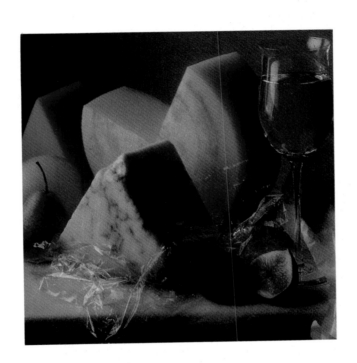